BIBLICAL INTERPRETATION
IN THE ERA OF THE REFORMATION

Biblical Interpretation in the Era of the Reformation

Essays Presented to David C. Steinmetz
in Honor of His Sixtieth Birthday

edited by

Richard A. Muller
John L. Thompson

WILLIAM B. EERDMANS PUBLISHING COMPANY
GRAND RAPIDS, MICHIGAN / CAMBRIDGE, U.K.

© 1996 Wm. B. Eerdmans Publishing Co.

255 Jefferson Ave. S.E., Grand Rapids, Michigan 49503 /

P.O. Box 163, Cambridge CB3 9PU U.K.

Printed in the United States of America

01 00 99 98 97 96   7 6 5 4 3 2 1

ISBN 0-8028-3819-7

Contents

v

CONTENTS

PART II
EXEGESIS AND INTERPRETATION IN THE EARLY REFORMATION

PART III
CONTINUITY AND CHANGE IN MID-SIXTEENTH-CENTURY BIBLICAL INTERPRETATION

Contents

PART IV
CONCLUSION

Preface

THE EDITORS AND AUTHORS of this volume wish to join in celebrating with David Steinmetz on the occasion of his sixtieth birthday. Each of us is either a colleague or a former student of his; some of us fall into both categories; and one colleague was once David's teacher.

The warmth of our congratulations is matched only by our respect for David's work, especially his studies of the history of biblical interpretation. David has drawn a host of students to this subject by his compelling statement of its themes and his inimitable gifts of presentation, and many of us have entered on careers impelled by an enthusiasm contracted from him. In dedicating this volume, we hope not only to advance David's special field of study but also to acknowledge his influence and legacy.

It is sometimes said that imitation is the sincerest form of flattery, and that can be true. Yet imitation may also be, by turns, both good pedagogy and good discipleship, for it is on the back of imitation that the treasures of tradition are often carried from one generation to the next. It is as heirs of the biblical tradition, then, that we offer these studies to a colleague, a teacher, and a friend.

RICHARD A. MULLER   JOHN L. THOMPSON
GRAND RAPIDS, MICHIGAN   PASADENA, CALIFORNIA

Curiosi te salutant:
A Premature Assessment

HEIKO A. OBERMAN

THIS VOLUME not only honors a dedicated scholar and effective teacher, but it also highlights a crucial field of investigation which he so firmly placed on the scholarly map that his name will continue to be associated with it. Over thirty-five years David C. Steinmetz, on an extended trek from Harvard to Duke, made a rich array of contributions which deserve to be acknowledged under a number of separate headings.

Before turning to a more precise description, however, a preliminary observation is in order. As long as I can recall, from his first seminar papers, he combined intensive efforts and native gifts in an uncommon desire to write creative English and thus overcome the treacherous deficit of the written word in the competitive arena of communication. Though during Steinmetz's graduate years Yale's Roland Bainton was a shining example of the historian able to address both the reader's intellect and his imagination, heavy Germanic influence at the Harvard of those days created such a climate of suspicion against the liabilities of evocation as *parfumierte Geschichte* that only the happy few could — and can — escape it untouched.

This precious aesthetic dimension is already evident in the substantial monograph on Johannes Staupitz (1968), thus initiating a series of publications that comprised the first of the three major thrusts in the scholarship of David Steinmetz. At once well written and closely argued, this book is still the best guide to Staupitz's thought — without necessitating the usual proviso "in the English language." Years later the critical editions of Staupitz's early works — produced by the expert Tübingen team of the Sonderforschungsbereich Spätmittelalter und Reformation (SuR 14, 1979; SuR 13, 1987) — have extended the source base and advanced improved textual readings, but they have substantially confirmed Steinmetz's well-documented findings: the center of Staupitz's theology — so appropriately captured in the main title — is the *misericordia Dei*. Moreover, in establishing this theme, Staupitz proves to be an acutely sensitive reader of the Scriptures and a well-informed adjudicator of the Church Fathers and the medieval tradition.

With this latter observation we touch upon the broader implications of this original thrust, going well beyond the technically limited field of Staupitz studies. Whereas former research had found its focus in Staupitz's self-understanding as *praecursor evangelii* and insofar as a forerunner of Luther, Steinmetz became a major agent in the recovery of the later Middle Ages as a period to be studied and appreciated in its own right — no longer as a mere backdrop to the Reformation, important as this dimension remained for Staupitz until the end (1525). As the *Handbook of European History 1400-1600* (Leiden, 1994; Eerdmans paperback, 1996) documents, the divide in 1500 — today sacrosanct only for incunabula collectors — has been successfully bridged in order to study a cohesive epoch with its many strands in terms both of continuity and discontinuity. Staupitz research is one of the first subfields to reap the benefits of this "epochal" reorientation.

His grasp of Staupitz's call for reform led Steinmetz in the ensuing phase into the wide world of sixteenth-century reform and reformation. The demands for specialization force most students of the Reformation era to dedicate themselves to one historical figure or one particular movement. *Reformers in the Wings* (1971) serves to protect the extensive parameters of early modern intellectual history, long threatened by confessional confinement, today no less at risk of caving in under professional pressure induced by the need to establish an academic profile.

The third thrust in the work of David Steinmetz demands special attention because it concerns a seemingly technical and limited subfield but one of still unmeasured potential: the history of biblical exegesis. In general terms this field is not new; the *Beiträge zur Geschichte der biblischen Exegese* established by Oscar Cullmann in 1959 could mine from its very beginnings a rich eighteenth- and nineteenth-century tradition. The shift in emphasis, however, from patristics to the confessionally much contested epoch of reform and reformation is an important new development closely associated with the name of David Steinmetz. In the interval between the end of the Second World War and the years immediately prior to Vatican II, scholars concentrated on the dogmatically charged issue of the relation of Scripture and Tradition, looking for antecedents to the *sola Scriptura* of the Reformers and "equal respect" for the oral traditions which paved the way for the Council of Trent. From that time on, new, detailed attention has been paid to the actual exposition of particular biblical narratives or specific texts. Most successfully carried through as a comparison between several exegetes, this approach proffers a precise recording of significant, at times even far-reaching variants, allowing for a controlled and accurate retracing of shifts in piety and mentality, which hitherto have gone unnoticed.

Quite apart from the immediate significance of such findings, the discipline of historical exegesis has given us a twofold methodological yield. In the first place, just as sermon collections have drawn fresh attention to their value in penetrating the mysteries of mentality, so exegetical literature can serve as a sensitive radar to spot "obvious" perceptions and apperceptions reflecting the experience of daily life. Not unlike the sermon, the exegetical genre — insofar as it is the product of a learned culture — presents a formidable challenge to historians seeking information of a broader social scope. But there is an additional psychological pitfall confronting the scholar intent on using exegetical sources to ferret out the underlying views of the author: the inclination to underestimate the degree to which the exegete is philologically committed to obeying the text concerned instead of speaking his/her mind. Even highly allegorical expositions are subject to such strict rules that exceptional skills are demanded to extrapolate the element of individuality in any given interpretation.

Perhaps even more important is the second methodological implication. In the intriguing relationship between intellectual and social history — ranging from partnership to divorce — a major point of contention has been the standards for convincing documentation in the service of reliable historical reconstruction. The Achilles' heel of intellectual history — even when shouldered by masters in the field — continues to be that the two essentially different poles, report and evaluation, are all too easily short-circuited so that the mind of the interpreter shines forth more brightly — or dimly, as the case may be — than the content of the interpreted source. No chiding of the social historian for a mindless reduction of complex realities to simple statistics can neutralize the intrinsic liability of (the best in) intellectual history: the potter forming the clay in his own image.

If actually prepared to sit down at the desk of the medieval or early modern exegete, the interpreter needs to be highly skilled in bringing to his tasks — beyond the necessary language tools — an intimate familiarity with the preceding exegetical tradition and the ability to draw on the same scholastic training which informed the exegetes chosen for analysis and comparison. Exactly at this juncture the comparative history of exegesis can play a new role by offering the intellectual historian modes of verification from within the field itself, holding out the promise of unmasking and destabilizing the interpretive paradigms drawn from "modern" philosophical or theological systems. A fine example of the effective execution of this task is Steinmetz's contribution to the Festschrift for Damasus Trapp (1991), in which the fierce and far-reaching debate between Karl Barth and Emil Brunner about Calvin's anthropology is clarified by comparing the exposition of one central passage (Romans 1:18-32) as presented by Denis the Carthusian, Melanchthon, Bullinger, Bucer, and Calvin.

Because of the large variety of skills required, only a limited number of players can work this field; all the more dependent are we on the expertise thus gathered. There is no way to forecast how modern historians of exegesis will shape our views of the epoch of reform and reformation, but change it they will. One of the signal features of this period is its discovery of the *bona curiositas*, rehabilitating the former mortal sin of "curiosity" into the essential quest for truth by experience and experiment. All who stand to profit from the endeavor so assiduously and creatively carried out by David Steinmetz may accordingly express their indebtedness in the telling departure from the classical farewell: *"Curiosi te salutant!"*

Abbreviations

ACW   Ancient Christian Writers. 56 vols. Westminster, Md., and New York: Newman, 1946-.

ANF   The Ante-Nicene Fathers. 10 vols. Buffalo and Edinburgh, 1885-96, but frequently reprinted.

ARG   *Archiv für Reformationsgeschichte.*

BHR   *Bibliothèque d'humanisme et renaissance.*

CCCM   Corpus Christianorum, Continuatio Medievalis. 127 vols. Turnhaut: Brepols, 1968–.

CCSL   Corpus Christianorum, Series Latina. 176 vols. Turnhout: Brepols, 1953-.

CH   *Church History.*

CHB   *Cambridge History of the Bible.* 3 vols. Cambridge: Cambridge University Press, 1963-70.

CNTC   Calvin's New Testament Commentaries. 12 vols. Edited by D. W. and T. F. Torrance. Grand Rapids: Eerdmans, 1959-72.

CO   Ioannis Calvini Opera Quae Supersunt Omnia. 59 vols. (= CR 29-88). Edited by G. Baum, E. Cunitz, and E. Reuss. Brunswick and Berlin, 1863-1900.

CR   Corpus Reformatorum. Vols. 1-28 comprise Philippi Melanchthonis Opera Quae Supersunt Omnia. Edited by C. G. Bretschneider. Halle, 1834-60. For CR 29-87 and 88-101, see CO and ZSW in this list.

CSEL   Corpus Scriptorum Ecclesiasticorum Latinorum. 85 vols. Vienna, 1866-.

CTJ   *Calvin Theological Journal*

CTS   Calvin Translation Society edition of Calvin's commentaries. 46 vols. Edinburgh, 1843-55. Frequently reprinted but variously bound; volume-numbers in the notes are therefore relative to each specific commentary and not to the entire set.

CWE   Collected Works of Erasmus. Toronto: University of Toronto Press, 1974-.

DTC   *Dictionnaire de théologie catholique*. 15 vols. Edited by A. Vacant, E. Mangenot, and E. Amann. Paris: Letouzey & Ane, 1899-1950.

FC   The Fathers of the Church. 92 vols. Washington: Catholic University of America Press, 1947-.

HTR   *Harvard Theological Review.*

HZW   Huldreich Zwinglis Werke. 8 vols. Edited by M. Schuler and J. Schulthess. Zurich, 1828-42.

LB   Desiderii Erasmi Roterodami opera omnia. 10 vols. Edited by J. Leclerc. Leiden [= Lugduni Batavorum], 1703-6.

LCC   Library of Christian Classics. 26 vols. Philadelphia: Westminster, 1952-69.

LCL   Loeb Classical Library. Cambridge, Mass.: Harvard University Press.

LW   Luther's Works [= "American Edition"]. 55 vols. St. Louis: Concordia, and Philadelphia: Fortress, 1955-86.

LWZ   The Latin Works of Huldrych Zwingli. 3 vols. 1912-29. Reprint, Durham, N.C.: Labyrinth, 1981-87.

MBW   Melanchthons Briefwechsel: Kritische und kommentierte Gesamtausgabe. Includes separate *Regesten* (8 vols.) and *Texte* (2 vols.). Stuttgart-Bad Cannstatt: Frommann-Holzboog, 1977-.

MQR   *Mennonite Quarterly Review.*

MSA   Melanchthons Werke in Auswahl [= "Studienausgabe"]. 7 vols. Edited by R. Stupperich. Gütersloh: Gerd Mohn, 1951-75.

NPNF   A Select Library of the Nicene and Post-Nicene Fathers. 28 vols. in two series. New York, 1886-1900, but frequently reprinted.

OS   Joannis Calvini Opera Selecta. 5 vols. Edited by P. Barth and W. Niesel. Munich: Christian Kaiser, 1970-74.

PG   Patrologia Graeca. 161 vols. Edited by J.-P. Migne. Paris, 1857-66.

PL   Patrologia Latina. 221 vols. Edited by J.-P. Migne. Paris, 1844-55.

SCJ	*Sixteenth Century Journal.*
SJT	*Scottish Journal of Theology.*
WA	D. Martin Luthers Werke: Kritische Gesamtausgabe. 66 vols. Weimar: Hermann Böhlaus Nachfolger, 1883-1987.
WABr	D. Martin Luthers Werke: Kritische Gesamtausgabe: Briefwechsel. 18 vols. Weimar: Hermann Böhlaus Nachfolger, 1930-85.
WADB	D. Martin Luthers Werke: Kritische Gesamtausgabe: Deutsche Bibel. 12 vols. Weimar: Hermann Böhlaus Nachfolger, 1906-61.
WATr	D. Martin Luthers Werke: Kritische Gesamtausgabe: Tischreden. 6 vols. Weimar: Hermann Böhlaus Nachfolger, 1912-21.
WTJ	*Westminster Theological Journal.*
ZSW	Huldreich Zwinglis Sämtliche Werke. 14 vols. (= CR 88-101). Edited by E. Egli et al. Berlin-Leipzig-Zürich, 1905-.

PART I

THE MEDIEVAL AND RENAISSANCE BACKGROUND

PART I

THE MEDIEVAL AND
RENAISSANCE BACKGROUND

Biblical Interpretation in the Era of the Reformation: The View from the Middle Ages

RICHARD A. MULLER

I. The Problem of the History of Exegesis

The history of exegesis in the era of the Reformation, or, as it might alternatively be identified, the history of the biblical commentary (as distinct from the history of the text and canon of Scripture), has seldom been adequately addressed. Farrar's old *History of Interpretation* is so profoundly biased against all forms of "precritical" exegesis that it is virtually useless to the understanding of the subject,[1] the *Cambridge History of the Bible* is notably silent on the issue of exegesis in the era of the Reformation,[2] and there are at present no studies of the history of biblical interpretation in the sixteenth century comparable in their scope and detail to the work of Margerie on the patristic period or to the works of Spicq, Smalley, and de Lubac on the Middle Ages.[3] This is a rather surprising fact, given the

---

1. Frederic W. Farrar, *History of Interpretation* (New York: Dutton, 1886; repr. Grand Rapids: Baker Book House, 1961).

2. In particular, Roland H. Bainton's essay "The Bible in the Reformation" (*CHB* 3:1-37) discusses the implications of *sola Scriptura*, the problem of the canon, and exegesis — but the discussion of exegesis is largely confined to hermeneutical principles and does not examine the actual procedures of interpreting the text, the resources used by the exegetes, or the various methods followed in Reformation-era commentaries.

3. Bertrand de Margerie, *Introduction l'histoire de l'exégèse*, I. *Les Pères grecs et orientaux*, IV. *L'Occident Latin* (Paris, 1980-90); Beryl Smalley, "The Bible in the Medieval Schools," in *CHB*

importance of Scripture and its interpretation to the Reformers and given the fact that biblical commentaries were the primary literary products of Reformers like Luther and Calvin, not to mention Vermigli, Oecolampadius, and Musculus.

Nonetheless, while there are numerous books and essays detailing, interpreting, misinterpreting, and advocating the Reformers' doctrine of Scripture, comparatively few works have given consideration to the detail and diversity of Protestant (not to mention Roman Catholic) exegesis in the sixteenth century, and, of the few extant studies, even fewer depart from the examination of doctrinal issues in the exegesis to investigate the sources and resources of sixteenth-century exegesis or the continuity and discontinuity between the Reformers and the older exegetical tradition. There are equally few presentations of the exegetical practices of lesser figures in the sixteenth century, writers whose work of biblical interpretation presumably promises to be less startling and, perhaps, more traditional than that of the great "movers and shakers" of Reformation thought.

Even the best-known large-scale studies of the exegesis of major Reformers, such as Bornkamm's classic study *Luther and the Old Testament*,[4] Pelikan's and Ebeling's examinations of Luther's hermeneutics,[5] Sick's monograph on Melanchthon's hermeneutic,[6] de Greef's *Calvijn en het Oude Testament*,[7] Parker's standard works on Calvin's Old and New Testament commentaries,[8] and Puckett's recent work on Calvin's Old Testament in-

---

2:197-220; idem, *The Study of the Bible in the Middle Ages* (Notre Dame: University of Notre Dame Press, 1964); Ceslaus Spicq, *Esquisse d'une histoire de l'exégèse latine au moyen âge* (Paris: J. Vrin, 1944); idem, "Pourquoi le Moyen Age n'a-t-il pas practiqué davantage l'exégèse littérale," in *Revue des Sciences Philosophiques et Théologiques* 30 (1941-42): 169-79; idem, "Saint Thomas d'Aquin: VI. Saint Thomas d'Aquin exégète," in *DTC* 15/1:694-738; Henri de Lubac, *Exégèse mediaevale: les quatre sens de l'Ecriture*, 4 vols. (Paris: Aubier, 1959-64).

4. Heinrich Bornkamm, *Luther and the Old Testament*, trans. Eric W. and Ruth C. Gritsch (Philadelphia: Fortress, 1969).

5. Jaroslav Pelikan, *Luther the Expositor: Introduction to the Reformer's Exegetical Writings* (St. Louis: Concordia, 1959); Gerhard Ebeling, *Evangelische Evangelienauslegung. Eine Untersuchung zu Luthers Hermeneutik* (Munich: Chr. Kaiser, 1942; 3d ed. [erweitert um ein Nachwort], Tübingen: J. C. B. Mohr [Paul Siebeck], 1991); idem, "Die Anfänge von Luthers Hermeneutik," *Zeitschrift für Theologie und Kirche* 48 (1951): 172-230.

6. Hansjörg Sick, *Melanchthon als Ausleger des Alten Testaments*, Beiträge zur Geschichte der biblischen Hermeneutik 2 (Tübingen: J. C. B. Mohr, 1959).

7. Wulfert de Greef, *Calvijn en het Oude Testament* (Amsterdam: T. Bolland, 1984).

8. T. H. L. Parker, *Calvin's New Testament Commentaries* (Grand Rapids: Eerdmans, 1971); *Calvin's Old Testament Commentaries* (Edinburgh: T. & T. Clark, 1986). Parker's survey of Romans commentaries, however, is an exception to this trend: *Commentaries on the Epistle to the Romans, 1532-1542* (Edinburgh: T. & T. Clark, 1986).

terpretation,[9] discuss the thought of the Reformers in relative isolation. These works, for all of their notable insights into the methods and practices of the great Reformers, make no attempt to tell us whether or not the exegesis of Luther or Calvin is original or highly traditional on a particular text or issue in Scripture. Nor do these works point us toward the commentaries of less famous predecessors and contemporaries to indicate lines of influence: this, despite the fact that we know that the Reformers did not do their exegesis in isolation but read widely in the works of the fathers and medieval doctors, as well as in the exegetical works of other Reformers.

It is certainly the case that the neat lines historians have tended to draw between the Middle Ages and the Renaissance, or between either the Middle Ages or the Renaissance and the Reformation, or between the Reformation and post-Reformation eras, were by no means visible in the sixteenth century. And it was far from obvious in the late fifteenth or sixteenth century (as is easily seen from the several printings of the work from that time) that Nicholas of Lyra's early fourteenth-century commentary on the text and gloss of the Bible was either textually or theologically out of date.[10]

The last two decades, however, have seen the flowering of a new interest in the detail of Reformation-era exegesis: we have seen several international colloquia on the subject as well as the appearance of the sixteenth-century volume of the massive *Bible de tous les temps*.[11] Moreover, major works in the history of interpretation and in the development of a method of comparative exegesis have come from the pens of David Steinmetz,[12] Elsie McKee,[13] and

9. David L. Puckett, *John Calvin's Exegesis of the Old Testament* (Louisville: Westminster John Knox Press, 1995).

10. E.g., Nicholas of Lyra, *Biblia sacra cum Glossa interlineari, ordinaria, et Nicolai Lyrani Postilla. . .* , 7 vols. (Venice, 1588).

11. Olivier Fatio and Pierre Fraenkel (eds.), *Histoire de l'exégèse an XVIᵉ siècle: textes du colloqui international tenu Genève en 1976* (Geneva: Droz, 1978); David C. Steinmetz (ed.), *The Bible in the Sixteenth Century* [Second International Colloquy on the History of Biblical Exegesis in the Sixteenth Century] (Durham, N.C.: Duke University Press, 1990); Irena Dorota Backus and Francis M. Higman (eds.), *Théorie et pratique de l'exégèse. Actes du troisieme Colloque international sur l'histoire de l'exégèse biblique au XVIe siècle, Genève, 31 aôut–2 septembre 1988* (Geneva: Droz, 1990); Guy Bedouelle and Bernard Roussel (eds.), *Le temps des Réformes et la Bible: Bible de tous les temps*, vol. 5 (Paris: Beauchesne, 1989).

12. David C. Steinmetz, *Luther and Staupitz: An Essay in the Intellectual Origins of the Protestant Reformation* (Durham: Duke University Press, 1980); idem, *Calvin in Context* (New York and Oxford: Oxford University Press, 1995).

13. Elsie Anne McKee, *John Calvin on the Diaconate and Liturgical Almsgiving* (Geneva: Droz, 1984); idem, *Elders and the Plural Ministry: The Role of Exegetical History in Illuminating John Calvin's Thelogy* (Geneva: Droz, 1988).

Irena Backus.[14] Kenneth Hagen has written extensively on the exegesis of Hebrews and Galatians.[15] Guy Bedouelle has examined the exegesis of Lefèvre d'Étaples.[16] Susan Schreiner has published an extensive examination of the history of the interpretation of Job.[17] Max Engammare has produced a significant examination of the Song of Songs.[18] A survey of major early sixteenth-century biblical interpreters has been offered by Wulfert de Greef.[19] John L. Thompson has placed Calvin's reading of Old and New Testament texts concerning women in historical perspective, and Timothy J. Wengert has performed a similar service for Melanchthon's interpretation of the Gospel of John.[20] In these works, not only have we seen detailed study of exegetical practice in the sixteenth century but also the beginnings of significant new methodologies for the history of exegesis — methodologies that recognize the complex dialogical process in which sixteenth-century exegetes engaged.

Before these recent studies appeared, two seminal essays by David Steinmetz had set the stage for investigation of "precritical" biblical interpretation. One of these essays, "The Superiority of Pre-Critical Exegesis,"[21] has been reprinted several times and has been consistently cited by other scholars in the field as a succinct statement of the churchly and tradition-

---

14. Irena Dorota Backus, Pierre Fraenkel, and Pierre Lardet, *Martin Bucer apocryphe et authentique: études de bibliographie et d'éxegèse* (Geneva: Revue de théologie et de philosophie, 1983); Martin Bucer, *Enarratio in Evangelion Iohannis,* ed. Irena Backus (Leiden and New York: Brill, 1988).

15. Kenneth Hagen, *A Theology of Testament in the Young Luther: The Lectures on Hebrews* (Leiden: Brill, 1974); idem, *Hebrews Commenting from Erasmus to Bèze, 1516-1598* (Tübingen: Mohr, 1981); idem, *Luther's Approach to Scripture as Seen in His "Commentaries" on Galatians, 1519-1538* (Tübingen: Mohr, 1993).

16. Guy Bedouelle, *Lefèvre d'Étaples et l'Intelligence des Écritures* (Geneva: Droz, 1976); idem, *Le Quincuplex Psalterium de Lefèvre d'Étaples: Un guide de lecture* (Geneva: Droz, 1979).

17. Susan E. Schreiner, *Where Shall Wisdom Be Found? Calvin's Exegesis of Job from Medieval and Modern Perspectives* (Chicago: University of Chicago Press, 1994).

18. Max Engammare, *Lire le Cantique des Cantiques a la Renaissance* (La Rochelle: Rumeur des Ages, 1994); idem, *"Qu'il me baise des baisiers de sa bouche": Le Cantique des cantiques à la Renaissance* (Geneva: Droz, 1993).

19. Wulfert de Greef, *"De Ware Uitleg": Hervormers en hun verklaring van de Bijbel* (Leiden: J. J. Groen, 1995). De Greef surveys Lefèvre, Erasmus, Zwingli, Bullinger, Oecolampadius, Capito, Bucer, Melanchthon, Vermigli, and Calvin, offering extensive bibliography on the history of exegesis.

20. John L. Thompson, *John Calvin and the Daughters of Sarah: Women in Regular and Exceptional Roles in the Exegesis of Calvin, His Predecessors and His Contemporaries* (Geneva: Droz, 1992); Timothy Wengert, *Philip Melanchthon's Annotationes in Johannem in Relation to Its Predecessors and Contemporaries* (Geneva: Droz, 1987).

21. David C. Steinmetz, "The Superiority of Pre-Critical Exegesis," in *Theology Today* 37 (1980-81): 27-38.

ary character of the older exegesis in its distinction from modern, higher-critical study of Scripture. The other essay, a set of ten theses written some four years earlier, presaged the argument for the "superiority of precritical exegesis" and neatly frames both Steinmetz's more recent work and the inquiries into Reformation-era biblical interpretation found in the present volume:

1. The meaning of a biblical text is not exhausted by the original intention of the author.
2. The most primitive layer of biblical tradition is not necessarily the most authoritative.
3. The importance of the Old Testament for the church is predicated upon the continuity of the people of God in history, a continuity which persists in spite of discontinuity between Israel and the church.
4. The Old Testament is the hermeneutical key which unlocks the meaning of the New Testament and apart from which it will be misunderstood.
5. The church and not human experience as such is the middle term between the Christian interpreter and the biblical text.
6. The gospel and not the law is the central message of the biblical text.
7. One cannot lose the tension between the gospel and the law without losing both law and gospel.
8. The church which is restricted in its preaching to the original intention of the author is a church which must reject the Old Testament as an exclusively Jewish book.
9. The church which is restricted in its preaching to the most primitive layer of biblical tradition as the most authoritative is a church which can no longer preach from the New Testament.
10. Knowledge of the exegetical tradition of the church is an indispensable aid for the interpretation of Scripture.[22]

The burden of the present volume is to examine the sources and resources and to illustrate the continuities and discontinuities in the exegetical tradition leading into and through the Reformation. Specifically, this collection of essays proposes to highlight the historical context of Reformation exegesis and to describe how a truly contextual understanding signals a highly illuminating turn in Reformation studies.

22. David C. Steinmetz, "Theology and Exegesis: Ten Theses," in *Historie de l'exégèse au XVIe siècle*, p. 382.

II. Reformation Exegesis in Medieval Perspective: Elements of Continiuity in Development

As already observed, much of the earlier literature on the history of exegesis is seriously defective. The problem is nowhere clearer than in Farrar's *History of Interpretation,* but it also emerges in such a relatively recent work as Kraus's well-known essay on Calvin's exegetical methods.[23] Farrar and Kraus share the assumption that the exegetical methods of the Reformers are a prologue to modern critical exegesis and that the hermeneutical assumptions of the Reformation were far more akin to those of twentieth-century biblical interpreters than to those of the medieval exegetes. And yet Kraus is almost nostalgic in his appreciation for precisely those theological and spiritual characteristics of Calvin's exegesis that cut across the grain of the modern biblical commentary, including such typical Calvinian assumptions as the identification of Christ as the *scopus* of Scripture and the need for the exegete to "go beyond the biblical wording" to identify the divine authorial intention. Kraus also notes favorably Calvin's interpretation of the Old Testament in terms of its fulfillment in the New, his understanding of Scripture as God's Word to the church, and his belief that the authority of Scripture is self-authenticated to the reader or hearer in and through the illumination of the Spirit.[24] What Kraus did not recognize is that these "theological" aspects of Calvin's exegetical program are not only integral to Calvin's stress on the literal sense of the text but they also and equally identify Calvin's method as belonging to a precritical model more in continuity with trajectories of medieval biblical interpretation than with tendencies in modern and so-called "critical" exegesis.[25] In short, Calvin's interests do not presage the nineteenth and twentieth century; they rather emerge from the legacy of his forebears.

Although often dismissed by modern exegetes as a form of excessive allegorism when understood in terms of its logic and its intentions rather than in terms of its abuses, the fourfold exegesis is not entirely discontinuous with the logic and the intentions of Reformation-era biblical interpretation. Thus, in the model inherited by Gregory the Great from Augustine and taught through the Middle Ages as an extension of Augustine's herme-

---

23. Hans Joachim Kraus, "Calvin's Exegetical Principles," *Interpretation* 31 (1977): 9-18.

24. Kraus, "Calvin's Exegetical Principles," pp. 9, 16-17.

25. Cf. Richard A. Muller, "The Hermeneutic of Promise and Fulfillment in Calvin's Exegesis of the Old Testament Prophecies of the Kingdom," in *The Bible in the Sixteenth Century,* pp. 68-82.

neutic (as described in his *De doctrina Christiana*), a fundamental relationship was assumed between the meaning of the text of the Law and the Prophets and the great commandment to love God and neighbor. From the literal or historical sense of the text, readers ought to be led to the right love of God, neighbor, and, therefore, of the self as well. This rightly ordered set of relationships could, moreover, be described in terms of the Christian virtues of faith, love, and hope. The text therefore points from its literal or historical meaning to what one ought to believe, do, and hope for — applications that correspond, respectively, to the allegorical, tropological, and anagogical senses.

As Spicq has pointed out in his survey of the history of medieval exegesis and as Schreiner has noted with specific reference to the exegesis of the book of Job, two directions have been taken in the course of medieval exegesis, the one toward a fourfold exegesis (literal, allegorical, tropological, and anagogical) that tended to emphasize allegory and trope, epitomized by Gregory the Great; the other, while hardly hostile toward the spiritual meanings of the text, nonetheless toward a "literal" interpretation of the text, well represented by Albert the Great and Thomas Aquinas.[26] Gregory himself described the model as threefold: "first we lay the foundation in history; then by following a symbolical sense, we erect an intellectual edifice to be a stronghold of faith; and lastly, by the grace of moral instruction, we as it were paint the fabric in fair colors."[27] The fourfold model appears in such writers as John Cassian, John of Salisbury, Thomas Aquinas, Hugh of St. Cher, and Nicholas of Lyra. Lyra repeated the couplet describing the *quadriga*, usually attributed to the Dominican, Augustine of Dacia (d. 1282): *Littera gesta docet, / quid credas allegoria, / Moralis quid agas, / quo tendas anagogia* — "The letter teaches what has happened, allegory what one believes, the moral meaning what one does, and anagoge where one is going."[28]

But there is another explanation of the fourfold exegesis found among medieval exegetes that inferred the model directly from the shape of the canon of Scripture and from the direction of sacred history: the Old Testa-

---

26. Spicq, *Esquisse d'une histoire de l'exégèse,* pp. 209-15, 273-78; Susan E. Schreiner, "Through a Mirror Dimly: Calvin's Sermons on Job," *CTJ* 21 (1986): 177.

27. Gregory the Great, *Ep.* 5.53a, trans. in F. H. Dudden, *Gregory the Great: His Place in History and Thought* (New York, 1905), 1:193.

28. De Lubac, *Exégèse mediaevale: les quatre sens de l'Ecriture,* 1:23. See also the surveys in R. E. McNally, "Exegesis, Medieval," in *New Catholic Encyclopedia,* 5:707-10, and Harry Caplan, "The Four Senses of Scriptural Interpretation and the Medieval Theology of Preaching," *Speculum* 4 (1929): 282-90.

ment is a figure of the New Testament, and the New Testament, albeit itself a fulfillment, contains figures of things still to come. When the Old Testament figures point toward teachings fulfilled in the New Testament, the meaning is allegorical. When either testament teaches things that Christians ought to do, whether by illustration in the Old Testament or by the example of Christ and the Apostles in the New, the meaning is tropological. And when the text presents figures of heavenly glory, the meaning is anagogical.[29]

For instance, in Aquinas's view, the literal or "historical" sense provides the foundation for all other levels of interpretation. Indeed, in some cases, Aquinas can insist that the literal meaning is the sole meaning of the text. Thus Aquinas will insist that metaphors and analogies must be understood as such — and that expressions such as the "hand" or "arm" of God in their literal sense refer to the power or activity of God and not to a physical hand or arm. A prophetic text like Daniel's reference to the stone cut out of the mountain refers in its literal sense not to a stone but to the thing signified by the stone.[30] For Aquinas, this literal meaning is to be gauged by the intentions of the divine author, as well as by the intentions and the stylistic characteristics of the human writer. The literal meaning of a prophecy, therefore, will be its fullfillment.

So, too, medieval exegetes understood, as Luther and Calvin did, that God is the primary author of Scripture but in such a way that the human "penmen" are also the authors of the text who express their own meaning in its words; thus Aquinas can write, "the principal author of Holy Scripture is the Holy Spirit . . . at the same time there is nothing repugnant in the notion that man, who is the instrumental cause of the Holy Scripture, should in one expression mean several things." Thomas goes on to note that the prophets "so spoke of present facts as to intend thereby to signify future things."[31] Such assumptions stand in an exegetical tradition that leads, by way of later exegetes like Nicholas of Lyra, toward the interpretive models of the sixteenth century.

Two further developments in pre-Reformation biblical interpretation served to increase emphasis on the literal meaning of the text and therefore

---

29. Hugh Pope, "St. Thomas as an Interpreter of Holy Scripture," in *St. Thomas Aquinas,* ed. Aelred Whitacre (Oxford: Blackwell, 1925), p. 133.

30. On Aquinas exegesis see Maximino Arias Reyero, *Thomas Aquinas als Exeget: Die Prinzipien seiner Schriftdeutung und seine Lehre von den Schriftsinnen* (Münster: Johannes Verlag, 1971); and see Paul Synave, "La doctrine de St. Thomas D'Aquin sur le sens littéral des Ecritures," *Revue biblique* 35 (1926): 40-65.

31. Thomas Aquinas, *Quodlibet* VII.14, ad 5m, as cited in Pope, "St. Thomas as an Interpreter of Holy Scripture," pp. 131-32.

illustrate aspects of the continuity between medieval and Reformation exegesis. First, Nicholas of Lyra, the early fourteenth century exegete who
worked in the Hebrew text of the Old Testament and studied the Jewish
commentators, argued for a simpler interpretive structure than the fourfold
exegesis, notably one that stressed the literal sense of the text: like Hugh of
St. Victor in the twelfth century and Thomas Aquinas in the thirteenth,
Lyra defined four senses of the text but stressed the use of the letter as the
norm. He also proposed a "double literal sense" extending to the prophetic
realization of a text and reflecting the movement from the sign in the text
to the thing signified.[32] Second, Faber Stapulensis (Lefèvre d'Etaples)
moved beyond this double to a single (and wholly spiritual) literal sense,
defining the literal meaning as that intended by the Holy Spirit.[33] Lyra's
intention was clearly to press the exegete toward the letter (the *historia* of
the text) as the basis for all spiritual or doctrinal understanding: from this
perspective he illustrates how nominally "scholastic" exegesis can point
methodologically toward the Reformation. By way of contrast, Faber's intention was to press the exegete away from the *historia*, particularly the
historia of the Old Testament, toward a christological meaning. Faber thus
illustrates how stress on the spiritual meaning of the Old Testament could
not only remain but also be of central concern to a "humanist" text-critic,
much of whose work focused on the establishment of the Hebrew text.

To press the point home, once it has been seen that Calvin consistently
understood the "literal" meaning of Old Testament prophecies of the kingdom to be not only the reestablishment of Israel after the exile but also the
establishment of the kingdom in the redemptive work of Christ, the further-
ance of the kingdom in the reform of the church in the sixteenth century,
and the final victory of the kingdom in Christ's second coming,[34] it can
also be seen that the "literal" meaning of the text, for Calvin, held a message
concerning what Christians ought to believe, what Christians ought to do,
and what Christians ought to hope for. This paradigm seems suspiciously
familiar. It is clearly not at all like the modern, higher-critical paradigm for
biblical interpretation. It asks that the exegete move past the rather bare
grammatical meaning of the text to doctrine, morality, and hope — in
short, from *littera* to *credenda, agenda,* and *speranda.* The exegetical practice

---

32. See James S. Preus, *From Shadow to Promise: Old Testament Interpretation from
Augustine to the Young Luther* (Cambridge, Mass.: Harvard University Press, 1969), pp. 62-71;
Eugene H. Merrill, "Rashi, Nicholas de Lyra and Christian Exegesis," *WTJ* 38 (1975/76): 66-79.
33. Preus, *From Shadow to Promise,* pp. 62-71, 137-49.
34. Muller, "The Hermeneutic of Promise and Fulfillment," pp. 74-79.

is far more textual, the hermeneutics is far more grammatical and philological, and (in justice to Calvin's intentions and actual procedure) the sense of the text is focused in its literal meaning, but the underlying assumption that the meaning of the text is ultimately oriented to the belief, life, and future of the church retains significant affinities with the *quadriga,* the basic pattern of the so-called "allegorical exegesis" of the Middle Ages.

A step back in time from Calvin to Luther makes the same point still more clearly. Luther's early exegesis in particular — as appears in his commentaries on the Psalter, on Hebrews, and on Romans — follows the standard medieval pattern of an extended gloss on the text, accompanied by scholia or postils in which issues of theological significance are addressed at greater length. But all Luther's commentaries, whether early or late, consistently address doctrinal and moral issues — *credenda* and *agenda.* What is more, they all consistently examine and dialogue with the patristic and medieval tradition, often as mediated by the *Glossa ordinaria.*

The point of these observations is not to claim either Luther or Calvin as a proponent of the *quadriga.* Rather, the point is to note a fundamental continuity of exegetical interest that remained the property of precritical exegesis as it passed over from the medieval fourfold model into other models that, in one way or another, emphasized the concentration of meaning in the literal sense of the text. The *quadriga,* after all, was never merely an allegorical interpretation. The history of medieval exegesis, moreover, evidences a shift toward the letter. Even so, Luther, Calvin, and their contemporaries did not simply trade allegory for literal interpretation. They strengthened the shift to letter with increased emphasis on textual and philological study, and then proceeded to find various figures and levels of meaning, indicating *credenda, agenda,* and *speranda* embedded in the letter itself. This passage from the fourfold exegesis toward an exegesis emphasizing the literal meaning of the text, therefore, marks a continuity — not a contrast — between sixteenth-century biblical interpretation and the exegesis of at least the preceding four centuries.

We need also to disabuse ourselves of the impression that the Reformers' reliance on the philological skills of the Renaissance humanists somehow marks a reversal of the tendencies and interests of the Middle Ages. Whereas it is certainly true that the biblical languages were not as widely or expertly known during the Middle Ages as they were in the sixteenth century, it is also the case that the humanist emphasis on the philological and textual examination of Scripture had medieval precedent. Not only can we point to the Hebraism of Nicholas of Lyra in the fourteenth century, we must also note the use of Hebrew and Greek in the Victorine school in the twelfth century and the concerted effort to establish a valid text of Scripture, through the use of Hebrew and Greek manuscripts, in the Dominican "Correctories" of the thirteenth century, the most notable of which was the work of Hugh of St. Cher.[35] Here, as in the shift from a fourfold or a spiritual exegesis to the more literal, grammatical methods of the Reformation, there was certainly a major change in emphasis with the Renaissance — and that change in emphasis carried over also into the Reformation. It was not, however, an unprecedented development; instead, it represents, together with the shift toward the literal sense, a significant trajectory in biblical study that links the Reformation to its past.

Finally, a continuity still more important than the presence of some knowledge of the biblical languages during the Middle Ages is the continuity of text. Despite the text-critical work of Erasmus and other scholars of the Renaissance, and despite the Protestant reaction to an increasing Roman Catholic emphasis on the normative character of the Vulgate, the Vulgate retained much of its status as the standard translation of Scripture even in Protestant circles until well into the sixteenth century. At the beginning of the Reformation there was little thought of replacing the Vulgate, if only because it was the text available not only in Latin bibles per se but also, more importantly, in the Gloss and in the commentaries then in use. Some Protestant exegetes, including the humanist Conrad Pellican, simply followed the Vulgate. Others, such as Calvin, whose commentaries offered their own translation, continued to reflect the language of the Vulgate in their own usage. After all, even in its original form it had been a rather fine translation and, as edited by the Dominicans in Paris during the thirteenth century, it was a much improved and for the most part accurate text. Even in the late sixteenth century, Beza would continue to refer to the Vulgate in his *Annotationes*, and not infrequently with considered respect.

III. Reformation Exegesis in Medieval Perspective: Elements of Discontiniuity and Change

Once the substantial continuity of development in medieval and Reformation exegesis has been noted, it can provide a baseline for ascertaining the nature of the change that took place as biblical interpretation moved through the Renaissance and the Reformation. If it now proves impossible

35. See Eugène Mangenot, "Correctoires de La Bible," in *Dictionnaire de la Bible*, 2/1, cols. 1022-26; and cf. Spicq, *Esquisse d'une histoire de l'exégèse*, pp. 165-72.

to identify sudden discontinuities in biblical interpretation — just as it has proved impossible, on a larger scale, to identify clear beginnings and endings of historical "periods" like the Middle Ages, Renaissance, and Reformation — it continues to be possible, indeed, necessary, to recognize the differences in exegetical approach that arose during the era of the Reformation.

The transition from the Middle Ages to the Reformation was not, certainly, a transition from precritical to modern "critical" exegesis: to document such a transition, we would have to look to the late seventeenth and the eighteenth century. It was a transition, however, from a precritical approach that could acknowledge spiritual senses of the text beyond the literal sense to a precritical approach that strove to locate spiritual meaning entirely in the literal sense. It was also a transition from a precritical approach that could distinguish (but seldom separated) scriptural meaning from traditional significance to an equally precritical approach that could identify, on occasion, wide diastasis between Scripture and tradition while remaining within the traditionary exegetical conversation.

So too, despite what has been said of the enduring significance of the Vulgate in Protestant circles, the transition from the Middle Ages to the Reformation did entail movement from a fairly uniform textual basis for theology (namely, the Vulgate) to a more diversified basis, with an increasing tendency for the more philologically capable commentators — again, Calvin is but an example — to offer their own translations of the biblical text. Here we can identify the major impact of Renaissance humanism on the history of exegesis: philological and rhetorical expertise, not absent from the field of medieval exegesis, became the norm with the rise of humanism. The task of establishing the text and of closely examining its grammar and syntax in the original languages became, by way of their humanistic training, one of the basic tasks in the Reformers' exegesis.

From the perspective, moreover, of the relative contrast between humanistic, philological interests and scholastic, theological, or dogmatic interests, it becomes possible to discern the dual heritage of Reformation-era biblical commentary and to characterize historically the various genres of biblical commentary found during the sixteenth century. Just as the Reformers' commentaries differ from medieval commentaries, so also are they seldom, if ever, precisely what one might call Renaissance humanist commentaries. The dual inheritance of the Reformation yielded a variety in the style or genre of the commentary that runs from theological analysis with little philological interest, such as can be identified in the *Glossa ordinaria*, to an essentially philological commentary, such as Erasmus's *Annotations,* in which theological interests are quite muted.

Luther's early efforts, for instance, notably his lectures on the Psalter, Romans, and Hebrews, follow quite closely the typical medieval format, moving from the identification of the text by citation of a phrase, to an extended amplificatory gloss, to elaborate *scholia* on significant issues or topics. From a purely formal perspective, Luther drew heavily there on the *lectio continua* and *enarratio* of the medieval classroom and thus reflects the method and the appearance of Nicholas of Lyra's commentary on the Bible. Stylistic transition, moreover, is quite noticeable over the course of Luther's career: his later commentaries and lectures no longer distinguish gloss from scholia and tend more toward an extended running comment on the entire text. This transition can be traced, at least in part, to the increased philological expertise of the comentator and the recourse to original languages, which rendered the traditional glosses obsolete. Of course, the gradual replacement of the Vulgate with other translations, particularly in the case of the New Testament with Erasmus's and eventually Beza's Latin versions, ultimately meant the demise of the old glosses as major reference points in Protestant circles.

The movement away from the traditional gloss and *scholia* not only through contact with philological concerns but also through the impact of humanistic rhetorical interests is also evident in the diverse patterns adopted by Bucer, Bullinger, Melanchthon, and Calvin.[36] Bucer apparently attempted to satisfy the requirements of all extant models, producing massive commentaries praised by his contemporaries for their content but criticized, notably by Calvin, for their unwieldiness. Bucer divided the commentator's task into *metaphrasis, enarratio, interpretatio,* and *observatio,* which consisted, respectively, in a paraphrase of the text; a running commentary addressing primarily the theological import of the passage; an analysis of specific issues in the text, often of a linguistic character; while the *observatio* or *observationes,* often prefaced with a *quaestio,* gave Bucer the opportunity to offer topical explanations of various questions raised in the text. This last section Bucer explicitly offered for the sake of those not profoundly educated in theology.[37]

36. See the extensive descriptions of the Romans commentaries of these and other early sixteenth-century exegetes in T. H. L. Parker, *Commentaries on the Epistle to the Romans 1532-1542* (Edinburgh: T. & T. Clark, 1986).

37. Cf. the extended description and outline in Parker, *Commentaries on Romans,* pp. 35-62.

Bullinger's commentaries can be described, without much exaggeration, as children of the gloss and scholion approach conceived in a world of Renaissance place-logic. Characteristic of Bullinger's efforts is his initial presentation of a unit of text, followed by a running commentary, and punctuated as necessary by theological *loci* in which the standard theological topics generated by the text are treated at some length. Thus, in his commentary on Romans, Bullinger inserts *loci* on the law and on the magistrate following his running commentary on chapters seven and thirteen, respectively. The gloss-scholion model is still visible, transformed into running commentary and *locus* by the concerns of sixteenth-century rhetoric and dialectic. Similar patterns can be discerned in Musculus's and Vermigli's commentaries.

Melanchthon, by way of contrast to both Bucer and Bullinger, strove for rhetorical clarity, offering analyses of the argument and disposition of an entire book. He provided discussion, however, not of the entire text, but only of the theological topics resident in the text. In his description of the argument and disposition, Melanchthon emphasized, first, the broad rhetorical forms in the text — exhortation, development, digression, confirmation of arguments, conclusion, and epilogue. Within these forms, Melanchthon indicated patterns of argument, including use of syllogisms, enthymemes, and so forth. His method might be characterized as a Renaissance descendant of the medieval scholion, fine-tuned by the humanistic sense of the priority of rhetorical over logical argument, and constructed around the use of rhetorical categories as primary categories for text analysis. Melanchthon's elicitation of topics or *loci* from the text, moreover, offered a paradigm for the movement from exegesis to theology, given the focus of theology on the identification and explication of the standard topics or *loci communes* of Christian discourse.

Calvin's commentaries present a fourth variant: his method is redolent of the gloss and the classroom *enarratio*, an approach evidenced in Luther's later lecture style, in the second division of Bucer's commentaries, and in the running comment found in Bullinger's exegesis. Yet, despite Calvin's explicit rejection of Melanchthon's concentration on the *loci*, Melanchthon's interest in the rhetorical structure of entire books of Scripture finds some reflection in Calvin's finely structured initial *argumenta*. Calvin also echoed Melanchthon's and Bullinger's sense that right understanding of the text must produce *loci* or topical discussion: he merely distinguished, somewhat pointedly, between the literary genre of the running commentary and that of the *loci communes* and then, accordingly, divided his labors between the writing of commentaries and the separate presentation of his *loci* as gathered in the *Institutes*.

IV. Prologue to the Present Volume

The two remaining essays in Part I of this volume offer, in greater detail than possible in the preceding survey, background perspectives on Reformation-era exegesis. Karlfried Froehlich leads off by examining the fourfold exegetical method presented on the eve of the Reformation by Johannes Trithemius (d. 1516). Froehlich provides a discussion of the varied history of scholarship on Trithemius and surveys the use and modification of the fourfold method in the centuries before Trithemius. Trithemius's work was rooted in Hugh of St. Victor's *Didascalion,* but consistently modified Hugh's threefold approach by adding *anagoge* to Hugh's description of a literal, allegorical, and tropological pattern of interpretation. Froehlich suggests that although Trithemius well sums up the old exegetical tradition, he also reduces it to a fairly rigid form, as evidenced, for example, by his failure to see how Hugh had understood the anagogical dimension as a broad hermeneutical principle rather than as a distinct meaning. In Trithemius's work, at least the method had run its course — and his treatise on interpretation points, if only negatively, toward the need for the infusion of new life into exegetical method.

In a second background essay, John B. Payne offers a view of Erasmus's exegetical method in its relation to the approaches of two Reformers, Zwingli and Bullinger. Here, as in the essays that follow, emphasis falls on the place and significance of a particular exegete in the history of biblical interpretation, as illustrated by his interpretation of a particular issue or passage in relation to his antecedents and contemporaries. What appears far more clearly in the context of these detailed examinations of the exegesis of particular passages than in any general survey of the development of exegetical method is a highly variegated picture of continuity and discontinuity between medieval and Reformation-era exegesis. Indeed, the acceptance or rejection of traditional exegesis on the part of a given Reformer becomes increasingly unpredictable as one moves away from the great debates of the Reformation to examine the vast array of passages in Scripture that played no particular role in doctrinal controversy. And even in the case of texts lying at the heart of sixteenth-century debate, the tradition is surprisingly nuanced.

Payne focuses on Erasmus's exegesis of Matt. 11:28-30, "Come to me, all who labor and are heavy-laden. . . ." There Erasmus's *Paraphrase* departs from Jerome's contrast between the heavy burden of the Mosaic law and the lighter burden of the law of Christ. Erasmus contrasts, instead, the law of Christ with the laws imposed by human beings, the "philosophy of

Christ" in its congruence with our nature as it ought to be over against the
burdensome regulations that beset our fallen nature. Significantly, this Erasmian interpretation recurs in Zwingli's understanding of the text as a juxtaposition of the gracious calling of Christ with the undue burdens of
human ordinances and teachings. Reliance on Erasmus's interpretation of
the text is even more pronounced in Bullinger's commentary on Matthew
— although here other influences, such as Chrysostom and Luther, appear
as well. Whereas several of the other essays in the volume document places
in which the Reformers stand in clear continuity with patristic or medieval
discussion of a passage, here we have a striking example of a marked change
of course, albeit still in conversation with the tradition.

With both medieval and Renaissance background in view, we move
on to the exegesis and interpretation of the early Reformation (Part II).
Here Kenneth Hagen's examination of Luther's many approaches to the
text of Psalm 116, "All men are liars," positions Luther both as a highly
original theological exegete and as a highly traditional churchman in close
dialogue with the exegetical tradition. This particular text nicely exemplifies
an exegetical development untouched by Reformation-era controversy in
which Luther sheds light on a text by drawing on and then refocusing the
tradition. As Hagen points out, Luther appears not as the precursor of
modern exegesis — nor even as the precursor of a dogmatic Lutheranism
— but as a late medieval exegete engaged in a churchly interpretive conversation that began as early as the Pauline juxtaposition of the Psalm, "All
men are liars," with the rejoinder, "God alone is true."

Carl M. Leth sets Balthasar Hubmaier's interpretation of the power
of the keys in Matt. 16:18-19 into the context of Hubmaier's rather pointed
polemic against "strange glosses" and scholastic "quarreling about words."
This particular text, of course, also stood at the center of a major Reformation debate. Despite the polemic, however, Leth is able to detect a striking
affinity between the Anabaptist Hubmaier's reading of the text and the
traditional Catholic assumption that Christ here grants "effective power"
to the church to remit sins. Among his contemporaries, Hubmaier resonates
far more clearly with Erasmus than with either Luther or Zwingli — although he shared with the latter two an assumption of the clarity and
simplicity of the meaning of Scripture.

Timothy J. Wengert takes on the issue of method, specifically of the
impact of humanist rhetoric on the exegetical method of Philip Melanchthon. Wengert shows how Melanchthon's humanistic rhetoric and philological skill conjoined in the production of a commentary no less indebted
than others of its day to the exegetical tradition but, at the same time, far

more closely attuned to the genre, organization, and detail of Paul's argument than any of its predecessors. In Wengert's words, "Melanchthon viewed Paul's epistle to the Romans as a letter, shaped by its author using common rhetorical methods to make a single theological point," namely, the letter's *scopus*. At the same time that Melanchthon offered theological evidence of "his own encounter with Luther's theology," his rhetorical analysis of the shape and contents of Paul's own argument "endowed evangelical theology with an apostolic authority it would not otherwise have had."

Irena Backus examines Martin Bucer's efforts to make sense of the difficult chronology of John 5–7 in the light of his dialogue with the exegetical tradition. The chronological problem of John 5–7 has troubled exegetes and theologians since Irenaeus, and it continues to trouble those scholars who hope even partially to reconcile the Johannine with the Synoptic view of Jesus' ministry. Whereas the Synoptic Gospels agree in placing the crucifixion some three years after the baptism of Jesus, the Johannine narrative can easily be construed as indicating a ministry of barely one year. Backus consults the writings of Irenaeus, Chrysostom, Cyril of Alexandria, Theophylact, Bede, Rupert of Deutz, Thomas Aquinas, Nicholas of Lyra, and Ludolph of Saxony, among others. Whereas Lefèvre and Erasmus simply adopt the solution of Chrysostom, Bucer stands as the first sixteenth-century exegete to take up the problem in detail — to the point that he was criticized by Oecolampadius for excessive meditation on the issue. What draws our attention here is the intensity of the exegetical conversation both among contemporaries and with the older tradition.

W. P. Stephens addresses Zwingli's understanding of John 6:63, a text crucial to his eucharistic debate with Luther, with particular attention to a scholarly line of argument that branded Zwingli with a dualistic understanding of flesh and spirit. Stephens illuminates Zwingli's exegesis with an examination of Augustine and Erasmus, noting points of contact and of disagreement between Zwingli and his two most influential sources. With this background in hand, Stephens then can trace out the development of Zwingli's views in controversy from 1523 to 1531 and conclude with a significant reappraisal of Zwingli's understanding of flesh and spirit.

Part III moves on to later generations of Reformers. Here Susan E. Schreiner places Calvin's eloquent definition of faith as "a firm and certain knowledge" into the context of sixteenth-century debate over the grounds of certainty. The problem of certainty relates both to salvation and to exegesis, given in particular the Reformer's need to rest assurance of salvation on an assured interpretation of Scripture. Calvin's views are contrasted with Zwingli's and Luther's arguments against Roman Catholic polemic. Perhaps more than Luther, and surely more than Zwingli, Calvin recognized the difficulty in an appeal to the work of the Spirit as a ground of certainty. Moreover, in polemic against both Roman Catholics and Quintinists, he "insisted that the spirit be always anchored in the Word." Schreiner reminds us of the difficulty of grounding the Protestant case in a context where argument was typically supported by traditionary or churchly authority — and, in particular, of the complex rootage of the Reformation watchword, *sola Scriptura.*

Craig S. Farmer examines the exegesis of the Bern theologian Wolfgang Musculus against the background of a catena of medieval readings of John 8 — the story of the woman taken in adultery. Here we encounter another necessary qualification of *sola Scriptura:* the term, Farmer concludes, "does not mean that Musculus, or other Reformation biblical scholars, had committed themselves to interpret Scripture armed only with their intellects and the guidance of the Holy Spirit." Reformation-era exegetes were immersed in the tradition of the biblical commentary; for all their objections to various aspects of medieval biblical interpretation, they stood not only in continuity but also in a relationship of dialogue with the earlier tradition.

Joel E. Kok takes up the question of Bullinger's status as an exegete in relation to Calvin, with a specific focus on the exegesis of Romans. Here Bullinger's work on the text preceded Calvin's, was read by him with interest, and was, perhaps, damned by Calvin with faint praise. Scholars have disagreed on the relationship between the two commentaries on Romans. Kok shows both agreement on major points and significant differences in emphasis as well as in method between the two exegetes.

John L. Thompson's presentation of the exegetical work of Peter Martyr Vermigli offers further evidence of the continuities of interpretive method during the transition from the Middle Ages to the Renaissance and the Reformation. Vermigli was certainly an example of a Reformer who had drunk deeply at the well of humanist philology. He was, by most accounts, more adept at Hebrew than Calvin was. But Thompson also reveals Vermigli as an assiduous cataloguer of exegetical opinion whose works often convey a wealth of information about the tradition of biblical interpretation: Vermigli's surveys of older opinion reference the rabbis, the church fathers, and the medieval doctors, as well as canon and Roman law. While his views of these older commentators are never uncritical, Vermigli seems more open to the strategic applications of allegorical readings than many of his Reformed contemporaries.

With Lyle D. Bierma's essay we pass from what might be called the second-generation Reformation exegetes — Calvin, Vermigli, Musculus, and their contemporaries — to a third generation of teachers whose work extended into the last two decades of the sixteenth century. Bierma looks to the theological understanding of Exod. 20:8-11 at the heart of Zacharias Ursinus's teaching on the Sabbath and sets it into the context of two Reformation-era trajectories for understanding the Sabbath: one stemming from Luther and Calvin, the other from Zwingli, Bucer, and Vermigli. Bierma is able to show a clear relationship between Ursinus's interpretation of the passage and aspects of the interpretations offered by Calvin, Vermigli, Bullinger, or Melanchthon. What is also evident here is the substantial rootage of Reformation views of the Sabbath in the medieval reading of the passage, as exemplified by Thomas Aquinas.

John Farthing's study of Girolamo Zanchi's interpretation of Gomer's harlotry introduces us to a side of Zanchi's work that has been almost entirely neglected and offers us a potentially surprising perspective on the way in which precritical exegesis addressed the role of women in the biblical narrative. On the one hand, Zanchi is nearly always mentioned as one of the chief contributors to the development of the Reformed doctrine of predestination — often through the clouded lens of a poor translation of his work made in the eighteenth century by A. M. Toplady. Farthing's examination of Zanchi's exegesis ought to give pause to those who would portray this Reformer as a speculative theologian of one doctrine. It ought also to underscore how the precritical understanding of the text as speaking a message to the church places Hosea's and Gomer's relationship into the context of salvation history and, given Zanchi's view of the present-day church as the ongoing people of God, into a homiletical context as well. By extension, we can point beyond Farthing's essay to another line of theological and exegetical continuity: the traditional understanding of the spousal relationship between God and Israel, Hosea and Gomer, as parallel to the relationship between God and the believer, so richly present in medieval spirituality and mysticism, also finds its place in Reformation exegesis.

Robert Kolb's essay on Nikolaus Selnecker concludes the exegetical essays with a view of Lutheran biblical interpretation in the decades just prior to the Formula of Concord, by one of the framers of that confessional synthesis. Selnecker's importance as an exegete rests in no small measure on his massive commentary on the Psalter. His commentary illustrates, perhaps even more clearly than the resolution of internecine controversies in the Formula of Concord, the ways in which Lutheran theology developed in dialogue with its own past. Selnecker's exegesis strongly reflects Luther's

— but it also reflects the earlier interpretive tradition, notably the thought of Bernard of Clairvaux. Although Selnecker's Psalter recalls the more discursive and homiletical style of Luther's later lectures, Kolb indicates that Selnecker elsewhere followed the more analytical, topical model of Melanchthon's exegesis. In addition, Selnecker clearly felt free to develop his own readings of texts (particularly in the form of analyses of theological implications) quite independently of both Luther's and Melanchthon's readings of the same texts, albeit certainly within the trajectory of late sixteenth-century Lutheranism.

Following a concluding essay by the editors, the final section of the volume, prepared by Mickey L. Mattox, presents a bibliography of the writings of David C. Steinmetz to the present.

· 2 ·

Johannes Trithemius on the Fourfold Sense of Scripture: The *Tractatus de Inuestigatione Sacrae Scripturae* (1486)

KARLFRIED FROEHLICH

I. Johannes Trithemius — His Life and Work

Johannes Trithemius (1462-1516) cannot be counted among the great Reformers, theologians, or even exegetes of the late Middle Ages. Undoubtedly, the *Abbas Spaenhemensis* was known and respected among his contemporaries. He was the friend, host, and correspondent of many church leaders, princes, and humanists. He had a significant part in the Benedictine reform movement of his time, and he published voluminously.[1] But there was nothing outstanding about him. This, of course, makes him extremely interesting to modern historians. They see him as a paradigmatic bridge person, a figure on the threshold between the Middle Ages and the Modern Age whose personality displays all the contradictions of the age, and whose

---

1. Important monographs on the life and work of Trithemius include Oliver Legipont, "Vita et Apologia Venerabilis Johannis Trithemii," in *Historia rei litterariae ordinis sancti Benedicti,* ed. Magnoald Ziegelbauer and Oliver Legipont (Augsburg: M. Veith, 1754), 3:217ff.; Isidor Silbernagl, *Johannes Trithemius: Eine Monographie* (Regensburg: Verlag Georg Joseph Manz, 1885); Klaus Arnold, *Johannes Trithemius (1462-1516),* Quellen und Forschungen zur Geschichte des Bistums und Hochstifts Würzburg, ed. Klaus Wittstadt, vol. 23 (Würzburg: Ferdinand Schöningh, 1971; 2nd ed., 1991); Noel L. Brann, *The Abbot Trithemius (1462-1516): The Renaissance of Monastic Humanism,* Studies in the History of Christian Thought, ed. Heiko A. Oberman, vol. 24 (Leiden: Brill, 1981). For the latest list of his works, see "Anhang I: Werkverzeichnis," and "Anhang II: Briefregister," in Arnold, *Johannes Trithemius,* 2nd ed., 1991, pp. 228-85.

written legacy, carefully catalogued and interpreted by himself in numerous autobiographical statements, can serve as a lens for the ambitions, preoccupations, and self-projections of his generation. With his encyclopedic mind, his love for books and stories, even fake and dubious ones, Trithemius was a receptive rather than a critical and original theologian and may reflect more accurately than others the manifold traditions and mentalities by which the world of ordinary church people at the end of the fifteenth century, of priests, monks, and lay teachers was shaped. This observation should be reason enough to present Trithemius's unremarkable and, as we shall see, quite unoriginal treatise as an introduction, so to speak, to this volume. It allows us to catch a glimpse of late medieval hermeneutics in its most normal, most traditional, and most trivial form.

Born to a winegrower's family at Trittenheim in the Moselle Valley in the night of February 1, 1462, "at the eleventh hour, the thirty-third minute" as he himself reports,[2] Trithemius pursued the *studia humaniora* at Trier and in the Netherlands, then at Heidelberg, apparently without ever acquiring a formal degree. Instead, he soon entered the undistinguished Benedictine Abbey of St. Martin at Sponheim near Kreuznach in the Rheingau under circumstances that he himself interpreted as providential. Not even two years later, at the tender age of twenty-one, he advanced to being elected abbot of the place, but he ended his days as abbot of an even smaller monastery, the Schottenkloster St. Jakob at Würzburg, where he found refuge and peace after having resigned his first charge in 1506 in the midst of incessant quarrels with his monks. It is quite clear that Sponheim enjoyed its greatest flowering ever under Abbot John's energetic and ambitious leadership. Beyond his local achievements, Trithemius was a staunch supporter of monastic reform through the institutions of the Bursfelde Congregation of Benedictine houses with which his monastery had affiliated under his predecessor. For many years he served the association as an untiring administrator, visitator, secretary, commission member, and co-chair of the annual chapter. During the 1490s, his fellow abbots invited him regularly to be the featured speaker at their meetings, where he treated them to ever new versions of his passionate plea for a true *philosophia monachorum* as an antidote to the ills of the time. His ideal was *bona vita cum scientia,* a monastic erudition of heart and mind, which meant first and foremost *scientia scripturarum.*[3]

---

2. See Arnold, *Johannes Trithemius,* p. 4, n. 2.

3. The term seems to go back to Jerome, whose epistles were for the young Trithemius a much admired model and an inexhaustible source of ideas, pet phrases, and elegant formu-

There was nothing really new in this program, but the combination of the traditional spiritual goal with his zealous advocacy of the study of the *litterae humaniores* rendered it appealing and relevant, according to the taste of the time, in the circles of his friends. Trithemius's aggressive rhetoric of asserting the superiority of this monastic humanism over all forms of secular knowledge — "true knowledge hides under the monks' cowls" *(latet scientia in cucullis)* — did not go unchallenged, however. It was the point at which his longtime friend Jakob Wimpheling fell out with him, defending the role of nonmonastic learning in church and culture: "False and fictitious is that proverb: True knowledge hides under the monks cowls, at the exclusion of seculars."[4] That Trithemius never appreciated this criticism of his monastic enthusiasm, because he saw it as an attack on the basic decisions of his own life, is an indication of the limitations of his character and the provincialism of his humanism.

During his lifetime, Trithemius fascinated his contemporaries primarily by the fame of the rich library he collected at Sponheim and the reputation of his vast learning, which included mastery of the three languages of the Cross but also the knowledge of the occult and magical arts. For subsequent generations, however, his fame rested on his writings as a historian, as the chronicler of his own monasteries of St. Martin and St. Jakob, of the great Abbey of Hirsau, of the Carthusian Order and the history of the Frankish nation, but most of all on his work as a literary historian. In the early modern period, Trithemius was the first author to revive a literary genre that had its precedents in Suetonius's and Jerome's *De viris illustribus.* His catalogues of ecclesiastical authors, of the writers of the Benedictine order, and of the literary heroes past and present of the German nation, based not only on secondhand information but also on firsthand inspection of a large part of the literature available in print and in manuscript at his time, have earned him the title "Father of Modern Bibliography." Especially the first of these works, his *De scriptoribus ecclesiasticis,* which circulated in manuscript form as early as 1492 and appeared in print in 1494, was an immediate success and proved its worth as an indispensable tool that generations of literary historians blindly

---

lations; *Ep. 125 ad Rusticum* is frequently mined in the extant writings of 1484-86. On the elements of the Abbot's reform program, see Brann, *The Abbot Trithemius,* esp. chap. 3.

4. Wimpheling, *De integritate libellus* (Strassburg, 1506), cap. 33; see Brann, *The Abbot Trithemius,* pp. 259-66, esp. 262. Trithemius claimed that the proverb originated at the time of Hrabanus Maurus: "Eo tempore proverbium illud verum exstitit quo dicebatur: *Scientia scripturarum in cucullis latitat monachorum . . .*" (PL 107:104). One should note, however, the replacement of *scientia* in general by *scientia scripturarum* in his version.

trusted.[5] All too blindly, as we know today. Suspected as a manipulator of historical evidence and fabricator of nonexisting sources by some contemporaries already, the learned abbot was finally and irrevocably indicted by the tribunal of nineteenth-century scholarship on at least two major counts of fraud: the invention of "Hunibald" and his supposed codex, the main source for Trithemius's bold reconstruction of the early history of the Franks, and the fiction of "Meginfrid," an alleged early chronicler of Fulda, to whose nonexistent treatise *De temporibus gratiae* he attributed much of the evidence for the claim that his ideal of monastic piety and erudition was being lived out by the monks of the ninth century already.[6] There were attempts to vindicate Trithemius's dependability, or at least his personal integrity, but the evidence was so devastating that it cast a deep shadow on everything he wrote, with good reason as we shall see.

The history of Trithemius scholarship since the disclosures of the late nineteenth century presents a model case for the dynamics of a developing historiographical consciousness. Its stages remind one of a grieving process.[7] At first, there was denial; then came anger, moral outrage at the enormity of the crime — the deception of generations of scholars by willful lies and outright fabrications. The Trithemius story became a prime illustration of pseudo-scholarship, the distortion of facts by a crook, an impostor with sinister intentions.[8] The next step was a

---

5. Arnold, *Johannes Trithemius,* pp. 117-132. See also Christel Steffen, "Untersuchungen zum 'Liber de scriptoribus ecclesiasticis' des Johannes Trithemius: Ein Beitrag zu den Anfängen der theologischen Bibliographie," *Archiv für Geschichte des Buchwesens* 10 (1970): 1247-1354. On the dedicatory letters: Brann, *The Abbot Trithemius,* pp. 221-28. The earliest known manuscript, containing a first revision of April 1492, is now at Yale's Beinecke Library, MS Marston 143. It is discussed by Hellmut Lehmann-Haupt, "Johannes Trithemius, Father of Bibliography: Notes on a Manuscript of his Liber de Ecclesiasticis Scriptoribus," in *Rare Books: Published for the Friends and Clients of H. P. Kraus* (New York, November 1957), 8:2.

6. On Hunibald and Meginfrid, see Arnold, *Johannes Trithemius,* pp. 167-79.

7. See the sketch in the important essay by Nikolaus Staubach, "Auf der Suche nach der verlorenen Zeit: Die historiographischen Fiktionen des Johannes Trithemius im Lichte seines wissenschaftlichen Selbstverständnisses," which was published as part of the three-volume *Festschrift* for Horst Fuhrmann, *Fälschungen im Mittelalter,* Teil I: *Kongreßdaten und Festvorträge: Literatur und Fälschung,* MGH Schriften, vol. 33, I (Hannover: Hahnsche Buchhandlung, 1988), pp. 263-316; here 264-70.

8. A telling example of this phase is the suggestion of Ludwig Traube, the great paleographer, that Trithemius "frequently took over the titles of actually existing writings from earlier lists but just invented the incipit." Traube's equally famous student, Paul Lehmann, criticized the excessive nature of this insinuation: "Die meisten Incipits existieren wirklich, sind nicht erfunden, sondern vorgefunden." See Paul Lehmann, "Merkwürdigkeiten des Abtes Johannes Trithemius," *Sitzungsberichte der Bayerischen Akademie der Wissenschaften, Philosophisch-Historische Klasse,* 1961:2 (München: Beck, 1961), pp. 1-75; here 57-58.

psychologizing phase. The reasons for the abbot's immoral behavior were sought in personality traits such as his self-conceit, vanity, and vivid imagination paired with a distorted sense of reality. These explanations allowed for a more balanced view; scholars could appreciate Trithemius's positive contributions and at the same time counsel caution. Recent scholarship has gone even farther. Klaus Schreiner pleaded for an understanding of Trithemius in the wider framework of the categories of late medieval historiography: History at that time was judged by its *utilitas*, and history writing was meant to serve moral goals and higher truths that were part of an author's deepest convictions.[9] More recently still, Nikolaus Staubach has broadened, and at the time concretized, this argument. He points to the patristic and medieval tradition of history as prophecy about events that are expected for the future as well as those that happened in the past; people were convinced that a revelation about the past could form part of personal revelations granted by God to inviduals. Trithemius, Staubach submits, may have been subjectively convinced that he had received such revelations, that visionary experiences had shown him the archetypal books of Hunibald and Meginfrid, just as he believed that Esdras received a revelation of the lost text of the Torah for the purpose of its restoration (4 Esdr. 14:21-41), Elizabeth of Schönau learned many names of the eleven thousand martyred virgins of Cologne from her angel, and the monk Hermann of Reichenau was granted the favor of seeing and reading Cicero's *Hortensius* in an ecstasy.[10] It is a small step from this interpretation to Frank Borchardt, who, in 1971, encouraged a new look at Trithemius's fictions as literary achievements in their own right.[11] In the course of the grieving process over the loss of the historian, the person and work of the abbot of Sponheim have been demystified and brought down to earth. It seems to be time for a "renaissance" of both.[12]

This does not mean, however, that the necessary task of Trithemian criticism has been completed. The careful scrutiny of Trithemius's literary notices on specific authors still yields annoying surprises. A case with

9. Klaus Schreiner, "Abt Johannes Trithemius (1462-1516) als Geschichtsschreiber des Klosters Hirsau. Überlieferungsgeschichtliche und quellenkritische Bemerkungen zu den 'Annales Hirsaugienses,' " *Rheinische Vierteljahresblätter* 31 (1966/67): 72-138.

10. See Staubach (above, n. 7), esp. pp. 300-315.

11. Frank L. Borchardt, *German Antiquity in Renaissance Myth* (Baltimore: Johns Hopkins Press, 1971), pp. 127-33.

12. The term is used by Klaus Arnold, "Additamenta Trithemiana. Nachträge zu Leben und Werk des Johannes Trithemius, insbesondere zu seiner Schrift De demonibus," *Würzburger Diözesangeschichtsblätter* 37-38 (1975): 239-67; here 239.

ramifications for the history of biblical exegesis is the fiction of Walahfrid Strabo as the author of the medieval *Glossa ordinaria* to the Bible. I have shown elsewhere that the ascription of this twelfth-century compilation, which originated in the French schools of Laon, Chartres, and Paris, to Walahfrid, a Carolingian author, goes back to Trithemius.[13]

After advancing the claim of Walahfrid's authorship of the *Glossa* in his *De scriptoribus ecclesiasticis* for the first time, the abbot repeated it in his *Catalogus illustrium virum Germaniae* as well as in the catalogue of Benedictine writers, thereby misleading scholars right down to Jacques-Paul Migne, who printed the *Glossa* under Walahfrid's works in the *Patrologia Latina*, using all his critical acumen to align the edition with the myth of Walahfrid's authorship, which Trithemius himself had probably created as part of his efforts to maximize the literary achievements of the Germanic *Vorzeit*. We need to keep the entire unfinished story of Trithemius scholarship before us if we want to appreciate the problems of the little treatise to which we now turn.

II. Trithemius on Scripture:
The *De inuestigatione scripturarum*

The text of the treatise *De inuestigatione scripturarum* survives in a single manuscript: Trier, Bibliothek des Bischöflichen Priesterseminars, MS 84.[14] Its fifteen leaves are bound as fols. 191r-205r (later foliation) with a number of devotional texts written by various hands of the late fifteenth century in a codex once owned by the Abbey of St. Matthias, a monastic center at Trier with which Trithemius was certainly in contact during his Sponheim years.[15] Many of the twenty-one pieces listed over washed-out entries from a monastic account book on an older parchment sheet (fol. 1r) are treatises,

13. "The Printed Gloss," in *Biblia Latina cum Glossa Ordinaria: Facsimile Reprint of the Editio Princeps, Adolph Rusch of Strassburg, 1480/81*, ed. Karlfried Froehlich and Margaret T. Gibson (Turnhout, Belgium: Brepols, 1992), pp. xii-xxvi; here xxiii-xxiv. "Walafrid Strabo and the *Glossa Ordinaria*: The Making of a Myth," in *Studia Patristica*, vol. xxviii, Papers Presented at the Eleventh International Conference on Patristic Studies held in Oxford 1991: Latin Authors (other than Augustine and his opponents), *Nachleben* of the fathers, ed. Elizabeth A. Livingstone (Louvain: Editions Peeters, 1993), pp. 192-96.

14. A brief description of MS Trier 84 is found in Jakob Marx, *Handschriftenverzeichnis der Seminarbibliothek zu Trier*, Trierisches Archiv, Ergänzungsheft, 13 (Trier, 1912), pp. 67-68. I am indebted to the library staff of the Priesterseminar for permission to check the codex in Trier during two visits (1992 and 1994), and to the staff of the Hill Monastic Manuscript Library at Collegeville, Minnesota, where I was able to consult a microfilm in 1993.

15. Lehmann (above, n. 8), p. 29; Arnold, *Johannes Trithemius*, p. 47, n. 69.

excerpts, and short notes of interest to a monk or priest involved in pastoral work. Folio 2ᵛ, for example, features a short note "De spectaculis in ecclesiis non faciendis." A treatise, *De septem viciis,* ends on fol. 179ᵛ, followed by eight empty leaves. Folio 189ʳ has a text entitled *De diebus egiptietis* (Incipit: "Nota quod in quolibet mense"); fol. 189ᵛ-190ʳ an *Epistula missa ad quendam Carthusiensem* (Incipit: "Quicquid salubrius et dulcius hauriri poterit"). Folio 190ᵛ displays three fragments: (a) six rhymed lines; (b) ten lines of prose, beginning "Ad hominem secularem pertinet"; (c) thirteen lines, "Nota signa hominis reprobati a deo." Our treatise, *De inuestigatione scripturarum,* is the final text in the codex; it is followed by four empty sheets, three of which are ruled the same way as our text. Incipit and explicit, written by the main scribe, give the title as "Tractatus de inuestigatione sacrae scripturae." Another hand, perhaps slightly later, added after the incipit: "Joannis abbatis spaenhemensis." The same hand apparently also added the entry at the end of the table of contents on fol. 1ʳ: "Item Tractatulus Johannis spaenhemensis• de inuestigatione sacræ scripturæ." The text, hardly an autograph,[16] is written in a strong bookhand of the late fifteenth century and is divided into twelve chapters. After the untitled prologue, the titles (in red) are regularly squeezed into the space of one or two lines at the end of the preceding chapter. The entire treatise is carefully rubricated. Large chapter initials are added in Green or Red, sentences are marked off by a red stroke through the capital letter at their beginning, and the rubricator has made several textual corrections in red.

While MS Trier 84 is the only surviving witness, external evidence for the existence of the treatise, and even for its date, is not lacking. Trithemius mentions the title among his works in the *Catalogus illustrium virorum Germaniae* and the Sponheim Chronicle.[17] The incipit is cited in two later lists of his writings, both dating from the Würzburg period, 1509 and 1512 respectively.[18] The composition, however, does go back to Trithemius's early years, as a correspondence in 1486 with Nicholas of Merneck, a friend from student days in Heidelberg, shows.[19] Nicholas was ordained to the priesthood

---

16. Brann, *The Abbot Trithemius,* p. 131, assumes that it is, but he cites no evidence. A number of scribal errors and corrections suggest that our manuscript was copied from another. Arnold discusses Trithemius's known autographs on pp. 64-68. I plan to publish the complete text of the treatise elsewhere in the near future.

17. See *Johannis Trithemii Opera Historica,* ed. Marquand Freher (Frankfurt: Typis Wechelianis apud Claudium, 1601; repr. Frankfurt: Minerva, 1966), pp. 183 and 401.

18. See Silbernagl, *Johannes Trithemius,* p. 261; Lehmann (above, n. 5), p. 72.

19. See the details in Silbernagl, pp. 24-31; Brann, *The Abbot Trithemius,* pp. 127-134; Arnold, *Johannes Trithemius,* pp. 47-48.

in the vicinity of Trier in April of 1486. The young abbot wrote him on that occasion,[20] and shortly thereafter sent him, apparently at Nicholas's request, a longer disquisition on the requirements of the priestly life that, in a revised and enlarged form, was printed frequently from 1494 on.[21] Section four of this tract deals with the duty and benefit of the study of Scripture for the priest. A priest must be erudite as well as devout, for a pious life without erudition does not suffice, and erudition without piety does not edify. The study of Scripture is the most efficient weapon against temptation; it nourishes the spirit and incites virtue. As he does elsewhere, Trithemius decries the ignorance of all too many priests: Instead of books *(libri)* they buy children *(liberi);* instead of their studies, they love concubines.[22] An undated letter written in response to Nicholas's somewhat cautious reaction in July refers to our treatise, a copy of which Trithemius apparently appended: "In order that you may know how to proceed more fruitfully with the study of the sacred book, I am sending you a treatise on this subject which I have recently composed at the request of some friends. In it, I have laid out in a comprehensive form many things concerning the investigation of the sacred Scriptures."[23] An undated letter to Nicholas later in the same year refers to it again: "Thus, if you want to approach the study of holy scripture more fruitfully, do not neglect the method in the little book which I sent you some time ago."[24]

It is clear that the treatise was written in the spring or early summer of 1486, but not for Nicholas. The "friends" at whose urging Trithemius composed it must probably be sought among his monks, and the biographical framework can be located with the help of the report that the abbot himself gave of the beginning of his literary activity in the *Nepiachus* ("childhood report") of 1507:[25]

> While I still concentrated my attention with most fervent love on the study of the Scriptures, as I mentioned before, and had gradually purchased as many of the books needed as I could, reading the purchased

20. See *Johannis Trithemii . . . Opera pia et spiritualia,* ed. Johannes Busaeus (Jan Buys) (Mainz: Ioannes Albinus, 1604), pp. 918-20.

21. See Arnold, *Johannes Trithemius,* pp. 47-48 and 238-39. Text: Busaeus, *Johannis Trithemii Opera,* pp. 765-83; here 774-76. The original letter of May 1486 is printed on pp. 925-31.

22. Busaeus, *Johannis Trithemii Opera,* p. 775a-b. The first part of the section clearly echoes Hrabanus Maurus's *De clericorum institutione.* See below, n. 33.

23. Busaeus, *Johannis Trithemii Opera,* p. 941b.

24. Busaeus, *Johannis Trithemii Opera,* p. 945a.

25. The text is printed in Johann Georg Eckhart, *Corpus Historicum Medii Aevi,* Tomus II (Leipzig: Apud Jo. Frid. Gleditschii B.Fil., 1723), cols. 1831-32 and 1842-44.

volumes most diligently day and night whenever I was given time and leisure, finally, in the year of our Lord 1484, on the day of St. Matthew the Apostle and Evangelist (= September 21), being twenty-three years old, I betook myself to writing. I was still a clumsy and rather confused writer and did not think that I could profit anyone by my elaborations. A master without much skill, I just wanted to make progress on my own, starting to collect in one work, but without any embellishment, passages from the holy fathers on all kinds of subject matter as it would occur — wonderful blocks for building, as it were. I undertook this compilation with an eye on my more mature years, so that I would always have at hand some thought on virtue or vice which I could present to my brothers as a word of exhortation. So I began by assembling plain, rather brief excerpts from the Fathers in the order of their subject matter like stones ready for some future building. But when this collection grew and grew and seemed like a wall set up without mortar, lacking all evenness, I began to insert the mortar of my own words and, like a new craftsman, continued building the wall, now with a smooth surface. From that point on, time and practice led to improvement in my dictation, step by step, and I began to compose orations, and later also treatises for my own devotional use without frequent citation of the doctors, although nothing can be said by me which has not been said before in a better way by them. Nevertheless, this childish activity did help me; through it, I became proficient, to the best of my ability, not just being guided by preceptors or rules, but also by imitation and long practice. I did not seek eloquence, neither did I care for stylistic brilliance and elegance. I decided to write as a monk for simple fellow monks, not for scholars; to edify souls rather than tickle the ears of readers. The first little pieces I wrote, rough and shapeless creatures, I threw into the fire after I had learned to publish somewhat more polished ones. Some of them dealt with the state and progress of monks. The others which I thought worthy of keeping, I have listed below; yet even they do not all seem sufficiently polished to me. Sometime, when I will have enough leisure, I shall see to it that they are published.

This account is remarkable in several respects. As Trithemius saw it, he started his literary career by buying books and reading them. In an earlier passage, he admitted that he was an insatiable consumer of books, a true bibliomaniac: "I confess my unrestrained love of study and books."[26] But

---

26. "Confiteor intemperatum ad studium et libros amorem meum," Eckhart, *Corpus Historicum*, II, col. 1829. Cf. Brann, *The Abbot Trithemius*, p. 113.

reading and writing were not the same thing. The reading phase belonged to the months of his novitiate:

> From that moment in which I first came into the Order there was nothing to me sweeter, nothing more pleasant, nothing more delightful than to apply my mind to the study of the Scriptures. . . . Every hour which I was able to steal for myself from the sleep, from the quiet, from the solace of my brothers I applied with the greatest fervor to the study of the Scriptures, so that I believed that I had squandered that day in which I had not learned something useful in my reading from the Holy Books.[27]

The term "Scriptures" includes not only the canonical books but also the fathers — an understanding that echoes Hugh of St. Victor, a writer whose footprints we will find time and again.[28] Trithemius began writing a month after he was elected abbot. That he can date this start to the day may reveal his interest in astrology and his self-image as a prophet; it certainly is related to his new status as well. We learn from a dedicatory letter that he regularly read before his brothers the literary exercises that he had penned the night before, little "exhortations," two books of which he collected in 1486 and kept for later publication.[29] His development as a writer is described in terms of an apprenticeship. Presumably in connection with his *lectio divina,* he began to set up files of patristic excerpts, organized by subjects that he thought might be appropriate for his admonitions to the monks. The building metaphor for the act of interpreting the Scriptures goes back to patristic times. Jerome and Gregory the Great used it, and in Hugh of St. Victor's hermeneutical writings it is the leading metaphor for the traditional threefold or fourfold sense of Scripture.[30] Hugh distinguishes the historical sense *(historia)* as the rough foundation stones from the allegorical sense *(allegoria)* as the smooth rows of hewn stones above ground. Trithemius's image of his own words as the mortar is an imaginative expansion and adaptation. It describes quite accurately what we should expect in a *tractatus*

---

27. Eckhart, *Corpus Historicum,* II, col. 1826. Brann, *The Abbot Trithemius,* p. 7 (Brann's translation).

28. *Hugonis de Sancto Victore Didascalicon de studio legendi: A Critical Text,* IV.1, ed. Charles Henry Buttimer (Washington, D.C.: Catholic University Press, 1939), p. 71:10-11: "Vetus Testamentum continet legem, prophetas, hagiographos, Novum autem evangelium, apostolos, patres."

29. See Busaeus, *Johannis Trithemii Opera,* p. 526. On the published editions: Arnold, *Johannes Trithemius,* pp. 37-38 and 231-32.

30. The material is discussed by Henri de Lubac, *Exégèse médiévale: Les quatre sens de l'écriture,* 4 vols. (Paris: Aubier, 1959-64), II/2:54-60.

from his beginning years: a wealth of excerpts from patristic and more recent writings with connecting phrases formulated by the young author, who tried to weld all of this together into a readable piece of oratory.[31] The abbot tells us that he had no literary ambitions; he just wrote for "simple fellow monks." Nevertheless, the goal of a "polished" product was clearly acknowledged, and he was striving to improve his writing, at least "by imitation." He would savor an elegant formula, an arresting phrase found in Jerome or elsewhere, and proudly use it himself. His Latin never reached the level of sophistication that characterized the style of many of his humanist friends. In our treatise, the "mortar" of his words is often easy to distinguish from the accomplished prose of his sources.

His prolific use of unacknowledged sources is, of course, particularly frustrating for the modern reader. Here, however, it is important to appreciate the perspective of the author-in-training. For Trithemius, it was the mark of real progress, a decisive step forward, to find that at a certain stage he was able to employ the language of the tradition without citing his sources *(postea etiam tractatus pro mea devotione sine crebra allegatione Doctorum inciperem);* he adds the disarming argument that a student once employed when he found himself confronted with my discovery that his paper was plagiarized: "But the book says it so much better than I can": *nihil a me dici queat, quod melius ab illis ante non sit dictum.* The treatise *De inuestigatione sacrae scripturae* is not a piece of late medieval academic scholarship. It is not even a piece of popularizing theological journalism. It must be read as a "school essay" of a person eager to learn and happy to share his learning, a rhetorical exercise without independent merit. Precisely as such, however, it is a precious document of late medieval monastic culture at its most basic level. We do not learn much about the author's theology but a great deal about his practical agenda in socializing simple monks into the world of biblical knowledge. We can find the traces of his reading and, in this way, gain an understanding of the hermeneutical tradition that shaped his mind and served as the norm he wanted to hand on to the coming generation.

In the manuscript, the treatise is subdivided into twelve chapters. The rubricator added titles for each one except for the introduction: (2) What is needful for those who want to acquire knowledge of Holy Scripture; (3) On the house of Holy Scripture, its seven columns and four walls, which

---

31. Arnold, *Johannes Trithemius*, p. 48, remarks on our treatise: "Wie in seinen anderen Frühwerken verarbeitet Trithemius auch in diesem 1486 entstandenen Traktat nur angelesenen Stoff gefällig, ohne Eigenes bieten zu wollen."

are the four evangelists; (4) On the fourfold way of Holy Scripture; (5) On the coincidence of these four and the frequent lack of coincidence; (6) On history and those who undertake to study it; (7) On allegory, tropology, anagogy, and the difference between them; (8) An example where four senses are found together; (9) An example of three together; (10) An example where only two senses occur together; (11) On the method and order of reading Holy Scripture; (12) On the impediments faced by those who study. Chapters 1–3 form the introduction, giving the rationale for the study of Scripture and stating the spiritual prerequisites on the part of the student. Chapters 4–11, the core of the treatise, focus on the fourfold sense, and the final chapter (12) completes the argument of the introduction by giving advice on how to avoid problems faced in any serious effort to study.

III. Introduction to Study: The *Scientia Scripturarum*

The treatise opens in a style reminiscent of a *recommendatio sacrae scripturae,* the traditional lecture that a new Master in Theology delivered at the beginning of his career.[32] The assigned topic was *laus scripturae,* an imaginative praise of Scripture as the foundational text in theology, and the rewards of its study. As a rule, the master would take a biblical verse or passage as his theme and develop his panegyric as an analysis of this text. There is no dearth of biblical allusions in Trithemius's introduction, but the absence of a stated biblical "theme" and its formal unfolding suggests that the young abbot may have other models on his mind. The precise object of his praise, moreover, is not Scripture but *scientia scripturarum,* Trithemius's key term for the double challenge of the monastic vocation: serious study and a holy life. This emphasis reminds one of Hrabanus Maurus's *De clericorum institutione,* which Trithemius had used in the epistolary treatise sent to his friend Nicholas in May of 1486.[33] Book III of Hrabanus's classic, itself reproducing much of Augustine's *De doctrina Christiana,* served as as an important handbook of biblical hermeneutics

---

32. On the exercises of academic "inception," which can be traced to the Parisian schools of the late twelfth century, see N. Spatz, "*Principia.* A Study and Edition of Inception Speeches Delivered before the Faculty of Theology at the University of Paris, ca. 1180-1286" (Ph.D. dissertation, Cornell University, 1992); see also her article, "Evidence of Inception Ceremonies in the Twelfth-Century Schools of Paris," *History of Universities* 13 (1994): 3-19.

33. A usable form is printed in PL 107:293-420. A more recent edition, *Rabani Mauri De institutione clericorum libri tres,* ed. Alois Knöpfler, Veröffentlichungen aus dem kirchenhistorischen Seminar München, 5 (München, 1905), also discusses the transmission of the text.

throughout the Middle Ages. Hrabanus states at the outset that religious leaders are under special obligation to show forth "fulness of knowledge, rectitude of life, and perfect erudition." They cannot afford to be ignorant of any aspect of their central task, which is to instruct themselves and others in the *scientia scripturarum*. Both things are necessary: Wisdom must illumine a pious life, and such a life must make a case for wisdom. *Scientia sanctarum scripturarum*, Hrabanus states, is the foundation, constitution, and perfection of practical wisdom.[34] As the verbal echoes in his earlier letter demonstrate, Trithemius was totally in tune with the venerable monastic teacher on these points and admired this particular text. Many of the themes that return throughout our treatise were already formulated by Hrabanus: the refusal to separate *sapientia* from *scientia*, the insistence on the church as the context for proper biblical interpretation, the "usefulness" *(utilitas)* of scriptural study for the fight against temptation and sloth, and the unity of truth found in Scripture and the *sapientes huius mundi*.

In the introduction, Trithemius does use Bible verses with some imagination. The interpretation of the woman of Rev. 12:1-2 as an image for *scientia sacrae scripturae* and the somewhat contrived "personification allegory" of Rachel being this *scientia*, with Jacob, "spurner of the world," as her suitor who must serve Laban, the "illumination" of the Holy Spirit, seem to be his own inventions. Jacob served Laban two times seven years, ridding himself of the seven mortal sins and practicing the seven virtues.[35] The abbot also reproduces classical school trivia: Knowledge of Scripture is not only true philosophy, it is also true ethics, logic, and politics. One wonders whether the opening image of an Arcadian landscape, "flowery meadows and open woods" *(Prata et nemorosa loca)*, belongs in the same context. *Pratum amoenitatis* certainly brings to mind the tradition of the *locus amoenus* in classical Latin literature.[36] A medieval source, however, seems to me even more likely: the *Speculum Virginum*.[37] Written around the middle of the twelfth century, this anonymous treatise addressed to

---

34. PL 107:379. Book III fills cols. 347-420.

35. As is frequently the case, the explanation of the names is derived from Jerome's *Liber interpretationis hebraicorum nominum*. On the practice of "personification allegory," see Grover Zinn in the introduction to his translation of Richard of St. Victor's *Benjamin Minor: Richard of Saint Victor: The Twelve Patriarchs. The Mystical Ark. Book Three of the Trinity*, trans. and intro. Grover Zinn, Classics of Western Spirituality (New York: Paulist Press, 1979), pp. 10-21.

36. See the material in the *Thesaurus Linguae Latinae* (Leipzig: Teubner, 1900), 1:1962-63.

37. The most important recent study is Jutta Seyfarth's introduction to her new critical edition: *Speculum Virginum*, ed. Jutta Seyfarth, CCCM 5 (Turnhout: Brepols, 1990), pp. 7*-55*.

religious women enjoyed enormous popularity in monastic circles. Trithemius must have been particularly fond of it. In his literary catalogues, he attributes it to Abbot Conrad of Hirsau (ca. 1070-1140), according to him one of the heroes of Benedictine reform. The same claim in the *Chronicon Hirsaugiense,* where he presents Hirsau as one of the greatest centers of monastic learning in German lands, is an indication of the high esteem in which he held this text. His unwarranted identification of Conrad as the author, however, once again has misled scholarship for centuries. The most recent editor, Jutta Seyfarth, argues convincingly that the manuscript tradition does not support any connection with Hirsau, let alone Abbot Conrad as the author.[38] That Trithemius knew the *Speculum* when he wrote *De inuestigatione* cannot be doubted. I have identified several long citations in chapters two and three, and traces of the work can be found everywhere in the first part. The *Speculum* is prefaced by an *Epistola* that already develops several themes echoed by Trithemius:

> Since variety delights the reader, while a uniform and continuous treatment softens and strains his or her resolve, I have divided this little work into twelve parts, so that the virgin of Christ, eager for the divine word, may stroll, so to speak, through these sections as through adjoining meadows and be charmed by a variety of flowers, I mean mystical senses. . . . The first section treats of the mystical flowers of paradise which grow from the one flower of the field and lily of the valley [Cant. 2:1], . . . and also of the form of that paradise with its four typical rivers, I mean the four evangelists and doctors who irrigate the whole church through their word and example.[39]

The first pages of Section One proceed to expand in full detail the image of the virginal life as the "flowers of paradise from the shoot of the church." The church, the spouse of Christ, is the paradise; she is the sealed fountain, the walled garden of the Song of Songs, full of flowers of every kind of color and fragrance, the fruits of virtue and a saintly life. Among Trithemius's earliest writings that he decided to discard was a compilation on the virtues and a treatise on virginity. The *Speculum Virginum* may well have been one of the most closely read books during his first monastic years. It must have made a deep impression.

The manuscripts of the *Speculum Virginum* were designed to be illustrated. All of them contain twelve full-page miniatures, normally on

---

38. CCCM 5:37*-42*.
39. Epistula, lines 58-69 (CCCM 5:3).

facing pages at the beginning of a new chapter.[40] The first picture is a Tree of Jesse, the second a Mystical Paradise with the four rivers, the four evangelists, and the four doctors, and the last one shows the House of Wisdom (Prov. 9:1). It is with this last image that Trithemius opens his second chapter: "Wisdom has built herself a house; she has hewn out seven columns" (Prov. 9:10). The columns are interpreted as the seven gifts of the Holy Spirit (Isa. 11:2-3) that rested first of all on Christ, who in turn bestowed them on the Scriptures. The interpretation here follows closely the beginning of Book XI of the *Speculum Virginum*.[41] The string of scriptural quotations is taken from that section, and entire sentences and phrases are incorporated. There are borrowings from other sources as well. Traces of the *Speculum Virginum*, however, remain visible throughout the chapter. The references to "Christian philosophers," Christ the "sun of righteousness," and especially the dialogue in the words of the Song of Songs between Wisdom as the longed-for spouse and the student of Scripture betray its constant presence. Because of his interest in *scientia scripturarum*, Trithemius does not follow the distinction between *sapientia* and *scientia* on which the *Speculum* insists.[42] Rather, like Hrabanus, he equates *sapientia* and *scientia scripturarum*, depicting ignorance and pride as their counterparts. It is in this context that we encounter a rare reference to the author's contemporary circumstances:

> Behold, knowledge is for sale and is being sold for most contemptible cash. For as the sophistication of the art of printing has grown, Wisdom has begun to shout even more vehemently in the streets, wanting to find a faithful beloved to whom she might address herself. Nowadays, there is little diligence among students. They all buy the mysteries of Holy Scripture in books for themselves and carry knowledge, not in their heart *(in corde)* but in their volume *(in codice)*.

This complaint about the consequences of books in print is somewhat puzzling. Brann has discussed in detail the vacillating pronouncements of the abbot on the value of the *ars impressoria:* In the context of his reform

---

40. See CCCM 5:33*-37*; a table of the location of the pictures in the various manuscripts is found on p. 136*. On the background and interpretation of the series, see Eleanor Greenhill, *Die geistigen Voraussetzungen der Bilderreihe des Speculum Virginum* (Münster: Aschendorff, 1962).

41. See *Speculum Virginum* XI.106-28, 175-82, 211-14.

42. "Sapientia est eternorum rerum cognitio intellectualis, scientia uero temporalium rerum cognitio rationalis. Illa pertinet in deo ad diuina contemplanda, ista ad humana propter deum disponenda." *Speculum Virginum*, XI.432-35.

ideas, Trithemius could wax enthusiastic about the potential of the printing press for a monastic literary culture, but at the same time he wanted to maintain the old-fashioned *scriptorium* and its spiritual function in the life of the monastery, as his well-known treatise, *De laude scriptorum,* demonstrates. The two tendencies were never reconciled.[43]

Chapter three opens by elaborating further on the prerequisites for the betrothal to Wisdom: "It remains for us now to discuss how one must espouse her." The expectant suitor must provide the appropriate wedding presents: the golden ring of an orthodox catholic faith with its jewel, the works of this faith; the crown of hope; and the precious robe of charity. The properly furnished house, his ready soul, is only the last of these requirements. With the house metaphor, however, Trithemius returns to the imagery of the *Speculum* and to another long excerpt from its text. As he always does, he ends the chapter with a final sentence of his own. It provides a somewhat clumsy transition to his real topic: "This true and holy Wisdom is contained in the divinely inspired sacred scriptures."

IV. The Practice of Biblical Interpretation

With chapter four, the abbot moves from the moral and spiritual prerequisites for the study of Scripture to the center of the treatise, the practice of biblical interpretation. Not surprisingly, the discussion of the four senses of Scripture forms the core of his argument. The chapter title added by the rubricator refers to them as the *quadruplex via sacrae scripturae.* Trithemius himself speaks of *modi intelligendi* and affirms the indispensability of the *quadriga* as well as its versatility: "All that one reads in Holy Scripture is understood through these modes. No part of Scripture fails to use them, meaning being ascertained either by all four modes at once, or by three together, by two or just one. Read what you want in Holy Scripture; in order to understand it, you will need at least one mode, or two, or three." In 1980, long before the new wave of postcritical hermeneutics, David Steinmetz published an article entitled "The Superiority of Pre-Critical Exegesis."[44] For many years, the provocative piece was required reading in Church History 01 at Princeton Theological Seminary. The main thesis was stated in a bold assertion: "The medieval theory of levels of meaning in the biblical text, with all its undoubted defects, flourished because it is true,

---

43. Brann, *The Abbot Trithemius,* pp. 142-49.
44. *Theology Today* 37 (1980): 27-35.

while the modern theory of a single meaning, with all its demonstrable virtues, is false." There can hardly be any doubt that the assumption of multiple meanings in the texts of the Old and the New Testament was indeed commonplace among early Christian writers. Origen and Jerome spoke of the "infinite forest of senses."[45] Gregory the Great compared the work of biblical interpreters to that of the goldsmiths who shape the same gold into a variety of ornaments — necklaces, rings, and bracelets.[46] John the Scot compared the "multiple and infinite understandings of the divine utterances" with the colorful feathers of the peacock.[47]

By the high Middle Ages, the multiplicity was more clearly defined as a quasi-normative quaternity of literal, allegorical, tropological, and anagogical senses, apparently for the purposes of instruction. The victory of this one systematization by no means excluded the continuing use, for example, of a system of three senses, a different sequence, or different designations for the four. In his magisterial study of medieval exegesis, Henri de Lubac endorsed Ceslaus Spicq's distinction of two main strands of the traditional theory: a threefold division, derived from Origen's anthropological model of body, soul, and spirit (historical, moral, and mystical sense or some similar constellation), that reached the Middle Ages through Jerome, Isidore, and Bede and was still very much alive in the twelfth century — Robert of Melun, Peter Abelard, Hugh and Richard of St. Victor, and Stephen Langton all taught it; and the "classical" fourfold division that Spicq traced back to Augustine and John Cassian with Bede and Hrabanus as intermediaries.[48] De Lubac's own interest was the rehabilitation of allegory and focused on the order of the senses. Against what he perceived as an early Protestant preference for moral interpretation, he demonstrated

---

45. See the instances cited in De Lubac, *Exégèse médiévale,* I/1:123, and Jerome's *Epist. 53.9 ad Paulinum:* "in verbis singulis multiplices latent intelligentiae" (CSEL 54:463.11).

46. "Sicut enim ex uno auro alii murenas, alii anulos, alii dextralia ad ornamentum faciunt, ita ex una sacrae scripturae scientia expositores quique per innumeros intellectus quasi uaria ornamenta componunt quae tamen omnia ad decorum caelestis sponsae proficiunt." *Epist.* III:62.42-46 (CCSL 140:212).

47. "Est enim multiplex et infinitus divinorum eloquiorum intellectus. Siquidem in penna pavonis una eademque mirabilis ac pulchra innumerabilium colorum varietas conspicitur in uno eodemque loco eiusdem pennae portiunculae." *De divisione naturae* IV.5 (PL 122:749).

48. De Lubac *Exégèse médiévale,* I/1:139-42; Spicq, *Esquisse d'une histoire de l'exégèse latine au moyen âge,* Bibliothèque Thomiste, 26 (Paris: Vrin, 1944), pp. 98-99. See also Ernst von Dobschütz, "Vom vierfachen Schriftsinn: Die Geschichte einer Theorie," in *Harnack-Ehrung: Beiträge zur Kirchengeschichte . . . Adolf Harnack dargebracht* (Leipzig: Hinrich, 1921), pp. 1-13; here 10-11.

that the majority of medieval listings placed the allegorical or mystical sense before the tropological.[49] On the other hand, he doubted the role Spicq attributed to Augustine; for while the bishop of Hippo used the number four in an interpretive *quadriga* of *historia, aetiologia, analogia,* and *allegoria,* he applied the schema to the interpretation of the Old Testament only and was aware that the terms had their place in the Greek rhetorical tradition.[50] The classical fourfold sense appears first in John Cassian's *Conferences* XIV.8 in the order: *historica interpretatio, tropologia, allegoria, anagoge.*[51] Cassian's illustration, the four meanings of "Jerusalem," points to Gal. 4:22-31 as the background of this particular division. Hrabanus cited Cassian in full in his commentary on Galatians.[52]

In the Middle Ages, Bede was widely regarded as the protagonist, even the originator of Cassian's formula. His most influential text was a remark about the wooden table in the tabernacle (Exod. 25:23): "The table of the tabernacle has four feet because the words of the heavenly oracle are customarily taken in either an historical, allegorical, tropological, or certainly an anagogical sense."[53] It was quoted in Hrabanus's commentary on Exodus 25 and often thereafter.[54] On the threshold of the twelfth century, the fourfold sense was clearly regarded as an "old" doctrine, part of the "rules of the ancient writers." In a precious passage of his autobiography, Guibert of Nogent (ca. 1055-1125) tells us how he learned about it:

> All too late I began to pant for the knowledge that had repeatedly been distilled for me by many good scholars: to busy myself, that is, with commentaries on the Scriptures, to study frequently the works of Gregory in which are to be found the best keys to that art, and, according to the rules of the ancient writers, to treat the words of the prophets and the gospels in their allegorical, their moral, and finally their anagogical

49. De Lubac, *Exégèse médiévale,* I/1:146-57.

50. De Lubac, *Exégèse médiévale,* I/1:177-87.

51. PL 49:962.

52. PL 112:330-31. On the history of the interpretation of Galatians 4, see Hartmut Freytag, "*Quae sunt per allegoriam dicta:* Das theologische Verständnis der Allegorie in der frühchristlichen und mittelalterlichen Exegese von Galater 4,12-31," in *Verbum et Signum. Erster Band: Beiträge zur medävistischen Bedeutungsforschung,* ed. Hans Fromm, Wolfgang Harms, and Uwe Ruberg (München: W. Fink, 1975), pp. 27-43.

53. "Item mensa tabernaculi quattuor habet pedes quia uerba caelestis oraculi uel historico intellectu uel allegorico uel tropologico, id est morali, uel certe anagogico solent accipi." *De tabernaculo* I.6.781-84 (CCSL 119A:25). The continuation offers descriptions of each sense and biblical examples.

54. *In Exodum* III.11 (PL 108:147-48).

meaning. In this work I had the special encouragement of Anselm, the abbot of Bec, afterward archbishop of Canterbury.[55]

With Gregory as his model, Guibert developed a definite preference for the tropological sense:

In my judgment, I thought that in our time moral interpretations were rather more useful than allegorical ones.[56]

It is interesting to note that a text from his treatise, *Quo ordine sermo fieri debet*, perhaps written as early as 1084, entered the *Glossa ordinaria* as the sixth *prothema*, "Quattuor sunt regulae," to the book of Genesis. It described succinctly the function of each of the four senses, and was often quoted as a standard definition, usually under the name of Bede.[57] One hundred years after Guibert, in a comment on the terse teaching style of the fathers, Peter the Chanter maintained that "Jerome expounded the entire Bible to Paula and Eustochium according to the four senses in the course of just one year."[58]

---

55. "Coepi igitur jam sero ad id quod saepe a plurimis mihi bonis doctoribus praestillatum fuerat anhelare; scilicet Scripturarum commentis intendere, Gregoriana dicta, in quibus artis hujus potissimum reperiuntur claves, crebrius terere, secundum veterum auctorum regulas ad allegoricum seu moralem quin et anagogicum sensum prophetica vel evangelica verba perstringere. In his praecipuum habui incentorem Beccensem abbatem Anselmum, postea Cantuariensem archiepiscopum. . . ." *De vita sua* I.17 (PL 156:874). English translation from *Self and Society in Medieval France: The Memoirs of Abbot Guibert of Nogent* (New York: Harper & Row, 1970), pp. 88-89. On this passage and the connection of Guibert's biblical hermeneutics with Anselm's psychology, see Klaus Guth, "Zum Verhältnis von Exegese und Philosophie im Zeitalter der Frühscholastik," *Recherches de théologie ancienne et médiévale* 38 (1971): 128-36.

56. ". . . quod iudicio meo allegoricis moralia satis hoc tempore utiliora putarem," *De vita sua* I.17 (PL 156:875).

57. "Quattuor sunt regulae sacrae scripturae, id est, hystoria, quae res gestas loquitur. Allegoria in qua aliud ex alio intelligitur. Tropologia, id est, moralis locutio, in qua de moribus ordinandis tractatur. Anagoge, id est, spiritualis intellectus, per quem de summis et caelestibus tractaturi ad superiora ducimur; his quattuor quasi quibusdam rotis, tota diuina scriptura uoluitur. Uerbi gratia: Hierusalem secundum hystoriam est ciuitas. Alleg{orice} ecclesiam significat. Secundum tropologiam, id est, moralitatem animam cuiuslibet fidelis, quae ad pacem aeternam anhelat. Secundum anagogen caelestium omnium uitam qui reuelata facie uident deum." *Biblia Latina cum Glossa Ordinaria* 1:6. For Guibert's text, see *Guibert de Nogent: Quo ordine sermo fieri debeat* etc. (CCCM 127:53.198-209). For an English translation see LCC 9:287-99 (here 291); for the date, see CCCM 127:7.

58. "Item: Idem [i.e., Jerome] in anni unius spatio totam bibliothecam historice, allegorice, tropologice, et anagogice Paulae et Eustochio exposuit." *Verbum Abbreviatum*, C. 2 (PL 205:26).

In the later Middle Ages, a widely used summary of the "doctrine" of the four scriptural senses was the famous mnemonic distich:

Littera gesta docet, / quid credas allegoria, /
Moralis quid agas, / quo tendas anagogia.[59]

Its first occurrence has been traced to the *Rotus Pugillaris* of Augustinus of Dacia O.P. (died 1285), but its great popularity was assured by its use in the prologues of Nicholas of Lyra's two postills. Martin Luther, who quoted it as early as 1516, probably knew it from a printed *Gloss* with Lyra that included Paul of Burgos's *Additiones* to Lyra with a third quotation.[60] Luther criticized the verse and its content as a scholastic game, a formal exercise of reduction and repartition. Neither the apostles nor the ancient doctors knew of these specific differences; they used the terms "rather indiscriminately."[61]

Luther had a point; the use of the distich and its content was part of a medieval tendency to reduce complicated theological subjects to simplistic formulas in order to make them readily available for popular consumption. But there was more to the system of the fourfold sense than this. Even at its beginnings, it was meant to explicate the dynamic of the two basic senses — or, more precisely, the two levels of the biblical text — in which Luther and the early fathers were interested: letter and spirit, word and meaning, history and mystery. Paul's use of letter and spirit in 2 Cor. 3:6 linked their dynamic not only to the dialectic of law and grace but also to the movement from the Old Testament to the New, the hermeneutics of promise and fulfillment. Origen interpreted the dynamic as *anagoge,* as the upward journey of the soul: from flesh to spirit, from life below to life above. His threefold sense merely elaborated this understanding in the consideration

---

59. On variations and parallels, see De Lubac, *Exégèse médiévale,* I/1:23-26. On the formal structure, François Châtillon, "Vocabulaire et prosodie du distique attribué à Augustin de Dacie sur les quatre sens de l'écriture," in *L'homme devant Dieu: Mélanges offerts au Père Henri de Lubac* (Paris: Aubier, 1962), pp. 17-28.

60. See the reprint of the Douai edition of 1617 in PL 113:25-50; here 28, 33, and 38. The reference comes in Luther's 1516-1517 lectures on Galatians, at 4:24 (WA 57/2:95:23-25).

61. Luther, *Vorlesung über den Galaterbrief* (WA 57/2:96; cf. his 1519 commentary on Galatians (WA 2:550.20-28), where the term "ludus" appears. For Luther, Augustine's interpretation of Paul's distinction between letter and spirit in 2 Cor. 3:6 embodied the correct understanding of different scriptural senses: "Letter, as Augustine says in *De spiritu et littera,* is any doctrine or any law when it comes without grace. . . . Therefore, it is plain that history as much as tropology and anagogy is 'letter', according to the Apostle, but 'spirit' is that very grace which is signified by the law, or that which the law requires" (WA 57/2:96.12-17).

of the function of Scripture for the Christian life. It should be clear that Augustine's basic hermeneutics in Book One of *De doctrina Christiana* described the same movement in terms of the soul's homebound journey of love.[62] In John Cassian's formulation, the dynamic of the two levels is clearly present. According to him, monastic spirituality in its preoccupation with the Bible subdivides into a practical and a theoretical science, the latter into "historical interpretation" and "spiritual understanding" of which tropology, allegory, and anagogy are subcategories; he may well have chosen them because they represented the Pauline triad of charity, faith, and hope. There could be more or fewer senses, but the dynamic would always move from concentration to expansion, from the limited to the unlimited, from that which is at hand to the world of God and Spirit.

The same division of the group of four senses into one plus three continued to dominate medieval thinking. John of Salisbury expressed it in this way:

> Although the surface of the letter is fitted to one sense only, a multiplicity of senses is hidden within, and from the same material allegory often builds faith and tropology [builds] character in many forms. Also, anagogy leads upward in manifold ways so that it endows the letter not only with words but with the things themselves.[63]

Salisbury's statement not only echoes Hugh of St. Victor but also anticipates Thomas Aquinas, who endorsed the traditional fourfold sense but set the literal sense apart from the others as the only one "from which arguments can be drawn."[64] When Aquinas speaks of the spiritual senses being "based" on the literal, he invokes the building metaphor that is so central to Hugh's hermeneutics. This metaphor always expressed the dynamic of the ascent. Like the ascent, building implies a sequence and a movement upward. Gregory the Great already described it as involving more than just two steps:

---

62. On Origen and Augustine, see the introduction to my *Biblical Interpretation in the Early Church* (Philadelphia: Fortress Press, 1984).

63. "Licet enim ad unum tantummodo sensum accommodata sit superficies litterae, multiplicitas mysteriorum intrinsecus latet. Et ab eadem re saepe allegoria fidem, tropologia mores variis modis aedificat. Anagoge quoque multipliciter sursum ducit ut litteram non modo verbis, sed rebus instituat." John of Salisbury, *Policraticus* VII.12 (PL 199:666).

64. Thomas Aquinas, *Summa theologiae* Ia, q. 1, a. 10, ad 1. On this and other hermeneutically significant texts in Thomas's works, see Maximino Arias Reyero, *Thomas von Aquin als Exeget* (Einsiedeln: Johannes-Verlag, 1971).

First we lay the foundation of history; then, by means of typical signification, we erect a mental structure to be a fortress of the faith; finally, through the grace of moral instruction, we cover the building with a coat of paint.[65]

This image remained a favorite description of the process of biblical interpretation right down to Hugh and Trithemius. It lies in the nature of the metaphor that the emphasis may shift: "first" can easily become "most important." Hugh, who explored the building metaphor at some depth both in his *Didascalicon* and in *De sacramentis,* inaugurated a trend of paying attention to the *realia* of the text, to *littera* and *historia,* and thus to the human authors of the Bible. Only a short time later, Andrew of St. Victor restricted his commentaries on the Old Testament to the literal sense; in his eyes, this was a gesture of humility and ascetic self-restraint, but it was also a response to the new scientific spirit of the age.[66] Beryl Smalley still regarded this trend as the sign of true progress in medieval hermeneutics.[67] This is a view from a rather limited perspective, however. True, the missing sense on Hugh's list of three is anagogy. But this does not mean that Hugh "secularized" exegesis or neglected the dynamic of the ascent. On the contrary, the *alter Augustinus* regarded the entire educational process of biblical interpretation in which he was involved as *anagoge,* a teachable movement upward that was meant to culminate in the contemplative life.[68] The central point was and remained the Augustinian insistence on the use of Scripture as the God-given vehicle, the effective means to embark on the soul's journey to God. If there

65. "Primum quidem fundamenta historiae ponimus; deinde per significationem typicam in arcem fidei fabricam mentis erigimus; ad extremum quoque per moralitatis gratiam quasi superducto aedificium colore vestimus." Gregory the Great, *Moralia in Iob, Epist. ad Leandrum,* cap. 3 (PL 75:513).

66. Rainer Berndt, *André de Saint-Victor (+1175). Exégète et théologien,* Bibliotheca Victorina, 2 (Turnhout: Brepols, 1991). On twelfth-century "literalism" and the reaction to it, see also Amaury d'Esneval, "Les quatre sens de l'Ecriture à l'époque de Pierre le Mangeur et de Hugues de Saint-Cher," in *Mediaevalia Christiana, XIe-XIIIe siècles. Hommage à Raymonde Foreville,* ed. Coloman Etienne Viola (Paris, etc.: Editions universitaires, 1989), pp. 355-69.

67. See her chapter on "Andrew of St. Victor," in *The Study of the Bible in the Middle Ages* (Oxford: Blackwell, 1952), pp. 112-85, and her essay "The Bible in the Middle Ages," in *The Church's Use of the Bible Past and Present,* ed. Dennis Nineham (London: SPCK, 1963), pp. 57-71.

68. Formally, one might argue that Hugh subsumed the anagogical sense under the allegorical: "Allegoria est cum per id quod factum dicitur, aliquid aliud factum sive in praeterito sive in praesenti sive in futuro significatur." *De sacramentis,* Prol. cap. 4 (PL 176:184).

was "progress" in the twelfth century, it consisted in the conviction that the ascent, the journey was *teachable,* not only through the practice of *lectio divina* in the monasteries but also in the "schools" that were entering the educational scene as a new factor to be reckoned with and were accessible to a much larger clientele. The consequences of "theology" being taught in the universities were immense, especially for the study of the Bible. John Van Engen has recently described the epochal changes that came with the phenomenon of the Bible being turned into a textbook for instruction in the schools.[69] One of the consequences certainly was an increased interest in the literal sense and everything that goes with it. But, given the unchanged goal of spiritual elevation and its experience in Christian life everywhere, the new situation also led to a renewed interest in the systematization of exegetical procedures beyond the letter, and thus in the four scriptural senses as a welcome tool. One might regret the *Verschulung,* this enthusiasm for the boundless potential of advancement through education. There clearly were dangers: to simple minds, the suggestion could be that if one only learned the correct methods, one would have it all. Trithemius wrote the bulk of his treatise with the intention of teaching basic methods, providing practical aids for people who wanted to learn how to read the Bible. The introductory chapters, however, provided the indispensable framework: the final goal of any *scientia scripturarum* was the incorporation of scriptural teaching into one's life, the undertaking of the journey, and practicing the ascent.[70]

V. The Fourfold Sense of Scripture

In his discussion of the fourfold sense, Trithemius did not draw on Lyra or the popular distich. He begins his fourth chapter with the image of the four rivers of paradise: "As the historians tell us, four rivers go forth from paradise by which all of Asia is irrigated abundantly." Again, the *Speculum Virginum* may be responsible for this turn. Its paradise picture

---

69. John Van Engen, "Studying Scripture in the Early University," in *Neue Richtungen in der hoch- und spätmittelalterlichen Bibelexegese,* ed. Robert E. Lerner (München: R. Oldenbourg, 1996).

70. In the article quoted above (n. 44), David Steinmetz spelled out the implication of Jacques Lefèvre d'Étaples's adaptation of Lyra's "double literal sense": "The problem of proper exegesis of Scripture is, when all is said and done, the problem of the regeneration of its interpreter" (p. 32). I would not see this as pushing Lyra's theory to "absurd limits." It seems to be an expression of the same Augustinian mentality as described here.

features the circle of the four rivers as they emerge from the one center, Christ; other symbolic figures, identified by inscriptions as four doctors, four cardinal virtues, and four evangelists, are placed around them: Geon with Gregory, Fortitude, and Matthew; Phison with Ambrose, Prudence, and John; Tigris with Augustine, Justice, and Mark; Euphrates with Jerome, Temperance, and Luke.[71] Of course, the biblical text does not really speak of four rivers; it speaks of a river going out of Eden (Vulgate: *de loco voluptatis*) to water the garden and subsequently dividing into four riverheads (Gen. 2:10). The one river as a symbol of Scripture nourishing the church was a commonplace in medieval exegesis.[72] The references in the *Speculum Virginum* show that the image easily evoked other passages, for example John 7:37-38 or Cant. 4:12-15. The four riverheads, on the other hand, were generally thought to symbolize the four Gospels or evangelists, a tradition that reached far back into patristic times[73] and often occurred in combination with other "moving fours": the four living creatures and the four wheels of Ezekiel's vision that can go in all directions (Ezek. 1 and 10); the four wheels of the trolleys in Solomon's temple (1 Kings 7:27-37); the four chariots of Zech. 6:1-8; and the strange *quadriga Aminadab* (Cant. 6:11, Vulgate). There was also, however, a tradition that saw in the four rivers of paradise a representation of the four senses of Scripture.[74] In the early thirteenth century we find it in a sermon of Innocent III for the feast of Gregory the Great who, as the pope claims, "produced the streams of the four interpretations from the fountain of scripture about which it is said mystically: 'A river went out etc.' (Gen. 2:10)."[75] Other references are found in Bonaven-

---

71. *Speculum Virginum*, ed. Seyfarth, plate 4. See also the references to the picture in the text: I.960-67, 988-1000; II.1-20 (CCCM 5:38-41).

72. De Lubac, *Exégèse médiévale*, I/1:36, n. 5. Pope Alexander IV even used it in a bull of October 7, 1255, "De fontibus paradisi flumen egrediens, exuberans videlicet sacrarum intelligentia scripturarum, . . . temporibus nostris largo profluxit laetitiae impetu super terram"; H. Dausend, "Das opusculum super missam des Fr. Wilhelm von Melitona," in *Aus der Geisteswelt des Mittelalters* (Festschrift Martin Grabmann), ed. Albert Lang et al. (Münster: Aschendorff, 1935), 1:558.

73. See Ernst Schlee, *Die Ikonographie der Paradiesesflüsse* (Leipzig: Hinrich, 1937). Also Anna C. Esmeijer, *Divina Quaternitas: A Preliminary Study in the Method and Application of Visual Exegesis* (Assen/Amsterdam: Van Gorcum, 1978).

74. See De Lubac, *Exégèse médiévale*, I/1:36 and 40.

75. "Hic de fonte scripturae quatuor expositionum rivos produxit. De quibus mystice legitur: Fluvius egrediebatur, etc. [Gen. 2:10]. . . . His autem fluminibus beatus Gregorius irrigavit paradisum, id est fecundavit ecclesiam." Innocent III, *Sermo IX de Sanctis* (PL 217:515).

ture,[76] Stephen Langton,[77] and the late medieval *Philosophia mona-chorum* that Trithemius may have known.[78] Innocent III already paired each sense with a particular river according to the etymology of its name: Geon means "fissure in the earth" *(hiatus terrae)* and stands for the historical sense; Phison, "mutation of the mouth" *(oris mutatio),* for allegory; Tigris, "swift" *(velox),* for anagogy; and Euphrates, "fruit-bearer," for tropology. Langton shows the same distribution.

The pairing of the four senses with the four doctors can also be found in the tradition. Bonaventure, in his treatise *De reductione artium ad theologiam,* ascribes special prominence to Augustine in allegory, to Gregory in tropology, and to Pseudo-Dionysius in anagogy. He does not mention Jerome, whom other writers name as the expert on the literal sense.[79] An anonymous late medieval *Apparatus* to Pseudo-Hrabanus's *Allegoriae in sacram scripturam,* apparently a school text, presents the idea in its simplest form:

> The Holy Spirit made provision for his church about the four doctors: Each one worked more eminently in one of the four senses than another,

76. "Sacra scriptura est ille fluvius qui egrediebatur e loco voluptatis ad irrigandum paradisum et fidelis animae et militantis ecclesiae; qui inde dividitur in quatuor capita, scilicet rivos historiarum, anagogiarum, allegoriarum, et tropologicarum." *Principium sacrae scrip-turae,* in *Sancti Bonaventurae Opera Omnia,* ed. A. C. Peltier (Paris: Vivès, 1867), 9:6b.

77. "Locus voluptatis est Spiritus Sanctus in quo est vera et summa plenitudo volup-tatis. Fluvius inde egrediens est Sacra Scriptura a Spiritu Sancto edita et eodem summi Dei digito depuncata. Dividitur autem fluvius ille in quatuor flumina, id est Sacra Scriptura in quatuor species, scilicet historiam, allegoriam, anagogen, tropologiam." Stephen Langton, *Glosa in Historiam Scholasticam,* ed. G. Lacombe, *Archives d'histoire doctrinale et littéraire du moyen âge* 5 (1930), p. 43.

78. "Lectio est fons egrediens de paradiso Dei et irrigat omnem terram quia diuina dictante Spiritu Sancto edita irrigat animam legentis ad fructificandum Deo. . . . Haec diui-ditur in quatuor flumina, scilicet historiam, allegoriam, moralitatem, tropologiam, ut qui de uno non poterit bibere, de alio bibat. Si paruulus es, Scriptura porrigit tibi lac in historia quo nutriaris ut grandescas; si subtilis ingenii es, occurrit tibi allegoria." Comment on *Regula Benedicti* 49:4, ed. Jean Leclercq, in *Etudes sur le vocabulaire monastique du moyen âge,* Studia Anselmiana, 48 (Rome, 1961), p. 149. Verbal echoes of this text in Trithemius's chapter four are unmistakable.

79. The passage draws further connections and celebrates Hugh of St. Victor's her-meneutics as the most comprehensive contemporary contribution: "In omnibus enim sacrae scripturae libris praeter litteralem sensum quem exterius verba sonant concipitur triplex sensus spiritualis, scilicet allegoricus. . . , moralis. . . , et anagogicus. . . . Primum maxime docet Augustinus, secundum maxime docet Gregorius, tertium vero docet Dionysius. Ansel-mus sequitur Augustinum, Bernardus sequitur Gregorium, Richardus sequitur Dionysium, quia Anselmus in ratiocinatione, Bernardus in praedicatione, Richardus in contemplatione. Hugo vero omnia haec." *De reductione artium,* cap. 5, in *Sancti Bonaventurae Opera Omnia,* 7:500b-501a.

as is manifest in their writings. Thus, the literal sense is Jerome's specialty, the tropological Gregory's, the allegorical Ambrose's, and the anagogical Augustine's who more than the others discussed heavenly subjects and those pertaining to the age to come.[80]

Trithemius coordinates the four rivers with both the four scriptural senses and the four doctors. His list differs from that of the *Speculum Virginum:* Geon stands with *historia* and Jerome; Phison with *allegoria* and Ambrose; Euphrates with *tropologia* and Gregory; and Tigris with *anagogia*[81] and Augustine. It is identical to that of Innocent III, but rests on a different etymology of the names. In fact, the abbot's geographical and onomastic explanations of the four rivers are taken straight out of Isidore's *Etymologies,* not from Jerome.[82] It seems that with the curious information provided by this encyclopedia, Trithemius is in his element. Details of the section such as the definitions of the senses ("history is the narrative of the order of events"; "allegory leads the understanding reader through the revelation of faith to the recognition of the truth," etc.) may still be owed to prior sources, but the composition seems to be his own. An indication is the unusually opinionated comparison of the four doctors: According to Trithemius, Jerome was the most eminent historian among them; Ambrose pursued allegory "more perfectly than the others"; Gregory was the "more perfect moralist"; and Augustine "flew around the mountain tops like an eagle." Of course, all four are needed; none is "inferior" to the other. Yet, "although everyone of them labored in all four of these understandings of Holy Scripture, each topped the others in one specific area." Toward the end of the chapter, Trithemius returns to the four doctors, this time pairing

---

80. "Providit Spiritus Sanctus Ecclesiae suae de quatuor doctoribus: quorum singuli in uno quatuor sensuum enixius altero laboravit, ut patet per eorum scripta. Unde Hieronymo appropriatur sensus litteralis, sensus tropologicus attribuitur beato Gregorio, sensus allegoricus Ambrosio, et sensus anagogicus beato Augustino qui inter caeteros de coelestibus et de his quae sunt futuri saeculi magis loquutus est," in *Apparatus Anonymi Scholastici,* cap. X, in *Spicilegium Solesmense,* ed. I. B. Pitra, vol. III (1855), pp. 436-55; here 438A. See Stegmüller, *Repertorium Biblicum Medii Aevi,* no. 7079. On the *Allegoriae* and their authorship, see below, n. 85.

81. Instead of the original Greek term *anagoge,* which Latin writers took over as a technical term, Trithemius uses the popular but incorrect form *anagogia.* The scribe of the manuscript seems unfamiliar with the word and is not sure about the spelling. He normally writes "anagoya" or "anagoia," but "anagya" or "anogya" also occurs. Protestant critics since Melanchthon took pleasure in pointing out that the Greek or Latin word *anagogia* is to be read as "an-agogia," meaning "lack of upbringing," "boorishness." See Châtillon (above, n. 59).

82. Isidore, *Etymologiae* XIII.21.7-10 (PL 82:490-91).

them with the elements of the building metaphor: Jerome the historian laid the foundation, Ambrose the allegorist erected the walls; Gregory the moralist decorated the building; and Augustine the anagogical eagle capped the structure with a roof.

This last activity, "putting on the roof," was not part of Gregory the Great's original analogy: laying the foundation, erecting the structure, and decorating the building. Its addition suggests still another source. The final image of the chapter, Scripture itself "building" its meaning by speaking in the fourfold way, is copied from it word for word. The source is the short prologue "Quisquis ad sacrae scripturae," attached to a biblical glossary, the *Allegoriae in sacram scripturam* — also a well-known "textbook" of medieval hermeneutics. Trithemius may have known it under the name of Hrabanus, among whose works it is printed in Migne's *Patrologia*.[83] The bulk of the *Allegoriae,* the so-called *Glossarium Angelus,* consists of an alphabetical repertory of biblical terms and their symbolic signification, which was composed in the later twelfth century either by Garnerius of Rochefort (ca. 1140-1225) or Adam of Dryburgh (Adam Scotus; d. 1212). At least the prologue must be credited to Adam.[84] Trithemius copied verbatim over half of this brief text in his chapters four and five. The image of the four scriptural senses as the "four daughters of Mother Wisdom," which he employs throughout chapter four, stems from there.[85] So does their description as food — the milk of history; the bread of allegory; the "savory refreshment" of tropology; the wine of anagogy; and again as the house of the soul. The discovery of this source points once more to the actual procedure and achievement of our author. By carefully weaving together excerpts from popular textbooks, using the connecting threads of his own words quite sparingly, he created a tool of undeniable usefulness — not only for his "simple" contemporaries who needed to be introduced to the tradition but also for our modern quest of a "normal" biblical

---

83. Incipit: "Quisquis ad Sacrae Scripturae notitiam desiderat peruenire," PL 112:849-51. André Wilmart, "Les allégories sur l'Ecriture attribuées à Raban Maur," *Revue Bénédictine* 32 (1920): 47-56, pointed out that the ascription to Hrabanus is not found in Trithemius's original catalogues. It appears, however, in the 1531 and 1556 Cologne editions of his *De viris illustribus* after the mention of Hrabanus's *De universo*.

84. See the article by Wilmart in the previous note, and A. Vaccari, "Esegesi di altri tempi. Correzioni e aggiunte," *Biblica* 18 (1937): 450-58. Friedrich Stegmüller is undecided: *Repertorium Biblicum,* nos. 7078 and 2364.

85. "Has namque quatuor intelligentias, videlicet historiam, allegoriam, tropologiam, anagogiam quatuor matris sapientiae filias vocamus." PL 112:849. The image is used by other late medieval writers, e.g., Jean Gerson; see his *Oeuvres complètes,* ed. Palémon Glorieux, V.377; VI:190.

hermeneutics at the dawn of the Reformation. The last sentence of the chapter connects the discussion back to the framework by sounding once more the themes of the introduction: "Finally, when the house has been built and perfected, the spouse whom you love, the understanding of Sacred Scripture, will come to you with all its riches, and will dwell with you eternally, protecting you here below from all evil and refreshing you with all the inestimable gifts of joy at home above."

Chapters five to ten present the actual guidelines for scriptural interpretation according to the fourfold sense. The section is clearly organized, easy to understand, and eminently practical. But alas, there is nothing original here either. Most of the text is a patchwork of excerpts, this time from a single source: Hugh of St. Victor's *Didascalicon*, a twelfth-century handbook that is itself full of unacknowledged citations.[86] Together with Augustine's *De doctrina Christiana*, the *Didascalicon* played a major role in shaping biblical hermeneutics after the twelfth century.[87] At the end of the fifteenth century, it had become a classic. The work falls into two parts: the first deals with the methodology of reading "secular" literature, the texts of the liberal arts (Books I-III); the second discusses the reading of the "divine" writings (Books IV-VI). Trithemius exploited the second part only, selecting and rearranging whatever seemed pertinent to his discussion of the senses. Chapter five begins by reproducing Hugh's warning in *Did.* V.2 that not every passage of Scripture can be interpreted in all four senses. Some "want to be interpreted spiritually only" — a point made by Origen already; others fit just one particular sense or a combination. To Hugh's illustration of music played on a string instrument,[88] Trithemius adds a clarification that is not in Hugh or in Hugh's sources: "On the zither, not all strings are touched at the same time, else they would emit a confused sound, not a

---

86. C. H. Buttimer's standard edition is cited above, n. 28. The English translation by Jerome Taylor, *The Didascalicon of Hugh of St. Victor: A Medieval Guide to the Arts*, Records of Civilization, 64 (New York: Columbia University Press, 1961), identifies many of the sources in the notes. Recently, Ivan Illich published a delightful study of the treatise: *In the Vineyard of the Text: A Commentary to Hugh's Didascalicon* (Chicago: University of Chicago Press, 1993). Much of the material in *Did.* IV-VI is repeated and partly condensed in Hugh's *De scripturis et scriptoribus sacris praenotatiunculae* (PL 175:9-28).

87. On the impact of Augustine's *De doctrina christiana*, see *Reading and Wisdom: The De doctrina christiana of Augustine in the Middle Ages*, ed. Edward English, Notre Dame Conferences in Medieval Studies, 6 (Notre Dame: University of Notre Dame Press, 1995), esp. the essays by Grover Zinn, Margaret T. Gibson, and Eileen Sweeney, which discuss the Victorines.

88. Buttimer (above, n. 28), 95.17–96.21; Taylor, *The Didascalicon of Hugh of St. Victor*, p. 120.

sweet-sounding harmony. The artist touches only those strings which con-tribute to the sweetness of the melody, sometimes one, sometimes two, sometimes three or more, as many as he deems sufficient for the production of his song." The point is underscored once more by the insertion of a long quotation from Adam of Dryburgh's prologue, which we mentioned earlier.

One major difficulty Trithemius encountered when quoting from the *Didascalicon* was that Hugh uses three senses only, as we already mentioned, leaving out anagogy.[89] The abbot's way of solving the problem is disarming: At every point where Hugh's text refers to the three senses, he supplies himself the "missing" reference to the fourth one. His almost mechanical formulations suggest that he did not grasp Hugh's subtle point about the comprehensive nature of the anagogical dynamic of all hermeneutics. For Trithemius the educator, anagogy, like the other senses, was defined by its specific subject matter. His summary of the criteria for discernment of the senses at the end of the chapter stands as an embarrassing witness to this simplistic understanding: "Any text which simply narrates the sequence of events belongs to history; any text useful for the edification of faith is treated as allegory; any text which promotes saintly behavior fits tropology; any text which speaks of the things above is marked off as belonging to anagogy." We are back to the easy systematization of the popular distich.

Chapter six drives home the foundational role of the literal sense: "Here we must point out that a person cannot arrive at the depths of allegorical understanding unless he is proficient in the historical narrative." The material basically excerpts and condenses *Did.* VI.3 with its emphasis on the correct procedure: One must begin with the foundation, with the effort to master the basic outline of the biblical story, the humble details, the what? how? by whom? where? of the historical narrative. History often seems boring and irrelevant *(inutilis)*. But knowledge is never superfluous. Everything learned will eventually have its use. Trithemius skips Hugh's wonderful boyhood reminiscences that illustrate this truth but picks up Hugh's advice about biblical books that the "beginning student in the school of Scripture" might read first: Genesis, Exodus, Joshua, Judges, Kings, Chronicles — he adds: "Esther, Judith, and similar books" — in the Old Testament; the Gospels and Acts in the New. Again, the abbot feels obliged to complete Hugh's references to the senses every time the fourth sense is missing: In history, Hugh says, you find the reasons to admire God's deeds,

---

89. The first sentence of *Did.* V.2, which Trithemius leaves out, reads: "Primum omnium sciendum est quod divina scriptura triplicem habet modum intelligendi, id est, historiam, allegoriam, tropologiam." Buttimer, 95.15-17.

in allegory to believe God's mysteries, in tropology to imitate God's perfection, "in anagogy," Trithemius adds, "what you can hope from God." He closes with the admonition not to expect shortcuts in the learning process: "No art is learned without a master." The pithy sentence comes from Jerome's Epistle 125.[90]

Didascalicon VI.4 provides the material for chapter seven, instruction about the spiritual senses. The opening quote of 2 Tim. 3:16-17, which is not in Hugh, makes the point that the "perfection" of the Christian who uses "all" of the inspired Scriptures comes through the complementarity of the senses: "What history cannot do, allegory can, and where allegory fails, the two other senses take over, promoting good behavior." Naturally, the investigation of the higher senses requires subtlety and prudence. With the words of Hugh, Trithemius turns to the building metaphor once more, recalling the activity of the stone mason who, once the rough foundation is in the ground, erects the structure by carefully laying his blocks course upon course, each course providing a "second foundation" for the following ones. While Hugh's text proceeds to explain the allegorical courses as the ordered arrangement of Christian doctrines that he later systematized in his *De sacramentis*, Trithemius breaks off at this point, saving the section on doctrines for his chapter eleven, where it is reproduced in full. Instead, he turns to practical examples: "In order that you may grasp the method of how you interpret scripture, I must give you some examples so that you may learn in which cases four of these senses converge and where you have three, two, or only one of them. Once you have digested these few examples, you can consider more easily the larger scene."

All the examples discussed in chapters eight to ten are Trithemius's own. I have not found any of them in the sources he seems to have used. Thus, they present a rare window, an unexpected opportunity for us to read the young abbot's own mind, to find out how he was coping personally with the need to "understand" the biblical texts he read, heard, and recited in his daily monastic experience. His example for a text combining all four interpretations is Ps. 50/51:20: "In your good pleasure, deal kindly with Zion, o Lord, and let the walls of Jerusalem be built up." This choice is introduced with a personal remark: "A brief verse comes to mind which is found in Psalm fifty and imposes itself boldly upon my gaze." The recital of Psalm 50, "Miserere," as part of the seven penitential psalms was a frequent experience in the monastery, especially during Lent, the season in

---

90. "Nulla ars absque magistro discitur." *Epist.* 125:15 (CSEL 56:133.10). The same quotation appears at the end of chapter eleven. See also above, n. 3.

1486 during which our treatise perhaps was composed.[91] The literal sense of the phrase is quite plain: "History is understood just as the words read." The allegorical meaning is unlocked by the key of etymology. "First one must know the meaning of the place names here." If Sion means "his seed" and Jerusalem "vision of peace,"[92] the verse begins to reveal its deeper meaning:

> David the prophet represents the righteous person who prays to the Lord and says: I implore you, o Lord, in your good pleasure deal kindly with Zion, that is, his seed. . . . Whose "his"? Christ's seed. What is this seed? The catholic church. Every Christian is the church of God as scripture says: God's temple is holy, and this temple you are [1 Cor. 3:17]. Thus, the righteous prays to God the Father in mystical words, as if he were saying openly: In your good pleasure, deal kindly, o Lord, with Zion, that is, every believer who is the seed of Christ your Son, and let the walls be built of Jerusalem, that is, the church militant, for if the Lord in his good pleasure had not come to the help of the nascent church, the walls of faith would have been destroyed by the perfidy of heretics and persecutors. But the omnipotent God himself in his compassion came to the rescue of the seed of the Christians at their beginnings, illumining some to be faithful Christians by inwardly drawing them to the faith, and outwardly showering them with signs and amazing teachings. In this way, apostles, martyrs, and finally the early doctors with whom the Lord shared his kindness, erected by their lives and teachings the walls of Jerusalem, the holy church militant, when, with the help of God, they rescued it from the jaws of the heretics.

These ruminations reveal more vividly than a formal theoretical treatise the actual preoccupations of the young leader: the place of Christ in his piety, his concern for righteous lives and right doctrine, for the church, its membership, its history and its tradition. They show the wealth of imagination that a simple Bible verse could release when even the first step of spiritual interpretation, allegory, was applied to it. Tropology built on this "second foundation." According to Trithemius, the principle of tropo-

91. See above, nn. 20, 23, and 24. The Roman Breviary expected the penitential psalms to be recited after Prime on all ferial days in Lent: Pierre Battifol, *History of the Roman Breviary* (London, etc.: Longmans, Green & Co., 1912), p. 170.

92. The main source for the etymology of Hebrew names in the Middle Ages was Jerome's *Liber interpretationis hebraicorum nominum;* see above, n. 34. Except for the opening of chapter four (above, n. 84), I have not been able to identify the exact origin of Trithemius's etymologies here and elsewhere, when they differ from Jerome.

logical interpretation was easy to grasp: "In tropology, the focus is on the soul." In the Psalm verse, the soul is praying: "Deal kindly with me in your good pleasure, that is, lead me according to your will, that I may please you and become Jerusalem, that is, a vision of the peace in which you rest." There is also a final step. Anagogically, the abbot suggests, not the individual soul but the universal company of the faithful is praying: "Deal kindly with Zion, that is, the church militant, inasmuch as all the righteous are her children to whom she gave birth, and let the walls be built of Jerusalem, that is, the church triumphant, for the construction of the kingdom of heaven consists in that the number of the elect is consummated."

Chapter nine introduces two examples of texts allowing for three senses in their interpretation: a short phrase from Ps. 121/22:6: "Pray for the things that are for the peace of Jerusalem," and the story of Judith. Trithemius had added the book of Judith to Hugh's reading list; he was obviously fond of it. The historical narrative, he says, is straightforward and has little to offer. Allegorically, however, Judith, "confessing" or "glorifying," stands for the church, and Holofernes, "infirmity of discession," for secular rulers like Nero who persecuted it. On the tropological level, Judith is the righteous soul, Holofernes the devil whom she kills through her confession and whose head she stores in her bag (Jdt. 13:11) "when she strips him of all his powers through her prayers and holy deeds and reduces him to nought." According to Trithemius, both texts have no anagogical meaning. In the case of the psalm verse, logic excludes it: "To pray for the peace of the heavenly kingdom would be superfluous and senseless since no turmoil exists there any more." On Judith, the abbot remarks wryly: "If you search for the anagogical sense of that story, look whether you find any. For me, it is enough to have ascended thus far."

Two very different texts serve as examples of two senses only in chapter ten: The first is the story of the rape of Dinah by Shechem (Gen. 34:1-2). According to Trithemius, it has only a literal and a moral sense. Predictably, one key to the tropology is etymology: "Sichem" means "hardworking" and stands for the devil "because he is always working to destroy the soul." No interpretation is given for the name of Dinah. In her case, the key is found in her reported activity: "She went out to see the women of the country." Thus, Dinah represents "the soul which went out to see various worldly longings and carnal desires," making herself vulnerable to the assaults of the evil one. The second passage is Rev. 21:2, which speaks of "the new Jerusalem having come down from heaven." This text has no historical referent "since that city of Jerusalem has nowhere descended from heaven." It allows, however, for an allegorical and an anagogical reading.

Allegorically, Jerusalem stands for holy mother church, the church of Christians, which descended from heaven when Christ, the Son of God, coming down from the Father, first founded her as he said himself in the Gospel that upon this rock, that is, upon himself, he would build his church.[93] Anagogically, because of what follows, you may understand this verse of the bliss of the saints in the kingdom.

At the end of his discussion of examples, Trithemius formulates the result: Any single sense and any combination is possible, especially when history is involved: history alone; history and one or more spiritual senses together. "The historical narrative in itself sometimes has no relevance, but still requires a spiritual reader *(misticum lectorem)*." Not the order of the texts but "exigency" decides which senses apply.

VI. Conclusion: Method and Order in the Study of Scripture

In chapter eleven, Trithemius returns to his source, the *Didascalicon*, taking up two final practical issues, the method *(modus)* and order *(ordo)* of the reading process. Both are essential because "where method is lacking, you have a defect, and where there is no order, one suspects shoddy work." For the method he reproduces the very brief chapter *Did.* VI.12 in which Hugh summarized what he had explained more fully in *Did.* III.9: Method in reading consists in analyzing the text by disassembling it into its constitutive parts and examining what is behind its terms. The notion of order receives much more attention. The initial material is provided by *Did.* VI.4. In his section on "history," Hugh had stressed the importance of studying, even memorizing the outline of the biblical story "from beginnning to end" as a first step. Now, after having discussed "allegory" and "tropology," he turns once more to the sequence of reading, this time under the aspect of the hermeneutical relationship between Old and New Testament. The "historical" reading had to proceed chronologically, from Genesis to the Revelation of John. "Allegorical" reading, however, must follow a different logic, a "cognitive order" in which the New Testament comes first because it holds the key to the hidden meaning of the Old; it moves from truth to figure, from open to hidden, from fulfillment to promise. With Hugh's help,

93. This was the traditional Augustinian interpretation of Matt. 16:18. See my article "Saint Peter, Papal Primacy, and the Exegetical Tradition, 1150-1300," in *The Religious Role of the Papacy, Ideals and Realities, 1150-1300*, ed. Christopher J. Ryan (Toronto: Pontifical Institute of Mediaeval Studies, 1989), pp. 3-44; here 7-12.

Trithemius formulates: "If a person wants to make headway in holy scripture, he must in his reading give priority to the New Testament in which the truth is openly proclaimed over the Old Testament and learn the truth before the figure; otherwise he will spend much effort and reap little benefit from it." Of Hugh's several examples he uses two. They seem to make the point pungently: How can one understand the prophecy of Isa. 7:14 ("Behold, a virgin will bear a son") if one has no knowledge of the angel's words to Mary (Luke 1:31-33)? How can one make sense of the vision in Dan. 7:13-14 if one has not read a passage such as Matt. 24:29-31? "Nobody could have understood these things by human reason, had not the Word made flesh by its light illumined everything that was hidden." A clear conclusion is to be drawn concerning order: "Train yourself first in the gospel doctrines so that you are clear about the truth; after that, you can turn to the shadow of the Old Testament."

With the reference to "doctrines," the way is open to return to Hugh's analogy in *Did.* VI.4 of the straight courses *(ordines)* of polished stones, the basic doctrines of the Christian faith, the *principia.* Hugh names eight: the Trinity, creation, the Fall, the mysteries *(sacramenta)* of restoration under natural law, then under the law of Moses, the incarnation, the new covenant, and Christ's resurrection. Trithemius skips the fifth, perhaps by mistake, and arrives at a total of seven. He reproduces, however, quite fully Hugh's admonition to keep to the "taut cord" of the basics as well as the warning to stay away from "perplexing speculations" on deeper theological issues and to refrain from reading beyond one's capacity when confronting "such a great sea of books and such manifold intricacies of opinions." Error lurks everywhere for the do-it-yourselfer. One needs the help of proven doctors and teachers. The abbot quotes all of this with obvious approval, drawing from it his own argument for humility: "Nothing impedes progress in one's studies as much as does presumptuousness."

This last sentence forms a bridge to the theme of chapter twelve, the third and last part of the treatise: Trithemius's reflections on the impediments that face the student of Scripture, and his advice on how to deal with them. His thoughts, however, are not only directed to the student of *scientia sacra.* The encouragement of study in every form is so much on the mind of the monastic leader that the chapter turns into a general harangue on vices in which the young abbot pulls out all the stops of his moralistic rhetoric, unloading on his readers an amazing range of classical and pseudoclassical citations and allusions. The result is a collection of commonplaces and trivialities less remarkable for its substance than for the personal engagement that one senses behind the pompous surface. The *Didascalicon* included a chapter on the same subject: *Quid studium impediat* (*Did.* V.5). Hugh named three major factors: negligence, imprudence, and circumstance. It seems that they were too theoretical, not practical enough for the young abbot and his experience with his monks. "What you need is not so much purity of the mind as moderate governance of the body." His list is quite explicit: anxiety, sensual pleasure, and idleness (*cura, uoluptas, ocium*). The first major enemy is sensuality in its various forms: "A full stomach has sleep on its mind and licentiousness, not reading." It seems that Trithemius regarded excessive drinking as particularly dangerous: "Believe me, nobody is susccessful in his studies if the wine cup is his constant companion." The diatribe against wine-drinking may be indebted to a passage in the *Speculum Virginum* that addresses the same problem in similar words.[94] Not much is said about anxiety; a small dose of it, the abbot submits, may even be beneficial to arouse the indifferent. With this thought, Trithemius is already close to his main concern on which he dwells extensively: idleness, *ocium*.[95] The remedy he recommends against this evil comes from Jerome: "Always find something good to do,"[96] with the stress on "always." The key to a successful struggle is persistence and constant practice: "Turn habit into nature." This point is driven home by a group of proverbial sayings on the value of *usus* and the perils of *inertia*. Many of them go back to well-known classical sources (Ovid, Horace, the *Disticha Catonis*); Trithemius hardly read them in the original. The sequence and wording of his citations suggest to me that they are taken from the *Polythecon*, a popular poetic florilegium of moral advice on a wide variety of topics, which dates from the thirteenth or fourteenth century.[97] The abbot is exploiting Book IX, chapter 13, entitled *De usu et exercitio*. The following two chapters deal with the other side: "Too much study wears down the body," and "From time to time, one must take a study break." Trithemius

94. *Speculum Virginum* V.662-701 (CCCM 5:136-37). The strong final exhortation, however, is not found there: "Fuge ergo vinum velud venenum, quia te ad sacre scripture studium prorsus reddit inabilem."

95. Later in the chapter, Trithemius quotes St. Benedict's Rule, cap. 48:1: "Ociositas inimica est animae." Brann, *The Abbot Trithemius*, gives considerable attention to the theme of *acedia*, the sin of sloth, in the writings of the abbot; see his "Index of Subjects," under *Acedia*.

96. "Semper aliquid boni facito." Jerome's orginal text is different: "Fac et aliquid operis," *Epist.* 125:11 (CSEL 56:130.6). Trithemius's version occurs as a manuscript variant, but without "semper." The section has influenced the abbot's argument throughout the chapter.

97. See the recent critical edition: *Polythecon*, ed. A. P. Orbán, CCCM 93 (Turnhout: Brepols, 1990).

incorporates appropriate quotations from these texts also. His citation formulas are very general: "I want you to remember that popular proverb," "someone says," "some secular sage said." A memorable one-liner, "Diligence softens the dullness of any task," is attributed to "a certain schoolmaster." This attribution betrays Trithemius's knowledge of still another source of proverbial wisdom: the Pseudo-Boethius treatise *De disciplina scholarium,* which may indeed be called a schoolmaster's handbook and where the line is found.[98]

After this ponderous display of secondhand wisdom, our author manages an elegant return to the more substantial concerns of Hugh's *Didascalicon.* The recommended rhythm of intensive study and necessary rest leads him to suggest a sequence of five activities for a healthy life of scriptural study: "Let meditation follow reading, manual labor meditation, prayer the manual labor, and contemplation of the heavenly gifts the prayer." The proposal is followed by a quotation from *Did.* V.9 in which Hugh laid out five steps to perfection, very similar in wording, but with the order of labor and prayer reversed. There is another difference: Hugh was really talking about four steps. He hesitated to include contemplation, which seemed to be qualitatively different from the others, a state "in which one has a foretaste, even in this life, of what the future reward of good work is."[99] Trithemius skips the hesitation. For him, all five steps are activities, exercises that anyone can do. Perfection is integrated into a course of action. It has become a curricular goal. Still following Hugh's words, the abbot speaks of "fruits," but he simply holds out the reward that those who submit to such a curriculum can expect. All five exercises are worthwhile "labor," and "the fruit of good labors is glorious; it is that wisdom which never withers." Wisdom, the mysterious, elusive bride, is not, as in Hugh, outside the scope of a methodological handbook. It is the natural prize of hard work, within reach of "anyone who pants for the *scientia sacrae scripturae*" and follows the right method. When Trithemius returns once more to Hugh in making the connection to the four senses, he quotes from an earlier chapter, where Hugh speaks of the fruit of the beginner's exegetical efforts:

---

98. *De disciplina scholarium (Ps.-Boethius),* I.7, ed. Olga Weijers, Studien und Texte zur Geistesgeschichte des Mittelalters, vol. 12 (Leiden: Brill, 1976), p. 95:19-20.

99. Hugh's chapter title reads "De quatuor gradibus," and the text begins: "Quattuor sunt in quibus nunc exercetur vita iuestorum et quasi per quosdam gradus ad futuram perfectionem sublevatur, videlicet lectio sive doctrina, meditatio, oratio, et operatio, quinta deinde sequitur, contemplatio, in qua quasi quodam praecedentium fructu in hac vita etiam quae sit boni operis merces futura praegustatur," Buttimer (ed.), *Didascalicon,* p. 109.12-18.

Twofold is the fruit of sacred reading *(lectio divina):* it instructs the mind with knowledge, and it equips it with morals (Trithemius: honors). It teaches what it delights us to know and what behooves us to imitate. Of these, the first, knowledge, has more to do with history and allegory, the other, instruction in morals, has more to do with tropology. The whole of sacred scripture is directed to this end.[100]

This seemed a compelling summary of the basics, exactly what the abbot wanted as a clear systematization of the traditional doctrine. The difficulty, of course, was that only three senses are discussed. We know why. Just as contemplation was not a fifth step in a curricular sequence for Hugh, anagogy was not a fourth sense in a teachable schema of scriptural interpretation. It was the essence of the interpretive process itself, the never-ending task of the Christian life. The part of *Did.* V.9 that Trithemius did not reproduce makes this point and clarifies the use of the other senses as well: "That we ascend is our goal; that we descend is for the sake of this goal. Not the latter but the former ought to be the principal thing." Trithemius may have been tempted to supply a reference to the "missing" sense once more himself. This time, however, he did not add anything. His formulation of the customary petition at the conclusion of the treatise sounds like a faint echo of what he surely read in Hugh but apparently was unwilling to integrate into his simplified course in biblical hermeneutics:

May the one who is Alpha and Omega, our Lord Jesus Christ, deign to lead us to the right and proper end.

Unlike other works of the Abbot of Sponheim, the *Tractatus de inuestigatione sacrae scripturae* had no perceptible impact. Its value consists in what it reveals about its author and the teaching of biblical hermeneutics at the time of its writing. Our analysis has shown that, just as we were led to expect by the author's own description of his early literary activity, the little work is an ambitious beginner's exercise, a patchwork of quotations artfully connected with the "mortar" of the young author's own words — nothing of which he would be proud, yet not totally useless either, as his references in the correspondence of 1486 and the existence of the manuscript copy indicate. The files of excerpts from which he drew did not contain rare treasures. They reveal that the abbot's main sources for the theory of biblical interpretation were Jerome, Book III of Hrabanus

---

100. Buttimer (ed.), *Didascalicon*, p. 104.20-25; Taylor, *The Didascalicon of Hugh of St. Victor*, p. 127.

Maurus's *De clericorum institutione* with its excerpts from Augustine's *De doctrina Christiana*, and some classics of the twelfth century: the *Speculum Virginum*, the prologue "Quisquis ad sacrae scripturae notitiam," and Hugh of St. Victor's *Didascalicon*. Neither Nicholas of Lyra, whom he mentioned in the correspondence as a model exegete,[101] nor the scholastic theologians, such as Thomas Aquinas, Bonaventure, or even Jean Gerson, were needed for the task. The concept of the fourfold sense of Scripture was an old, venerable tradition of hermeneutical thought that had nourished the mind of the young Bible-loving abbot and which he intended to hand on. But the true superiority of this "method" could no longer be recognized in the simplified instructional systematization through which he tried to make it available even to the least among his brethren in the monastery or any contemporary who shared in the conviction of the value of education and was willing to learn. It seems that a new kind of Reformation was needed. It may still be needed today.

---

101. "Nicolaus de Lira ordinis Minorum totam Scripturam sacram ad litteram per modum postillatoris sufficienter exposuit. Quod opus tamquam aedificii spiritualis funda-mentum pro intellectu litterali caeteris est anteponendum, et his maxime qui litteralis intel-ligentiae adhuc sunt expertes. Hunc pro modico aere impressum poteris comparare." Busaeus, *Johannes Trithemii Opera*, p. 945b.

Erasmus's Influence on Zwingli and Bullinger in the Exegesis of Matthew 11:28-30

JOHN B. PAYNE

Erasmus of Rotterdam (1466-1536) was the prince of the Christian humanist movement in northern Europe. As a Christian humanist, he was concerned to bring about a spiritual and moral renewal of the church and society by a revival of the ancient classical and Christian literature — Scripture and the church fathers. Erasmus considered his work upon the New Testament, which included the preparation of a critical edition of the Greek text with fresh Latin translation accompanied by *Annotations* and the *Paraphrases,* to be his most important contribution to this reform program. His *Novum Testamentum* was published first in 1516 and then subsequently in 1519, 1522, 1527, and 1535 with ever expanding annotations. In 1517 the *Paraphrase on Romans* inaugurated the publication of the *Paraphrases on the New Testament,* which was completed in 1524. Both his *New Testament* and the *Paraphrases* had widespread influence upon the Reformation. All of the Reformers read them and made some use of them. Luther based his translation in 1522 upon Erasmus's 1519 New Testament. Zwingli made a pocket copy of Erasmus's Greek text and virtually memorized it. He obtained the *Paraphrases* on the New Testament as soon as they appeared. Erasmus's Greek text, inferior as it was from the standpoint of modern textual criticism, underlay the *Textus Receptus* ("the received text"), which was the principal basis of nearly all the vernacular versions well into the nineteenth century. The translations of the *Paraphrases* and some of the *Annotations* into the vernacular made possible a more popular influence.[1] This article provides a glimpse of the influence of Erasmus's New Testament exegesis in annotation and paraphrase upon two prominent Swiss Reformers.

Matthew 11:28-30 — "Come to me, all who labor and are heavy-laden, and I will give you rest. Take my yoke upon you, and learn from me; for I am gentle and lowly in heart, and you will find rest for your souls. For my yoke is easy and my burden is light" — was a capital text for exegetes in the period of the Reformation. That for Erasmus this was a central pericope is indicated by his lengthy annotation on 11:30 *(iugum suave)* in 1519, his wide-ranging explication of it in the preface to a Latin edition of his New Testament in 1521, and his extended paraphrase of the whole pericope in 1522. Luther preached at least five sermons on the whole section, Matt. 11:25-30, including his last sermon at Eisleben just before

---

1. The most complete standard edition of Erasmus's works remains *Desiderii Erasmi Roterodami opera omnia* (Leiden, 1703-6; photo reprint: Hildesheim: Ohms, 1962), 10 vols., cited as LB. The *New Testament* with the *Annotations* appears in vol. 6, and the *Paraphrases on the New Testament* in vol. 7. The *New Testament* and the *Paraphrases on the New Testament* have not yet been published in the new critical edition *Opera omnia Desiderii Erasmi Roterodami: Recognita et adnotatione critica instructa notisque illustrata* (Amsterdam: North Holland Publishing Company, 1969–), hereafter cited as ASD. The critical edition of the letters remains that of P. S. Allen, H. M. Allen, and H. W. Garrod (eds.), *Opus epistolarum Des. Erasmi Roterodami* (Oxford: Oxford University Press, 1906-47), 11 vols. plus index by B. Flower and E. Rosenbaum (Oxford: Oxford University Press, 1958), hereafter cited as Allen. The letters are in process of translation in the *Collected Works of Erasmus* (Toronto: University of Toronto Press, 1974), cited as CWE. For a facsimile of the final edition of the *Annotations* with earlier variants, see Anne Reeve (ed.), *Erasmus' Annotations on the New Testament: The Gospels* (London: Duckworth, 1986); Anne Reeve and M. A. Screech (ed.), *Erasmus' Annotations on the New Testament: Acts, Romans, I and II Corinthians* (Leiden: Brill, 1990); and idem, *Erasmus' Annotations on the New Testament: Galatians to the Apocalypse* (Leiden: Brill, 1943). The *Paraphrases of Mark, John, Acts, Romans,* and *Galatians* and the *Annotations on Romans* have so far appeared in the Toronto edition. On Erasmus's New Testament scholarship see Jerry H. Bentley, *Humanists and Holy Writ: New Testament Scholarship in the Renaissance* (Princeton: Princeton University Press, 1983), and Erika Rummel, *Erasmus' Annotations on the New Testament: From Philologist to Theologian* (Toronto: University of Toronto Press, 1986). On the *Paraphrases on the Gospels,* see *Humanistische Evangeliensauslegung: Desiderius Erasmus von Rotterdam als Ausleger der Evangelien in seiner Paraphrasen* (Tübingen: Mohr, 1986). On the origin and character of the *Paraphrases,* and the history of their publication in Latin and their translation into English, see CWE 42:xi-xxiv. On German translations of the *Paraphrases* and some of the *Annotations,* see Heinz Holeczek, *Erasmus Deutsch 1: Die volkssprachliche Rezeption des Erasmus von Rotterdam in der reformatorischen Öffentlichkeit 1519-1536* (Stuttgart: Frommann-Holzboog, 1983), pp. 45-128. On Erasmus's hermeneutics see Manfred Hoffmann, *Rhetoric and Theology: The Hermeneutics of Erasmus* (Toronto: University of Toronto Press, 1994). For up-to-date articles and reviews see the *Erasmus of Rotterdam Society Yearbook* (1981–).

his death.[2] It is well known that Matt. 11:28 was so dear to Zwingli that he placed it on the title page of his writings. He made use of it throughout his writings and wrote a substantial exegesis of it in his posthumously published commentary on Matthew. His successor in Zurich, Heinrich Bullinger, expanded upon it at great length in the preface to his own commentary on Matthew of 1542 and wrote a substantial explanation of it within the commentary itself, even though his own favorite verse (used as a subtitle for all his writings) was Matt. 17:5. My article is limited to an analysis of the interpretations of Erasmus as well as those of Zwingli and Bullinger, both of whom were influenced by Erasmus's exegesis.

I. Erasmus on Matthew 11:28-30

In Erasmus's annotation, most of which was written in 1519 (though there are major additions in 1522 and quite minor ones in 1535),[3] Erasmus is concerned to contrast the easy yoke of Christ (he prefers *commodum* to the Vg. *suave*) with the hard yoke of the law and even more with the vexing burden of human laws that have been added to the yoke of Christ. He nods in passing to the tradition on this verse when he refers to Jerome's question as to how the evangelical law is lighter and milder than the Mosaic since the latter punishes the dead whereas the former punishes also the will, but Erasmus does not think that Jerome really solved what he proposed. Jerome had argued that the yoke of the gospel is lighter than that of the law because the gospel commands those things that we can do, such as not coveting, and punishes an action only when the will is involved. On the other hand, the law punishes the deed regardless of the will. He gives the example of a virgin who in time of persecution became a prostitute against her will. According to the law she is condemned; according to the gospel, however,

---

2. See the register in WA 22:xlix-l. Luther wrote an extended comment upon it in his *Annotationes in aliquot capita Matthaei* in 1536 (WA 38:526-30).

3. I use the Leiden edition of Erasmus's works (text in LB 6:63-65), which has been compared with the collation of editions by Anne Reeve, *Erasmus' Annotations of the New Testament: The Gospels*. A German pamphlet version of this 1519 annotation was first published by Schoeffler in Mainz in 1521: *Herr Erasmus von Roterdam verdeutschte ausslegung über das gottlich trostlich wort vnsers lieben herrn vnnd seligmachers christi Nement auff euch mein Joch vnd lernet von mir.* Heinz Holeczek lists a total of eleven editions from 1521 to 1523. *Erasmus Deutsch,* pp. 82-83, 292-93. See also Paul A. Russell, *Lay Theology in the Reformation: Popular Pamphleteers in Southwest Germany 1521-1525* (Cambridge: Cambridge University Press, 1986), pp. 270, 239 n. 78.

she is sustained.[4] Apparently, Erasmus did not care much for this reasoning. But he does agree with the tradition since Augustine that the Mosaic law, once a temporary restraint on a superstitious and rebellious people, was, as Peter in Acts 15 stated, "a heavy burden which neither they [the Jews] nor their fathers were able to bear."[5]

But it is not traditional in the exegesis of this passage to stress, as Erasmus does, the sharp contrast between the easy and pleasant yoke of Christ and the burdensome laws that have been added to this yoke by human beings, though Erasmus does find some support for his position in Augustine. Like Augustine, he identifies the light burden of Christ with the law of love, which sweetens whatever is bitter; but unlike Augustine, he emphasizes that the burden of love cannot be understood as light except as made possible by the gift of the Holy Spirit.[6] Erasmus stresses that the law of love is easily borne because it is according to nature. "Nothing is more congruent with human nature," he says, "than the philosophy of Christ, which is concerned with almost nothing other than the restoration to innocence and sincerity of a fallen nature,"[7] a sentiment that echoes the famous statement in the *Paraclesis:* "Now what is most in accord with human nature easily penetrates into the souls of all. What else, however, is the philosophy of Christ, which he himself calls rebirth, than the restoration of a nature created good?"[8] Similar statements are found elsewhere in Erasmus's writings.[9]

The greater portion of his annotation is devoted to a long complaint concerning the burdensome doctrines and laws that in the course of time the church has added to the simple and easy yoke of Christ. As in the preface to his edition of Hilary and in the *Ratio verae theologiae,*[10] he bemoans the

---

4. Jerome, *Comm. in Mattheum* 11:30 (PL 26:78).

5. Erasmus, *Annotatio in Matt.* 11:28-30 (LB 6:63C); Augustine, *Sermo* 105.6 (CCSL 24A:653.70-71); Radbertus, *Expos. in Matt.* (PL 120:453); Rupert of Deutz, *In opus de gloria et honore Filii Hominis super Matthaeum* (PL 168:74); Nicholas of Lyra, *Postilla super totam Bibliam* (Frankfurt/Main: Minerva, 1971); reprint of 1492 Strassburg edition), sig. d-iii[v].

6. Augustine, *Enarr. in Ps. 67:18* (CCSL 39:881.17ff.).

7. Erasmus, *Annotatio in Matt.* (LB 6:63D).

8. Erasmus, *Paraclesis* (LB 5:141).

9. See, e.g., Erasmus, *Epistola de philosophia evangelica* (LB 6:*5[r]): ". . . Evangelica doctrina sit instauratio simul et perfectio naturae, ut erat primum condita sincere, mirum videri non debet, si Philosophis quibusdam Ethnicis datum est, naturae vi quaedam animadvertere, quae cum doctrina Christi consentiant. . . ." On the dialectic of nature and grace in Erasmus's thought, see J.-C. Margolin, "L'Idée de nature dans la pensée d'Erasme," in idem, *Récherches Erasmiennes* (Geneva: Droz, 1969), pp. 31-41.

10. Ep. 1334.362-69 (Allen 5:180-81; *Ratio verae Theologiae,* LB 5:92D).

multiplication of doctrines beyond the teachings of Christ and those of the Apostles as summarized in the Apostles' Creed. This process began already in the early church on account of the divisions of the heretics. All the more does he satirically rail against the growth of theological speculation among the scholastics, "when there are many kinds of things which it is impious for a human being to define,"[11] a theme that is also frequent in his writings.

Before launching into a diatribe against the accumulation of oppressive laws, Erasmus, as a sort of self-justification, refers to the letter of Augustine to Januarius in which Augustine regrets that so many wholesome practices sanctioned in Holy Scriptures are neglected and so many superstitious rites are so highly esteemed. The Bishop of Hippo accepts in addition those practices that the council of bishops and the custom of the universal church authorize, but the endless variety of custom in different places he deplores as weighing down the Christian religion with slavish burdens, which God in his mercy wished to be free. Christianity should have only very few and very clear sacramental celebrations. The condition of the Jews is more bearable, who, though they had not known the time of liberty, were subject only to the burdens of the law, not to human prescriptions.[12]

Erasmus must have delighted in discovering this statement of Augustine that he could cite as supporting his attack upon laws contrived by human beings. Naturally, he does not note Augustine's conclusion that the church, founded in the midst of much chaff, tolerates many things except for those that are contrary to faith and morals, and indeed, though he wishes that there did not exist so much variety of custom in the church, Augustine recommends that it be endured as long as it does not contradict faith and morals. Erasmus notes that Augustine was upset on account of certain frivolous barefooted processions. "But what if he [Augustine] saw that free people of Christ ensnared by so many laws, so many ceremonies, so many chains, oppressed by the plain tyranny of human beings, of secular princes, bishops, cardinals, popes, and most of all, their satellites, who," he adds in 1522, "assuming the image of religion, pursue the business of the stomach."[13] Then Erasmus cites a long litany of what were for him burdensome and even oppressive or superstitious medieval laws and customs, including fasting, the observance of feast days, the colors of vestments in worship, the chains of vows and of marriage, the burden of confession, the

---

11. Erasmus, *Annotatio in Matt.* (LB 6:63).
12. Augustine, Ep. 55 (CSEL 34:209.18-210.14).
13. Erasmus, *Annotatio in Matt.* (LB 6:64).

abuse of the authority of the popes for excommunications, absolutions, dispensations, and indulgences, and the neglect of the gospel by a priesthood more concerned to master Aristotelian philosophy.

He recognizes that Paul held that love endures all things, but thinks that evils that are inflicted from without are more bearable than those that are suffered from within, not only by the members but also by the rulers of the church. He mentions that for the healing of such evils the customary remedy was the General Council, but rather than calling for the convening of such a council, he expresses the hope that Christ might inspire popes and princes, theologians and preachers, with a large consensus to teach "prudently and calmly those things which in Christ's eyes are worthy."[14]

At the end of the 1519 portion of the annotation Erasmus stresses that the Pauline doctrine of the liberty of Christ should not be embraced in order to give license to the flesh, but rather that we should shake off the heavy human yoke, so that we might be burdened "by the truly pleasant yoke of Christ," to which he adds in 1522: "The love of the Gospel commands less, but accomplishes more."[15] And then, lest his words of 1519 incite an uproar, he urges that tumult should be avoided and evil princes endured, though he closes with an appeal once more that Christ might inspire his Vicars to prefer for Christ to rule by the gospel laws rather than to maintain tyranny by human decrees.[16] In his response to Albert Pio (1525), who had criticized this Annotation's attack upon human laws, Erasmus regrets that he had not written more circumspectly, but insists that he could not have surmised such things as have arisen in more recent times.[17]

In the *Paraphrase* of 1522, Erasmus takes quite a different approach to the passage. There is no mention here of the burden of human laws or even of the Mosaic law. Rather, the burdens are those of the world, broadly conceived: poverty, disease, old age, a distorted care for riches,

---

14. Erasmus, *Annotatio in Matt.* (LB 6:64).

15. LB 6:64. As pointed out by Erika Rummel, Erasmus's critique of ecclesiastical law here closely parallels his letter of 1522, *Epistola de interdicto esu carnium deque similibus hominum constitutionibus*, which was occasioned by the controversy concerning the law of fasting in Basel in 1522; see *Erasmus and His Catholic Critics*; 2 vols. (Nieuwkoop: De Graaf, 1989), 1:181-83. For this text see ASD IX-1:19-50.

16. Erasmus, *Annotatio in Matt.* (LB 6:64-65).

17. *Responsio ad epistolam Pii* (LB 9:11183A). On Erasmus's conflict with Pio see Rummel, *Catholic Critics*, 2:15-123; and Myron P. Gilmore, "Erasmus and Alberto Pio, Prince of Carp," in *Action and Conviction in Early Modern Europe* (Princeton: Princeton University Press, 1969), pp. 299-318. The comments in criticism of human laws in the *Epistola de interdicto esu* drew much more attention from Erasmus's critics than the annotation. See Rummel, *Catholic Critics*, 1:183. Cf. *Paraphrasis in Marcum* 2:19 (LB 7:177; CWE 49:42).

a tortured love or hatred, the confusion of false opinions, and the consciousness of sins. Whereas the Western tradition since Jerome had named sin as the principal burden intended here, Erasmus sets it down as but one burden among others.[18] To be sure, Chrysostom had adopted a wider interpretation, but not so far-ranging as that of Erasmus. Having applied the invitation to "all that are in anxiety, in sorrows, in sins," even he had held that it was the consciousness of sin that especially weighed down the soul.[19]

The focus of Erasmus's exegesis is upon the *tranquillitas animi* that the yoke of Christ brings in contrast with the lures of this world. This term, a favorite of Cicero and Seneca,[20] Erasmus uses three times in the place of *requiem*, which was his own translation in his *Novum Testamentum* well as that of the Vulgate.[21] In the *Enchiridion* Erasmus had already connected the idea of *tranquillitas* with this passage, though he uses only the adjective, not the noun. There he compares the ways of the world, which lead to distress, with the way of virtue, "which is not difficult to begin with and grows easier with practice" and leads to immortal life.[22] The former with maximum labor leads to everlasting travail, the latter with moderate toil to everlasting peace *(otium)*. But even if the path of virtue *(pietas)* were more laborious, "nevertheless the harshness of the struggle would be alleviated by the hope of a reward. . . ." And then, after quoting Matt. 11:29-30, he states: "In brief, no pleasure is lacking where there is a tranquil *(tranquilla)* conscience; but no misery is absent where an unhappy conscience torments us."[23]

18. Erasmus, *Paraphrasis in Matt.* (LB 7:69); Jerome, *Comment. in Matt.* (PL 26:78).

19. Chrysostom, *Hom. in Matt.* 38.3 (PG 57:432; NPNF 10:252-53).

20. Cicero, *De oratore* 1.1.2; *Tusculanae disputationes* 4.5.10; *Orationes de lege agraria* 1.8.21; *De officiis* 1.20.69; *Oratio pro L. Murena* 27.55; Seneca, *De tranquillitate animi* 2.3ff.

21. Erasmus, *Annotatio in Matt.* (LB 6:69).

22. Erasmus, *Enchiridion* (LB 5:24; CWE 66:59). Compare with Rabanus and the *Glossa ordinaria*, who harmonize this passage with Matt. 11:14 ("for the gate is narrow and the road is hard that leads to life") by arguing that the way is at first narrow and difficult, but that over the course of time it becomes enlarged by the sweetness of indescribable love. Rabanus, *Comm. in Matt.* 11:28 (PL 107:918): "Pater noster Benedictus ait, non est nisi angusto initio incipienda, processu vero conversationis et fidei dilatato corde inenarrabili dilectionis dulcedine curritur via mandatorum Dei; and *Biblia cum Glossa ordinaria et expositione Lyre literali et morali nec non Pauli Burgensis additionibus ac Matthiae Thoringi replicis* (Basel: J. Petri and J. Froben, 1498) 5:f-5ᵛ: "Item quomodo jugum suave, cum supra dicitur: Arcta via est quae ducit ad vitam. Sed angusta, quia non nisi angusto initio incipitur, processu vero temporis ineffabili dilectionis dulcedine dilatatur." In contrast with Rabanus and the *Glossa Ordinaria*, Erasmus thinks that the yoke is not difficult to begin with.

23. Erasmus, *Enchiridion* (LB 5:24; CWE 66:59).

In the *Paraphrase* he stresses that it is the taking on of Christ's yoke willingly and eagerly that brings tranquillity.[24] That yoke consists of the appropriation of his teaching and the imitation of his life, which displays itself in no aspiration for riches or honors, humility, gentleness and non-requiting love,[25] and a complete dependence on the Father. Such a yoke "to unbelievers seems harsh and heavy, but to those who trust in the divine goodness with all their heart, and have taken in the fire of the gospel love," it is "mild and easy." In contrast with the statement in the *Enchiridion*, he mentions faith as lightening the burden of the Christian life, but, as in the *Enchiridion*, he also adds that the certain hope of rewards renders the yoke sweet. He concludes that a good conscience, free of all care and confident in the rewards of eternal life, cannot be disturbed.[26]

Erasmus's notion of tranquillity here in the *Paraphrase* is more shaped by Scripture and Christian tradition than it is by Stoicism; yet there is Stoic coloring in the language concerning the tranquil soul as free from all disturbance from within brought on by ambition, anger, greed, pleasures of the flesh, etc., and as calm in the midst of storms raging about him.[27] The sea metaphor was a favorite of the Stoics for the tranquillity as well as the agitation of the soul.[28]

In his *New Preface* to his Latin New Testament (1520),[29] the text of

24. Erasmus, *Paraphrasis in Matt.* (LB 7:69D).

25. Cf. Rabanus, *Comm. in Matt.* 11:28 (PL 107:917B): "Discendum ergo nobis est a Salvatore nostro ut simus mites moribus et humiles mentibus, ut neminem laedamus, neminem contemnamus . . .'; and *Glossa ordinaria*, 5:f-5ᵛ: "Quia nullum ledo moribus. Quia nullum despicio mente."

26. LB 7:69-70. Cf. Seneca, *De tranquillitate animi* 3.4.

27. LB 7:69.

28. Cicero, *Tusculanae dispuutationes* 5.16: "ut maris igitur tranquillitas intelligitur nulla ne minima quidem aura fluctus commovente, sic animi quietus et placatus status cernitur, cum perturbatio nulla est qua moveri queat"; Seneca, *De tranquillitate animi* 2.1: "Horum . . . non parum sanum est corpus, sed sanitati parum adsueuit, sicut est quidam tremor etiam tranquilli maris, utique cum ex tempestate requieuit." On tranquillity as free from all storms or disturbances, see Cicero, *De officiis* 1.20.69; *De oratore* 1.1.2.

29. According to Holeczek, this *Nova Praefatio* first appeared in his Latin New Testament edition published by Froben in 1520 (*Erasmus Deutsch*, 4.64 n. 1). I have seen a 1521 copy in the Basle University Library, *Novum Testamentum omne...* (Basileae: Apud Io. Frobenium, An. M.D. XXI), a 2ʳ-a4ᵛ. It is to be found in the Leiden edition under the title *Praefatio tertiae editionis novi testamenti an. M.D. XXIV* (LB 6:*2ᵛ-*3ʳ). It exists in two different German versions, the one translated by Nikolaus Krumpach, pastor in Querfurt, and the other, an anonymous translation. It is astonishing that this short piece was published twelve times from 1522 to 1525. Its frequent and widespread publication parallels the interest shown in the annotation on Matt. 11:29 and must, therefore, have been regarded as useful in the Reformation *Flugschrift* propaganda war of the early 1520s. See Holeczek, *Erasmus Deutsch*, pp. 73-79 and 291-92.

Matt. 11:28 serves as the point of departure for Erasmus's remarks. He first emphasizes the universality of the invitation. It is given to all, whether male or female, young or old, slave or free, rich or poor, priest or lay, monk or nonmonk. As in the *Paraphrase*, it applies to a wide range of burdens, and he names several of the very same ones: ambition, anger, envy, evil desire, wretched love or hatred, poverty, disease, and old age, and, as in the 1519 annotation, he names the burden of human laws. There is no mention here of *tranquillitas* as the gift of Christ, but rather of *refrigerium*.[30] But the weight of the explication of the text in this preface is upon how and where to reach this Christ who graciously invites all who are burdened to come to him. "The way to him," he says, "is not by the feet, but by the affections: nay by the feet, but by the feet of the soul, not the body." As pointed out by André Godin,[31] Erasmus here appropriates a favorite figure of Origen. He emphasizes the immediacy of the presence of Christ by referring to Luke 17:21, "The Kingdom of God is within you," and in an inexact manner to Rom. 10:8: "The word is near you in your lips and in your heart," which in his *Annotations* he exegetes in an Origenistic manner as meaning that the Word (that is, Christ) is within you.[32] Since Christ is within the soul, to be led away by bodily things is to be led away from oneself and from Christ. No one comes to Christ unless the Father (John 6:44) and Christ draw him and unless he approaches with sincere faith and hungering and thirsting for righteousness.

Christ is especially present to his own, and more effectively than he was in body to the Jews, in the Gospels and the apostolic letters. Here we have the purest pulses of his mind. These may be approached as often as we like. They are accessible to all, not just to theologians, he implies, just as Christ's gracious invitation is open to all. With a familiar metaphor, Erasmus refers to Scripture as the pure *fontes* or *venae* of the Savior, which alone assuage thirst, and he asks: "Why, neglecting these, do we willingly drink from the wasted pools of others filled with broken rocks, in which there is more lime than water?" He goes on to criticize the preference for human rules such as that of St. Francis or St. Augustine over the philos-

---

30. LB VI:*2ᵛ.

31. A. Godin, *Erasme lecteur d'Origène* (Geneva: Droz, 1982), p. 127. The anonymous German translation picks up the implied criticism of pilgrimages in this text and entitles the preface *Von walfart, Erasmi Roterodami, Vermanung, wo Christus und sein reich zu suchen ist*; see Holeczek, *Erasmus Deutsch*, pp. 75-80 and 291. Holeczek, however, is not as inclined, as I am, to think that this text was the occasion for this German title.

32. *Annotatio in Romanos* 10:8 (LB 6:618; CWE 56:283). Cf. K. H. Schelkle, *Paulus: Lehrer der Väter* (Düsseldorf: Patmos, 1956), p. 369.

ophy of Christ — which alone satisfies — to be discovered in these writings.[33]

II. Zwingli on Matthew 11:28-30

That Zwingli was probably influenced by Erasmus's treatment of Matt. 11:28 should not be surprising, for he specifically refers to Erasmus's poem concerning Jesus in his explanation of Christ as the only mediator in his *Auslegen und Gründe der Schlussreden* (#20) of July 1523. In a famous passage, he describes the decisive impact that Erasmus's poem had upon him. He says that when some eight or nine years ago he read the poem (namely, the *Expostulatio Jesu cum homine suapte culpa per eunte*,[34] though he doesn't give the title), which describes Jesus with beautiful words as "the source of all good and as the bringer of salvation and the consolation and treasure of the soul," he was struck by the truth of the words and wondered why we seek help from any creature. He did not permit other poems of Erasmus dedicated to the saints Anna and Michael to deter him from the knowledge that Christ is alone the treasure of our poor souls.[35] It is in the context of the discussion of this article concerning Christ as the one mediator — who alone intercedes for us, to whom we alone pray, in whom alone we place our confidence — that Zwingli sets the gracious call of the Savior. Matthew 11:28 expresses Zwingli's conviction that Christ, the deeply humiliated one, who knows our distress and anxiety, the one who graciously calls us and whom we may confidently call upon, is the source of mercy and rest for us sinners, he and no one else. To call upon another creature is idolatry.[36] Elsewhere in the *Auslegen und Gründe*, Zwingli makes use of this text in an Erasmian manner to criticize those who burden themselves with unwise laws *(unwysen gsatzen)* and then again attacks human teachings and ordinances *(menschen leere und satzungen)* as not useful for salvation since they do not bring comfort. Only Christ's friendly invitation of God's grace does that.[37]

---

33. Erasmus, *Nova Praefatio* (LB 6:*2ᵛ-*3ʳ). For other passages that contrast the pure fountains of Scripture with the wasted pools of human doctrine, see Ep. 373:161-63 (Allen 2:170; CWE 3:203); Ep. 384:52-54 (Allen 2:185; CSEL 3:222) and the references in Allen 4:33 n. 15.

34. Erasmus, *Expostulatio Jesu* (LB 5:1319-20).

35. Zwingli, *Auslegen und Gründe* (ZSW 2:217.8-21).

36. *Auslegen und Gründe* (ZSW 2:221.7-222.9). Zwingli also quotes this text in his earlier discussion of this article, where he stresses that it is directed to those who are burdened by sin (ZSW 2:194.28-195.3).

37. *Auslegen und Gründe* (ZSW 2:66.1-16; 76.6-77.31).

The twin themes of Christ as the foundation of grace and of Christ as the sole mediator, often accompanied by a polemic against other so-called mediators or intercessors, are frequently associated with Matt. 11:28 in his writings. Already in the *Von Erkiesen und Freiheit der Speisen* of April 1522, the passage is set in the context of a discussion of law and grace. The law that oppresses and kills is not only that of the Old Testament but also that of the New. Matthew 5:22 ("But I say unto you, that whosoever is angry with his brother shall be in danger of the judgment") is a severe word if taken literally and impossible for weak human beings to keep. But Zwingli's solution to this predicament differs from that of Jerome and Erasmus, coming closer to that of Augustine and Luther. Christ has given us the law that "we might recognize our sickness *(prästen)*,[38] and then take refuge alone in him, who mercifully pitied our weakness or sickness *(prästen)*, when he said, 'Come unto me, all who labor. . . .'" Whoever does not know this easy *(ringen)* way to God's grace seeks to fulfill the law by his own powers and prescribes for himself specific ascetic practices and abstinences.[39]

Just a few months later in the *Von Klarheit und Gewissheit des Wortes Gottes,* he again sounds the themes of grace and of Christ as the only sure way of salvation in connection with this passage. When Zwingli ridicules seeking salvation by entering various religious orders, he parallels Erasmus's critique of adopting a monastic rule instead of the rule of Christ that he set forth in the new preface to his Latin New Testament. But whereas Zwingli stresses grace, Erasmus emphasizes the call to discipleship as the way of Christ. Zwingli goes on to deride indulgences from the pope or making pilgrimages to Compostella as means of salvation, and then quotes Matt. 11:28 as offering us the one assurance of salvation. "O glad news, which brings with it its own light, so that we know and believe that it is true. . . ."[40] Similarly, under the heading of the gospel in *Eine kurze Christliche Einleitung* (1523), Zwingli refers to the text twice, to stress, first, salvation by grace, not by works; and, second, Christ as the sole mediator.[41]

---

38. On this controversial term see Gottfried W. Locher, *Zwingli's Thought: New Perspectives* (Leiden: Brill, 1981), pp. 202-3; W. P. Stephens, *The Theology of Huldrych Zwingli* (Oxford: Oxford University Press, 1986), pp. 140 n. 1, 149 n. 41; and R. Pfister, *Das Problem der Erbsünde bei Zwingli* (Leipzig: Heinsius, 1939), pp. 23-25.

39. Zwingli, *Von Erkiesen und Freiheit der Speisen* (ZSW 1:104.3-9).

40. Zwingli, *Von Klarheit und Gewissheit des Wortes Gottes* (ZSW; trans. G. W. Bromiley in LCC 24:84).

41. Zwingli, *Eine kurze Christliche Einleitung* (ZSW 2:639.20-35, 645.8-20).

In two writings of 1524, Zwingli combines the themes of grace and mediatorship in connection with this passage. In August, responding to Emser on the question of making intercessions to the saints, Zwingli once again uses the text to stress Christ as the only way to the Father.[42] As pointed out by Gottfried Locher, Zwingli's July 18 letter to the Toggenbergers not only closely associates idolatry with works righteousness but also connects Christ as the sole fountain of grace with Christ as the sole mediator in its treatment of Matt. 11:28.

> Was it not great blindness that God Almighty, who created us, has so often made known to us that he is our Father, and finally even gave his Son for us; and he himself stands there and calls us poor sinners, saying "Come to me, etc." And we went and turned to the creature, and thought God to be so rough and cruel that we dare not come to him, and though we called him Father, we did not do so in the spirit of Christ; that is, we did not regard him as Father and we did not expect all grace from him; for we did not recognize the secret of his grace, in that he gave his Son for us; and we did not ascribe salvation to the grace of God even though his only Son, Jesus Christ, true God and man, has redeemed us by the virtue of his suffering, which he bore for us. But we have inferred our righteousness, and therefore our salvation, from our own works. . . .[43]

In the words that follow concerning the neglect of the divine commandment of love in favor of the prescriptions of human beings and concerning "trusting in the priests' vestments, singing, murmuring, even gluttony, whoring and greed" rather than in the laws of God, we detect a radicalized Erasmianism for which Erasmus himself provided the material in his annotations of 1519 and 1522 on Matt. 11:29 and in the new preface to his Latin New Testament.

In the *De vera et falsa religione commentarius* (1525) he puts the accent on the sheer gift of Christ's coming and dying for us by reference to this text. If we could gain life by our merits, there would be no need for Christ. But Christ came into the world that we might have life and have it most abundantly, and he himself said, "Come unto me. . . ." The statement "All who labor and are burdened" indicates that he came to save sinners and that the consciousness of sin that weighs us all down should not prevent us from coming to him.[44] With his stress here upon the consciousness of sin as the principal burden,

---

42. Zwingli, *Adversus Hieronymum Emserum antibolon* (ZSW 3:272.33-34).
43. ZSW 8:207-8, quoted in Locher, *Zwinglis Thought*, pp. 160-61 nn. 44, 45, 46.
44. Zwingli, *De vera et falsa religione commentarius* (ZSW 3:652.17-32).

Zwingli is in line with the mainstream of Western interpretation, in contrast with Erasmus, who interprets sin as one burden among others.

The most extended exegesis of Matt. 11:28-30 occurs in Zwingli's *Commentary on Matthew,* published by Leo Jud in 1539.[45] His exegesis here is rather surprisingly set in the context of a discussion of humanity as created in the image of God and as sinner, which, in the polished Latin version of Jud, has a strong humanist color. Because God has stamped his image on all human beings, all of them, even the wicked, fear God (here he treats a theme that he had already touched upon in the *Von Klarheit und Gewissheit des Wortes Gottes*).[46] The human conscience is aware that God is just and will not allow sin to go unpunished. This mark, which has been stamped upon human beings by God, is called the image of God in the Scriptures, but by the heathen it is called *informatio,* a certain innate or preconceived notion of God. Here Zwingli quotes a passage from Cicero's *De natura deorum,* which identifies what Cicero calls a certain *anticipatio* or *informatio deorum* with what Epicurus calls πρόληψις.[47] The con-

---

45. Text reprinted in HZW 6/1. Additional exegetical material on Matthew is found in the so-called *Additamenta,* provided also in HZW 6/1, from a manuscript previously regarded as lost but recently discovered in the Zurich Central Library (ZV 370). Max Lienhard, "Aus der Arbeit an Zwinglis Exegetica zum Neuen Testament," *Zwingliana* 18 (1991): 310 n. 1. There is yet another manuscript in the Zurich Central Library, which contains Zwingli's exegesis on Matthew, Mark, and John (CAR II:181). These manuscripts have not been published. To be sure, excerpts of the latter manuscript have been published by Oskar Farner, but Farner's work has been criticized as full of errors. See O. Farner, *Aus Zwinglis Predigten zu den Evangelien Matthaus, Markus und Johannes* (Zürich: Zwingli, 1957); Lienhard, "Aus der Arbeit," p. 310 n. 4; Ulrich Gäbler, *Huldrych Zwingli* (Munich: Beck, 1983), p. 148. Max Lienhard reported in 1991 that the critical edition for the Corpus Reformatorum of the texts previously published by Schuler and Schulthess and of the manuscripts has made much progress but remains incomplete. Lienhard, "Aus der Arbeit," pp. 310-11. My analysis rests therefore upon the two renditions in HZW 6/1. How true the version of Jud may be to Zwingli's actual lectures and preaching on Matthew, which Walter Meyer dates as taking place in 1529-30 ("Die Entstehung von Huldrych Zwinglis neutestamentliche Kommentaren und Predigtnachschriften," *Zwingliana* [1976]:287), is not exactly clear. As pointed out by Schuler and Schulthess and by Meyer, the *Additamenta,* in contrast with the scholarly Latin commentary published by Jud, contains German as well as unpolished Latin and no Greek (HZW 6/1:395; Meyer, "Entstehung," pp. 297-99). The German has the character of the spoken word. In spite of the difference in style and language the two examples of Zwingli's Matthew exegesis agree in substance as far as Matt. 11:28-30 is concerned.

46. Zwingli, *Von Klarheit* (ZSW 1:347.3-24).

47. Zwingli, *Annotationes in Evangelium Matthaei* (HZW 6/1:281-82); Cicero, *De natura deorum* 1.16.43. On this term in Epicurus and on Cicero's correct understanding of it, see *M. Tulli Ciceronis de natura deorum, liber primus,* vol. I, ed. A. S. Pease (Cambridge: Harvard University Press, 1955), pp. 296-97n.

sequence of this innate preconception or presentiment of God, from which the fear of God arises in all, is that all fall into despair, for all are sinners and know themselves worthy of eternal punishment. The Ciceronian and Epicurean natural knowledge of God is therefore quickly qualified by the biblical doctrine of human sin.[48]

Over against the predicament of humanity Zwingli sets the work of God's redemption in Christ. God succors human weakness by sending his only Son, not as he did at the time of Abraham in his impassible nature, but rather as one whom God made common with us, sending him to live many years among us as a weak human being subject to all the necessities of our nature except for sin. The *Additamenta* is more graphic than the Latin commentary. It even ascribes *Presten* to the human Christ, the controversial Zwinglian word for the weakness or sickness of human nature that inclines to sin. "He wanted to experience in himself all our disease *(Presten)* with sin excluded, insult, shame, pain and toil." Both texts set forth the characteristically Zwinglian doctrine of the twin natures of God as revealed through his act of redemption in Christ: his mercy and his righteousness. Under the latter theme, Zwingli affirms the Anselmian doctrine of the atonement: "Righteousness indeed which does not allow the sin to go unpunished, nor spares his own Son, but hands him over to death for all of us gathering all the sins of the world in him and expiating them in him."[49]

The gracious invitation of Matt. 11:28 he interprets as being issued from the cross by the Savior to "despairing and anxious consciences." He stresses here that the gift Christ offers in this passage is consolation, peace, and tranquillity for disturbed consciences, a gift received by "a certain trust and undoubted faith." His interpretation here is more in line with that of Luther, Melanchthon, and Bucer than it is with that of Erasmus.[50]

---

48. The *Additamenta* mentions the fear of God in the conscience of humanity that gives rise to the acknowledgment of the just judgment of God against evil human beings, but it contains no reference to Cicero and Epicurus and the innate knowledge of God in all human beings. See HZW 6/1:421.

49. Zwingli, *Annotationes in Evangelium Matthaei* (HZW 6/1:282, 421). On Zwingli's use and modification of the Anselmian atonement tradition, see Locher, *Zwingli's Thought*, pp. 164-65, and Stephens, *Theology of Zwingli*, pp. 118-20.

50. Cf. Luther, *Predigt am Sonntag nach Maria Reinigung* (WA 17/1:43.13-17, 27-32, 44.21-26, 45.32-34); *Evangelium am Mattiastage*, Matthew 11 (WA 17:2.396.5-21). Melanchthon, *Annotationes in Evangelium Matthaei*, MSA 4:175.15-19); Bucer, *Enarrationes perpetuae, in sacra quatuor evangelia* (Strasbourg, 1530), fol. 113ᵛ.

In the spirit of Erasmus and of Chrysostom, though not with either's exact words in the exegesis of this passage, Zwingli states that "the yoke of Christ is nothing other than to be zealous for the will of God and blamelessness."[51] Like Chrysostom, he contrasts the heavy yoke of a love for riches and self-indulgent pleasure with the light yoke of those serving Christ, who, though harassed by persecutions from without, are inspired from within by a wondrous joy so that they cheerfully and serenely endure all things to the end, knowing that they please God.[52] Zwingli applies the double theme of mercy and righteousness to the yoke of Christ. It is of mercy that God came to the assistance of our infirmity through the toil and death of his beloved Son, bearing all things obediently for our sake and satisfying the divine righteousness. It is of righteousness that we bear our own cross, that we take his yoke upon us and learn from him to bear all things for the sake of his glory and righteousness and for the sake of the neighbor. By following in Jesus' path, we shall find rest for our souls, a theme that is similar to Erasmus's paraphrase. There is a tension here between rest for consciences as issuing from the gracious act of God in Christ's death and rest as resulting from one's imitation of Christ.[53]

III. Bullinger on Matthew 11:28-30

If Zwingli's interpretation of Matt. 11:28-30 is partly indebted to Erasmus, the exegesis of this text by his successor, Heinrich Bullinger, owes all the more to the great humanist, as Bullinger himself acknowledges. Matthew 11:28-30, as translated and interpreted by Erasmus in his annotation, sets the theme for almost the entire preface to Bullinger's *Commentary on Matthew*. Though he does not specifically refer to Erasmus's annotation on

---

52. Cf. above, p. 68 for Erasmus's understanding of Christ's yoke in his *Paraphrase;* and for Chrysostom see *Hom. in Matt.* 38 (PG 57:431). Chrysostom interprets the yoke of Christ as adopting Christ's path of humility, meekness, and gentleness.

52. Chrysostom, *Hom. in Matt.* 38 (PG 57:432-33).

53. The *Additamenta* elaborates on *Et invenietis requiem* somewhat more than the 1539 commentary: "So verr ir thund wie ich gethan habe alle Ding, ja auch den Tod um üwer willen erlitten: also lernend von mir auch grosse Ding thun um der Wahrheit willen, alle Ding, ze liden um des Rechten willen, und so in solcher Mass lebind, wie ich auch gethan han: so werdend ir Ruw finden in üweren Seelen und Conscientzen." HZW 6/1:422; cf. Zwingli, *Annotationes in Evangelium Matthaei,* HZW 6/1:283: "Si quemadmodum ego omnia propter vos feci, vos quoque ob gloriam dei et proximi facere et pati prompti fueritis, tranquillitatem et pacem conscientiis vestris invenietis"; and Erasmus, *Paraphrasis in Matt.,* 11:29-30 (LB 7:70).

this verse, toward the end of the preface he does acknowledge his overall debt both to Erasmus's *Annotations* and his *Paraphrase,* something, he says, he has "never hidden" in his work. In fact, Bullinger places Erasmus first among the exegetes — including Bibliander, Pellican, Bucer, Jerome, Chrysostom, and Augustine — who have assisted him with his interpretation and bestows upon him the highest praise.[54]

Like Erasmus in his annotation, Bullinger uses Matt. 11:28-30 as his springboard to contrast the simple doctrine of Christ (clearly comprehended in a limited number of articles and expressed in a few words) with the varied, complex, burdensome, and obscure human doctrines — traditions set forth with laborious loquacity — an argument that Bullinger himself makes, however, with much repetition and prolixity. He illustrates this argument with several examples of summary statements of doctrine and piety in the New Testament, drawn from the teachings of Jesus in the Gospels of Matthew and John, from the speeches of Peter in Acts, and from the letters of Paul. In his brief exegesis of Matt. 11:28-30 itself, he uses the familiar Erasmian expressions of Christ as the heavenly teacher and his teaching as the heavenly philosophy that will bring consolation, healing, correct instruction in the truth, and true tranquillity of soul. He stresses that Christ calls all those who are entangled, burdened, and afflicted not to heavy burdens, but to an easy and light yoke, a very simple kind of doctrine.[55]

Bullinger cites John 3 and Jesus' words to Nicodemus as an example of this simple and brief kind of doctrine: namely, that anyone aspiring to eternal life must be born anew from heaven. This new birth he interprets as meaning that human beings possess nothing of themselves to prepare for righteousness and salvation. They require the illumination and transformation of the Holy Spirit in order to perceive their corrupt natures and flee to the mercy of God, who gave his only begotten Son so that everyone who believes on him might not perish but have eternal life. "What," he says, "could be spoken about this matter more briefly, more clearly, or more fully?" In Matthew, he admits, the exposition of the law is somewhat more

---

54. Bullinger, *In Sacrosanctum Iesu Christi Domini nostri Euangelium secundum Matthaeum, Commentariorum libri XII per Heinrychium Bullingerum* (Zurich: Froschauer, 1554), sig. aaa 6ᵛ; the preface is dated 1542, the date of the first edition; hereafter cited as *Comm. in Matt.* See *Heinrich Bullinger Bibliographie,* ed. Joachim Staedke, in *Heinrich Bullinger Werke,* vol. 1, ed. Fritz Büsser (Zürich: Theologischer Verlag, 1972), Nr. 144.

55. Bullinger, *Comm. in Matt.* sig. aaa 2ʳ-aaa 2ᵛ. The theme of simplicity in doctrine is apart from his annotation a frequent theme in Erasmus's writings. See John B. Payne, *Erasmus: His Theology of the Sacraments* (Richmond: John Knox, 1970), pp. 14-15.

extended, but it is summarized in one sentence, in the Golden Rule: "Do unto others as you would have them do unto you." And in John: "This is my commandment, that you love one another, just as I have loved you." Similarly, in Paul: "You owe nothing to anyone except to love one another. For he who loves the other, fulfills the law." Bullinger asks: "Who says that this is prolix or involved or obscure?"[56]

After citing a number of similar passages, Bullinger stresses that in Christ the Father gave us all that is necessary concerning salvation, justification, and the Christian life: "short indeed," he says, "but clear, plain, full, and perfect in every part." What pertains to doing good, prayers, and fasting, the Lord Jesus has set forth in Matthew 6, where nothing burdensome or inexplicable is discovered such as you find in the disputations of the sophists. Bullinger is also eager to point out that the Lord commended very few sacraments, only baptism and "the symbol of his body and blood," the celebration of which he describes in Erasmian style as characterized by no sumptuousness or splendor and as attesting to the memory of his death and the mutual concord among Christ's people.[57]

What Peter preached in Acts before Cornelius was likewise set forth in few words and contained nothing about auricular confession, satisfaction, indulgences, masses, invocation of the saints, worship of idols, and pilgrimages. And in Acts 15 at the Apostolic Council, the Apostles permitted nothing from the law to be added to accomplish justification except for the fourfold prohibition, and that only *pro ratione temporis* and *pro moribus eius seculi hominum*. The thought again echoes Erasmus, who had connected this temporary injunction with the burdensome law concerning confession, which he held could likewise be regarded as only a temporary law that could be changed.[58] Paul taught the same point in Acts as well as in his Epistles, namely, that in Christ the faithful have all that is necessary for salvation and for the perfection of virtue, and that there is no need for other mediators besides Christ. Here of, course, he touches on a characteristic Zwinglian theme.[59]

He thinks that there are also human testimonies for his argument here, and he refers to two: Lactantius's *Divine Institutes* on true worship and Augustine's letter to Januarius. He points out, as Erasmus had not in

---

56. *Comm. in Matt.*, aaa 2^v-aaa 3^r.

57. *Comm. in Matt.*, aaa 3^r-aaa 3^v. For Erasmus's view see Payne, *Erasmus*, pp. 133-36.

58. *Comm. in Matt.*, aaa 4^r; cf. Erasmus, *Responsio ad Notationes Eduardi Lei in Erasmum Novas* (LB 9:255E).

59. *Comm. in Matt.*, aaa 4^r-aaa 4^v.

his annotation, that Augustine had held in that letter that the sacraments were very few in number and very easy of observation.[60] But more important than such human testimonies is the witness of Scripture, to which he abruptly returns. From the testimonies of the Gospels, Acts, and the Epistles, it is clear, thinks Bullinger, what are the limited chief matters of the gospel, which do not burden, but perfect the Church: faith in God, love of the neighbor, public justice, patience in suffering, saintliness of life, overflowing beneficence, pure and faithful prayer, and a devout use of the sacraments.[61]

Toward the end of his preface Bullinger provides another more extended and rather different summary of the essentials necessary for the perfection of the church. First place is given to the apostolic doctrine or the gospel or Holy Scripture. Next are the ministers of the church, who are interpreters and teachers of the Word and of morals. For this office schools are needed where languages and the liberal arts are taught and catechism and discipline are carried on.[62] Then there must be presbyters to execute the discipline and the magistrate and laws to regulate worship and morals in society.[63] Finally, at somewhat greater length he describes the last item, the sacraments, which he says do not justify, since justification is by faith, but rather exercise and arouse faith.[64] In the New Testament they contain nothing difficult or sumptuous or of worldly splendor. He had earlier interjected that, though there is foundation in the New Testament for schools, there is none for cantors and singing.[65] For other items that he lists here, such as magistrates for regulating worship and morals, he does

---

60. *Comm. in Matt.*, aaa 5ʳ; Lactantius, *Institutiones divinae* 5.13; 6.1.

61. *Comm. in Matt.*, aaa 4ᵛ, aaa 5ʳ.

62. Concerning Bullinger's work as *Schulherr* and as chronicler of the schools in Zürich and its environs, see Kurt Rüetschi, "Bullinger als Schulchronist," in *Heinrich Bullinger 1504-1575: Gesammelte Aufsätze zum 400. Todestag,* ed. Ulrich Gabler and Erland Herkenrath (Zürich: Theologischer Verlag, 1975), pp. 141-59.

63. But in contrast with Oecolampadius in Basel and Calvin in Geneva, Bullinger did not think that presbyters should carry out their discipline independently of the magistrate. See J. Wayne Baker, "In Defense of Magisterial Discipline: Bullinger's 'Tractatus de Excommunicatione' of 1568," in *Heinrich Bullinger 1504-1575*, pp. 141-59.

64. For Bullinger's mature view of the sacraments, see his *Confessio Helvetica Posterior* (1566), as translated in *Reformed Confessions of the 16th Century,* ed. Arthur C. Cochrane (Philadelphia: Westminster, 1966), pp. 277-88, and for an analysis see Ernst Koch, *Die Theologie der Confessio Helvetica Posterior* (Neukirchen-Vluyn: Neukirchener Verlag des Erziehungsvereins), pp. 267-326.

65. Bullinger, *Comment. in Matt.*, aaa 5ᵛ-aaa 6ʳ. On Bullinger's attitude toward singing in worship and its lack of basis in the New Testament, see Markus Jenny, "Reformierte Kirchenmusik? Zwingli, Bullinger und die Folgen," in *Das Reformierte Erbe [Gottfried W. Locher]*, *Zwingliana* 19/1 (1992): 193-95.

not attempt to derive a New Testament basis. Bullinger perhaps realized that the previous summaries he had set forth as apostolic and fundamental for the perfecting of the church were rather varied; thus he thought it best to provide one more that would capture all that he held most dear for the upbuilding of the church and that conformed to the practice in Zurich.

Like his preface, Bullinger's commentary on this passage owes much to Erasmus, especially to his *Paraphrase*, though there are also evidences of influence from Chrysostom and, not surprisingly, from his former colleague, Zwingli. Concerning verse 28: "Come to me, all who labor and are heavy laden, and I will refresh you," he states that there are two chief matters here: whom Jesus calls and for what he calls them. Bullinger follows Erasmus and Chrysostom in stressing the universality of the invitation to every kind of human being afflicted with whatever sort of condition. Like Zwingli, he stresses the "to me" and not to anyone else of the invitation. Also like Zwingli, he links the Christ who invites here in Matthew with the Christ whom Paul describes as reconciling us to the Father by his death upon the cross. With Chrysostom, Zwingli, and Luther, he emphasizes more than Erasmus did that Christ's gracious invitation applies only to those who are truly burdened, that is, those who are conscious of their sin.

According to Bullinger Christ comprehends the goal of his invitation in one word, which he translates after Erasmus as *refocillabo* or *recreabo* vos. He mentions Chrysostom's point that Christ did not say, " 'I shall save you,' but rather what is much greater, 'I shall establish you in all peace.' " He adds at the end of his discussion on this verse that they are teachers of falsehood who maintain that "rest and safety are to be sought in the intercessions of the saints, celebrations of masses, and other similar trifles of the papists."[66]

He commences his exposition of verses 29 and 30 ("Take my yoke upon you," etc.) with the point also made by Chrysostom that these words signify the reciprocal demand made upon those who are recipients of the gracious invitation for whom Christ sacrificed himself. For the explication of "learn from me because I am meek and lowly in heart," Bullinger lifts verbatim a long passage from Erasmus's *Paraphrase* that he freely acknowledges.[67] The passage contrasts the yoke of the world, which is at first sight alluring (but in reality, grievous and bitter), with the easy and mild yoke of Christ, that is, with the learning of his teachings and the imitation of

---

66. Bullinger, *Comm. in Matt.*, 115ᵛ-16ʳ; Chrysostom, *Hom. in Matt.* (PG 57:431).
67. Erasmus, *Paraphrasis in Matt.* (LB 7:69).

his life, which bring peace and tranquillity to the soul. With Erasmus he uses the term *tranquillitas* more than once, but without any Stoic connotations. He states with Erasmus and Chrysostom that the Lord demands of his heirs that they serve him with humility, kindness, and blamelessness; so to serve him is not difficult since Christ demands nothing of us that is inhuman and since to live according to the gospel "not only leads to the attaining of eternal life in the age to come, but in the present renders our life sweet." After naming several sins that corrupt our lives and involve us in irreparable calamities, he quotes from Erasmus's *Annotation* the famous passage: "Whatever is according to nature is easily borne, and nothing more agrees with human nature than the philosophy of Christ, which is concerned with almost nothing other than the restoration to innocence and sincerity of a fallen nature." He also quotes from Erasmus's annotation: "Nothing is so bitter that love does not make pleasant and sweeten."[68]

Bullinger concludes that Matt. 11:28-30 not only gives the summary of the gospel in a very few words but answers decisively to two kinds of human beings: first, those who dare to oppress the church "with the most vexing, stupid, bitter, and absurd laws," against whom he says Erasmus wrote "with great learning" in his *Annotation* on this passage; and, second, those who, having heard that we are justified by faith in Christ, give up all zeal for virtue and lapse into Epicureanism.[69] For him the text opposes two contrasting evils: oppressive ecclesiastical legalism and irresponsible Christian living.

IV. Conclusion

In spite of the fact that both Zwingli and Bullinger reveal a greater sense of the consciousness of sin as the "burden" of which Jesus speaks in this text and of consolation as the gift offered than does Erasmus, both adopt Erasmus's view of the heavy yoke as evocative of the myriad medieval laws and traditions that oppress human consciences and of the mild yoke of Christ as the life of love and virtue to which Christ has obligated all his disciples. Bullinger agrees more with Erasmus than does Zwingli that this mild yoke of Christ is truly easy since it agrees with human nature and since love renders all things sweet. It is therefore remarkable that Bullinger, the second-generation Reformer, shows an even greater dependence on

---

68. Bullinger, *Comm. in Matt.*, 116ʳ; Erasmus, *Annotatio in Matt.* 11:29 (LB 6:63).
69. Bullinger, *Comm. in Matt.*, 116ᵛ.

Erasmus than does Zwingli. On the basis of the narrow scope of this essay sweeping conclusions are not justified, but one might suggest the need for a closer assessment of the continuing influence of Erasmus on the mature Bullinger not only for the humanistic form but also for the theological content of his exegesis, especially in the light of the judgments by Staedke and Hausammann that the young Bullinger was little shaped by Erasmus's theological exegesis.[70]

70. Joachim Staedke, *Die Theologie des jungen Bullingers* (Zürich: Zwingli, 1962), p. 36: "Er [Bullinger] hat den grossen Humanisten stets geehrt und geliebt, aber in der theologischen Sachfrage hat er nicht nachgegeben"; Susi Hausammann, *Römerbriefauslegung zwischen Humanismus und Reformation* (Zürich: Zwingli, 1970), p. 144: "Wenn wir nun auf die am Anfang dieses Vergleiches gestellte Frage zurückkommen, ob sich in methodischer oder sachlicher Hinsicht in wesentlichen Punkten von Erasmus führen und bestimmen ließ, so müssen wir sie aufs Ganze gesehen verneien."

PART II

EXEGESIS AND INTERPRETATION
IN THE EARLY REFORMATION

· 4 ·

Omnis homo mendax:
Luther on Psalm 116

KENNETH HAGEN[1]

TRAINED IN THE CLASSICAL medieval tradition as a *doctor in Biblia,*
Martin Luther also stood at the watershed between the medieval and
emerging modern approaches to the Christian Scriptures, where he partic-
ipated in the increasing attention to the "literal" sense of Scripture characteristic of his age. Nevertheless, as a biblical interpreter Luther remained
firmly rooted in the medieval approach to the text, the so-called "spiritual
reading" *(lectio divina).* As professor of Scripture at the University of Wittenberg from 1513 to his death in 1546, Luther spent his entire career
wrestling with the whole Bible, but returning again and again to those texts
that he loved best: the Psalms, the letters of Paul, and the Gospel of John.[2]

1. This tribute, dedicated to an old friend and colleague in the field of exegetica, is an
attempt to say something (truthful) about Luther's ALL-or-nothing theology. New research
and writing took place at Hill Monastic and Manuscript Library, Collegeville, Minnesota,
where I was plunged into the marvelous world of medieval manuscripts. The good folks in
Collegeville, at HMML, Alcuin Library, the Watrys at St. John's University Special Collections,
the Benedictines (Cyril, David, Gregory, Kilian, Peregrin), and, above all, our sponsors at the
Institute for Ecumenical and Cultural Research deserve thanks for their splendid cooperation.
     2. Among the many Luther biographies that one might cite, the most comprehensive and
up-to-date is probably Martin Brecht's three-volume *Martin Luther,* trans. James L. Schaaf
(Minneapolis: Fortress Press, 1985-93). Still helpful, however, is Julius Köstlin's classic study,
revised by Gustav Kawerau, *Martin Luther, sein Leben und seine Schriften,* 5th rev. ed. (Berlin,
1903). For an in-depth study of Luther's development after 1521, see Heinrich Bornkamm,
Luther in Mid-Career 1521-1530, trans. Theodore E. Bachmann, ed. Karin Bornkamm (Philadelphia: Fortress Press, 1969). The best English-language introduction to Luther studies remains

Led by Gerhard Ebeling's pioneering studies of Luther's hermeneutics, the tendency in Luther studies generally has been to distance Luther from his medieval context. Indeed, Ebeling's claim that Luther departed from medieval allegory (1519) has dominated the modern picture of Luther as a biblical interpreter.[3] My own research, however, has called into question any connection between Luther and Enlightenment approaches to the biblical text. On the contrary, we now know that Luther was deeply rooted in the traditional monastic approach to Scripture as the *sacra pagina*. Like his patristic and medieval predecessors, for example, Luther saw Christ as the heart of the Psalter.[4]

I. *Omnis homo mendax* — "Everyone is a liar":[5] Psalm 116:11 in the Exegetical Tradition

Study of patristic and medieval commentators helps one to appreciate better what Luther was doing when he came to comment on Ps. 116:11.

Mark U. Edwards, Jr., "Martin Luther," in *Reformation Europe: A Guide to Research*, ed. Steven Ozment (St. Louis: Center for Reformation Research, 1982), pp. 59-83. Essential for advanced research is Kurt Aland's aptly titled *Hilfsbuch zum Lutherstudium*, 3d rev. ed. (Witten: Luther-Verlag, 1970). Current Luther studies may be tracked through the annual *Lutherjahrbuch*, which contains over a thousand bibliographic entries. In addition, the *Luther Digest* annually condenses about thirty-five Luther studies (about half originally written in German).

3. See his *Evangelische Evangelienauslegung. Eine Untersuchung zu Luthers Hermeneutik* (Munich: Chr. Kaiser, 1942; 3d ed. [erweitert um ein Nachwort], Tübingen: J. C. B. Mohr [Paul Siebeck], 1991); idem, "Die Anfänge von Luthers Hermeneutik," *Zeitschrift für Theologie und Kirche* 48 (1951): 172-230; idem, "Luther und die Bibel," in idem, *Lutherstudien* (Tübingen: J. C. B. Mohr [Paul Siebeck], 1971), 1:286-301. The standard introduction to Luther as a biblical interpreter is Jaroslav Pelikan's *Luther the Expositor: Introduction to the Reformer's Exegetical Writings* (St. Louis: Concordia, 1959). Among the many specialized studies of Luther's biblical interpretation, one might also mention Heinrich Bornkamm, *Luther and the Old Testament*, trans. Eric W. and Ruth C. Gritsch, ed. Victor I. Gruhn (Philadelphia: Fortress, 1969); Scott H. Hendrix, *Ecclesia in Via: Ecclesiological Developments in the Medieval Psalms Exegesis and the Dictata Super Psalterium of Martin Luther* (Leiden: E. J. Brill, 1974); James Samuel Preus, *From Shadow to Promise: Old Testament Interpretation from Augustine to the Young Luther* (Cambridge, Mass.: Harvard, 1968); and David C. Steinmetz, *Luther and Staupitz: An Essay in the Intellectual Origins of the Protestant Reformation* (Durham, N.C.: Duke University Press, 1980).

4. See Kenneth Hagen, "What did the term *Commentarius* mean to sixteenth-century theologians?" in *Théorie et pratique de l'exégèse biblique*, ed. Irena Backus and Frances Higman (Geneva: Droz, 1990); idem, *Luther's Approach to Scripture as Seen in His "Commentaries" on Galatians, 1519-1538* (Tübingen: J. C. B. Mohr [Paul Siebeck], 1993).

5. In deference to contemporary sensitivities about gender and language, wherever

The numbering of the Psalms varies, especially Psalm 116, which in some Vulgates is entitled "a continuation of the previous Psalm." In the Latin Vulgate and for the tradition in which Luther worked, it is known as Psalm 115, without any formal verse numbering.

Psalm 116 was a favorite psalm of Luther's because it expresses a central theological truth about the Truth.[6] Moreover, because of the way Paul repeated the Psalm in Rom. 3:4, "Every person is a liar," and filled out its meaning with the phrase "God alone is true," Luther frequently pondered the theological truths about *homo* and God contained in just three Latin words: *omnis homo mendax*. Given the repetition of the Psalter in Paul, the echo of Scripture within and throughout Scripture, and Luther's own hermeneutical assumption that Scripture is its own interpreter, he believed that Psalm 116 is made clear in Romans 3. Together with Luther's paradoxical theology and the unity of Scripture, one could say, therefore, that Rom. 3:4 is actually on the *sacra pagina* of Ps. 116:11.[7]

Did Luther change his mind about any theological or technical aspects of the Psalm verse? No. His rendering of the German text is the same in 1524, 1528, 1531, and 1545.[8] The variations in the Latin Psalters on this verse for over a thousand years are inconsequential. His comments on the text are consistently the same from 1513 onward; what he calls the various senses in the *Dictata,* for example, *literaliter*[9] and *moraliter,*[10] turn up with exactly the same emphases and content later.

Examination of patristic and medieval authors places Luther's exegesis of Psalm 115 (116) in its proper historical context: Luther knew and used the work of such authors as Jerome, Augustine, Arnobius the Younger,

---

possible I will render *homo* as "everyone." Where I need to contrast "man" with God, I use man since in the Psalter and in Luther man/homo *(mendax)* is such a derogatory term and contrasts with the *verax* (true) so well. Also, where the contrast comes in between "man" as the former self under the wrath of God and the "god" we become in faith, "man" as the individual person needs to be used in order to convey that I am no longer such a man, but a child of the Most High.

6. Cf. Luther, *Römerbriefvorlesung,* on Rom. 3:4 (WA 56:212.12): "confessio veritatis Dei."

7. At HMML, *Omnis homo mendax* was always my starting point as a way of focusing on the Psalter as a whole; the number of known manuscripts seems to be endless. Time and eternity seem to blend together in the Psalter. The monks copied the Psalters and sang them. Prayer and work blended together in their devotion to God. Working with manuscripts, especially Psalms manuscripts, brings one closer to the church at work in the Middle Ages.

8. The marginal note to *lügener* is the same for 1531 and 1545 (WADB 10/1:489): "Das ist, es ist auff keinen menschen zu bawen, Er kan doch zu letzt nicht helffen, und mus feilen."

9. Luther, *Dictata super Psalterium* (1513-16), on Ps. 116:11 (WA 4:268.29).

10. Luther, *Dictata* on Ps. 116:11 (WA 4:269.3).

Gerhoh of Reichersberg, Peter Lombard, Rusch's Strassburg Bible, and Faber Stapulensis. Furthermore, much of what was written in medieval works on the Psalter, including Luther's comments, is a continuation of what Jerome and Augustine said. Since Augustine used the Gallican Psalter of Jerome, we will consider Jerome first.[11]

Jerome's first examination of our text occurs in his *Brief Commentary on Psalms.*[12] We now switch to the Vulgate numbering (Psalm 115). To paraphrase Jerome: Pope Symmachus and the Septuagint render the Psalm, "I said in the excess of my mind: Everyone is a liar" *(Ego dixi in excessu mentis meae: omnis homo mendax).* The liar *(mendax)* in Hebrew is KIVZHB, which Symmachus renders falsehood *(mendacium)*[13] and elsewhere failure *(defectio).* Isn't this saying that not only are we *mendax* but also *mendacium* and *defectio,* and that our life is quickly over since the next verse reads, "I will receive the cup of salvation"?[14] Yes, since he goes on to say that the God who made me out of nothing *(de nihilo)* and sustains me deserves to be offered in return what he, my creator, has given me. Jerome lines up the *mendax* with the *ex nihilo* of creation, which is behind us as then our life moves on — to become as gods, as Jerome proposes in his later *Treatise on the Book of Psalms.*[15]

What is important for the medieval tradition on the Psalter in Jerome's Preface to the Hebrew Psalter *(Praefatio in libro Psalmorum iuxta Hebraeos)* is his assertion that this Book of Hymns is one book and is to be read in the church of Christ as one book, whereas with Jews (he says) it consists of single words with disastrous consequences.[16]

---

11. In addition to the Roman and Gallican Psalters associated with Jerome, his third Psalter (late fourth century) was translated from the original, hence known as "Hebrew Psalter." *Psalterium iuxta hebraeos Hieronymi,* ed. J. M. Harden (London: SPCK, 1922) p. v. For a discussion of the scholarship on *Hebraica Veritas* and Luther on Jerome, see Christoph Markschies, "Hieronymus und die 'Hebraica Veritas' — Ein Beitrag zur Archäologie des protestantischen Schriftverständnis?" *Die Septuaginta zwischen Judentum und Christentum,* ed. Martin Hengel and Anna Maria Schwemer (Tübingen: J. C. B. Mohr [Paul Siebeck], 1994), esp. pp. 176-81.

12. Text of Jerome's *Commentarioli in psalmos* is found in CCSL 72:177-245.

13. *Mendacium* is derived from *mendax: mendacium* is the lie or falsehood produced by *mendax,* the liar. KIVZHB is Jerome's attempt to transliterate KŌZĒB: see CCSL 72:234.

14. The verses that follow "our" Psalm 115 verse (Vulg.) are sometimes in different order: sometimes the *Calicem* verse, sometimes the *retribuam* verse follows. Sometimes the numbering of the whole Psalm can vary in manuscripts; I have seen 115 as 114.

15. See CCSL 72:234.1-12 on Ps. 115 for this paragraph.

16. Donatien De Bruyne, *Préfaces de la Bible Latine,* ed. Auguste Godenne (Namur: Auguste Godenne, 1920), pp. 46-47. For bibliography, see Samuel Berger, *Les préfaces jointes aux livres de la Bible dans les manuscrits de la Vulgate* (Paris: Imprimerie Nationale, 1804).

Jerome's *Treatise on the Book of Psalms*[17] begins with a question, "What is earth and the ruin of destruction? I said in my excess: Everyone is a liar."[18] That truth *(veritas)* is not in our substance, but shadow *(umbra)* is, is a prominent theme throughout this section. *Mendacium* is in corporeal substance, not in the soul. Considering all the diverse errors in the human condition, I will not find truth in this world but rather falsehood, shadow, and phantom.[19] The long and short of it is that all we have on this earth is puff and poof.

Then (which can also serve as a summary of Jerome's exposition) he asks if David, as shadow, is telling the truth when he says, "Everyone is a liar"; or is that Psalm verse itself a lie, that is, not true? Whatever way Jerome looks at this question, the end result is contradiction. How do we know that a phantom is not lying when it says, "Everyone is a liar"? Let's turn to Aristotle. After turning syllogisms around some more à la Aristotle, Jerome remembers Col. 2:4 and the deception of philosophy and so declares: David is telling the truth because he is no longer a shadow. As long as we are "men," we lie; when we become gods, we cease to be liars (see Ps. 81:6). When you are made god, you cease to be man and do not lie.[20]

St. Augustine treats *Omnis homo mendax* throughout his immense *Enarrationes in Psalmos*[21] as well as at Psalm 115 itself.[22] Thus, Ps. 36:19, "They will not be confounded in the evil time." What does this mean? In the day of tribulation, when hope was lacking, they did not hope in God but in "man" *(in homine)*. Cursed is he who puts his hope *in homine*, hence

17. Text of Jerome's *Tractatus in Librum Psalmorum* is found in CCSL 78:3-352.

18. Psalm 115: "Quid autem est terra et cinis? *Ego autem dixi in excessu meo: omnis homo mendax.*" The Hebrew Psalter reads, "Ego dixi in excessu meo: Omnis homo mendacium"; Jerome, *Tractatus* on Ps. 115 (CCSL 78:240.15-18).

19. "Mendacium hic dixit, quasi umbram, quasi imaginem. . . ." Now we can say, Omnis homo mendacium: hoc est, omnis homo umbra. We have the Hebrew and the Septuagint; I follow the church [on the matter of *mendax*]: *Ego dixi in excessu meo: omnis homo mendax;* see Jerome, *Tractatus* on Ps. 115 (CCSL 78:240.27–241.35).

20. Jerome, *Tractatus* on Ps. 115 (CCSL 78:241.36–242.63).

21. Augustine's *Enarrationes in Psalmos* comprise vols. 38, 39, and 40 in the CCSL.

22. Augustine uses v. 11 ("Everyone is a liar") for the First Sunday after Easter; see William L. Holladay, *The Psalms through Three Thousand Years* (Minneapolis: Fortress Press, 1993), p. 167. I would say that if one were to come to the Psalter in Romans (3:4) from within the Greek and Latin traditions, from the early centuries (CE) on, one could hardly say, as Holladay does (p. 122), that Paul "alludes" to Ps. 116:11; he is citing it: ἄνθρωπος ψεύστης. See the excellent chapter on the utilization of the Psalms in the first Christian centuries by Pierre Salmon, *Les "Tituli Psalmorum" des Manuscrits Latins* (Paris: Les Éditions du Cerf, 1959), 10-15; for Rom. 3:4, p. 11.

in falsehood and deception.[23] If you put your hope in your God, you will not be confounded because he in whom you hope cannot deceive.[24]

Similar is the comment on Ps. 52:1, "The fool said: There is no God. You are 'man,' the liar; he is God and God is true. Separate your heart and life from those who are abominable in their lies."[25] Or again, Ps. 91:5 and John 8:44: He who speaks *mendacium* speaks of himself. Every sin is a *mendacium* against the law and against truth. Therefore it says in Rom. 3:4, "God alone is true *(verax)*; everyone else, however, is a liar." Be careful not to lie since you are a man. In order to be *verax*, drink truth; taste of God, and you will be true.[26]

These texts provide some background for Augustine's reading of Ps. 115:11, *Ego autem dixi in ecstasi mea: omnis homo mendax*. The *ecstasi* is the voice of a martyr. What pertains to everyone is *mendax*; it is the grace of God that effects *verax*, lest one fall just as Peter fell and speak not what one believes but what one negates.[27] Concerning humankind, nothing should be taken for granted. Well, therefore, are they who see in *pavore suo* (their holy awe, awesome fear) that everyone is a liar. By the gifts of God we do not fall. Thus it is most truly said: *Omnis homo mendax*, but God is true who says, "You are gods, sons of the Most High" (Ps. 81:6).[28] If all are liars, the only way they can cease being liars is to become gods and sons of the Most High.[29]

---

23. "Confunderis, quia fefellit te spes, fefellit spes posita in mendacio; omnis enim homo mendax"; Augustine, *Enarratio* on Ps. 36 (CCSL 38:352.9.7-8).

24. Augustine, *Enarratio* on Ps. 36 (CCSL 38:352.9.1-10).

25. Augustine, *Enarratio* on Ps. 52 (CCSL 39:640.4.22-28).

26. Augustine, *Enarratio* on Ps. 91 (CCSL 39:1283.6.10-18).

27. "Hoc itaque considerans deuotissimus populus fidelium testium, quomodo infirmitatem humanam Dei misericordia non relinquat, in cuius infirmitatis pauore dictum est: *omnis homo mendax*, quomodo consoletur humiles, et impleat spiritu fiduciae trepidantes, ut pene mortuo corde reuiuiscant, nec in semetipsis fidentes sint, sed in eo qui suscitat mortuos, et linguas infantium facit disertas, qui ait: *Cum autem tradent uos, nolite cogitare quomodo aut quid loquamini: dabitur enim uobis in illa hora quid loquamini; non enim uos estis qui loquimini, sed spiritus patris uestri qui loquitur in uobis:* haec ergo omnia considerans ille qui dixerat: *ego dixi in pauore meo: omnis homo mendax*, et uidens gratia domini se factum ueracem, *quid retribuam*, inquit, *domino, pro omnibus quae retribuit mihi?*" Augustine, *Enarratio* on Ps. 115 (CCSL 40:1654.4.1–1655.4.15).

28. "Proinde uerissime dictum est: *omnis homo mendax;* sed Deus uerax, qui ait: *Ego dixi: Dii estis, et filii Altissimi omnes; uos autem sicut homines moriemini, et sicut unus ex principibus cadetis.*" Augustine, *Enarratio* on Ps. 115 (CCSL 40:1654.3.19-22).

29. "Si enim omnis homo mendax, in tantum non erunt mendaces, in quantum non erunt homines; quoniam dii erunt, et filii Altissimi." Augustine, *Enarratio* on Ps. 115 (CCSL 40:1654.3.25-27).

Much of medieval commenting on this Psalm verse focuses on the various renderings and meanings of liar. Next to the amount of time spent on the word for liar, medieval commenting pays attention to the word for the condition of the speaker; that is, the one who says *Omnis homo mendax* does so in a state of ecstasy *(ecstasi)*; or. . . ? Augustine says that *ecstasi* is *pavor* because the Psalm verse is the voice of a martyr facing impending suffering and death. The verse is said by someone "whose fearful awe of infirmity God's mercy does not abandon." Thus it reads *ego dixi in pauore meo: omnis homo mendax,* which seems quite different from the usual *Ego autem dixi in ecstasi mea;* in fact, isn't it the opposite? On the face of it, *pavor* is fear, anxiety, panting for fear. Pursuing the matter further, *pavor* can mean religious fear, that is, awe; and, earlier in classical Latin, *pavor* can mean joyful trembling. *Pavor* is on the fearful side of amazement; whereas ἔκστασις *(ekstasis)* in Greek, the origin for *ecstasis* in Latin, is on the wondrous side of amazement; *ekstasis* basically means both astonishment and terror. For example, *ekstasis* was the amazed reaction at Jesus' healing the twelve-year-old girl (Mark 5:42); it is used in Gen. 27:33 (LXX) — Isaac trembled.

Again Augustine opens an aspect of the text that had not been clear to me before. Augustine's reading has the opening phrase saying: If indeed everyone is a liar, dead because of sin and, as men and women all, everyone is never anything as *homo* but a liar without hope of anything except eternal death, then we are in a deadly serious situation as *humana.* Such a situation calls forth from the depth of *humana infirmitas*[30] a loud exclamation that expresses both a sickness unto death (the fearful tone) and an almost joyful yelp of amazement that this *mendax* by the grace of God is no longer a *homo*. This is precisely Luther's point about the liar-man. In Christ I am no longer a man. In Augustine's citation of Ps. 81:6, I am a god among the children of the Most High.

The *mendax* verse comes in *Enarrationes*, finally, in connection with Ps. 115:13: "I will receive the cup of salvation and call upon the name of the Lord." O *homo*, in your sin you are *mendax*; by the gift of God, *verax*; thereby, no longer *homo*. Who gives to you the cup of salvation? It is none other than the one who said: "You will be able to drink the cup I will drink."[31]

Arnobius, who died after 451, is hard to locate in time, place, and position; he did write his *Comments on the Psalms* sometime in the fifth

---

30. Augustine, *Enarratio* on Ps. 115 (CCSL 40:1654.3.4).
31. Augustine, *Enarratio* on Ps. 115 (CCSL 40:1655.5.1-8).

century.[32] On Ps. 115:11, he writes, "Albeit (or however much) he says that man is to be subject to the interchange of his benefits, everyone is a liar."[33] To paraphrase Arnobius: Before he says what he is to say, he [the Psalmist] expresses his faith; "I have believed," he said. What did you believe? Birth and death; and because I have believed, therefore I am humbled. Because I have believed, this I have said: If the Lord again humbled himself and for me took on the form of a servant, how wretched I make (myself). How do I repay to the Lord for all he has repaid me? As much as he says that man is to be subject to the interchange of his benefits, every man is a liar. What is the worth of man's repayment to the Lord, except perhaps by compensating passion with passion.

Some question exists about Arnobius the Younger and his position on the spectrum between Augustine and some kind of semi-Pelagianism. Arnobius's comments on Psalm 115 indicate a fair amount of exchange that is to take place between the wretch and his redeemer, an emphasis not seen so far on this verse.

The *Anonymous Gloss on Psalms* (Seventh Century) contains what seems to be a standard biblical text and comment;[34] it turns out, however, to have a different combination of comments. The Gloss speaks in the voice of the church: I am greatly humiliated, as if the church says, because I both believe and preach thus, I will endure tribulation. EGO DIXI IN EXCESSU MENTIS MEAE: OMNIS HOMO MENDAX. Others read, "in extasi mentis," but *ekstasis* in Greek is what in Latin means *alienatio mentis*. The alienation of the mind means to transcend the physical senses as did Peter and Paul (*mentis excessus*, Acts 10:10-11), and Paul in 2 Cor. 12:2-3 (*raptum . . . ad tertium caelum*). The church seeks to despise (to be alienated from in the sense of *alienatio sensus corporis*) the five exterior senses and to contemplate God with interior gifts. *Omnis homo mendax* means that whatever is of us is *mendacium*, and whatever is of God is of *veracio* (truth). When we cleave to God we are then *veraces*, or, as 1 Cor. 6:17 puts it: "Whoever adheres to God is one spirit."[35] Simply put, to be true is to be in Truth, who is God.

---

32. Arnobius, *Commentarii in Psalmos* (CCSL 25:1-258).

33. "Quantumuis dicat se homo seruire ad uicissitudinem beneficiorum eius, omnis homo mendax est"; Arnobius, *Commentarii* on Ps. 115 (CCSL 25:183).

34. *Anonymi Glosa Psalmorum ex Traditione Seniorum*, Teil II: Psalmen 101–150, ed. Helmut Boese, Vetus Latina, Die Reste der altlateinischen Bibel, vol. 25 (Freiburg: Verlag Herder Freiburg, 1994).

35. *Anonymi Glosa* on Ps. 115, p. 82.1-19.

Gerhoh of Reichersberg's (1093-1169) *Commentarius in Psalmos*[36] should probably be placed before Peter Lombard's work on the Psalter.[37] Gerhoh's commentary offers us the following: Psalmus CXV, *De confessione Martyrum.* [Vers. 11] *Ego dixi in excessu mentis meae: Omnis homo mendax.* The excess of mind is taken in two ways, either *pavore* or *inspiratione.* The *pavor* means human infirmity and death; in confessing Christ, we remember his death. *Omnis homo mendax* is said in fear; since I am a man, I am not able to be fulfilled in the truth. In Hebrew *Omnis homo mendacium,* that is, in this life everyone is shadow, an imitation *(imago),* not true and not the truth. Everyone in sin is a liar; true by a gift of God.[38]

Peter Lombard's *Commentary on the Davidic Psalms* (115)[39] indicates that the *proprium* (property) of man is that he is *mendax,* which is not easily known except in *excessu mentis* — a comment I have not seen before. The *exstasi mea* is mental rapture unto the eternal. The essence of human stuff is liar *(Omnis homo mendax est ex se).* The ecstasy is both *pavore* and *inspiratione.* Nothing of good is our *proprium.* Thank goodness for the power of God who makes us true.[40]

Rusch's Strassburg Bible (1480-81)[41] provides a significant exemplar of the glossed text of Psalm 115. Here, the interlinear gloss has *ex se,* meaning in and of ourselves we are all liars, whereas in and of God we are true *(ex Deo verax).* A more extended interlinear gloss of *omnis* is given: "I have suffered many tribulations on account of the word of God which I will hold firmly, whence the truth shines more brightly."[42]

The *Glossa ordinaria* records the comment of Augustine and provides other standard readings found in medieval expositions.[43] At "What shall I render to the Lord?" Augustine is cited: "The power and grace of God shall conquer weakness and he shall not be consumed."[44] The *Glossa ordinaria* provided Luther with a wealth of resources, as did Faber Stapulensis.

---

36. Paris: Beauchesne, 1986. Also, HMML project no. 2770. Gerhoh of Reichersberg's *Opera* (vol. 1): *Commentarius in Psalmos 1–20* contains the typical dedicatory to the Trinity.

37. See *Dictionnaire de Spiritualité,* s.v. "Psaumes."

38. "*Omnis homo* peccando est *mendax,* dono Dei verax," Gerhoh of Reichersberg, *Commentarius in Psalmos* on Ps. 115 (PL 194:717-20).

39. Peter Lombard, *Commentarius in Psalmos Davidicos* (PL 191:55-1296).

40. Peter Lombard, *Commentarius* on Ps. 115 (PL 191:1029-30).

41. *Biblia Latina cum Glossa Ordinaria,* Facsimile Reprint of the Editio Princeps Adolph Rusch of Strassburg 1480/81 (Brepols: Turnhout, 1992). At CXV (2:604, hand-numbered), *Ego dixi in excessu meo: omnis homo mendax.*

42. *Biblia Latina cum Glossa Ordinaria,* 2:604.

43. *Biblia Latina cum Glossa Ordinaria,* 2:604.

44. *Biblia Latina cum Glossa Ordinaria,* 2:604.

The origin of Faber Stapulensis' *Qvincvplex Psalterium*[45] (Five Psalters) stemmed from Faber's philological interest in establishing a clear and intelligible Psalter, needed in and of itself, and needed in the French Church since the Breviary of the day contained psalms that were obscure and unintelligible. The *Vetus* (Old), a very literal translation of the LXX, is pre-Vulgate, established from Old Latin versions, beginning probably around A.D. 150; it existed in a plurality of versions. The *Vetus* was used, for example, by Augustine, who said the *Vetus Itala* was the best version,[46] and by Cyprian.[47] The *Psalterium Romanum* is still used today in the Holy Office at St. Peter's in Rome. The Gallican version was widely used, contra the *Hebraica*. The *Textus conciliatus* is a "new text, established by a comparison of the readings supplied by all the witnesses," by all the evidence or readings supplied from before Jerome.[48] So the *Conciliatum* is a reconciliation of many Latin versions with the Hebrew text of Jerome, available in Latin translation at St. Germain since the ninth century, that Faber prepared for his *Quincvplex Psalterium*. In his *Ad Reverendissimum* (preface to his patron), Faber says that he added or changed a few things *ad gallicum*, by which effort this Psalter *(Conciliatum)* accords more accurately and beautifully with the Hebrew original.[49]

A literal translation of the *Argumentum*[50] would read, "A Psalm, which Christ always resolved to be heard by God, concerning his ecstasy in which he renews [i.e., refreshes his mind about] the *errata* of every person, and concerning his great humiliation and cup of passion that he took up for our redeeming, which pure host of his body he offered for the whole people of Israel in the middle of the people at Jerusalem to God the Father and the highest divine Trinity."

The Hebrew version has *mendacium;* the others have *mendax.* The *Conciliatum,* Gallican, and Roman Psalters have *excessu;* the *Vetus* has *ex-*

45. *Qvincvplex Psalterium. Gallicum. Romanus. Hebraicum. Vetus. Conciliatum* (Paris: Henricus Stephan, 1509).

46. Augustine, *De doctrina Christiana,* 2.15.22 (CCSL 32:47-48).

47. It is probable that Tertullian used the Old Latin, but "certain" that Cyprian did; see Ernst Würthwein, *The Text of the Old Testament: An Introduction to the Biblia Hebraica,* trans. Erroll F. Rhodes, 2d ed. (Grand Rapids: Eerdmans, 1995), p. 91.

48. E. Amann, "Lefèvre d'Etaples," *DTC,* 9/1:136-37.

49. Faber, *Quincvplex Psalterium,* p. 3 of preface.

50. "ARGVMENTVM. Psalmus, quod semper Christus certus esset exaudiri a deo, de eius extasi in quo omnium hominem errata novit, de nimia humiliatione eius & passionis calice quem pro nobis redimendis suscepit, quod hanc puram sui corporis hostiam vidente vniuerso Israelis populo in medio populi Ierusalem deo patri & superdiuinae trinitati obtulerit." See *Quincvplex Psalterius.*

stasi, and the Hebrew, *stupore.*[51] Faber's Epilogue to the Psalms says that Psalm 115 speaks of the ecstasy of Christ and his chalice. Does *exstasi* mean joy here? Yes, *exstasis* by 1500 can easily be ecstasy in the American sense as well as fear, fright, and agony.[52]

II. Luther's Interpretation of Psalm 116:11

Luther's exegesis of Psalm 116 (115) should be treated chronologically. From the beginning, Luther knew the two sides of *excessus* ("In my excess I said" conveys both fear and joy), the contrast between the liars and the gods (and how one moves from being a liar to being true), and the tradition of the martyrs.[53] In his *Annotations* (1513-) on Faber's *Quincvplex Psalterium,* Psalmus CXV, Luther identifies "my excess" as being in an elevated state, illumined to see how one is nothing; and Luther identifies how we through faith and the martyrs are gods, no longer liars but the truthful ones.[54]

In his *First Lectures on Psalms* (1513-15), the *Dictata super Psalterium,* reflecting what the literature calls the double-literal sense of Scripture, Luther says the Psalm is spoken in the person of the Psalmist and in the person of the Lord Christ *(in persona sua et domini Christi).*[55] The note in the Gloss adds the reference to 2 Cor. 4[:13] that shows that, although

51. "Psalmus CXV

VET.: Ego autem dixi in exstasi mea: omnis homo mendax.

CONCIL.: Ego dixi in excessu meo: omnis homo mendax.

GALL.: HALELVIA.CXV. Ego dixi in excessu meo: omnis homo mendax.

ROM.: HALELVIA.CXV. Ego dixi in excessu mentis meo: omnis homo mendax.

HEB.: Ego dixi in stupore meo: omnis homo mendacium."

52. *peur, effroi, angoisse.* See Albert Blaise, *Dictionnaire Latin-Français des Auteurs Chrétiens,* ed. Henri Chirat. Gerhoh says *excessu* can be *pavore* or *inspiratione* (PL 194:718). In a variety of Latin dictionaries consulted, the meaning of *exstasis* ranges from great rejoicing, through terror and amazement, to stupor.

53. Luther, *Annotationes Quincuplici Fabri Stapulensis Psalterio manu adscriptae* (1513ff.) (WA 4:466-526).

54. Luther, *Annotationes,* on Ps. 116:10-18 (WA 4:519.26-30): *"Ego dixi in excessu meo. Iste est excessus, quando homo elevatur super se secundum Ieremiam et illuminatus videt quam sit nihil, et quasi de supra respicit in seipsum in suas nebulas et tenebras, tanquam in monte positus infra respiciens, supra ps. 30 in fine. Omnes homo mendax: nos autem sumus dii, ideo veraces, sicut martyres."*

55. In the *Dictata,* it is "Glossa: Psalmus CXV [CXVI v 10-19.]" (WA 4:265.15-17).

Augustine says that the Psalm is the voice of martyrs, the early church of Corinth understood that the Psalm referred to Christ.[56] After liar, Luther comments that everyone is such because God alone is true along with those born of God;[57] only those who believe are the truthful ones because faith is truth.[58]

In the Gloss on *in excessu meo,* Luther identifies *excessu* as ecstasy. He speaks of it, first, as the meaning of faith *(sensus fidei),* which exceeds the literal sense, the domain of unbelievers (remember: only those of the Spirit understand the words of the Spirit). Second is the rapture of the mind unto a clear knowledge of faith, which is ecstasy proper. Third is the mind's awesome fear in persecution. Fourth is *excessus,* in which reference is made to Luke 9[:31], speaking of the *Die Verklärung Jesu* and of Jesus' *Ausgang* to Jerusalem (in Luther's German Bible) that martyrs make.

The Scholia contain an amazing section on "I have been humbled exceedingly" *(Ego humiliatus sum NIMIS).* "When I speak on account of the word of faith, they persecute me. Why are you not then silent so as to avoid affliction? Because I believe; because of what I believe, I speak. Faith compels me to speak against every lie in the world." Luther was and is famous for his rhetoric. Even though more often than not he attacks dialectic, Luther engages in fierce analysis of what I call elsewhere "the logic of faith," because to do otherwise would aid the opposition. The opposition will rise up; faith is a battle with the evil ones. Luther must speak out. A silent faith is a theological oxymoron. "The zeal and fervor of faith and truth does this to me and makes this happen, just as the apostles opposed Jews, as doctors opposed heretics *(Apostoli contra Iudeos, doctores contra hereticos),* as up to today every Christian opposes false Christians, so Psalm 39 'I have not concealed your truth from a great council.' "[59]

"If I speak and if my zeal consumes and compels me, what happens?" This is Luther's lead into the Psalm verse: "I said in my excess: Everyone is a liar." Liar means without faith; the status as true comes about through the confession of faith. As long as I was a man I did not see that everyone is a liar. Liars by definition are blind. Now that I believe and am *in excessu* and made spiritual through faith, I see that they who are not *in excessu* are the liars. Some very strong synonyms for "liars" come roaring off the page:

---

56. Luther, *Dictata* on Ps. 116:11 (WA 4:265.22): *"in excessu meo raptu mentis seu pavore passionis."*
57. Luther, *Dictata* on Ps. 116:11-12 (WA 4:266.1-2).
58. Luther, *Dictata* on Ps. 116:11 (WA 4:266.25-28).
59. Luther, *Dictata* on Ps. 116:10 (WA 4:267.6-13).

stulti, vani, mali; then the all-powerful "etc." The *veraces* are righteous and wise.[60]

Luther employs the two-kingdom distinction to say that many of the most truthful people on earth *(coram hominibus)* are liars *coram deo* since they do not say, "I have believed." And it also goes the other way: Those who are the truthful ones through the truth of faith are persecuted and humiliated in this world *(coram hominibus).*[61]

In commenting on the remaining verses, Luther continues to emphasize the strong contrast between truth and lie.[62] If there is the realm of God, the "sons of men" are not there. Luther's strongest Latin, albeit avoiding scatological overtones, goes in opposite directions; one way to the "gifts of God," the reverse to the idiot, the fool, *homo* the liar, the libeler.[63] On verse 16, "O Lord, for I am your servant," three exclamations *(Trinitas)* are expressed in this confession: *pater, o domine fili,* and *o domine spiritus sancte.*[64] The Psalter was a major source of trinitarian theology in the early and medieval church.[65] Either God is three in one or he is not; three in one from day one to all eternity is the claim of faith.

In his *Vorwort zu Bugenhagens In Librum Psalmorum Interpretatio* (1524)[66] Luther offers the broadly applicable hermeneutical comment that the bishop of the Church of Wittenberg offers the Psalter in the spirit of Christ who is the key *(clavis)* to David.[67]

---

60. Luther, *Dictata* on Ps. 116:11 (WA 4:267.16-22). The same analysis of *Ego dixi* is given again in a paragraph entitled "Literaliter" (WA 4:268.29–269.2). Under "Moraliter" Luther writes: "Quod intelligitur de mendacio, non quo coram hominibus est mendax, sed coram deo" (WA 4:269.10-12).

61. Luther, *Dictata* on Ps. 116:11 (WA 4:269.12-15).

62. Luther, *Dictata* on Ps. 116:14-15 (WA 4:270.16–271.8).

63. Luther enters into the medieval discussion using the various senses: in addition also *spiritualiter* [*sacramentaliter*], set in brackets but the Latin requires it, and *explariter*. The last refers to the martyrs: Luther, *Dictata* on Ps. 116:15 (WA 4:271.12-15).

64. Luther, *Dictata* on Ps. 116:16 (WA 4:271.18-21).

65. An ancient discipline was "prosopologique": to discern the Psalms that apply to God the Father, to Christ, and by extension to the church. Working with *prosōpon* and persona comes Augustine's dictum: "una persona (una quaedam persona) et nos transfiguravit in se (Christus)"; see *Dictionnaire de Spiritualité*, 12:2567.

66. Luther, "Vorwort zu Bugenhagens In Librum Psalmorum Interpretatio" (WA 15:8).

67. Luther, "Vorwort zu Bugenhagens" (WA 15:8.9-13). Luther holds David, Isaiah, Paul, and John on the same level (WA 15:8.30). See Luther's preface to Roth's German translation of his *Operationes in Psalmos* ("Vorrede zu 'Das erste Theil der lateinischen Auslegung des Psalters D. M. Luther [*Operationes in Psalmos*] verdeutscht durch Stephan Roth," 1527. Prefatory Title: "Allen meinen lieben herrn und brudern ynn Christo Ihesu" (WA 23:389.1-31).

In his *Summaries* (the *Summarien über die Psalmen und Ursachen des Dolmetschens,* 1531-33), Luther writes on the psalms and the matter of translation. Psalm 116 is a *Danckpsalm,* as are 114 and 115. He is so thankful that God has heard his prayer. This Psalm engages in extremely deep *anfechtung.* He confesses his faith and the Truth of God *(die warheit Gottes).*[68] All men are false (line 22). The pious must suffer in the world. Again, Luther starkly contrasts between truth and those who would be holy but are false.[69]

The only sermon on Psalm 116:10 I could find is from Luther's *Predigt am Montag nach Trinitatis* (1534).[70] The thrust of the sermon is that to utter "I said in my excess" is the work of the devil; whereas the purpose of the Psalm verse is to utter praise to God. The devil seeks to bring us only to *anfechtung,* not to truth.[71] The devil would have us see how sour Christ is. In such a situation comes the judgment that the whole world is full of liars *(totus mundus sit lügner).* And there is nothing worse than being a liar. The world is not able to hear that God gives grace. These people are not in faith; they bear lies, are dumb, and live in false faith. Luther will preach the word of the cross *(verbum crucis).*

III. Luther's Originality in the Light of His Predecessors' Exegesis

By Luther's time, Scripture as its own interpreter had taken on various configurations of meaning — including various combinations of the sufficiency, clarity, efficacy, and authority of Scripture alone. Among others earlier, whether in the Gospel of John, Augustine, or Aquinas, the same principle of Scripture-interprets-Scripture obtained, but the configuration of issues congealed differently. For Luther the authority of Scripture alone focused on "what drives Christ" *(was Christum treibt),* seeing that the unity of Scripture is grounded in the unity of the Trinity.

For a proper interpretation of Luther, it is important to note that Rom. 3:4 used and explained Ps. 116:11 (RSV) and that Ps. 116:11 actually says what Paul said. Therefore, it is necessary to have some understanding

---

68. Luther, *Summarien* on Ps. 116 (WA 38:56.21).

69. Luther, *Summarien* on Ps. 116 (WA 38:56.20-24).

70. Luther, "Predigt am Montag nach Trinitatis" (edited in WA 37:419.15–424.30). The title also includes "1. Juni 1534. Lunae post Trinitatis." It is found in the WA section entitled "Predigten des Jahres 1534." Under *Credidi, ideo locutus sum* is a chatty style with a mixture of German and Latin.

71. Luther, "Predigt am Montag nach Trinitatis," on Ps. 116:11 (WA 37:423.18).

of Scripture as a whole in order to understand any of its parts. That everyone is a *mendax* (liar) is not an assertion about human nature, nor is it a pessimistic anthropology; rather, it is an optimistic assertion about God in the form of doxology. Paul (Rom. 3:4) makes it clear that there is more to the Psalm than first meets the eye. The "more" is its opposite, namely, God alone is true *(verax)*. Opposites express theological truth in Paul and, therefore, in Luther. When the text says liar, Luther sees Truth.

The Psalter repeats over and over the basic truth that everyone is a liar and God alone is true. Sometimes, as in the case of Psalm 116, only "Everyone is a liar" appears. No more need be said. Both parts of the contrast are the message even though only one appears at this point on the page. As Luther saw it, the message of Scripture is consistent and not everything has to be said over and over. Praise of the truthfulness of God is the central message of the Psalter, which is why Psalm 116 was such a favorite of Luther's throughout his life.

Luther resonated with Psalm 116 not only because the *mendax/verax* contrast expressed a truth about the Truth, but also because the contrast was so reflective of the biblical, and later patristic and monastic, view of the two ways (wickedness/righteousness), presented in the form of contrasts. While Luther shares with his predecessors all the exegetical particulars about the verse, perhaps unique to Luther on this Psalm is that he uses the form of contrast to drive the wedge deep between the opposites of lie and truth. The contrast is the basis for his paradoxical way of practicing theology as the discipline of the sacred page. I do not see the overall theological constructs of Augustine, Jerome, Lyra, and Faber built on constructs of sharp antithesis; if Luther is paradoxical or antithetical (supply your favorite term) through and through, the others mentioned here are not so in their whole theological program. For Luther the sacred page is full of paradox; focus on the lie casts the truth into the clearest of light. In the truth of Christ, my lie ceases to be.

In sum, Luther worked on the Psalter with Moses and David in one breath and then with Jerome and Faber in another in order to sing the praises of *verax* by way of contrast with *mendax*.

IV. Concluding Reflections

(1) The lie and the liar are theological terms with reference to the *coram Deo* in Luther's famous distinction between "before God" and "before human beings." In the exegetical tradition there is some speculation about

whether the Psalm verse *(Omnis homo mendax)* is itself a lie. For Luther, the answer is "No." Clearly not. Liar, just as sinner, is apparent only to the person of faith. It is the law that brings the lie to light. In Paul's mind, as Augustine and Luther knew well, there is a cosmic battle between the forces of Satan and the call of the Holy Spirit. No neutrality. For Luther, keeping silent about the lies amounts to complicity with Satan.

(2) The Psalm verse in Latin uses the generic word for humankind *(homo)*, neither the Latin word for a male person *(vir)* nor the Latin word for a female person *(mulier)*. The Hebrew text says that each person *(hā'ādām)*[72] is a liar; that is, we humans are untrustworthy and ultimately unable to create or redeem Israel to be a Light to the Nations.

In other words, this Psalm verse does not engage in constructive or philosophical anthropology. Luther constantly emphasizes that what Aristotle does in logic is fine for philosophy, but Aristotle is not a theologian since the test of one's standing as a theologian is whether or not one gives honor and glory to the Almighty Creator and Redeemer. Since Aristotle does not give God the glory, he is no theologian. Luther recognizes the other disciplines of philosophy, medicine, and law; and he emphasizes that, while all are needed, medicine is not theology. Paul is clearly the theologian since he gives God the glory in his doxological Rom. 3:4, "God alone is true, everyone is a liar."

Homo, therefore, is a theological term equivalent to pagan or sinner. When a person actually says something that is true, the operative linguistic category is adjective. Given Luther's attachment to the Gospel of John, however, Truth is God, a person — "I am the Way, the Truth, and the Life" — and not an adjective. Those who live in the Truth are truthful in their speaking. The reverse does not work, for that would be Aristotle; that is, by speaking truthful words, a good habit to maintain to be sure, one does not become truth. As good as good habits may be, habits do not save; only God saves.

(3) *Omnis* is a key word in this verse that is often overlooked — *omnis* excludes no one. Outside of Christ, all fall short of the glory of God. Luther

---

72. In Gen. 1:27, the "*hā-'ādām* is not one single creature who is both male and female but rather two creatures, one male and one female." Since a shift occurs from singular to plural pronouns, humankind "from the beginning" consisted of two creatures, both equal and free (to lie). Genesis 1:26 RSV: "Let us make humankind *('ādām)* in our image, after our likeness; and let them have dominion. . . ." For a discussion of Genesis, see Phyllis Trible, *God and the Rhetoric of Sexuality* (Philadelphia: Fortress Press, 1978), esp. p. 18. For an analysis of *'adham* in the Psalter and Ps. 116:11, see G. Johannes Botterweck and Helmer Ringgren (eds.), *Theological Dictionary of the Old Testament* (Grand Rapids: Eerdmans, 1974), 1:82.

spoke in outrage against all, be they Turk or Schwärmer, against all false brethren who besmirch the holy name of Jesus. Luther did not and could not, given his Augustinian presuppositions, entertain the possibility of salvation outside of Christ; and as *doctor ecclesiae* he felt compelled to take a stand on the side of Truth. To be silent, in his worldview, meant complicity with the other side, which is every bit as evil as the lie. Without Truth, serious sickness is close at hand. This coincides with Luther's ALL-or-nothing theology.

(4) Everyone is interested in truth, in knowing, being, and seeing it. The question is, How does one arrive at Truth? This is a theological, spiritual, and epistemological question. The theological move that Luther most often makes is to move to the goal by way of the opposite. Contemporary parlance usually dubs it a dialectical or dualistic thought-structure. For Luther it would be better to term this move paradoxical; theology "through *(per)* antitheses" is antithetical theology. Luther uses the strongest German and Latin idioms possible to make a point. At one point, in 1531, Luther even says that *Lugner ist zu schwach.*[73]

(5) Truth involves both reality and the perception of reality. When 1 Kings (RSV) 10:6 says, "And the Queen of Sheba said to Solomon, 'The report was true which I heard in my own land of your affairs and of your wisdom. . . ,' " was the report true, that is, historically accurate (by anybody's understanding of history)? No, only half true, or only the half of it, as v. 7 goes on to say. What is the "it"? Truth and reality are often thought of as a philosophical problem. The central claim of the Bible (Rom. 3:4: God alone is true) is that God's words are true; only God can be trusted never to tell a lie. The words of those in the status of "men" are always lies, not completely and consistently trustworthy, because "men" are not God, only God is God, and "men" are against God. If Luther were asked, "Are you a man?" his answer, consonant with Paul, would be, "I was a man; now, in Christ, I am no longer a man of my former ways." Luther is talking about our relationship with God *(coram Deo, von oben)*. When that relationship is out of kilter, then everything else is also off. To make such a statement offends us all because it is making a religious judgment that goes to the core of our being. If we are at heart liars, we are awful, putrid, sick unto death — some of the milder of Luther's idioms. But is that not exactly what

---

73. That is, that " 'Liar' is too weak a term"; see Luther, "Revisions-Protokoll zum Psalter 1531" (WADB 3:145.30). Although the note says that Luther stayed with *Lügner,* it occurs already (without umlaut) in, e.g., *Psalterium . . . in linguam germanicum translata* (1456; Codex Vindobonensis Palatinus 2671; HMML, no. 15, 924), fol. 246^r.

is ailing our world — deep, serious, sickness, sickness of the soul? People cease to be liars when they are claimed by God.

(6) The effort to situate Luther as the first modern historical-critical exegete does not work; neither does it work to make Luther the first Lutheran.[74] After working on Luther and hermeneutics, sometimes together, more often separately, for over twenty-five years, I have come to see Luther as part of his medieval, Roman Catholic, Augustinian-Benedictine, Bernardian traditions. Like any good late-medieval theologian, Luther had to pick and choose his way through the issues he confronted. Given his near genius talents of language, in which I would include logic as well as Greek, his conclusions are there for all who wish to ground their contemporary theology in Scripture.

---

74. See my *Luther's Approach to Scripture*, n. 4, above.

• 5 •

Balthasar Hubmaier's "Catholic" Exegesis: Matthew 16:18-19 and the Power of the Keys

CARL M. LETH

BALTHASAR HUBMAIER was the most prominent theologian of the first generation of Anabaptists. Wrestling early with the challenge of the radical reformulation of the Reformation, Hubmaier was a creative contributor to the theological dialogue of the period.[1] Though his views were not uniformly adopted or applauded by later leaders of the Radical reforms, he did contribute significantly to the theological formation of Anabaptism, particularly Swiss and South German Anabaptism. Hubmaier's theology reflects his own synthesis of catholic, nominalist, humanist, and Reformation influences.[2]

Hubmaier's background made him an unlikely prospect and an unusually capable theological resource for the Anabaptist movement. A con-

1. For a discussion of Hubmaier's place in the early Anabaptist movement, see John H. Yoder, "Balthasar Hubmaier and the Beginnings of Swiss Anabaptism," *MQR* 33 (1959): 5-17; "The Believer's Church Conferences in Historical Perspective," *MQR* 65 (1991): 5-19. The character of Hubmaier's movement to reform and the importance of these influences on his theological understanding are variously interpreted. See Hans J. Hillerbrand, "The Origin of Sixteenth-Century Anabaptism: Another Look," *ARG* 53 (1962): 152-80; Kenneth R. Davis, "Erasmus as a Progenitor of Anabaptist Theology and Piety," *MQR* 47 (1973): 163-78; Jarold Knox Zeman, "Anabaptism: A Replay of Medieval Themes or a Prelude to the Modern Age?" *MQR* 50 (1976): 259-71; and James William McClendon, Jr., "Balthasar Hubmaier, Catholic Anabaptist," *MQR* 65 (1991): 20-33.

2. For discussion of Hubmaier's contribution to Anabaptist thought, see Rollin Stely Armour, *Anabaptist Baptism* (Scottdale: Herald Press, 1966); and Christof Windhorst, *Täuferisches Taufverständnis* (Leiden: E. J. Brill, 1976).

temporary of the early Reformation leaders, Hubmaier first appears in the historical record in 1507 when he enters the University of Freiburg at Breisgau.[3] It was here that he established a special relationship with his teacher, John Eck, and became a student of nominalism.[4] In these early years Hubmaier also developed ties to humanism that would continue and have lasting impact on his thought.[5] When Eck went to Ingolstadt in 1510, Hubmaier was named his successor at Freiburg. In 1512 Hubmaier followed Eck to the University of Ingolstadt. He was awarded his doctorate in theology there in the same year and was named Professor of Theology. Though apparently successful in his academic career, Hubmaier left the University in 1516 to become cathedral preacher in Regensburg. A popular (though controversial) figure, Hubmaier remained solidly Catholic during this period. In 1520 he left Regensburg for reasons that remain unclear to go to Waldshut, a small city on the Rhine in the area of Schaffhausen, to serve as the city's senior pastor. In the years 1520-23, Hubmaier became increasingly active in humanist and reform circles. By 1523 he had been identified with the Reformers and supported Zwingli's reforms in Zurich. In 1524 Hubmaier instituted a Zwinglian reform of the church in Waldshut, but soon developed different, and conflicting, theological views from Zwingli and his supporters. On Easter Sunday, 1525, Hubmaier instituted baptismal reform in Waldshut, baptizing some 60 adult believers, including himself. Following political reversals at Waldshut and open conflict with Zwingli at Zurich, Hubmaier made his way to Nikolsburg, in Moravia. Here he again

3. For a more complete study of Hubmaier's life and career see Torsten Bergsten, *Balthasar Hubmaier — Seine Stellung zu Reformation und Täufertum 1521-1528* (Kassel: J. G. Oncken, 1961). A shorter version is available in English edited by W. R. Estep, Jr., *Balthasar Hubmaier, Anabaptist Theologian and Martyr* (Valley Forge: Judson Press, 1978). David Steinmetz offers a brief introduction in *Reformers in the Wings*, "Balthasar Hubmaier — Free Will and Covenant" (Grand Rapids: Baker Book House, 1981), pp. 197-208. The standard edition of his works is Balthasar Hubmaier, *Schriften*, ed. Gunnar Westin and Torsten Bergsten (Gütersloh: Mohn, 1962), hereafter cited as *Schriften*. Most of these writings are now available in English, in *Balthasar Hubmaier — Theologian of Anabaptism* (trans. H. Wayne Pipkin and John Howard Yoder (Scottdale: Herald Press, 1989), hereafter cited as Pipkin-Yoder. Wherever possible, published English translations will be cited, followed by references to original-language editions.

4. Bergsten, *Hubmaier*, p. 74. For a study of the lasting impact of nominalism on Hubmaier's thought see David C. Steinmetz, "Scholasticism and Radical Reform: Nominalist Motifs in the Theology of Balthasar Hubmaier," *MQR* 45 (1971): 123-44; and Walter L. Moore, Jr., "Catholic Teacher and Anabaptist Pupil: The Relationship between John Eck and Balthasar Hubmaier," *ARG* 72 (1981): 68-97.

5. Bergsten, *Hubmaier*, pp. 70, 97, 99, 101; cf. p. 103: "Der Humanismus hatte ihn in seiner Entwicklung zum Reformator und Täufer wesentlich beeinflußt, und der Eindruck . . . war bleibender Art."

attempted the reform of the church and produced most of his theological writings. He was ultimately burned as a heretic in 1528 at Vienna.

I. Hubmaier's Principles of Biblical Interpretation

Before we consider Hubmaier's interpretation of a specific text, we want to understand the principles of his approach to biblical interpretation. His treatise "On Baptism" (considered his best and most complete theological work) serves well as an introduction to Hubmaier as an interpreter of Scripture.

Hubmaier begins with an emphatic conviction of the self-evident meaning of Scripture. He finds Scripture to be "clear, bright and plain."[6] In consequence, it is the task of the interpreter to seek the "simple" meaning of the text. "We want to present the text in the simplest way of all."[7] Scripture will reveal its meaning to the simple, unsophisticated believer who earnestly seeks understanding. The obscuring glosses and interpretations of the scholastics are the enemies of such a straightforward understanding of Scripture. "Away with quarreling about words! We want to take the correct sense and meaning for ourselves, so that we do not confuse anybody with strange glosses."[8]

The interpreter's most helpful ally is Scripture itself. Interpreting Scripture in the light of other Scripture is Hubmaier's favored method. "One only needs to bring Scripture to Scripture."[9] Hubmaier's treatise on baptism certainly reflects this principle. Some sections are little more than a sequence of passages from Scripture cited in whole or in part or simply alluded to without critical or interpretive comment. Another favored method of scriptural interpretation is contextual study. Hubmaier encourages careful attention to the sequence of the text and the context of meaning. "I admonish the reader to watch for the sequence of word, meaning and understanding."[10] His own interpretive work reflects a concerted

6. Balthasar Hubmaier, *On Baptism* (Pipkin-Yoder, p. 98, cf. also pp. 111, 120, 148-49; *Schriften*, p. 110, cf. also pp. 131, 139).

7. Hubmaier, *On Baptism* (Pipkin-Yoder, p. 112, also pp. 98, 113; *Schriften*, p. 132, also pp. 120, 133).

8. Hubmaier, *On Baptism* (Pipkin-Yoder, p. 109, also pp. 98, 110, 111, 113). Cf. *Schriften*, p. 130 (also pp. 120, 130, 131, 133): "Vah mit dem worter zanck, wir wöllen den rechten sentenz vnd synn für vns nemmen, das wir nyemants mit frembden glosen verwirren."

9. Hubmaier, *On Baptism* (Pipkin-Yoder, p. 119, also pp. 104-5, 109, 143). Cf. *Schriften*, p. 138 (also pp. 126, 130, 158): "Man muoß nun schrifft schrifft bringen."

10. Hubmaier, *On Baptism* (Pipkin-Yoder, p. 106, also pp. 114, 135; *Schriften*, pp. 127-28, also pp. 133-34, 150-51).

effort to interpret Scripture contextually. Hubmaier employs a simple, commonsense methodology that is consistent with his concern for the immediate accessibility of Scripture to the unsophisticated disciple.[11]

Though infrequently, Hubmaier does make use of traditional interpretive tools. In "On Baptism" he uses the distinction between the letter and the spirit of the text to distinguish the preaching of John the Baptist from the gospel of Christ.[12] Noah's ark is recognized as a "figure" of baptism.[13] He defends the "spiritual" interpretation of the literal text in defense of adult baptism. The children Jesus invites to himself and commends (Matt. 19:14) should be understood as "children in evil." He justifies such a spiritual interpretation as following Christ's example.[14] He also maintains that he is not opposed to the use of language skills in interpretation, only to their misuse in obscuring the text or withholding it from common readers.[15] It should be noted, however, that Hubmaier himself makes little use of such linguistic tools.

Hubmaier also refers to other sources of authority in interpreting Scripture, but only occasionally. "On Baptism" includes passing reference to Erasmus (as a translator), canon law, Augustine, and Thomas Aquinas.[16] These points of reference are the exception rather than the rule, and Hubmaier dialogues very little with specific traditional interpretations. Indeed, traditional authorities are broadly dismissed or ignored. Hubmaier shows little interest in justifying himself or his views in light of traditional authorities.[17] Hubmaier's point of active reference in this treatise is Ulrich Zwingli in their debate on baptism. In his effort to confute Zwingli he repeatedly calls him to "strive for the clear, plain, and pure Word of God from which alone your faith comes."[18]

---

11. Hubmaier, *On Baptism* (Pipkin-Yoder, pp. 142-43; *Schriften*, p. 157).

12. Hubmaier, *On Baptism* (Pipkin-Yoder, pp. 102-3; *Schriften*, p. 124).

13. Hubmaier, *On Baptism* (Pipkin-Yoder, p. 134; *Schriften*, p. 150).

14. Hubmaier, *On Baptism* (Pipkin-Yoder, p. 141; *Schriften*, p. 156).

15. Hubmaier, *On Baptism* (Pipkin-Yoder, pp. 99, 142-43). Cf. *Schriften*, p. 120 (also p. 157): "Ob wol ich auch zuo erclärung der tunckelen schrifften die zungen oder sprachen nit verwürff, aber zuo den sonnenscheinlichen worten bedarff man weder zungen noch lungen."

16. Hubmaier, *On Baptism* (Pipkin-Yoder, pp. 132, 138-39, 141; *Schriften*, pp. 148, 153-54, 156).

17. Clearly Hubmaier is quite capable of citing traditional and historic authorities, as he does at some length in *The Opinion of Ancient and New Teachers* (Pipkin-Yoder, pp. 245-74; *Schriften*, pp. 224-55). This is, however, the exception rather than the rule.

18. Hubmaier, *On Baptism* (Pipkin-Yoder, pp. 148-49). Cf. *Schriften*, p. 163: ". . . trachtend nach dem hellen, claren, lautern wort Gottes, darauß alleyn eüch der glaub kompt."

Hubmaier is willing, however, to bring extrabiblical resources to the task of interpretation. Understanding the simple, clear message of Scripture depends upon the illumination of the Spirit. Presumably, in an interpretive tautology, the illumination of the Spirit is verified by the simple, clear understanding of the biblical message.[19] This "simple" understanding of Scripture, of course, consistently reflects Hubmaier's theological perspectives. Such a self-evident theological understanding is not necessarily limited by Scripture. "Even if there were no Scripture on earth which states that faith should precede water baptism, its meaning and understanding would still be enough."[20] The simplicity and straightforward manner of Hubmaier's biblical interpretation is conditioned, at times, by his own theological presuppositions.[21]

The study of Hubmaier as a biblical interpreter is limited by his relatively small corpus of works, especially the absence of biblical commentary. Although his writings are filled with biblical citations, most of them are only lists devoid of discussion or interpretive comment.[22] It is, however, possible to trace his interpretation of some significant biblical texts and ideas through his use and application of them. That is what we will attempt to do with Hubmaier's interpretation of Matt. 16:18-19.[23] This is the narrative in which Christ grants the power of the keys. It is also a text whose interpretation became an intersection for theological systems. Hubmaier's treatment of it offers a window into his theological system as he interacts with the divergent views of his contemporaries.

II. Matthew 16 among Hubmaier's Contemporaries

We want to begin by placing Matt. 16:18-19 in the interpretive context in which Hubmaier would have worked. In late medieval Catholicism this text

---

19. Hubmaier, *On Baptism* (Pipkin-Yoder, p. 103; *Schriften*, p. 124).

20. Hubmaier, *On Baptism* (Pipkin-Yoder, p. 135; *Schriften*, p. 150).

21. The difficulty in this "simple" interpretive method is noted in Windhorst, *Taufverständnis*, pp. 45-46.

22. His most extended biblical treatments are focused on baptism. For a study of his interpretive treatment of the baptism of John the Baptist see David Steinmetz, "The Baptism of John and the Baptism of Jesus in Huldrych Zwingli, Balthasar Hubmaier and Late Medieval Theology," in *Continuity and Discontinuity in Church History*, ed. F. F. Church and T. George (Leiden: E. J. Brill, 1979), pp. 169-81.

23. It is impossible to study the interpretation of Matt. 16:18-19 apart from Matt. 18:18, which, in fact, is more frequently cited. However, since it is in Matt. 16:18-19 that the power of the keys is explicitly promised, we will base our study on that text.

was traditionally associated with the priestly practice of sacramental absolution. Since the interpretation of the keys has a long and diverse history, we will focus on two central figures in the tradition, Peter Lombard and Thomas Aquinas.[24] The *Sentences* of Peter Lombard identified the power of the keys as given to Peter and his successors.[25] Exercised by the priest, the keys signify a twofold spiritual power: both the knowledge to discern and the power to judge *(discernendi scientia et potentia iudicandi)* who is worthy of the kingdom and who is not. The power of the keys did not actually extend to remitting guilt but to declaring absolution for those already forgiven by God, who alone had the power to remit the guilt of sin.[26] The keys included the remedial power of excommunication and discipline but did not convey independent authority to the priest.[27] Thomas Aquinas refined that view to convey actual instrumental power to the priest in the sacrament of absolution.[28] The power of jurisdiction, however, which is the basis of authority in the granting of indulgences, was given specifically to Peter and his successors (that is, to the pope).[29]

It was this last application of the power of the keys that prompted Martin Luther's emphatic response. In June of 1519, Luther delivered a sermon at Leipzig on Matt. 16:13-19 in conjunction with his disputation with John Eck. Luther's rejection of indulgences was reinforced by his explanation of the proper understanding of the power of the keys. Following Augustine, Luther maintained that the keys were given to Peter as a personification of the church rather than to him personally. The priest is a servant of the keys, using them in the service of the church, and the proper use of the keys is for the reassurance of the conscience.[30]

24. For a helpful overview of the treatment of this passage in the patristic period see Joseph Ludwig, *Die Primatworte Mt. 16,18.19 in der altkirchlichen Exegese* (Münster: Aschendorffsche Verlag, 1952).

25. Peter Lombard, *Libri IV Sententiarum* 4.18.1 (Rome: Collegii S. Bonaventurae, 1916), p. 857.

26. Lombard, *4 Sent.* 18.2, 18.4 (pp. 858-61). Cf. 4.18.4 (p. 861): "Deum solum per se peccata dimittere."

27. Lombard, *4 Sent.* 18.7, 18.8 (pp. 862-66). Lombard discusses the use of the keys in dist. 19, pp. 866-72.

28. Thomas moves to this position later in his life. His earlier agreement with Lombard is reflected in the supplement to the third part of the *Summa Theologiae*, q. 18, esp. art. 1 (London: Burns, Oates & Washbourne, 1928), 18:249-53. His later writing expressly grants instrumental power to the priest in absolution; see *Summa Theologiae*, IIIa.84.3, 86.6, and 89.1 (Blackfriars edition [1966], 60:13, 17, 97, 137).

29. Aquinas, *Summa Theologiae*, IIIa (supplement), 20.1, 25.1, 26.2.

30. Luther, *Sermon on Matthew 16:13-19* (LW 51:59; WA 2:248-49).

This, you see, is what the keys do for you; what the priests were ordained for. When you feel your heart wavering or doubting whether you are in grace in God's eyes, then it is high time that you go to the priest and ask for the absolution of your sin, and thus seek the power and the comfort of the keys.[31]

By reassuring the penitent of God's grace and encouraging faith, the keys offer peace and confidence. In this way the power of the keys is rightly administered.[32]

Luther offers a more thorough and systematic treatment in his treatise *On the Keys*.[33] Here Luther identifies the two keys Christ grants to the church. One is the binding key, which is the "divine threat with which God threatens the hardened sinner with hell."[34] The redemptive intent of the use of the first key is to move the sinner to cling to the second key. This key is God's "divine promise with which he promises to the humble sinner the kingdom of heaven."[35] He rejects the interpretation that preaching or teaching should be understood as a key.[36] Preaching and teaching draw their scriptural authority from Luke 11:52 and Matt. 23:13, not Matt. 16:18-19, and are addressed to all. Peter's keys, in contrast, "only apply to some, namely to sinners."[37] Their rightful power is exercised in focusing our hope on the certain promises of God and his Word, alone. Even "to make repentance the basis of the forgiveness of your sins and of corroborating the work of the keys, is to abandon faith and deny Christ."[38]

---

31. Luther, *Sermon on Matthew 16:13-19* (LW 51:59); cf. WA 2:259: "Sihe, hie zu dinen dir die schüssel, da zu sein die priester einfetzt. Wan du fülest dein herz, das es wandt odder zweifelt, du seiest nit in gnaden vor gottis augen, da ist hoche zeit, das du zum priester gehest und begerest ein absolution über deine sund und sucht also die gewalt und trost der schlüssel."

32. Luther, *Sermon on Matthew 16:13-19* (LW 51:60); cf. WA 2:249: "Also hilfft die gewalt der schlüssel nicht die prister als prister, sundern allein die sundliche und blöde gewissen, die da gnad durch den glauben empfangen und ir hertz zufriden und guter zuvorsicht gegen got gesetzt wirt."

33. Although this treatise was written in 1530, after Hubmaier's death, it elaborates positions implicit already in 1519 and serves to fill out our understanding of Luther's interpretation of Matt. 16:18-19.

34. Luther, *On the Keys* (LW 40:329; WA 30[II]:468).

35. Luther, *On the Keys* (LW 40:329; WA 30[II]:468).

36. Luther does not identify whose interpretation he is rejecting. A likely prospect would be Ulrich Zwingli's; however, this treatise is a detailed and developed response to Catholic interpretations of the keys, without explicit or obvious references to Zwingli (or Hubmaier).

37. Luther, *On the Keys* (LW 40:358; WA 30[II]:492).

38. Luther, *On the Keys* (LW 40:364); cf. WA 30[II]:496.36-40: "Rewen soltu (das ist war), Aber das darumb die vergebunge der sunden solt gewis werden, und des schlüssels werck bestettigen, das heisst den glauben verlassen und Christum verleugnet. Er wil dir die

Ulrich Zwingli explains his view of the keys in his *Auslegen und Gründe der Schlußreden* (1523) and his *Commentary on True and False Religion* (1525). The importance of this issue is highlighted when he declares that "the subject of the keys is not only closely related to the Gospel but is really nothing else than the Gospel itself."[39] He rejects the traditional association of the power of the keys with priestly absolution. He also maintains that the keys were promised to all disciples rather than to Peter, individually, or to the church, corporately. "From all this it is evident that Christ promised the Keys not to Peter alone, but to all who on being asked recognized that He is the Son of God."[40] Christ himself is the rock upon which the church is to be built.[41] The keys are promised in Matt. 16:18-19, but were actually given at Jesus' resurrection in conjunction with the Holy Spirit.[42] The keys are understood to be virtually synonymous with the Word, specifically the Word as preached.[43] This Word, proclaimed to both believers and unbelievers, brings the despairing heart to trust in Christ.

> Christ, then, metaphorically called Keys the delivering and comforting of the soul; and these take place when under the illumination of the Holy Spirit we understand the mystery of Christ and trust in him. To loose, therefore, is nothing else than to raise to sure hope the heart that is despairing of salvation; to bind is to abandon the obstinate heart.[44]

---

sunde nicht umb deinen willen, sondern umb seins selbs willen, aus lauter gnaden durch den schlüssel vergeben und schenken."

39. Zwingli, *Commentary on True and False Religion* (LWZ 3:157; ZSW 3:723).

40. Zwingli, *Commentary* (LWZ 3:158-59; ZSW 3:725-27). Zwingli's position is similar to Origen's, but it is not clear whether the similarity is incidental or evidence of Origen's influence.

41. Zwingli, *Commentary* (LWZ 3:161-63; ZSW 3:728-30); cf. also idem, *Auslegen und Gründe der Schlußreden* (ZSW 2:369).

42. Zwingli, *Commentary* (LWZ 3:167; ZSW 3:734); cf. also idem, *Auslegen und Gründe* (ZSW 2:381).

43. Zwingli, *Commentary* (LWZ 3:160, 172; ZSW 3:726, 738). The latter text reads, in part: "Verbum ergo dei, quo nos ipsos cognoscere discimus, quoque deo fidere docemur, claves sund, quibus ministri erbi liberant; nam qui eo docti omnem fiduciam in deum collocant, iam vere liberi sunt." Cf. also idem, *Auslegen und Gründe* (ZSW 2:374).

44. Zwingli, *Commentary* (LWZ 3:167; ZSW 3:734); cf. also idem, *Auslegen und Gründe* (ZSW 2:388-89). There is a striking similarity to Luther's description of the pastoral function of the keys in *Auslegen und Gründe* (ZSW 2:412): "Geloubt nun der mensch recht und sicher in got, so würdt im verzigen, und darff darzu niemans denn gottes. Ist er aber imm glouben nit styff, so gange zuo dem priester, das er im die spyß der seel zuodiene, das ist: rechte underrichte; und so er dem heilsamen wort glouben gibt, so ist er von stund an rein."

The effectual power of the keys is conditioned by the free initiative of the Holy Spirit. The preaching of the Word might be best understood as creating an appropriately conducive context in which the Spirit might be expected to work.[45] It is the ministry of the keys to preach the hope-giving Word that directs our faith to Christ in the confidence that the Holy Spirit will make the word effective, producing faith and assurance of salvation in the hearer.[46]

The final contemporary of Hubmaier to be considered is Erasmus. While he does not treat the issue of the keys at length, he does address their meaning and use in two treatises from the early 1520s. In his *Paraphrase of the Gospel of Matthew* (1522), Erasmus asserts that the rock upon which the church will be built is the firm profession of faith in Christ that Peter originally expressed, prompting Jesus' declaration.[47] Later, in his *Inquisitio de Fide* (1524), Erasmus explains that the keys are given to the church, which Erasmus identifies as the community of those making a confession of faith, committed to discipleship, practicing the exercise of discipline, and having unity in the Holy Spirit.[48] The church to which Erasmus refers, then, is a visible church but not to be understood simply as the institution of the Catholic church. He effectively describes a form of believer's church, ascribing to it — both locally and generally — the power of the keys.[49] The power of the keys is tied both to the remission of sins and to entry into the church through confession and baptism, as well as to postbaptismal discipline.[50] Erasmus gives special attention to the importance of confession and commitment to discipleship in association with baptism. He does not reject infant baptism but struggles to reconcile the practice with his desire for a form of confessing baptism.[51] The issue of baptism

45. Zwingli, *Commentary* (LWZ 3:175; ZSW 3:740). This reflects the understanding of the relation of human and divine initiative that pervades Zwingli's theological system.

46. Zwingli, *Auslegen und Gründe* (ZSW 2:411): "Uß der krafft der schlüsselen, das alle sünd dem gleubigen und rüwenden menschen verzigen werden, nit von dem pfaffen, bischoff, münch oder bapst, sunder durch Jesum Christum, so man inn gloubt unser pfand des heils sin, und got umb sinetwillen erforddret oder in sinem namen."

47. Erasmus, *Paraphrase* of Matt. 16:18-19 (LB 7:92-93). On the significance of the *Paraphrases*, see Roland H. Bainton, "The Paraphrases of Erasmus," *ARG* 57 (1966): 67-76.

48. Desiderius Erasmus, *Inquisitio de Fide*, ed. Craig R. Thompson (New Haven: Yale University Press, 1950), pp. 69, 71; cf. idem, *Paraphrase* of Matt. 16:18-19 (LB 7:92).

49. Bainton, "Paraphrases," pp. 72-73, 75; Davis, "Erasmus as a Progenitor," pp. 171-73.

50. Erasmus, *Paraphrase* of Matt. 16:18-19 (LB 7:93): "Haec mea peculiaris est potestas, condonare peccata: sed hanc potestatem tibi quadantenus impartiam, ut quod tu meis clavibus acceptis solveris super terram apud homines, solutum sit & in coelis apud Deum." Cf. also idem, *Paraphrase* of John 20:20-23 (LB 7:644) and *Inquisitio* (LB 7:71).

51. Erasmus is troubled by baptism without understanding and commitment. He even proposes re-baptism of young adults who would be able to undergo catechism and make a public confession with their re-baptism; see Bainton, "Paraphrases," pp. 73-74.

is considered by Erasmus in the context of the power of the keys and "binding and loosing," associating baptism with (an adult) confession and submission to discipline.

III. Hubmaier and the Power of the Keys

Hubmaier develops his understanding of the power of the keys most fully in his *On the Christian Ban,* published in Nikolsburg in 1527.[52] He maintains that the keys were given to the church, not to Peter personally. In his paraphrase of Matt. 16:19, Hubmaier changes the "you" from singular to plural, apparently to accommodate Christ's intention to "indicate that many men shall be gathered together in this unity of faith and Christian love," that is, the church, to whom Christ promises the keys.[53] The keys were not actually given to the church until after Jesus' resurrection, the granting of the keys being recorded in Matt. 28:19-20, Mark 16:15-16, and John 20:22-23.[54] As these texts indicate, the giving of the keys is tied to the commission to make disciples and baptize them, and to the forgiveness of sins. The keys are given to the church, therefore, to create a believing community of the baptized. Hubmaier explains the initiatory function of the first key:

> Namely, to preach the gospel, thereby to create a believing congregation, to baptize the same in water, thus with the first key opening to her the door of the Christian church, admitting her [namely, the believing congregation] to the forgiveness of sins.[55]

It is not coincidental that the forgiveness of sins is treated in the context of admission to the believing community. Hubmaier is fond of noting that there is no salvation outside the church, and in his *Twelve Articles on the Christian Faith* the exercise of the authority of the keys over the believing community is considered in the section on remission of sins.[56] The second key is the binding aspect of the power of the keys.

---

52. While most of Hubmaier's interpretation of the keys is drawn from this treatise, significant comments are also found in *A Christian Catechism* (1526), *The Twelve Articles of the Christian Faith* (1527), and *On Fraternal Admonition* (1527).

53. Hubmaier, *On the Christian Ban* (Pipkin-Yoder, p. 412; *Schriften,* p. 368).

54. Hubmaier, *On the Christian Ban* (Pipkin-Yoder, pp. 412-13; *Schriften,* pp. 368-69).

55. Hubmaier, *On the Christian Ban* (Pipkin-Yoder, p. 412; *Schriften,* p. 368).

56. Hubmaier, *The Twelve Articles of the Christian Faith* (Pipkin-Yoder, p. 239; *Schriften,* p. 219): "... das wölhen die Christenlichen Kirchen also aufflöse auff erden, das derselb gwißlich auffgelöset, vnd von seinen sünden entbunden sey, auch in den himelen. Herwiderumb wölhen

It is the authority to exclude again persons who had been received and admitted into the Christian congregation if they should not will to behave in a right and Christian way, and to close the doors behind them.[57]

Hubmaier understands the power of the keys to be effective, freely exercised by the (believing) church.

The basis of this power and authority is the power and authority of Christ. Prior to the incarnation, this authority was exercised by God the Father. It was granted to Christ during his bodily existence, and he then exercised it "in preaching and in deed."[58] During this time Christ administered the gospel and forgiveness directly, exercising the power of the keys to loose and bind.[59] Following his resurrection, in preparation for his bodily absence, Jesus granted to the church those powers that he had been given by the Father. "Thereafter he turned the same over to the Christian church and let her deal, practice, dispose, and authorize, as she possesses and will possess and use it until the coming of the Lord."[60] In the (bodily) absence of Christ, the church exercises those powers freely and with full authority.[61] When Christ returns in the second coming, the church will return all authority to Christ, who will render the final judgment. "When that has all happened, then Christ will again render and give back his authority and keys to God his heavenly Father."[62]

Hubmaier is less explicit in identifying the church to whom this authority is given. It is possessed by the "particular and visible church, gathered together in part bodily and yet completely in the Spirit, even

---

die Kirch binde, vnd auß irer gmainshafft auß schliesse auff erden, das derselb auch gebunden sey vor Got in den himeln vnd auß der all gmainen Christenlichen Kirchen, (ausserhalb wölher khain hail ist) auß geschlossenn, Wie denn Christus seiner Gesponß vnd lieben Braut, die baid Schlüssel selbs an die seytten gehenckt, vbergeben vnd beuolhen hat, als er noch was auff erden." Cf. also idem, *A Christian Catechism* (Pipkin-Yoder, p. 341; *Schriften*, p. 307), and *On Fraternal Admonition* (Pipkin-Yoder, p. 374; *Schriften*, p. 339). This strikingly catholic interpretation is nonetheless proposed without reference to its traditional precedents and roots this authority exclusively within the church of confessing believers.

57. Hubmaier, *On the Christian Ban* (Pipkin-Yoder, p. 414; *Schriften*, p. 370).

58. Hubmaier, *On the Christian Ban* (Pipkin-Yoder, p. 411; *Schriften*, p. 368).

59. Hubmaier, *On the Christian Ban* (Pipkin-Yoder, pp. 412-13; *Schriften*, p. 369).

60. Hubmaier, *On the Christian Ban* (Pipkin-Yoder, p. 413; *Schriften*, p. 369). Hubmaier's paraphrase of John 20:23 here reads, "Jch gib euch yetz die Schlüßlen vnnd allen gwalt, gleich wie ich den selben bißher von meinem vater entpfangen hab zuo verzeyhung der sünden."

61. Hubmaier, *On the Christian Ban* (Pipkin-Yoder, p. 414; *Schriften*, p. 370): "Eruolgt, das die Christenlich Khirch eben disen Gwalt hat zuo verzeihen vnd zuobehalten die sünnd yetz hie auff erden, biß zuo der anndern zuokunfft des Herrens, gleich wie den selben Christus leiblich auff erden selb auch ghebt hat."

62. Hubmaier, *On the Christian Ban* (Pipkin-Yoder, pp. 415-16; *Schriften*, p. 371).

though only two or three are together in the name of the Lord Jesus and all of the others on the other hand are in error."[63] The problem of determining whether a local congregation is gathered "completely in the Spirit" and which two or three are gathered in the name of Christ, but not in error, is left unaddressed. Hubmaier assumes a community of baptized believers, committed to the Rule of Christ[64] and guided by the Holy Spirit, who will exercise the power of the keys correctly.

Hubmaier insists that the proper understanding of the keys is foundational to the proper understanding and practice of the sacraments. This is especially critical to the understanding of the Lord's Supper. Since the basis of the authority of the church (exercised through the power of the keys) is the authority and power of Christ exercised in his absence, any doctrine of Christ's presence in the Supper strikes at the heart of that authority. The teacher of Christ's presence in the Supper "thereby unbuckles the keys from the side of the Christian church, which Jesus with serious words attached to her side gave her and commended to her until he come again."[65] Hubmaier's theology of the Supper, then, hinges ultimately upon his defense of the *absence* of Christ rather than his presence.[66]

The understanding of the keys also affects the practice of baptism. The confession and commitment of the baptizand must include his or her willing submission to the Rule of Christ and thus to the exercise of the power of the keys. It is in this way that one may properly identify the true constituency of the church.[67] Indeed, without submission to the Rule of Christ and to the discipline of the (believing) congregation there is no church.[68]

---

63. Hubmaier, *On the Christian Ban* (Pipkin-Yoder, p. 414; *Schriften*, p. 370).

64. The "Rule of Christ" is the commitment of the disciple to live a Christ-directed life under the authority of the congregation. While it includes the sense of a call to life lived according to the will of Christ, the use of the term tends to focus more specifically on the exercise of admonition and discipline, i.e., the ban.

65. Hubmaier, *On the Christian Ban* (Pipkin-Yoder, p. 413; *Schriften*, p. 369): "Er gürtet auch ab die Schlüßlen von der seitten der Christenlichen Kirchen, die Jr doch Christus mit ernstlichen worten vmbgürtet, geben vnd beuolhen hat, biß er widerumb kumme."

66. John D. Rempel offers an informative and stimulating discussion of the critical role of Christ's absence in Hubmaier's thought in *The Last Supper in Anabaptism — A Study in the Christology of Balthasar Hubmaier, Pilgrim Marpeck and Dirk Philips* (Scottdale, Pa.: Herald Press, 1993), pp. 65-89.

67. Hubmaier, *On Fraternal Admonition* (Pipkin-Yoder, pp. 374, 383, 385; *Schriften*, pp. 339, 345, 346); and *On the Christian Ban* (Pipkin-Yoder, pp. 410, 413; *Schriften*, pp. 367, 369).

68. For a discussion of this formative understanding see Kenneth R. Davis, "No Discipline, No Church: An Anabaptist Contribution to the Reformed Tradition," *SCJ* 13 (1982): 43-58.

IV. Conclusion

Balthasar Hubmaier interprets Christ's granting of the power of the keys in light of his ecclesiology and Christology. The power of the keys is given to the church. The church, however, is specifically identified as the fellowship of confessing believers. This community consists of those who are committed to the Rule of Christ and have willingly submitted to the discipline of the community. Remission of sins and, ultimately, salvation are necessarily linked to incorporation into this community. The initiatory event that gains entry into this saving community is baptism. Confession of faith in Christ, submission to the Rule of Christ, and acceptance of the disciplinary authority of the believing community are requisite for that baptism. The fidelity of the believer to these commitments and to the demands of the gospel is maintained by the discipline of the community and the use of the ban. The power of the keys grants to the community the effective power over salvation by its authority to include or exclude persons from this salvific fellowship. This power is emphatically identified with the power exercised by Christ and is, in fact, the same power that has been entrusted to the church in Christ's bodily absence. The authority of the church hinges upon this delegation of authority in the power of the keys. This makes the denial of Christ's sacramental presence a defense of the foundational authority of the church. It also makes this passage, and Hubmaier's interpretation of it, a core element in his thought.

What can we learn by placing Hubmaier's interpretation of Matt. 16:18-19 in the context of the other interpreters we have considered? Surprisingly, Hubmaier stands much closer to the Catholic tradition than to Luther and Zwingli in his understanding of the keys granting effective power associated with the remission of sins. In fact, he shares with Thomas Aquinas the belief that the power of the keys may be effectively exercised through human initiative. While he shares with Luther the interpretation that the keys are given to the church, their respective understandings of what that means are quite different. He includes preaching, as Zwingli does, within the function of the keys, but preaching is clearly secondary to the role of the keys as constitutive of the church. His emphasis on human initiative is diametrically opposed to Zwingli's emphatic defense of the divine initiative. The virtual absence of any shared ground between Hubmaier and these two Reformers is striking, suggesting that Hubmaier's understanding of the keys is drawn from other than Reformation sources.

While Hubmaier's lack of agreement with Luther and Zwingli is evident, his broad agreement with Erasmus is also clear. Hubmaier closely echoes Erasmus's interpretation of the meaning and use of the keys. Both understand the church — as a visible community of confessing believers — to be the sole recipient of the power of the keys. They share a similar understanding of the role of the keys in constituting and maintaining that community of faith. Baptism, remission of sins, and admission into the salvific community are connected together and with the power of the keys. Erasmus and Hubmaier offer similar interpretations of the power of the keys and how they function in a congregation of committed disciples. It goes beyond the scope of this study to claim or prove that this interpretation in Hubmaier is the result of Erasmus's influence. There is clearly, however, a remarkable similarity in their understanding of the keys.[69]

One aspect of Hubmaier's interpretation that does not correlate clearly with Erasmus, however, is his understanding of the delegation of Christ's power in the giving of the keys. Erasmus understands that Christ has granted real power, in some degree, to the church. But Hubmaier's understanding of the total transfer of Christ's own authority, exercised fully in his absence, is nowhere to be found in Erasmus's discussion of the keys. John D. Rempel suggests that Hubmaier's Christology developed out of a eucharistic doctrine that denied any real presence.[70] It is tempting to speculate whether we might find some roots for this distinctive interpretation in his nominalist background.[71] In any case, this unusual aspect of Hubmaier's theology reflects some other source than Erasmus.

What do Hubmaier's treatment of Matt. 16:18-19 and his interpretation of the power of the keys tell us about his work as a biblical commentator? On the one hand, his interpretive work is free of reference to glosses,

69. The absence of clear evidence of direct influence by Erasmus should not preclude the possibility of his influence on Hubmaier's thought. For a discussion of this problem and of possible Erasmian influence on Anabaptism generally, see Hillerbrand, "The Origin of Sixteenth-Century Anabaptism," pp. 157-61. Of particular interest is Hillerbrand's treatment of Erasmus's *Paraphrase of Matthew* as evidence of his influence on Anabaptism. A systematic study comparing Erasmus's views there and Hubmaier's interpretation of those issues would offer clearer evidence regarding Erasmian influence.

70. Rempel, *The Last Supper*, p. 73. Whether Hubmaier's sacramental theology determines his Christology or not, Rempel ably shows the direct interrelation of these with the issue of the power of the keys. Any sacramental understanding that affirms the presence of Christ undercuts the authority of the power of the keys. Having been entrusted to the church in Christ's absence, his presence would require the church to relinquish that authority. Without that authority the church cannot be rightly constituted or maintained. Therefore, protection of the necessary authority granted with the keys dictates a sacramental theology of Christ's absence.

71. George H. Williams, in fact, suggests this connection in *The Radical Reformation* (Philadelphia: Westminster, 1975), pp. 220-21.

traditional authorities, or scholastic debate. He gives little attention to linguistic study or technical issues. He appears to appeal to common sense, offering a simple explanation of the meaning of the text. On the other hand, Hubmaier's "simple" meaning is both theologically creative and conditioned by his theological presuppositions. Given those presuppositions, the meaning of the text appears quite clear to Hubmaier. This "self-evident simplicity" frees him to exercise considerable creativity in his interpretive work. This is not in any way to imply conscious manipulation of the text on Hubmaier's part, for he seems quite sincere in his conviction that his interpretation derives from the "simple, clear" meaning of the text.

For all of the commentators we have considered, the interpretation of Matt. 16:18-19 is finally a theological (rather than exegetical) issue. It could not, in fact, be resolved on the basis of the text or on the basis of the "literal" reading, but ultimately required an appeal to more abstract and less immediately exegetical considerations. Hubmaier's interpretation of the power of the keys reveals him as much more than a simple biblical interpreter following in the footsteps of Luther and Zwingli. He appears, at least in this case, to be more closely following Erasmus. He also displays some rather creative theological thinking. In sum, Hubmaier emerges as a thinker in critical dialogue — and significant continuity — with Catholic sources. His treatment of the keys offers insight into his method of biblical interpretation and provides a window into the theology of this important Reformation figure.

· 6 ·

Philip Melanchthon's 1522 Annotations on Romans and the Lutheran Origins of Rhetorical Criticism

TIMOTHY J. WENGERT

THIS ESSAY INVESTIGATES what, for sixteenth-century readers, would have made Philip Melanchthon's first published interpretation of Romans such a contrast to other expositions of Romans then available in German bookstalls and libraries. Melanchthon combined his humanist training in the analysis of ancient texts with a single-minded conviction regarding the central point of Romans. As a result, he produced a commentary that to contemporary readers, who were also steeped in humanism's rhetorical techniques, would have sounded like the Apostle Paul's own voice commenting from the first century on the sixteenth century's most critical theological debates. For these readers Melanchthon's method rendered the exegete and the exegetical tradition nearly invisible by inviting them to consider Paul's dialectic and rhetoric in the light of the very rules for argument and speech being taught by Melanchthon in Wittenberg's classrooms. Melanchthon blended evangelical theology and humanist method and placed both in the authoritative mouth of St. Paul himself.[1]

---

1. Here I disagree substantially with the way these rhetorical and historical insights are dismissed by Ernst Bizer in his *Theologie der Verheißung: Studien zur theologischen Entwicklung des jungen Melanchthon (1519-1524)* (Neukirchen: Neukirchener Verlag des Erziehungsvereins, 1964), p. 133, where he writes, "Man mag darin [namely, in this rhetorical understanding of Romans] den Anfang einer historischen Betrachtungsweise erkennen, doch hat sie für den Kommentar selbst kaum Konsequenzen gehabt." He does provide a comparison of Luther's

I. Melanchthon's Biography[2]

Philip Melanchthon was born 16 February 1497 in Bretten, an important town on a south German trading route running between the Danube and Rhein river basins. His father, the armorer George Schwarzerdt, died when Philip was only eleven, so the family sent the precocious child to Pforzheim, to attend the Latin school of George Simler. There he lived with a relative (by marriage), Elizabeth Reuchlin, the sister of the German humanist, Johannes Reuchlin. To further the young prodigy's work in Greek, Reuchlin gave Philip a copy of a Greek grammar and translated the budding scholar's name from German, Schwarzerdt ("black earth"), into Greek (Μέλαν χθών).

Melanchthon studied at the University of Heidelberg, where he received his Bachelor of Arts in 1511, and at the University of Tübingen, where he received his Master of Arts in 1514. While teaching in the arts faculty at Tübingen, he also attended lectures in theology and law and worked at the printshop of Thomas Anshelm. During this time he also published an edition of Terence that received favorable comment from, among others, Erasmus of Rotterdam. In 1518, the Elector of Saxony, acting on the suggestion of Reuchlin, called Melanchthon to fill a newly created professorship of Greek at the University of Wittenberg.

---

lectures on Romans with Melanchthon's annotations on Romans. Like other scholars of the time, Arno Schirmer, *Das Paulusverständnis Melanchthons 1518-1522* (Wiesbaden: Franz Steiner, 1967), also ignores this historical context in search of theological parallels.

2. The best biography in English is still Clyde L. Manschreck, *Melanchthon: The Quiet Reformer* (Nashville: Abingdon, 1958). For recent German literature see Heinz Scheible, "Melanchthon, Philip," in *Theologische Realenzyklopädie* 22:371-410 and the extensive bibliography listed there. The most extensive bibliography of works about Melanchthon is the three volumes of Wilhelm Hammer, *Die Melanchthonforschung im Wandel der Jahrhunderte*, Quellen und Forschungen zur Reformationsgeschichte, vols. 35, 36, and 49 (Gütersloh: Gerd Mohn, 1967-81). The 1521 edition of his *Loci communes theologici* is available in English in LCC 19:18-152. This version does not replace the more faithful translation of Charles Leander Hill, *The Loci Communes of Philip Melanchthon* (Boston: Meador, 1944). The 1543 version is available in an error-filled translation entitled *Loci Communes 1543*, trans. J. A. O. Preus (St. Louis: Concordia, 1992). A partial translation into English of Melanchthon's own German translation of the third edition of the *Loci* is published under the title *Melanchthon on Christian Doctrine: Loci communes 1555*, trans. Clyde L. Manschreck (Oxford: Oxford University Press, 1965; repr. Grand Rapids: Baker, 1982). Also available in English is Melanchthon's 1540 *Commentary on Romans*, trans. Fred Kramer (St. Louis: Concordia, 1992). For Melanchthon's original works, researchers still rely on CR 1-28, on the *Supplementa Melanchthoniana* (Leipzig: R. Haupt, 1910-29), and on MSA 1-7. Many of his important works have not been published since the sixteenth century.

Once at Wittenberg Melanchthon was quickly won over to Luther's theology and even assisted him at the Leipzig debates against John Eck in 1519. He remained a professor at Wittenberg for the rest of his life and taught in both the arts and theology faculties. His *Loci communes theologici,* first published in 1521 and revised in 1522, 1535, and 1543, stands as the first evangelical systematic theology. Having accompanied the Elector of Saxony to the Diet of Augsburg in 1530, he became the chief writer of the *Augsburg Confession.* When negotiations between the Roman and evangelical parties broke down after the Emperor's acceptance of the *Roman Confutation,* Melanchthon quickly penned a defense, the *Apology of the Augsburg Confession,* published in 1531. An appendix to the Augsburg Confession, the *Treatise on the Power and Primacy of the Pope,* written in 1536, was the third document penned by Melanchthon to be published in 1580 as part of the Lutheran *Book of Concord.*

With the Smalcald War of 1547, the Elector of Saxony John Frederick lost most of his lands and his electorship to his victorious cousin, Maurice. This meant that the University of Wittenberg changed hands as well. Maurice, an evangelical prince who fought on the Emperor's side, had hoped that the church in his new territories might be allowed to maintain the confession delivered to the Emperor in Augsburg. However, the triumphant Emperor insisted that all evangelical lands subscribe to an interim agreement for regulating churches in the Holy Roman Empire, called the Augsburg Interim after the location of the 1548 imperial Diet. Melanchthon, working to preserve evangelical churches in Saxony, proposed for his new prince a compromise, nicknamed by Lutheran opponents the "Leipzig Interim." Thus began thirteen years of controversy among Lutherans in Germany (almost without exception Melanchthon's own students) over the importance of church practices in times of persecution (the adiaphoristic controversy), over original sin and free will (the synergistic controversy), over the necessity of good works for salvation (the Majoristic controversy), and over the Lord's Supper (the crypto-Calvinistic controversy). Long before these controversies saw any resolution, on 19 April 1560 Melanchthon died.

II. Melanchthon's Early Encounters with Paul

From 1518 through 1522 Philip Melanchthon was completely preoccupied with the Apostle Paul and especially his letter to the Romans — a letter, as Melanchthon often stated, that provided the "scopus et methodus" for the entire Scripture. If ever any Reformer could be accused of "Paulinocentrism," it was the young Melanchthon during these years.[3] In August 1518, as part of his Wittenberg *Antrittsrede*, he announced lectures on the Greek text of Titus as part of his duties as teacher of Greek in the arts faculty.[4] These were followed by lectures on the Greek text of Romans and Galatians.[5] On 9 September 1519, under the direction of Martin Luther, Melanchthon defended his theses for the Baccalaureus Biblicus, the first theological degree.[6] This gained him the right to lecture on the Latin Bible and its content and not simply on the Greek text and grammar. By 11 December he reported lecturing on Matthew.[7]

On 25 January 1520, as part of the customary celebrations of the Conversion of St. Paul, Melanchthon delivered an oration entitled "Declamatiuncula in divi Pauli doctrinam."[8] By 27 April he reported completing lectures on Matthew and preparing for lectures on both Romans and what he called "Obelisci," an equivalent for lectures on the *Sentences* of Peter Lombard.[9] In the same letter he described how it had occurred to him to abandon the medieval form of commenting on the *Sentences* in favor of Paul's *methodus*, combining Paul's structure in Romans with *loci communes*.[10] In

3. The myth reducing Protestant theology to Paul and Romans may have its origins here but certainly does not apply to Luther or other Reformers. Melanchthon's single-mindedness is unique.

4. Horst Koehn, "Philip Melanchthons Reden: Verzeichnis der im 16. Jahrhundert erschienenen Drucke," *Archiv für Geschichte des Buchwesens* 25 (1984): 1277-1495. Melanchthon's speeches are conventionally cited according to Koehn's numbering system, as (here) Koehn, no. 46. The full text is found in MSA 3:29-42. The preface, Melanchthon to Otto Beckman (before 16 Oct. 1518), is published in MBW, no. 30, *Texte* 1:84-86 (hereafter cited conventionally, as MBW 30 [T1:84-86]).

5. Melanchthon to Johannes Schwebel (11 Dec. 1519), MBW 68 (T1:158-59). It is not clear whether any trace of the lectures on Romans has survived. Peter Barton, "Die exegetische Arbeit des jungen Melanchthon 1518/19 bis 1528/29: Probleme und Ansätze," *ARG* 54 (1963): 52-89, argues that these lectures are the *Theologia Institutio Philippi Melanchthonis in Epistolam Pauli ad Romanos* (Bizer, *Texte* [below], pp. 89-99). For Galatians, see Ernst Bizer (ed.), *Texte aus der Anfangszeit Melanchthons* (Neukirchen-Vluyn: Neukirchener Verlag des Erziehungsverein, 1966), pp. 31-37 (hereafter cited as Bizer, *Texte*).

6. Printed in MSA 1:23-25. See also Luther to Johannes Staupitz (3 Oct. 1519), WABr 1:514.

7. MBW 68 (T1:159.12). These lectures were published without Melanchthon's permission in 1523 as the *Annotationes in Evangelium Matthaei iam recens in gratiam studiosorum editae* (MSA 4:133-208).

8. Originally published in February 1520. See MSA 1:26-53 (Koehn, no. 51).

9. Perhaps in connection with the second theological degree, the Baccalaureus Sententiarius. See Melanchthon to Johannes Heß (27 Apr. 1520), MBW 84 (T1:189-97).

10. The initial result of these lectures was probably the *Theologia institutio* and finally the *Loci communes theologici*, published in 1521.

preparation for lectures on Romans Melanchthon had Melchior Lotter print a copy of Erasmus's Latin text of Romans that included some marginal notes by Melanchthon on the rhetorical *dispositio* of the text. Lotter also added Melanchthon's own "Adhortatio ad Paulinae doctrinae studium," a second declamation on Paul.[11] By 13 June Luther reported to Spalatin that the lectures were well underway.[12] On 20 February 1521 Melanchthon himself could write to John Hess that he had reached chapter ten.[13] In April or May 1521 Melanchthon published the printed text of 1 Corinthians and stated in a preface to the readers that he had just completed work on Romans.[14] At nearly the same time, however, in anticipation of another set of lectures in the Greek language, he published a copy of the Greek text of Romans, dedicated to a new arrival in Wittenberg, John Bugenhagen.[15] In July 1522, after the completion of lectures on 1 and 2 Corinthians, Luther, over Melanchthon's objections, saw to the publication of his lectures on the Latin text of all three books.[16] After this, Melanchthon did not again lecture on Paul until 1526, when he began lectures on Colossians.[17]

---

11. Two prefaces by Melanchthon grace this publication, which probably appeared in May 1520. See Melanchthon to Andreas Camicianus (May 1520: Preface to *Adhortatio ad Paulinae doctrinae studium*), MBW 94 (T1:209-10); Melchior Lotter [writer: Melanchthon] to the reader (May 1520: Preface to the text of Erasmus's Latin translation of Romans), MBW 94a (T1:211-12); and, for the text, CR 11:34-41 (Koehn, no. 54).

12. Luther to Georg Spalatin (13 June 1520), WABr 2:122-23.

13. Melanchthon to Johannes Heß (20 Feb. 1521), MBW 126 (T1:258-61). Cf. Melanchthon to Tilemann Plettener (Mar. 1521: Preface to the *Loci communes theologici*), MBW 132 (T1:267-72), where he pointed out that he had begun the lectures the previous year.

14. Melanchthon to the reader (Apr./May 1521: Preface to Melanchthon's Latin edition of 1 Corinthians), MBW 138 (T1:279-80).

15. Melanchthon to Johannes Bugenhagen (ca. May 1521: Preface to the Greek edition of Romans), MBW 142 (T1:292-93). Glosses to this text from Melanchthon's lectures were published in Bizer, *Texte*, pp. 39-85.

16. First printed on 23 October 1522 by John Stuchs of Nuremberg. See Luther to Melanchthon (29 July 1522: Preface to *Annotationes in epistolas Pauli ad Romanos et ad Corinthios*), MBW 230 (T1:473-77). The edition used for this study is the Strasbourg edition of 5 May 1523: ANNO ‖ TATIONES PHILIPPI ‖ Melanchthonis in Epistolam Pau ‖ li ad Romanos unam, Et ad ‖ Corinthios duas. ‖ ARGENTORATI APVD ‖ Iohannem Heruagium. Anno ‖ M.D.XXIII. Colophon: ARGENTORATI APVD IOHAN= ‖ NEM HERVAGIUVM TERTIO ‖ NONAS MAII ANNO ‖ M.D.XXIII. Octavo, woodcut on title page, 144 leaves. Henceforth cited as *Ann. Rom.* Melanchthon's objections had to do with what he considered their crude Latin style.

17. See my work (in preparation) on Philip Melanchthon's exegetical opposition to Erasmus of Rotterdam. The chronology and the documents referred to in the preceding paragraphs have often been disputed. Peter Barton in both MSA 4:10-11 and his *ARG* article

Melanchthon's early fervor for Paul has been preserved in various ways. Outside the lost work on the Greek text of Romans from 1519, we possess the two declamations, notes, and glosses on the published Latin and Greek texts, and various rhetorical outlines of the Pauline texts preserved in student notebooks, to say nothing of the works leading up to the *Loci communes theologici*. But clearly Melanchthon's work in the *Annotations on Romans* had the greatest impact on his contemporaries. Although published without his consent and rejected by him in the commentary on Romans of 1532,[18] these lectures and their subsequent publication formed an important literary event in the history of the sixteenth-century exegesis of Romans. It was an immediate best-seller by any measure, rivaled only by the 1518 paraphrase of Romans by Erasmus.[19] The error-filled first edition was soon replaced by a corrected copy in 1523. The *Ann. Rom.* formed the cornerstone for the Wittenberg theologians' commentary on the entire New Testament from 1522 to 1524.[20]

III. The *Annotations on Romans* and Other Commentaries on Romans

Luther himself noted the importance of the *Ann. Rom.* in his preface to the published version, which was based on a copy of the lectures Luther himself stole and gave to the printer. After lodging hefty critiques of Thomas Aquinas and of Erasmus's favorite patristic exegetes, Origen and Jerome

---

mistakes the later Greek lectures for the *Ann. Rom.* Bizer speculates that the *Artificium* is the forerunner of the *Loci*. The editor of WABr 2 thought that Melanchthon lectured continuously on Romans from 1519 through 1522 in an attempt to correct an earlier error by Karl Hartfelder, *Philipp Melanchthon als Praeceptor Germaniae* (Berlin: A. Hofmann, 1889). The debate over Melanchthon's earliest lectures has also been driven by theological concerns. See especially the exchange between Lowell Green, "Die exegetischen Vorlesungen des jungen Melanchthon und ihre Chronologie," *Kerygma und Dogma* 3 (1957): 140-49 and Adolf Sperl, "Eine bisher unbekannte Vorlesung Melanchthons über den Römerbrief im Herbst 1521," *Zeitschrift für Kirchengeschichte* 69 (1958): 115-20, and idem, "Nochmals zur Chronologie der frühen exegetischen Vorlesungen Melanchthons," *Kerygma und Dogma* 4 (1958): 39-40.

18. MSA 5:26.5-8. This rejection in no way undermines its earlier importance despite the mistaken assumptions of some modern scholars.

19. MBW 230 (T1:473-75) lists eleven separate printings between 1522 and 1525, with six in 1523 alone. There were also three separate printings of two German translations. For details see Timothy J. Wengert, *Philip Melanchthon's "Annotationes in Johannem" in Relation to Its Predecessors and Contemporaries* (Geneva: Droz, 1987), p. 255.

20. Wengert, *Melanchthon's "Annotationes,"* pp. 31-42.

("mere trifles and ineptitude compared to your *Annotationes*"), Luther had to counter Melanchthon's own reluctance toward publishing this work.

> You say, "Scripture alone must be read instead of commentaries." You speak the truth concerning Jerome, Origen, Thomas and others like them. For they wrote commentaries in which they handed down their own thoughts rather than Pauline or Christian ones. No one would call your *Annotationes* a "commentary" but at most an "index" for the reading of "Scripture" and the "knowing" of Christ, regarding which not even one of the commentaries extant up until now is better.[21]

The point is not that Melanchthon was any less a commentator or any less indebted to the exegetical tradition than any other exegete. Rather, given his readers' expectations and training, Melanchthon's method provided his commentary a certain transparency that Luther himself sensed and praised.

Plenty of other important theologians had wrestled with Paul's letter to the Romans early in the sixteenth century. Besides John Colet and Luther, whose works went unpublished in that century, the most important commentaries on Romans available by 1520 were those of Jacques Lefèvre d'Étaples, the French humanist whose commentary Luther had used, and Erasmus of Rotterdam, whose paraphrase, translation and annotations on Romans were available by 1519. In addition, works by Nicholas of Lyra, Thomas Aquinas, Augustine, and John Chrysostom were widely available. Chrysostom's work, however, was exegesis in the midst of homily; Augustine's, in *De spiritu et litera*, exegesis intermingled with polemic. Lyra, whose work depended on Thomas, provided the best of medieval exegesis: a running set of glosses on the text organized on the basis of the medieval *divisio*. Although Lyra's comments assumed that Paul shaped the text, the shape Lyra described would have looked decidedly scholastic to sixteenth-century interpreters.[22]

---

21. MBW 230 (T1:477.24-29). For Melanchthon's own criticism of commentaries, see his preface to the *Loci communes theologici* of 1521 (MBW 132 [T1:271-72]).

22. His gloss on Rom. 3:23 shows the influence of Aristotelian categories. "Hic consequenter ostenditur modus iustificationis huius per causam formalem, efficientem, et finalem et temporis congruentiam." His preface focused on historical issues, not rhetorical ones. He asked three questions: to whom the letter was sent (the Romans), from where it was sent (Corinth), and the "causa finalis vel quare scripta est causa motiua." To this question Lyra provided a scholastic answer: the letter contained a "reuocatio ab errore falsitatis" and an "inuitatio ad cognitionem veritatis." For an analysis of this approach, see A. J. Minnis, *Medieval Theory of Authorship*, 2d ed. (Philadelphia: University of Pennsylvania Press, 1988). Melanchthon criticizes scholastic method in his letter to Bernhard Maurus (Jan. 1519: preface to *De rhetorica libri tres*), MBW 40 (T1:101.34-48), where he contrasts Lyra and others to Johannes Reuchlin, Erasmus, and Luther.

Lefèvre's work used humanist techniques to investigate the Vulgate text and to fashion his own elegant commentary (no stodgy glosses for him!). The first part was cluttered with detailed indices, including one arranging Paul's comments according to the Apostles' Creed and another listing rejected heresies and heretics. A lengthy middle section provided parallel texts of the Vulgate and his own Latin version corrected by the Greek. The commentary, besides giving detailed analysis of the criticisms of the Vulgate at the end of each chapter, alternated excerpts from Paul's text with Lefèvre's comments. Only in the conclusion to each of these sections of commentary, which introduced the topic of the next biblical passage cited (often in the form of a question), did Lefèvre consistently give the reader the impression Paul was moving the discussion in a particular direction.[23]

Erasmus used the annotations of 1519 to defend his new Latin translation of the text and thus continued to develop the humanist tradition of textual criticism pioneered by Lorenzo Valla and Lefèvre. Outside of the initial *argumentum,* however, the words and their proper translation over against the Vulgate, not the Apostle, took center stage. The paraphrase of Romans by Erasmus deserves special comment, and not simply because Melanchthon criticized it.[24] The whole point of paraphrase, an art cherished by humanists,[25] was to allow the author to speak. Yet the form could also destroy the *methodus* of the original author and trumpet instead the linguistic abilities of the exegete. The very fact that Erasmus thought his paraphrase could be judged only by those with a thorough knowledge of the fathers would also seem to indicate that even he viewed it as a thoroughly traditioned text, that is, one that could be interpreted only through the patristic consensus. He strove not simply for faithfulness to

23. Jacobus Faber Stapulensis [Jacques Lefèvre d'Étaples], *S. Pauli epistolae XIV ex Vulgata, adiecta intelligentia ex graeco, cum commentariis* (facsimile reprint of 1512 Paris edition; Stuttgart: Frommann-Holzboog, 1978). For example, in introducing comments on Rom. 1:16-17 Lefèvre writes, p. 68, "At quo modo fructificabat Christo? Euangelizando. Ideo ostendit [Paulus]: quid euangelium sit dicens. . . ." Otherwise, Paul often takes second place to discussions of the exegetical tradition.

24. Cf. Melanchthon's lame apology to Erasmus (5 or 9 Jan. 1519), MBW 38 (T1:95-97), and Erasmus's miffed response (22 Apr. 1519), MBW 53 (T1:119-21). See also my article "'Qui vigilantissimis oculis veterum omnium commentarios excusserit': Philip Melanchthon's Patristic Exegesis," in a forthcoming collection of essays published by the Herzog August Bibliothek, Wolfenbüttel.

25. See Melanchthon's praise of Erasmus's ability in this regard in *De rhetorica libri tres* (Leipzig: Valentin Schumann, 1521) in a section entitled "De enarratorio genere" (sig. C-5ᵛ).

Paul but for faithfulness to the fathers' interpretations of Paul, an aim quite different from Melanchthon's.[26]

IV. The *Annotations on Romans* and Rhetorical Analysis of Romans

Melanchthon's starting point seems innocent enough, given the exegetical revolution it sparked. It arose squarely out of his training as a humanist, where speeches and letters of the ancients were routinely the stuff of school-children's exercises, and out of his critique of medieval practices of commenting.[27] Simply put, Melanchthon viewed Paul's Epistle to the Romans as a letter, shaped by its author using common rhetorical methods to make a single theological point, the letter's *scopus*. Thus, everything Melanchthon found in Romans, and everything he subsequently told his students about, arose from Paul. It was Paul's point, Paul's language, Paul's argument, Paul's structure. At the same time, Melanchthon linked this Pauline exegesis to his own encounter with Luther's theology and thus endowed evangelical theology with an apostolic authority it would not otherwise have claimed. Melanchthon's own exegesis thus achieved a timeliness unmatched by other interpretations.[28]

Melanchthon had, of course, certain forerunners. Augustine's anti-Pelagian arguments, Lyra's scholastic Paul, Lefèvre's rhetorical turns, and Erasmus's Pauline paraphrase certainly demonstrated other ways an exegete could allow Paul to find his voice through Romans. Moreover, the *argumentum* used in both Erasmus's annotations and his paraphrase put the letter

---

26. MBW 53 (T1:120.8-10).

27. MBW 40 (T1:101.38-40). "Quibus [nugis] factum est, ut pro apostolicis literis sophisticas habeamus. . . ."

28. As David Steinmetz has pointed out in his more general discussion of precritical exegesis ("The Superiority of Pre-Critical Exegesis," *Theological Studies* 37 [1980]: 27-38), it is important to understand that the scriptural text itself allows for such an interpretation as Melanchthon's. It is not as if this interpretation of Paul were not "in the text" but simply imposed upon it. Melanchthon was not simply reading something into the text, as certain modern literary critics might imagine of all interpretation, but he was reading something new out of the text. Patristic, medieval, and humanist scholars all knew that Romans was a letter (on Paul's eloquence see Augustine, *De doctrina Christiana* 4.7.12-15); Melanchthon was the first to make his treatment of Romans as a letter the heart of his exegesis. Susan E. Schreiner, *Where Shall Wisdom Be Found? Calvin's Exegesis of Job from Medieval and Modern Perspectives* (Chicago: University of Chicago Press, 1994), pp. 8-21, makes a similar argument in the case of precritical interpretation of Job.

within an appropriate historical context.[29] Nevertheless, Melanchthon provided for readers of his *Ann. Rom.* new and unique access to the Apostle Paul.

The first and arguably the most important level of that access came from Melanchthon's conviction that Romans was a letter and, like all other letters, could be analyzed using rhetorical tools.[30] A first step in rhetorical analysis for Melanchthon was always determining the genre of speech employed by an author or speaker.[31] When it came to Romans, Melanchthon's opinion varied, in part as a result of his adding a fourth genre (the didactic) to the traditional three (demonstrative, deliberative, and judicial). Occasionally he placed Romans in the "genus iudicale," since that genre comprised texts involving controversies and litigation. Although in *De rhetorica libri tres* of 1519 Melanchthon had argued that Romans belonged in the deliberative genre under the subgrouping of didactic (as opposed to persuasive),[32] in the *Inst. rhet.* he used Romans as an example of the judicial kind of speech, despite the fact that earlier in the same book he had for the first time defined a separate didactic genre.[33] In what may have served as the preface to his dictated glosses on the Latin text, most likely delivered in May 1520, Melanchthon put Romans in the newly independent didactic genus.[34] He did the same in both his introductory comments to his lecture

29. Nevertheless, even here there are broad divergences between the two. See Wilhelm Maurer's more detailed analysis in his *Der junge Melanchthon*, vol. 2: *Der Theologe* (Göttingen: Vandenhoeck & Ruprecht, 1969), pp. 125-27.

30. Modern rhetorical criticism is merely reiterating arguments already investigated by Melanchthon and especially by his epigone, George Major.

31. For definitions this essay relies on Melanchthon's *Institutiones rhetoricae* (Strasbourg: Johannes Herwagen, 1523), his Wittenberg lectures on rhetoric from 1520-21 first published at the end of 1521 (henceforth cited as *Inst. rhet.*). For a synopsis of rhetorical categories, see the list compiled by Rolf Schäfer at the end of his edition of Melanchthon's 1532 commentary on Romans, MSA 5:379-92. For arguments similar to these, based on the Romans commentary of 1532, see Rolf Schäfer, "Melanchthons Hermeneutik im Römerbrief-kommentar von 1532," *Zeitschrift für Theologie und Kirche* 60 (1963): 216-35.

32. *De rhetorica libri tres*, sig. C-viii[v].

33. *Inst. rhet.*, fol. 8[v]. He made the same point in the *Theologica institutio* (reprinted in Bizer, *Texte*, p. 97), where he also noted the sections of such a speech: exordium, narratio, and confirmatio. The *Inst. rhet.* defined in more detail the same parts but prefaced the entire section with a discussion of the *status*.

34. The *Artifitium Epistolae Pauli ad Romanos a Philippo [Melanchthone]*, a manuscript of Melanchthon's early lectures now in the Karlsruher Landesbibliothek and published in Bizer, *Texte*, p. 20. Bizer seems to confuse this text with the *Theologica institutio* and the forerunners of the *Loci communes theologici* of 1521, a position corrected in MBW. It seems more likely to represent his first attempt to provide a *dispositio* for Romans, and perhaps it simply preserved Melanchthon's introduction to the glosses on the text that immediately preceded the lengthier *scholiae* found in the *Ann. Rom.*

on the Greek text in 1521 and in the opening remarks to his annotations on 1 Corinthians.[35]

Melanchthon's indecision arose in part out of his changing assessment of the purpose of Romans. If Paul wrote the letter simply to refute his opponents, it belonged to the *genus iudiciale;* if to instruct the church, the *genus didacticum.* Linking the letter to the *Loci communes theologici* tipped the balance in favor of the didactic, so that Melanchthon eagerly pointed out Paul's dialectical proofs and method of teaching. Nevertheless, as we shall see, he was by no means insensitive to the prosecutorial nature of some material. He even realized that a portion of the book (Rom. 6:8-23), what he called a "digressio hortatoria," fell into the deliberative, that is, persuasive genus.[36]

V. The *Scopus* of Romans

Having determined its genus, the second step in rhetorical analysis consisted of analyzing a work's structure, or *dispositio.* This concern, reflected already in the *Artifitium* (probably Melanchthon's introduction to the Romans lectures of 1520), resulted in the publication of a separate commentary on the text in 1529.[37] However, in both the *Ann. Rom.* and the 1532 *Commentarii in Epistolam Pauli ad Romanos* (MSA 5), Melanchthon also investigated at length the various sections of Paul's letter and their coherence.

Before outlining a work's *dispositio* an exegete had to determine the *status* of a work. According to the *Inst. rhet.,* this was especially necessary for speeches belonging to the *genus iudicale.* The *status* "is a summary sentence concerning the point of contention and thus is a brief pronouncement or proposition containing the sum of the controversy to which all

---

35. The former, entitled ΠΑΨΟΔΙΑΙ ΕΝ ΠΑΥΛΟΥ *ad Romanos,* is also printed in Bizer, *Texte,* p. 45; the latter is found in MSA 4:16. There Melanchthon states, "Epistula ad Romanos didactica est, docens, quid evangelium, adeoque unde sit iustificatio, estque veluti totius scripturae methodus consistitque tota in uno loco, unde sit iustificatio."

36. *Ann. Rom.,* fol. 32[r-v]. "Apostolus usus est locis et argumentis suasorijs," beginning with an argument "a caussa peccati" and following it with an argument "a facili." In the *Inst. rhet.,* fol. 7[r], he defines the *genus deliberativum* as "quo suademus" and lists two of the *loci* under the *confirmatio* as "utilitas" (fol. 8[v]: "nascitur ex ipsa caussa") and "facile" (fol. 8[v]: "huc pertinent possibile & impossibile").

37. The *Dispositio orationis in Epistola Pauli ad Romanos* (Haguenau: John Setzer, 1529).

proofs and arguments are referred."[38] The *status* here corresponds to the *thema* in the *genus didacticum*.[39] Melanchthon's conviction concerning the *status* of Romans gave his *Ann. Rom.* its coherence, sealed the centrality of Paul's role as author of the letter, and provided a direct link between the Pauline text and the sixteenth-century debates over justification. It also spelled a rejection of a certain alternative construal of Romans, championed by Erasmus and Jerome, that limited Paul's argument to Jewish ceremonial law, especially circumcision.[40]

The readers of the *Ann. Rom.* would first have encountered Melanchthon's rhetorical approach to Paul in the *argumentum*, a brief introduction to the letter.[41] Here, like Jerome and Erasmus, he discussed the occasion for writing the letter. However, unlike his two models, Melanchthon glossed over historical matters and zeroed in on the theological issue: Paul wanted to "describe and express" Christ and his benefits. Melanchthon also mentioned that Paul answered both Jews and Gentiles who wanted to trust their own righteousness by condemning all human strength and merit and by arguing that righteousness came "gratis . . . per Christum," so that the one who believes is saved.[42] He then provided an overview of the letter's *dispositio*. In the first eight chapters Paul

> treats grace, law and sin in the most apt order and plainly with a rhetorical method. The *status* of the case is that we are justified by faith. This opinion *(sententia)* is proved with many arguments. . . . In the last part of the letter he treats predestination and the call of the Gentiles. At the end he adds some παραινέσεις, that is, admonitions that shape the common life.[43]

Melanchthon's view of Romans' *status* was disarmingly simple. "The *status* of the case is that we are justified by faith. This opinion *(sententia)*

---

38. *Inst. rhet.*, fol. 8ᵛ.

39. *Inst. rhet.*, fol. 2ᵛ.

40. One could perhaps argue that Krister Stendahl's more recent arguments along the same lines ("The Apostle Paul and the Introspective Conscience of the West," *HTR* 56 [1963]: 199-215) may demonstrate his theological disposition toward Erasmus and Jerome (and away from Luther and Augustine) rather than any new insight into the text.

41. The idea of using such prefaces came originally from Jerome's introductions to the biblical letters, carefully imitated and commented upon by medieval exegetes like the *Ordinary Gloss* and Nicholas of Lyra and, more importantly, from the new introductions provided by Erasmus to his paraphrases and annotations of the New Testament.

42. *Ann. Rom.*, fol. 3ʳ.

43. *Ann. Rom.*, fol. 3ᵛ.

is proved by many arguments."[44] He repeated the point over and over. To make the transition from Rom. 1:17 to the rest of the letter, he began: "The sum *(summa)* of the *narratio:* The proposition and *status* of this disputation is that only faith in Christ is imputed for righteousness. He [Paul] puts this proposition together out of some others by using rhetorical expansion *(amplificatio)*."[45] At Rom. 3:21 he stated that "The sum *(summa)* of this text and *status* of the disputation is that righteousness is through faith in Christ."[46] Finally, at Rom. 4:1 he summarized the foregoing verses by stating, "The proposition, in which the *status* of the speech's order *(dispositio)* in this letter is contained, is concluded in chapter three, namely righteousness is faith."[47]

In this way Melanchthon communicated Luther's Reformation insight to his listeners and readers. But here, unlike even in the *Loci communes theologici,* Melanchthon was not proof-texting to demonstrate the scriptural soundness of this or that theological argument, as if to say, "What Luther said Paul says, too." Instead, he was arguing that Paul in the whole book of Romans was making Luther's very point, thus confronting the hearer or reader with a much more powerful argument: "Luther's theology witnesses to and returns to Paul's entire argument in Romans." Thus when he summarized the entire sweep of arguments in the first eleven chapters, Melanchthon wrote:

> Up to this point the Apostle has disputed concerning Grace, the Law and Predestination — *loci* so necessary for Christianity, that whoever ignores them cannot be called a Christian. And in sum, up to this point [he] has disputed concerning the gospel, that is to say, justification.[48]

Melanchthon replaced the scepticism of Erasmus regarding justification that Luther later challenged in *De libero arbitrio,* the investigation of a variety of topics found in Lefèvre or Lyra, and the unfocused glosses or homilies in patristic sources with a single theme, central to Christianity itself, which Melanchthon claimed was woven throughout the Pauline text, not simply plucked randomly out of a few verses.

This approach had far-reaching consequences for the rest of Melanchthon's exegesis. For one thing, it meant that difficult verses could be inter-

---

44. *Ann. Rom.*, fol. 3ᵛ.
45. *Ann. Rom.*, fol. 9ʳ. We will discuss the technical terms "narratio" and "amplificatio" below.
46. *Ann. Rom.*, fol. 17ᵛ.
47. *Ann. Rom.*, fol. 19ᵛ.
48. *Ann. Rom.*, fol. 63ᵛ.

preted by using the *scopus* of the letter. For another, verses thought to be less important could be and were passed over in silence, a practice about which even Calvin complained. Third, Melanchthon also used this approach with other books of the Bible.[49] These three points may clarify how Melanchthon's exegesis utilized a "canon within the canon." However forced or strained such an exegetical principle may appear today, for Melanchthon it would have involved not only discovering the *scopus* for the entire Scripture, which in his eyes was none other than the book of Romans itself, but also discovering the *scopus* for each individual book and relating it to every other book. Thus, far from doing damage to the text's meaning, this approach to the "canon within a canon" arises from Melanchthon's exegesis and sharpens the exegete's ability to discover meaning and priorities in the biblical text.

VI. The *Dispositio* of Romans

There are two other consequences of how Melanchthon concentrated the *scopus* of Romans. Melanchthon's focus upon what he considered the main themes of Paul's argument on justification — sin, law, and grace — led to the development of the *Loci communes theologici* itself, a small step toward developing a biblical theology that Melanchthon contrasted to Lombard's *Sentences*.[50] Finally, by defining the *scopus* of Romans, Melanchthon could then show how it affected Paul's message and structure for the entire book, that is, how it affected the letter's *dispositio*. Although Melanchthon did not publish a separate text showing the outline of Romans until 1529, student notes have left a remarkable monument to his attempts to provide such an outline for his early auditors.[51] Contemporary readers of the *Ann. Rom.* would also have noted numerous references to Romans' *dispositio*.

Romans 1:1-7 was labeled with the Greek term *epigraphé*. Here Melanchthon noted that Paul added a commendation of his office and a description of the gospel.[52] Romans 1:8-17 consisted of Paul's exordium, including (as a good Ciceronian exordium should) sections of *benevolentia* (praising the worth of the Romans) and *attentio* (stressing the importance

---

49. See Wengert, *Melanchthon's "Annotationes,"* pp. 183-89.

50. MSA 2/1:19. This attempt very quickly changed with the second edition of 1535, when Melanchthon shifted to a more credal organization of the *Loci*.

51. See *Texte*, pp. 20-30, 97-99.

52. *Ann. Rom.*, fol. 3ᵛ. These divisions also influenced the glosses in Luther's German translation of the New Testament.

of listening to a particularly difficult theme).[53] Paul concluded with the *propositio* or *status* in Rom. 1:17, cited above. What followed, from 1:18 to 3:20, was a "rhetorica amplificatio," to use Melanchthon's description of the *narratio*, the second main section of a speech. The first part of this *amplificatio*, namely, that Gentiles sinned, concluded in Rom. 1:32.[54] The second, coming after a *digressio* in 2:1-16, began in 2:17 with Paul's arguments that Jews also could not keep the law.

Melanchthon's comments on Rom. 3:1-8 demonstrated how important he considered this rhetorical method for clarifying obscure portions of the text.

> The beginning of chapter three is rather obscure. For this reason let us diligently consider the composition of the speech [*sermo*] and the counsel of the writer. . . . A Jew could boldly interject . . . "How do the circumcised compare with the Gentiles?" Paul responds to this objection through a rhetorical *occupatio*.[55]

Melanchthon employed a similar appeal in explaining the meaning of Rom. 2:14. Those who take this verse out of the context of Paul's overall argument abuse Paul. Thus here, too, the "ordo et ratio sermonis" must be observed.[56]

In Rom. 3:9 Paul returned to the third part of his proposition by combining the two previous sections and arguing that all people were under sin.[57] Romans 3:19 and 20 contained two further *occupationes*, before Paul reintroduced the *status disputationis* in 3:21.[58] Paul began the third section of his speech, the *confirmatio*, in chapter four. Melanchthon noted that Paul organized this section "not in a simple fashion but with *Rhetorica subiectio*,"

---

53. *Ann. Rom.*, fol. 6ʳ. In the *Inst. rhet.*, fol. 3ᵛ, Melanchthon stated that "Exordium non modo in hoc genere [demonstratio] sed in alijs etiam tribus locis constat: Beneuolentia, Attentionis, Docilitatis."

54. *Ann. Rom.*, fol. 10ᵛ.

55. *Ann. Rom.*, fol. 14ʳ. An *occupatio* is a response to an opponent's anticipated objection.

56. *Ann. Rom.*, fol. 12ʳ. "Quare cum sententia scriptorum potius petenda sit ex tota disputatione, quam ex uno aliquo uersu. Abutuntur Paulo, qui hunc unum uersiculum pro iusticia uirium humanarum probanda iactant. Iam & hic spectandus est ordo, et ratio sermonis." He mentioned a similar objection in his discussion of 1 Tim. 2:4 (fol. 52ʳ): "Proinde haec ad Timoth. sententia, sic exponenda est, ut ne pugnet cum reliquis scripturae sententijs." The appeal to context has a long tradition among literal commentators in the Middle Ages, among them Lyra, based upon Augustine's comments in *De doctrina Christiana* 3.2.4. (I am grateful to my colleague, Philip Krey, for pointing this out.)

57. *Ann. Rom.*, fol. 15ᵛ.

58. *Ann. Rom.*, fol. 17ᵛ.

in which he responds "to the Jews and everyone else who seeks a Pharisaical righteousness, merited by what they call good works."[59] In 4:16 Melanchthon recognized an "Epilogus Argumentorum" and principal conclusion, but in 5:1 Paul introduced another *propositio* to serve as a second epilogue.[60] Although Melanchthon did not employ the technical term *confutatio,* it appears that he categorized chapters 6–11 in those terms. That is, he discovered three objections "a sensu carnis" to which Paul responded. The first appeared in Romans 6, the second in Romans 7, and the third in Romans 9–11.[61]

One detects a certain shift in the tenor of the analysis here from rhetoric to dialectic, that is, from a judicial to a didactic form of speech. Paul was writing to instruct. It is little wonder that Melanchthon's introductions to these sections reflected more closely the topics in the *Loci communes theologici.* In Rom. 7:1, for example, Melanchthon discovered an axiom (7:1) followed by an *applicatio* in the rest of the chapter. In 7:8 he described what Paul had taught *(docuit)* up to this point regarding how the law reveals sin and how human nature thereby becomes angry with the law and God. In the next section Melanchthon discovered that "he declares the same notion now using a rhetorical antithesis."[62]

In 8:1 Melanchthon provided a clearer statement of Paul's arguments, using captions also found in the *Loci communes theologi:* the power of the law and sin (chap. 7) and the power of grace (chap. 8).[63] To introduce Paul's new argument, Melanchthon provided for the first time in the *Ann. Rom.* a series of numbered theses, demonstrating the power of grace and written much more in the style of didactic speech, a technique he also used in the *Loci communes theologici.*[64] As he informed his readers, his goal was "ut exacte cognoscas," the kind of clarity gained only through the proper use of dialectic.[65] In 8:6, using "splendid and plainly heroic words," Paul brought his disputation to a close with the "Rhetorical schema" of a *contentio* or *collatio,* comparing nature to the spirit.[66] From 8:12 to the end of

---

59. *Ann. Rom.,* fol. 19[v]. In the *Inst. rhet.,* fol. 21[v], Melanchthon defined a *subiectio* as "when we respond to our own question," and he gave Paul in Romans as an example.

60. *Ann. Rom.,* fols. 25[v] and 26[v].

61. *Ann. Rom.,* fols. 30[v], 34[r], and 52[v].

62. *Ann. Rom.,* fol. 37[r]. 7:10 was an epilogue to this argument (fol. 37[v]).

63. *Ann. Rom.,* fol. 39[v]: "SVPERIORI CAP. Vim legis & peccati tractauit Apostolus. Hic describit uim gratiae, quam ut exacte cognoscas, repetenda sunt quae supra dixit."

64. *Ann. Rom.,* fols. 39[v]-40[r].

65. See Wengert, *Melanchthon's "Annotationes,"* fols. 192-94.

66. *Ann. Rom.,* fol. 43[r]. A *contentio,* according to *Inst. rhet.,* fol. 23[v], is an antithesis; a *collatio* the comparison of two antithetical things. The example Melanchthon used was the *collatio* in 1 Corinthians between wisdom of the flesh and the spirit.

the chapter Paul again "rhetorico more" added a suasorial, hortative section, complete with a *propositio* (8:13), an *argumentum ab exemplo* (8:19), an *argumentum a facili* (8:26), and an *argumentum ab utili* (8:28-39), which also formed a brief *conclusio* on predestination.

Romans 9–11 dealt with the third set of "objections of the flesh" to justification, this time centering around predestination. These arguments included a *digressiuncula* in 10:14-21 and a *consolatio* for distressed consciences in 11:1-36.[67] In Romans 12–15, the disputation having been concluded, Paul turned, as was his custom, to paraenesis for the justified.[68] With that Melanchthon's comments in the *Ann. Rom.* on the *dispositio* of Romans came to a halt.

By gathering these scattered references together, we can begin to measure the true impact of Melanchthon's rhetorical method for analyzing Paul's letter. It gave the letter a powerful unity by relating everything back to the central *scopus*. It also left Paul in control of the letter as a master rhetorician and teacher, weaving his various arguments together to make a single point. Finally, it gave added punch to the polemic, by placing Paul's authority over against those who taught justification by any form of merits or works.

Another level of rhetorical analysis concerned the actual words used. Here, too, Melanchthon stressed Paul's effort. For example, when Paul employed the expression "works of the law" in Rom. 3:20, Melanchthon introduced his explanation (that the phrase denoted our attempts to fulfill the law by our own powers) with, "Paulo mos est. . . ."[69] When in Rom. 3:27 Paul spoke of the "law of faith," he was consciously misusing the term "law."[70] The notion that works receive a reward was a "vulgaris modus loquendi . . . scripturae," used not only by Paul but also by Christ.[71]

Melanchthon also discovered that Paul used other rhetorical tropes, including examples,[72] allegory,[73] and logical arguments.[74] One of the most fascinating uses of this aspect of rhetorical method came in comments on Rom. 10:6-8, where Paul had clearly "misread" Moses by referring to faith

67. *Ann. Rom.*, fols. 60^r and 60^v.
68. *Ann. Rom.*, fol. 63^v. "Hic enim fere mos est Apostolo. Primum fidem praedicare, per quam iustificatio est. Postea bona opera. Atque hoc interest inter Christianam doctrinam, et pharisaicam theologiam."
69. *Ann. Rom.*, fol. 16^v.
70. *Ann. Rom.*, fol. 19^r.
71. *Ann. Rom.*, fol. 11^v.
72. *Ann. Rom.*, fol. 60^v.
73. *Ann. Rom.*, fol. 71^v, on Rom. 13:11.
74. *Ann. Rom.*, fol. 22^r, on Rom. 4:13.

and the gospel what Deut. 30:12-13 had said about the law.[75] The options from earlier exegetical tradition, namely, to treat the text of Deuteronomy and Romans as examples of letter and spirit or of prophecy and fulfillment, had already been rejected, as we shall see below. To explain this contradiction Melanchthon turned to the practice of rhetoricians:

> Although Moses is speaking about the Law, Paul is speaking about the Gospel. . . . First it can be responded to grammatically. In this place Paul is not citing the intent [*sententia*] of Moses but is using his words in another argument altogether. As when we, too, sometimes write, we refer to the words of Cicero or Virgil, but not their intent [*sententia*].[76]

VII. The *Loci* Method

Melanchthon also found in the text of Romans Pauline definitions of terms. These went beyond rhetorical discussions of a *modus loquendi* to the heart of Melanchthon's *loci* method, that is, viewing the scriptural text as suggesting a variety of basic theological concepts. One text could suggest a variety of *loci*, or it could define a particular term and hence a particular *locus*. We find both aspects of this method operative in the *Ann. Rom.*[77] Romans 6:1 serves as a good example of the former, where Melanchthon stated that "to this text many *loci communes* run together: death, penance, baptism, burial, sabbath and similar works of the captive nature: the old and new creature; their conflict."[78]

The latter combined Melanchthon's belief that Romans belonged to the didactic genre (and hence that Paul was a teacher) with the Reformer's own work as a teacher in Wittenberg's classroom. Here again evangelical theology and Pauline thought converged and were used to refute alternative interpretations of Romans. These "Pauline" definitions of terms were also directly related in Melanchthon's mind to the *status* of Romans. Paul defined the meanings of Law, Gospel, Righteousness, Sin, Letter and Spirit, Old and New Creature, Faith, Grace — the very categories that defined the *scopus* of Romans.[79]

---

75. This had already given Nicholas of Lyra problems.

76. *Ann. Rom.*, fol. 57[r].

77. See Wengert, *Melanchthon's "Annotationes,"* pp. 182-91. The former mirrors more closely Erasmus's definition of *loci* as nestlets *(nidulae)*, that is, as general topics or categories.

78. *Ann. Rom.*, fol. 31[r].

79. Here are some examples from the *Ann. Rom.*: Gospel: fols. 5[r], 5[v], 7[v], 26[v]; Law and Gospel: fol. 7[r]; Righteousness of the Law and of Faith: fol. 7[v]; Signs: fol. 21[r-v]; the human

Comments on Rom. 1:16, 17 aptly demonstrate this method of definition. Melanchthon began his exegesis of these verses by defining the righteousness of the law as one of works and human strength and by arguing that with the gospel the "veil of Moses" had been removed and the righteousness of works condemned. He then provided two definitions, one after another, demarcated by the traditional "hoc est." "That is, that righteousness by which God justifies us, which is not of our works but of faith." There followed a second: "That is, righteousness, by which God reputes us as righteous and accepts us, is not to work but to believe." He concluded with a comment central to Luther's Reformation insight and crucial to Melanchthon's *loci* method.

> First, therefore, notice this common practice of the Scripture, that the righteousness of God is a term not for that which is in God . . . but for that by which God justifies, reputes us righteous, and accepts us.[80]

Definition not only elucidated the *scopus* and the important *loci* of Romans, it also provided Melanchthon an important vantage point from which to criticize the tradition. For example, when he encountered the word *litera* in the text of Rom. 2:27 and 7:6, he immediately contrasted it to *spiritus* and defined it as "every work, every teaching, which does not live in the heart through the Spirit."[81] At the same time he contrasted that definition to a competing one. "Here you will chiefly observe two words, letter and spirit. For the letter does not signify the literal or historical sense, as Origen thinks."[82] Here the crucial hermeneutical battle, being waged at the same time by Luther against Jerome Emser, was joined by Melanchthon at the level of definition. Once the words no longer carried the medieval, Origenistic freight, the "Pauline" (read: "evangelical") meaning could be recovered.[83] Moreover, it was precisely the *scopus* of Romans (justification by faith alone) that supported this change in definition. To Melanchthon "letter" suggested works-righteousness, not simply historical or literal.

The *loci* method Melanchthon employed also helps explain another feature of the *Ann. Rom.*, namely, the piling up of citations from other

---

being: fols. 31^r and 35^r (misnumbered 25^r); Law: fols. 23^r-25^r, 41^v; Predestination: fols. 48^v-52^v; Faith: fols. 26^r, 57^v-58^r; Cross: fol. 65^v; Magistrates: fol. 70^v.

80. *Ann. Rom.*, fol. 7^v. Cf. Martin Luther's preface to his Latin works, WA 54:179-87.

81. *Ann. Rom.*, fols. 13^r and 35^v (misnumbered 25^v)-36^r.

82. *Ann. Rom.*, fol. 13^r.

83. We will discuss Melanchthon's use of sources more fully below. In contrast, Erasmus's preface to Romans (LB 7:773-78) praised Origen's work.

portions of Scripture. At first, this may strike the modern reader as a heavy-handed form of proof-texting. However, two features stand out. First, the passages cited often support the purported Pauline argument itself. In this way Melanchthon attempted to show that Paul's argument was not unique to Scripture. In fact, the citations supported his claim that Romans was the key to Scripture. Second, the practice itself was a rhetorical technique, called a *congeries*, which Melanchthon defined in his *Institutiones rhetoricae* as "an accumulation of diverse things" around a single theme, giving Rom. 1:18-31 as an example.[84] This technique was an important component for constructing *loci communes* from the Bible.[85]

In the context of Melanchthon's own pedagogy, we must note that another purpose of his lectures was not simply to adumbrate Paul's theology but to arm his hearers against those who misused certain Pauline texts, especially in arguments against the evangelicals. Here Paul receded into the background and the needs of sixteenth-century listeners took center stage. Comments on Rom. 13:1-7 demonstrate this well. Here Melanchthon sounded a much more clearly scholastic tone, beginning with a distinction ("Dupliciter Deus [not Paul!] dicit constituere magistratum, expresso mandato [= preaching the Word], et sine mandato [= the rule of the sword]").[86] He then went to great lengths to indicate under what circumstances one must not obey the magistrates and especially papal laws, a topic completely absent from the text itself.[87] This urge to teach related directly to Melanchthon's construal of *loci communes*. Since a text belonged to a larger commonplace, the exegete could take leave of the immediate text and its author to deal with the larger, biblical topic.[88]

---

84. *Inst. rhet.*, fol. 23ᵛ.

85. Thus, Melanchthon also used the term in the *Loci communes theologici* itself at the conclusion of lists of biblical passages. See MSA 2/1:76.25 and 84.4.

86. *Ann. Rom.*, fol. 70ᵛ.

87. *Ann. Rom.*, fol. 71ʳ, where he wrote, "Si obijciatur: Obtemperandum esse legibus Papalibus propter hunc Pauli textum . . . Responde. . . ." He provided a six-point argument. For a broader discussion of this topic, see David C. Steinmetz, "Calvin and Melanchthon on Romans 13:1-7," *Ex Auditu: An Annual of the Frederick Neumann Symposium on Theological Interpretation of Scripture* 2 (1986): 74-81.

88. See Wengert, *Melanchthon's "Annotationes,"* pp. 170-91. This interpretive move, linked to Melanchthon's use of dialectics in the didactic genre, undermined the very unity of the text uncovered by his rhetorical method by treating each text as suggesting a different theological topic. Thus Melanchthon located the meaning of the text not in Paul's rhetoric but in a prefabricated set of *loci communes*.

VIII. The Exegetical Tradition in the *Annotations on Romans*

At this stage in Melanchthon's career rhetorical method still predominated, even in his use of the exegetical tradition. Although a thorough examination of Melanchthon's sources in the *Ann. Rom.* goes beyond the scope of this essay, the few explicit references to the tradition paint a vivid picture of Melanchthon's threefold engagement with the history of interpretation of Romans.[89] First, where Melanchthon's interpretation took on the flavor of classroom lecture and focused on a particular *locus communis*, he used patristic exegesis and authority to support his theology and terminology. This was particularly the case for comments on predestination, where he used Augustine's argument that God did things "non permissiue, sed potenter" to reject scholastic terminology and where he cited both (pseudo-) Augustine and Ambrose to interpret the text of 1 Tim. 2:4.[90]

Second, Melanchthon could also employ the exegetical tradition in ways that supported his own exegetical method. An older exegete could be baffled by a text that Melanchthon's method easily interpreted.[91] Or he could delight in Paul's argument.[92] This enjoyment of Paul's arguments was, of course, precisely what Melanchthon hoped his approach would also accomplish in his hearers and readers. Thus Augustine's own delight gave just that much more authority to Melanchthon's method. Or an ancient interpreter could, like Melanchthon, simply have gotten it right in contrast to the later tradition.[93]

Third, Melanchthon could also take on the exegetical tradition. Origen misunderstood the nature of Paul's servitude in Rom. 1:1.[94] He also

---

89. Among his sources were Luther, Erasmus, Theophylact (who summarized Chrysostom), and Augustine. He certainly also knew exegetical arguments found in Nicholas of Lyra.

90. *Ann. Rom.*, fols. 50^r and 51^r, respectively. In the same context (fol. 49^r), he also referred to Hilary's interpretation of Psalm 113 (Vulg.) and Augustine.

91. *Ann. Rom.*, fol. 12^r. "Torsit haec sententia [Rom. 2:14] Augustinum, varie & multipliciter."

92. *Ann. Rom.*, fol. 22^v, citing *De spiritu et litera*. "Hoc Enthymema [in Rom. 4:13] mire delectauit Augustinum." An enthymeme was a type of syllogism, used in the didactic genre of speech. See the *Compendiaria dialectices ratio* (CR 20:743-45), first published in 1520.

93. On Rom. 4:16 (*Ann. Rom.*, fol. 25^v) Augustine "acute illum locum enarrat" in contrast to those who defined penance in terms of our own satisfactions (fol. 26^r). Melanchthon also cited Theophylact positively on Rom. 5:3 (fol. 28^r).

94. *Ann. Rom.*, fol. 4^v. "Quare quae de seruitute legis hic disserit Origines, parum ad rem faciunt." Erasmus was not nearly as critical, stating merely that he preferred "simpler things." See *Erasmus' Annotations on the New Testament: Acts — Romans — I and II Corinthians*, ed. Anne Reeve and M. A. Screech (Leiden: E. J. Brill, 1990), p. 335.

failed to grasp the Pauline contrast of letter and spirit. Jerome's statement anathematizing those who claimed the law was impossible to fulfill had been abused by the later tradition, so Melanchthon glossed the saint's opinion by limiting it to what was possible *per gratiam*.[95] In one case he even objected to Erasmus's translation (Rom. 13:11).[96]

These objections marked Melanchthon off from Erasmus and others who preferred to work with a consensus of authorities in their interpretation of the biblical text.[97] Here Melanchthon began to articulate a view of church history that saw the gospel under continual attack and in constant need of restoration by God, who worked through chosen instruments (the prophets, Christ, Augustine, Luther). Origen and those who followed him, such as Jerome, were most suspect. The *sententia Pauli* or *scopus epistulae* stood opposed to those exegetes like Origen who, misled by human reason, did not understand the law in Romans to include moral commands and could not properly distinguish law and gospel or letter and spirit.[98] However, Melanchthon was not simply concerned with past exegetes but with the impact such wrongheaded interpretation was having in the present. For example, on Rom. 6:14 he complained,

> The disputation concerning the law is well-known, in which nothing correct has been produced by modern theologians, who speak only of the abrogation of ceremonies and claim that [in the gospel] the moral law not only is not abrogated but also actually increases.[99]

Comments on Rom. 7:1-6 echoed the same sentiment in connection with the *scopus* of Romans. After reminding his listeners of the topics covered in the earlier parts of Romans, he concluded that philosophy's link between virtue and law was broken by the simple example from experience given by Paul.

---

95. *Ann. Rom.*, fol. 41^v.

96. *Ann. Rom.*, fol. 69^v. "Erasmus legit tempori seruientes, alias legitur domino seruientes. Lectio uetus magis arridet mihi. . . ." It does not seem that he even used Erasmus's translation in his lectures on John. See Wengert, *Melanchthon's "Annotationes,"* pp. 124-34.

97. Cf. n. 24.

98. For the explication of this central vision in Melanchthon, see Peter Fraenkel, *Testimonium Patrum: The Function of the Patristic Argument in the Theology of Philip Melanchthon* (Geneva: Droz, 1961).

99. *Ann. Rom.*, fol. 32^v. This formed an entire section in the *Loci communes theologici* (MSA 2/1:125-37).

We have already said more than enough concerning the nature and power of the law, because it is the law's property to show sin and by showing sin to increase it. By this approach [*sententia*] the whole of philosophy and indeed all human reason is overturned, which figures the law is nothing else than a means to attain virtue. . . . Not one of all the books by any of the pagans or scholastics has been produced that had to do with this nature of the law, despite the fact that even experience itself [in the remarriage of widows] teaches this.[100]

This comment brings us full circle. Not only Luther in his epistle dedicatory, but Melanchthon himself argued that something new had transpired in his annotations on Romans. The hegemony of Aristotelian philosophy and the consensus of theologians (especially those under Origen's spell) had broken down in favor of what he viewed as a simple and clear reading of the Apostle. The key to that reading — rhetoric — far from being an arcane method privy to a few, was at the beck and call of every student with an arts degree, perhaps especially the ones trained under Melanchthon at the University of Wittenberg. Paul had finally become the orator Augustine had wanted him to be, and as orator Melanchthon made him speak to the theological debates of the Reformation in a clear, evangelical voice. In the history of biblical interpretation scarcely any exegetes have produced as seamless a translation for their audience.

100. *Ann. Rom.*, fol. 34$^\text{v}$.

The Chronology of John 5–7:
Martin Bucer's Commentary (1528-36)
and the Exegetical Tradition[1]

IRENA BACKUS

VIRTUALLY ALL THE Reformers found themselves employed in a remarkable diversity of roles, but Martin Bucer illustrates the tendency especially well. Deeply impressed by his encounter with the writings and person of Martin Luther, Bucer was released from his Dominican profession in 1521 and within a few years had risen to prominence among the Reformers of Strasbourg. Bucer's Lutheranism was soon replaced by more Zwinglian inclinations, though he attempted to mediate between the two at Marburg; indeed, in later years he often journeyed afar in his efforts to reconcile Lutherans and Catholics with Reformed Christians. In 1549, however, the unpleasant terms of the Augsburg Interim induced him to leave Strasbourg for Cambridge, where he offered his services to Cranmer and the English Reformation until his death. For thirty years, then, Bucer labored variously as a Reformer, pastor, teacher, writer, liturgist, ecumenist, and diplomat.[2]

---

1. Except for the introductory paragraph and some minor revisions, this essay originally appeared (in French) in *Bucer apocryphe et authentique: Études de bibliographie et d'exégèse*, Cahiers de la Revue de théologie et de philosophie, 8 (Geneva-Lausanne-Neuchâtel: Revue de théologie et de philosophie, 1983), pp. 41-50. This translation was prepared by John L. Farthing.

2. Bucer's life has received a fair amount of attention, including several notable biographies. In English, shorter accounts may be found in David C. Steinmetz, "Martin Bucer (1491-1551): The Church and the Social Order," in *Reformers in the Wings* (Philadelphia: Fortress, 1971), pp. 121-32; and David F. Wright, "Martin Bucer 1491-1551: Ecumenical

But above all, it was his work as an interpreter of Scripture that undergirded his other interests and efforts, and in the course of his career he composed commentaries (sometimes more than one) on Judges, the Psalms, Zephaniah, all four Gospels, Romans, and Ephesians.[3] This essay will examine a distinctive feature of his commentary on the Gospel of John, which first appeared in 1528 but was revised in 1530 and again in 1536.

In the first edition of his commentary on the Fourth Gospel,[4] commenting on John 7:1ff., Bucer proposes a change in the chronological order of the events narrated in John 5–7:

> Earlier in the fifth chapter [cf. John 5:16] the Evangelist has said that the Jews wished to kill the Lord for healing on the Sabbath a man who had been sick for thirty-eight years [John 5:5] and for making himself equal to the Father [John 5:18]. These things he recalls here with just a word to indicate the reason why he was in Galilee at that time. In the previous chapter, the Evangelist describes the miracle of the loaves as taking place just as the feast of the Passover was drawing near [cf. John 6:4], and he does not record whether Jesus actually went up to the feast in Jerusalem. Hence I conjecture that the Evangelist has made a μετάστασις, that is, a transposition, in his narrative. For the things that are described in chapter five as taking place during a feast of the Jews happened, I believe, at the feast of Pentecost, whereas previously, when the Passover was approaching, he had fed the five thousand in Galilee, beyond Lake Gennesaret, which the Evangelist calls "the Sea of Tiberias" (John 6:1). In this seventh

Theologian," in idem, *Common Places of Martin Bucer* (Abingdon: Sutton Courtenay Press, 1972), pp. 17-71. The standard English biography is still Hastings Eells, *Martin Bucer* (New Haven: Yale University Press, 1931), but there are several more recent specialized studies of Bucer's career and teachings, particularly Martin Greschat, *Martin Bucer. Ein Reformator und seine Zeit* (Munich: Beck, 1990); and Christian Krieger and Marc Lienhard (eds.), *Martin Bucer and Sixteenth-Century Europe*, 2 vols. (Leiden: Brill, 1993).

3. Of Bucer's commentaries, only the one on John has appeared in a modern edition (*Enarratio in Evangelion Iohannis*, ed. Irena Backus [Leiden: Brill, 1988]). The critical edition of Bucer's works is *Martini Buceri Opera omnia*, comprising three still-incomplete series: the *Deutsche Schriften* (Gutersloh: G. Mohn, 1960-), the *Opera Latina* (Leiden: Brill, 1982-), and the *Correspondance de Martin Bucer* (Leiden: Brill, 1979-). Bibliography pertaining to Bucer is indexed in several works, most notably Robert Stupperich, *Bibliographia Bucerana*, Schriften des Vereins für Reformationsgeschichte, 169 (Gütersloh: C. Bertelsmann, 1952), pp. 39-96; cf. also "Bucer-Bibliographie 1951-1974," in *Bucer und seine Zeit: Forschungsbeiträge und Bibliographie*, ed. Marijn de Kroon und Friedhelm Krüger (Wiesbaden: Franz Steiner, 1976), pp. 133-65.

4. *Enarratio in Evangelion Iohannis* (Strasbourg: Ioh. Hervagius, April 1528), fol. 151[r-v]. The following passage has been translated from Bucer, *Enarratio in Evangelion Iohannis*, ed. Backus, pp. 289-90, where the text is from Bucer's third edition (Strasbourg: Ioh. Hervagius, September 1536), with variant readings from previous editions noted in the apparatus.

chapter the things are mentioned by which Jesus had aroused the Jews, in the fifth chapter, to want to kill him; clearly, then, it is reasonable to suppose that the things narrated in this chapter took place in that Feast of Tabernacles which came right after the Pentecost in which, as I see it, Jesus did the things that are mentioned in the fifth chapter.

For it does not seem to me likely that Jesus would have been absent from any feast in Jerusalem that the Law required him to attend. Since, therefore, we find here a description of his reason for being in Galilee (because the Jews desired to kill him) and since it is clear from the contents of chapter seven that their desire to kill him was based on the things mentioned in the fifth chapter, namely, his violation of the Sabbath, it may be inferred that the Lord did not appear in Jerusalem after the festival at which he had healed the sick man [cf. John 5:16]. Now if it is not fitting to say that he simply disregarded the Law, it must be admitted that the feast in which he healed the sick man was just before the Feast of Tabernacles; hence it was the Feast of Pentecost. Otherwise we would have to say either that Jesus was not in Jerusalem for a whole year, and thus violated the Law twice, or else that he had been there but that no charges had been lodged against him for violating the Sabbath. That, however, would seem highly improbable. The fact that the people of Jerusalem were saying, "Is this not the one whom they are seeking to kill? And here he is, speaking openly," etc. (John 7:25-26) and also the fact that the Lord explicitly apologizes for what the Jews regarded as a violation of the Sabbath (John 7:23), suggests that in reality the things narrated in the fifth chapter happened not long before the events recounted in this chapter. But no one who has looked quite carefully at the writings of the Evangelists will be surprised to find such transposition of events in the evangelical histories. For they were intent upon extolling the excellence of Christ, and not upon describing each thing in precise sequence.

In other words, according to Bucer, this is the real chronology of John, chapters five to seven:

- John 6: the feeding of the five thousand in Galilee just before Passover.
- John 5: the healing of the sick man in Jerusalem at Pentecost.
- John 7: Jesus addresses the Jews in Jerusalem at the Feast of Tabernacles shortly after Pentecost.

The passage cited above remains unchanged, except for certain grammatical corrections, in the two later editions of *John* (1530 and 1536)

143

that appeared during Bucer's lifetime.[5] Here we will discuss, first, the chronology of chapters 5–7 as presented in the Johannine commentaries,[6] both patristic and medieval, that were accessible to Bucer, and then the specific characteristics of Bucer's appropriation of the patristic and medieval traditions, as compared to that which is seen in his contemporaries who also wrote commentaries on the Fourth Gospel (Lefèvre d'Etaples [1523], Philip Melanchthon [1523, 1546], Erasmus [1524, 1527], Iohannes Brenz [1528], and Iohannes Oecolampadius [1533]).

I. The Patristic Tradition

Irenaeus's *Adversus haereses* was published for the first time at Basle in 1526, in an edition prepared by Erasmus.[7] Here the bishop of Lyons discusses the chronology of John 5–6 in the context of his attack on a heresy according to which Christ would have been crucified sometime during the twelfth month after his baptism. He arranges the events in the following order: Christ went up to Jerusalem for the first time on the occasion of the Passover after he had changed the water into wine (John 2:23). When he went to Jerusalem for the second time, it was also "on the day of the Feast of the Passover," when he healed the sick man at the pool (John 5:1ff.). *After* this miracle, says Irenaeus, Christ went across the Sea of Tiberias, and it is there that he fed the five thousand (John 6:1ff.).[8] Finally, he returned to Jerusalem for the third time, again for the Passover, shortly before his death (cf. John 12:1; 13:1).[9] By counting the month of the paschal feast as the first month of the year, Irenaeus implies that the ministry of Jesus Christ lasted about two and a half years, not one year, as the Gnostics would have it.

John Chrysostom's commentary on the Fourth Gospel was accessible to Bucer in a Latin version by Franciscus Aretinus, published at Basle by

5. *Enarrationes perpetuae in sacra quatuor Evangelia* (Strasbourg: Georg Ulr. Andlanus, March 1530) and *Enarrationes . . .* (Basel: Ioh. Hervagius, September 1536): both of these works include Bucer's commentary on the Synoptic Gospels, first published in 1527, together with his commentary on John.

6. In the preface to the first edition (fol. 8^r), Bucer mentions the commentaries of Chrysostom, Augustine, Erasmus, and Melanchthon. In 1536, he added Brenz's commentary to the list. Nonnus's *Paraphrase* (edited in 1527 by Melanchthon) is frequently cited in Bucer's text.

7. *Opus eruditissimum divi Irenaei . . . emendatum opera Des. Erasmi Roterodami* (Basel: Froben, 1526).

8. Some of the Greek manuscripts omit all reference to τὸ πάσχα in John 6:4; cf. Aland and Nestle, in loc., and C. K. Barrett, *The Gospel According to St. John* (London, 1958), p. 228.

9. Irenaeus, *Adv. haeres.* 2.22 (PG 7:782-83).

Andreas Cratander in 1522.[10] In commenting on John 5:1, Chrysostom takes the view that "the feast day of the Jews" is the Pentecost, but he furnishes no proof for this conjecture.[11] He affirms that Jesus was *often* (but not always!) present at the legal feasts, so as not to violate the law and also to attract a greater number of hearers. He says, moreover, that a year passed between the healing of the sick man in John 5:1ff. and the Feast of the Passover mentioned in John 6:4.[12]

To explain the absence of Jesus from the Feast of the Passover in John 6:4, Chrysostom is content to say that he abolished the law little by little, all the while taking advantage of the spitefulness of the Jews.[13] With regard to John 7:1, Chrysostom explains that five months passed between the events described in John 6:4 (which took place at the time of the Passover) and the Feast of Tabernacles, which provides the context for John 7. According to the Greek father, this interval does not signify a lack of activity on Jesus' part, and he emphasizes that the task of the Evangelists was not to relate all the events in the Savior's life but to focus on those that make manifest the opposition of the Jews.[14] Thus, according to Chrysostom, the chronology is as follows:

- John 2:23 — The Passover in the spring of the same year in which Jesus was baptized.
- John 5:1 — The Feast of Pentecost in the summer of the same year.
- John 6:4 — The Passover of the following year.
- John 7:1 — The Feast of Tabernacles of the same year as John 6:4.

Keeping in mind John 12:1 and 13:1, we establish that, according to Chrysostom (who agrees here with Irenaeus), the ministry of Jesus lasted for about two and a half years.

The John commentary by Cyril of Alexandria was published for the first time in 1508 in a Latin translation by George of Trebizond.[15] Cyril,

10. Published in a Latin version in the *Opera* of Chrysostom; cf. Dom Chr. Baur, *Saint Jean Chrysostome et ses oeuvres dans l'histoire littéraire* (Louvain/Paris, 1907), p. 152 (no. 76).

11. Chrysostom, *Homilia* 36 (35) in PG 59:203.

12. Chrysostom, *Homilia* 42 (41) in PG 59:239-40.

13. Chrysostom, *Homilia* 42 (41) in PG 59:239-40.

14. Chrysostom, *Homilia* 48 (47) in PG 59:269-70.

15. Bucer may have had access to the 1524 edition, published in Basel by Cratander: *Divi Cyrilli . . . In Evangelium Ioannis commentaria. . . . In quibus multa habentur adiecta . . . praesertim in quatuor libris intermediis, ad eosdem commentarios per Iudocum Clichtoveum superadditis. . . . Opus insigne quod thesaurus inscribitur. . . . Insuper in Leviticum libri XVI. . . .*

like Irenaeus, identifies the "feast day" of John 6:4 as Pentecost. He justifies this conjecture by saying that Pentecost is the feast that directly follows the paschal feast mentioned in John 2:23.[16] The text of the Gospel that he, like Irenaeus, is following omits all reference to the paschal feast in John 6:4; accordingly, Cyril views the events of this chapter as the direct consequence of the healing of the sick man in John 5:1ff.[17] With little concern for problems of chronology, he interprets the flight of Jesus (in John 6:1ff.) as an example that authorizes Christians to flee in times of persecution. He does not raise the question of chronology in John 7:1ff.

Among the Latin fathers available to Bucer, Augustine's commentary on John and his *Harmony of the Gospels (De Consensu Evangelistarum)* make no reference to questions of chronology in John 5–7. Jerome, who raises the problem in his commentary on Daniel,[18] follows Eusebius in affirming that according to the witness of the Fourth Gospel the ministry of Jesus lasted three and a half years. Jerome does not enter into a detailed discussion of the Johannine chronology. We can arrive at a total of three and a half years, however, only by assuming that John 5:1ff. took place during the Passover — which implies a total of four Passovers (John 2:23; 5:1; 6:4; 13:1).

II. The Medieval Tradition

Bucer had access to the works of Theophylact (considered in the sixteenth century to be one of the ancient fathers) in a translation by Oecolampadius.[19] In his commentary on John, Theophylact follows the chronology of Chrysostom in identifying the feast mentioned in John 5:1ff. as the Feast of Pentecost.[20] The *Pascha* in John 6:4 is the Passover of the same year.[21] As in Chrysostom's commentary, there is an interval of five months between the *Pascha* of John 6:4 and the Feast of Tabernacles mentioned in John

16. Cyril, *In Evangelium Ioannis* 5:5-6 (PG 73:337-38).

17. Cyril, *In Evangelium Ioannis* 6:2-4 (PG 73:441-44).

18. Jerome, *In Dan.* 9:24ff. (PL 25:547-58; CCSL 75A:875-78). The *Opera omnia* of Jerome were available in Erasmus's edition (Basel: Froben, 1516).

19. *In quatuor Evangelia enarrationes Joanne Oecolampadio interprete* (Basel: A. Cratander, March 1524).

20. Theophylact, *In Iohannem* 5:1ff. in loc. in PG 123:1257-58. Like Chrysostom, Theophylact emphasizes that Jesus was present there so as not to transgress the law and in order to attract a large audience.

21. Theophylact, *In Iohannem* 6:4 in loc. in PG 123:1283-84.

7:1ff. Theophylact's explanation of this interval and the absence of Jesus from the paschal feast in John 6:4 is the same as Chrysostom's.

St. Thomas Aquinas, in his commentary on the Fourth Gospel, associates himself with the chronology and exegesis of Chrysostom. The feast of John 5:1ff. is once again interpreted as Pentecost: Jesus is present in order to obey the law and to proclaim the gospel to the greatest possible number of hearers.[22] According to Thomas (who agrees here with Chrysostom), the absence of Jesus from Jerusalem in John 6:4 indicates that he intended to abolish the law gradually.[23] Here again an interval of five months separates the Passover of John 6:4 from the Feast of Tabernacles in John 7:1ff. This interval is justified by reference to Chrysostom. Hence it comes as no surprise that Chrysostom's commentary serves as the principal source for St. Thomas's *Golden Chain (Catena aurea)* in all questions regarding the chronology and exegesis of John 5–7. On John 5:1, the text cited by Thomas is Chrysostom's Homily 36 (35), where reference is made to Pentecost.[24] Commenting on John 6:4, Thomas bases his discussion on Chrysostom's Homily 42 (41), which affirms that one year passed between the healing of the sick man in John 5:1ff. and the Passover, at which Jesus was not present, because he abolished the law "gradually" *(paulatim)*. On the question of the annulment of the law, Thomas adds the witness of Theophylact, who emphasizes that "when the truth comes, every shadow passes away" *(veritate adveniente omnis cessat figura)*. Finally, he cites the witness of the Venerable Bede, who shows, on the basis of the report in Matt. 14:13, that a year elapsed between the beheading of John the Baptist and the passion of Christ, and that both events took place at the time of the Passover.[25] On John 7:1, it is once again Chrysostom who is cited (in Homily 48 [47]) to support the view that five months elapsed between John 6:4 and John 7:1.[26] We may conclude, therefore, that Thomas is more concerned with chronological questions in his *Catena* than in his commentary on John; he follows Chrysostom's chronology, while appealing to Bede for his interpretation of the interval between the events of John 6:4ff. and the passion of Christ.

---

22. Thomas Aquinas, *In Iohannem Evangelistam Expositio* 5:1ff. in loc.: *Lectio prima*, in Thomas Aquinas, *Opera omnia* [Editio Piana] (Rome, 1570-71), vol. 14:2, fol. 30^r, col. A-B.

23. Aquinas, *In Iohannem* 6:4ff. in loc.: *Lectio prima, Editio Piana* 14:2, fol. 36^v, col. B.

24. Thomas Aquinas, *Catena aurea*, ed. Guarienti, 2 vols. (Turin and Rome, 1953), 2:397, col. A.

25. Aquinas, *Catena aurea*, 2:412, col. B–2:414, col. A.

26. Aquinas, *Catena aurea*, 2:432, col. A-B.

According to Thomas, the ministry of Jesus comprised two and a half years.

The *Ordinary Gloss* makes no mention of chronology.[27] Nicholas of Lyra follows Chrysostom in placing the healing of the sick man at Pentecost. Commenting on John 6:4, he mentions the Passover, but his main purpose is to account for the absence of Jesus. For this he sees two main causes. First, those who had mortal enemies *(inimicitias capitales)* were excused from the feasts prescribed in the law. Second, Christ was obligated to obey the law according to his human nature, but he was also obliged to violate it from time to time in order to show his divine nature. On John 7:1, Nicholas of Lyra makes no reference to the question of chronology.

We find a curious testimony from Rupert of Deutz, whose commentary on the Fourth Gospel was published for the first time in 1526 at Cologne in an edition by Johannes Cochlaeus.[28] Rupert places the events of John 5:1 at the time of the Passover. He justifies this suggestion by referring to John 4:35, which speaks of a harvest that is to take place in four months. This means, according to Rupert, that John 4:35 took place two months before the Feast of the Passover,[29] which was the one mentioned in John 5:1. Commenting on John 6:4, Rupert is especially concerned to present the Jewish Passover as a prefiguration of the death of Christ[30]; the question of chronology is not taken up again in John 7:1.[31] Placing John 5:1 at the time of the Passover, Rupert is following in the steps of Eusebius and Jerome. In light of John 2:23 and 13:1, this means that according to Rupert, along with Jerome, the Gospel of John mentions four paschal feasts; thus the ministry of Jesus lasted not for two and a half but for three and a half years.

In the fifteenth and early sixteenth centuries, the most important source for the life of Jesus was the *Vita Christi* by Ludolphus of Saxony, who flourished around 1330.[32] Bucer himself owned a copy of the 1516

27. *Opus praeclarum totius Biblie cum glosulis tam marginalibus quam interlinearibus* (Basel: I. Froben, 1502), vol. 4, in loc.

28. Rupert of Deutz, *Commentaria in Evangelium Sancti Iohannis* (Cologne: F. Birkmann, 1526). There are a few traces of influence of this commentary in Bucer's, but it would be incorrect to argue that it was one of his principal sources.

29. Rupert of Deutz, *Commentaria in Evangelium Sancti Iohannis,* John 4:35 in loc. in PL 170:390 (CCCM 9:241).

30. Rupert of Deutz, John 6:4 in loc. in PL 170:440 (CCCM 9:304).

31. Cf. Rupert of Deutz, John 7:1 in loc. in PL 170:502 (CCCM 9:383-84).

32. I refer here to the modern edition: *Ludolphus de Saxonia: Vita Jesu Christi,* ed. L. M. Rigollot, 4 vols. (Paris/Brussels, 1878), with thanks to P. Fraenkel and R. G. Hobbs for having drawn my attention to Bucer's use of this work.

edition of the *Vita*.[33] In the *Preface*, Ludolphus explains the method that he has adopted for elaborating his chronology of the life of Jesus:

> But before we proceed to the narrative of the Gospel, you should know that some things were beneficially presented by the Evangelists, at the direction of the Holy Spirit, sometimes anticipating or foreshadowing things that were going to be said afterward and sometimes repeating or recapitulating things that had already been said. It would not be fitting for these things to be written differently than they were written by these authors, as they were expressed in the way that was most advantageous. For according to Augustine it is likely that each of the Evangelists believed that he had to follow the order that God saw fit to suggest to his recollection. Yet in order to avoid disturbing the devotion of the weaker brethren, in places where it was deemed necessary, because either the event itself or perhaps the most suitable way of expressing it seemed to require a different order, some episodes are located in the midst of events that followed them in the actual historical sequence. Yet I do not affirm that this is the true and certain and due order of the reported events as they actually happened, since such exactitude is hardly to be found in any account.[34]

According to Ludolphus, then, there are two levels of interpretation of the Gospels: (a) the divine truth that remains independent of all historical questions, and (b) the matter of chronology. Historical and chronological details may be modified "insofar as the matter itself or narrative considerations seem to require it, so that the faith of the weaker brethren may not be disturbed." And in fact he does modify the order of the events in John 5–7. The Feast of the Passover in John 6:4 comes a year after that of John 2:23,[35] although the healing of the sick man in John 5:1 takes place at Pentecost, a few months *after* the Passover of John 6:4.[36] The Feast of

---

33. Printed in Paris by J. Badius. This edition was identified by Peter Fraenkel as being Bucer's on the basis of the pagination given in the Strasbourg Reformer's *Florilegium Patristicum*, ed. P. Fraenkel (Leiden: Brill, 1988).

34. Ludolphus of Saxony, *Vita Jesu Christi*, 1:10, col. A-B; cf. Eusebius (-Rufinus), *Hist. eccl.* 3.24 (Griechischen christlichen Schriftsteller 9:2.245-49).

35. Ludolphus of Saxony, *Vita Jesu Christi*, pars I, cap. 67 (ed. Rigollot, 2:166, col. A): "Istud erat secundum festum paschale, et in eo non fuit Dominus in Ierusalem. Sicut enim servando Legem ostendebat se esse verum hominem de filiis Israel secundum carnem: sic aliquando, praetermittendo observationem eius ostendebat se esse Deum, supra Legem."

36. Ludolphus of Saxony, *Vita Jesu Christi*, pars I, cap. 78 (ed. Rigollot, 2:243-44): "*Post haec erat* [etc.] scilicet Pentecostes. . . . Ad dies festos Iudaeorum Dominus ascendit homo cum hominibus solemnitates celebrans, et cum eis dies festos agens, ne Legi contrarius videretur, et ut populis undique tunc confluentibus fidei doctrinam annuntiaret. . . ."

Tabernacles in John 7:1 is positioned after the healing of the sick man.[37] Ludolphus remains in the tradition of Chrysostom in identifying the feast of John 5:1 as Pentecost,[38] but he cites no authority for changing the chronological order. This change means that Jesus' ministry still includes three paschal feasts (John 2:23; 6:4; 12:3), the events of John 5:1 taking place at Pentecost in the same year as the Passover of John 6:4.

III. The Sixteenth-Century Tradition: The Johannine Literature, 1523-28

The commentators of this era reveal, in general, very little interest in questions of chronology. Lefèvre d'Etaples follows Chrysostom in locating the "feast day" of John 5:1 at Pentecost of the same year as the Passover of John 2:23. He also says that the Feast of the Passover mentioned in John 6:4 is the *second* after the baptism of Christ.[39] Melanchthon, in his *Annotationes* on John published at Basle in 1523, makes no reference to chronology; the same is true for the *Annotationes* of Erasmus.[40] In the *Paraphrases* of 1524, Erasmus follows Chrysostom and Cyril in locating the "feast day" *(dies festus)* of John 5:1 at Pentecost,[41] but the whole question of chronology is once again ignored. Brenz, in his commentary on John, published for the first time by J. Secerius at Hagenau in 1527 and reissued in January 1528, merely mentions Pentecost as the context of John 5:1 without discussing the chronological details.[42]

Bucer is the only exegete of this period who tries to establish the chronology of John 5–7. He follows the tradition of Chrysostom (and Cyril)

---

37. Ludolphus of Saxony, *Vita Jesu Christi*, pars I, cap. 82 (ed. Rigollot, 2:273ff.).

38. This is also the case in Petrus Comestor's *Historia scholastica*, cap. 81 on John 5:1 (PL 198:1578), which nevertheless does not change the order of events in John 5–7. In the *Monotessaron* (printed as early as 1480) Pseudo-Gerson does not identify the feast of John 5:1, and his chronology includes three Passovers (John 2:23; 6:4; 13:1). Nor does he makes any further attempt to alter the order of events in John 5–7; see *Opera omnia . . . in V tomos distributa*, ed. E. L. DuPin (Antwerp, 1706), tom. 4, cap. 18, col. 111; cap. 47, col. 130; cap. 50, col. 132; cap. 77, cols. 148-49; cap. 137, col. 183.

39. Lefèvre d'Etaples, *Commentarii initiatorii in quatuor Evangelia* (Basel: A. Cratander, 1523), John 5:1 (fol. 306ʳ); John 6:4 (fol. 313ʳ).

40. Melanchthon does not so much as mention the textual variant of John 6:4, even though he knows Cyril and Irenaeus.

41. Erasmus, *Paraphrases*, John 5:1, in loc. (LB 7:533).

42. Johannes Brenz, *In D. Iohannis Evangelion I'is B'ii Exegesis per autorem diligenter revisa ac multis in locis locupletata* (Hagenau: Ioh. Secer, 1528), fol. 75ᵛ.

in identifying the feast of John 5:1 with Pentecost, and he transposes the order of John 5 and John 6 (here following Ludolphus's *Vita*). Like Ludolphus, he sees nothing illegitimate in these chronological changes, since the divine truth of the Gospel remains intact. Nevertheless, Bucer's narrative differs from that of Ludolphus in several important respects. It is remarkable that Bucer justifies a change in the sequence of events by referring to the internal coherence of the Gospel narrative. In John 5:1 and in John 7:1ff., the Jews seek to kill Jesus because he has violated the Sabbath. Here is the proof, says Bucer, that Jesus was absent from Jerusalem after the healing of the sick man at Pentecost, and that he came back to Jerusalem for the following feast (in the same year), which was the Feast of Tabernacles. Bucer is opposed to Chrysostom's chronology, which retains an interval of one year between John 5:1 and John 6:4. This would imply, says Bucer, either that Jesus was absent from *two* feasts required by the law (the Feast of Tabernacles, which came *immediately after* Pentecost, in John 5:1, and the Passover in John 6:4), or that he would have visited the city without any attempt at retaliation on the part of the Jews. This latter hypothesis is highly improbable in light of John 7:23-26. With regard to the suggestion that Jesus was absent from two feasts in the same year, Bucer rejects out of hand Chrysostom's idea that Christ was obliged in his human nature to be present at only some of the Jewish feasts, since, according to his divine nature, he was about to abolish the law. That is why Bucer here places greater emphasis on the human nature of Christ than do his predecessors and contemporaries. This exegetical approach is not difficult to explain if we bear in mind that his commentary is to a great extent a work of anti-Lutheran polemic, even if he did see fit, in the third edition, to suppress some of the polemical materials *(excursus)* that were especially offensive after the Concord of Wittenberg (29 May 1536).[43] It is clear that Bucer wrote his commentary in response to that of Brenz.[44] And it is quite remarkable to find that Brenz, commenting on John 6:4 and John 7:1, stresses the divine nature of Christ and his first mission, which was to *abolish* the law.[45]

43. This concerned particularly the eucharistic passages — John 6:53ff.; cf. Ian Hazlett, "Zur Auslegung von Johannes 6 bei Bucer während der Abendmahlskontroverse," in *Bucer und seine Zeit*, ed. M. de Kroon and F. Krüger (Wiesbaden, 1976), pp. 74ff.

44. This is particularly evident when one examines closely the textual relationships between the two commentaries on John 6:53ff.

45. Cf. Brenz, *In D. Iohannis Evangelion*, John 7:1ff. in loc.: "Atque hoc festum in Lege septem diebus semel in anno in praeteriti beneficii a Deo accepti monumentum celebratum est: non enim habemus hic manentem civitatem sed celestem patriam quaerimus."

IV. The Commentaries of Oecolampadius (1533) and Melanchthon (1546)

In his commentary, published in Basle in 1533, Oecolampadius criticizes Bucer's preoccupation with chronology (without, however, mentioning him by name).[46] Commenting on John 5:1ff. (fol. 143ᵛ), he says:

> Some think that the feast was Pentecost, and thus that in a few days Christ went up to Jerusalem again [for the Feast of Tabernacles]. But it is more likely that it was the Passover. But, as he went up to Jerusalem again in the following year, it is normally concluded that Jesus preached for three years and a half, based on the number of his visits to Jerusalem. The feast day *(dies festus)* of John 5:1, however, is unspecified; it provides no evidence, therefore, bearing on the question of chronology.

In John 6:4 (fol. 110ᵛ), Oecolampadius simply says, without being very specific, "It is certain that this miracle took place at some time from Christ's first going up to Jerusalem." But he returns to a critical approach in John 7:1ff. (fol. 143ᵛ): "Certain ones [i.e., Bucer] deem the order of events to be in some way confused, as this happens not infrequently with the Evangelists. This, however, is by no means certain, etc." In the reference to "a few days" *(paucis diebus)* of John 5:1, Oecolampadius can mean only Bucer's chronology, since, according to Chrysostom's reckoning, there would have been an interval of more than a year (at least according to the Gospel narratives) before Jesus' next visit to Jerusalem. Oecolampadius himself tends toward the chronology of Eusebius and Jerome (as reported by Rupert of Deutz), according to which the ministry of Jesus would have lasted three and a half years. When he mentions, in commenting on John 7:1, "those who find that the order of events is confused," he seems to be warning Bucer against modifications that are too daring.

It is not entirely clear to what degree Melanchthon's commentary represents a response to Bucer.[47] It is in this commentary that Melanchthon attempts to elucidate the chronology of John 5–7 and the length of Jesus' ministry. He maintains the order of the Gospel narrative and claims that the healing of the sick man in John 5:1 took place at Pentecost, explicitly

---

46. Johannes Oecolampadius, *Annotationes piae ac doctae in Evangelium Ioannis* (Basel: A. Cratander, 1533).

47. First published in Strasbourg in Caspar Cruciger's edition. We follow the text in CR.

basing his opinion on the authority of Cyril.[48] Melanchthon specifies that this miracle took place in the first year after the baptism of Christ. In his comments on John 6:4, Melanchthon inserts a longer excursus on the subject of chronology. Following in the footsteps of the Venerable Bede, he shows that, according to the witness of the Synoptics (Matt. 14:13ff.; Mark 6:3ff.; Luke 9:10ff.), the paschal feast mentioned here took place shortly after the death of John the Baptist.[49] The question under consideration here concerns the second Passover after the beginning of Jesus' ministry, the first having been mentioned in John 2:23. Like Chrysostom and St. Thomas, Melanchthon affirms that there is an interval of one year between John 5:1 and John 6:4. The feast marks the beginning of the third year from the commencement of the ministry of John the Baptist. At this very moment, says Melanchthon, Christ had already been preaching for about eighteen months. Without explicitly saying so, Melanchthon suggests that, since Jesus died at the Passover of the following year (cf. John 12:1, 13:1), his ministry lasted around two and a half years. On John 7:1 (following, as always, Chrysostom and St. Thomas), Melanchthon writes that "while a great part of the history" of Jesus' activity "has been omitted, the Evangelist now adds an account of the winter of the last year of Christ's preaching."[50] Melanchthon shows himself to be more concerned than his predecessors not only to specify the details of Chrysostom's chronology but also to establish the duration of Jesus' ministry.

V. Conclusions

With respect to the order of the events of John 5–7 and the duration of Jesus' ministry, the following hypotheses had been advanced prior to 1536:

48. Melanchthon, *Annotationes in Evangelium Ioannis*, CR 15:115: "Ex serie historiae apparet adhuc agi primum annum a baptismo Christi, et festum, cuius hic fit mentio, scribitur a Cyrillo esse Pentecoste. . . ."

49. Melanchthon, *Annotationes in Evangelium Ioannis*, CR 15:129-31.

50. Melanchthon, *Annotationes in Evangelium Ioannis*, CR 15:154. It is striking to record that Melanchthon does not indicate the issue of a five-month interval between John 6:4 and John 7:1. We call attention also to the testimony of Cajetan whose *Commentarii in quatour Evangelia* was first published in Paris in 1536. Cajetan does not alter the chronological order. In John 5:1ff. he identifies the feast with a "festus temporis hyemalis"; in John 6:4 he specifies that the ministry of Jesus extended over three Passovers (John 2:23; 6:4; 12:1), namely, over two and a half years. He also indicates that John 7:1ff. took place six months after John 6:4. Cajetan, thus, takes up the tradition of Chrysostom, while modifying some of its details.

(1) According to Irenaeus, John 5:1 is situated at the time of the second Passover of Jesus' ministry. The paschal feast is not mentioned in John 6:4, and the ministry of Jesus lasts for two and a half years. This interpretation was not taken up again in the sixteenth century.

(2) According to Chrysostom, John 5:1ff. should be understood as describing events that took place at the time of Pentecost of the same year in which Jesus was baptized; there is an interval of one year between John 5:1 and the paschal feast of John 6:4. John 7:1 also is located in the second year of Jesus' activity. Once again his ministry extends over two and a half years. This chronology is taken up, with some modifications, by virtually the entire medieval tradition and by Lefèvre d'Etaples. Toward 1536, Melanchthon renews and elaborates this view, all the while citing Cyril, not Chrysostom, as his primary source for identifying the "feast day" *(dies festus)* of John 5:1 as the Feast of Pentecost.

(3) According to Cyril of Alexandria, who here agrees with Chrysostom, John 5:1ff. took place at Pentecost. Along with Irenaeus, Cyril makes no reference to the paschal feast in connection with John 6:4; he regards the flight of Jesus in this chapter as a direct consequence of John 5. Erasmus, in his *Paraphrases*,[51] takes up certain elements of Cyril's exegesis of these passages, but without adopting his chronology.

(4) Eusebius and Jerome, whose chronology is taken over by Rupert of Deutz and, later on, by Oecolampadius, situate John 5:1 at the second paschal feast after the baptism of Jesus. In that scenario, John 6:4 takes place at the time of the third Passover and the entire ministry of Jesus covers three and a half years. In his commentary on the Fourth Gospel, Bucer remains in the tradition of Chrysostom (and Cyril) by locating John 5:1 at Pentecost. He follows a medieval source, the *Vita Christi,* in transposing the order of chapters 5 and 6, but he justifies this step with arguments that

---

51. Cf. Erasmus, *Paraphrases,* John 6:4 in loc. (LB 7:542): "Verum ut imagine quadam rerum significaret, fore ut ob incredulitatem Hierosolymitis adversus Deum rebellibus sua domus relinqueretur deserta. Deinde proinde iam evangelica pietate cessaturum omnem carnalem illorum cultum, atque ibi demum pure celebratum iri Pascha ubicunque relictis mundanis affectibus, ad coelestium rerum amorem transferretur animus, maluit esse apud Galileos in desertis quam Hierosolymis in Templo." Cf. Cyril, *In Evangelium Iohannis* (1524), John 6:2 in loc.: "Cum ab Hierosolymis abierit Dominus, ut apud prophetas dictum est: dereliqui haereditatem meam, cum ab infrenato Iudaeorum populo ad alienigenas pervenit, tunc magna sequitur eum turba. Ipse vero in montem ascendit, ut re ostendat quod dixit: si exaltatus fuero, omnia ad meipsum contraham. Exaltatus vero aliter est, cum in altum quasi montem, in honorem et gloriam deitatis ascenderit. Non enim ut Hebraicus populus, quasi hominem, nos, nudum contemnimus: sed ut Deum et Salvatorem et Dominum adoramus." Cf. PG 73:441.

are his own and implicitly makes Jesus' ministry last two and a half years. Bucer's concern for chronology seems to have a very specific polemical and theological purpose: Bucer is not primarily interested in the exact duration of Jesus' ministry; he is, however, determined to show that Jesus would have not been absent from as many as *two* of the feasts required by the law. Thus he emphasizes the importance of the human nature of Christ in opposition to the christological doctrine of Brenz.

• 8 •

Zwingli on John 6:63:
"Spiritus est qui vivificat, caro nihil prodest"

W. P. STEPHENS

I. Introduction

The Bible was central to Zwingli's ministry in Zurich — in his preaching, his disputations, and in the Bible-study meetings known simply as *Prophezei* or "prophecy."[1] His ministry there opened in January 1519 with his preaching through Matthew and then in the months and years that followed through other books of the Old and New Testament. At the First Disputation in January 1523 the Bible was present in Hebrew, Greek, and Latin, so

---

1. The standard bibliography of Zwingli is U. Gäbler, *Huldrych Zwingli in 20. Jahrhundert* (Zürich: Theologischer Verlag, 1975). Details of books and articles since 1972 are published in *Zwingliana* and those before 1896 in Georg Finsler, *Zwingli-Bibliographie* (Zürich: Orell Füssli, 1897). The main biography of Zwingli in English is G. R. Potter, *Zwingli* (Cambridge: Cambridge University Press, 1976). A shorter recent study is U. Gäbler, *Huldrych Zwingli: His Life and Work,* trans. Ruth C. L. Gritsch (Philadelphia: Fortress Press, 1986). See also O. Farner, *Huldrych Zwingli,* 4 vols. (Zürich: Zwingli Verlag, 1943-1960), and G. W. Locher, *Die Zwinglische Reformation im Rahmen der europäischen Kirchengeschichte* (Göttingen and Zürich: Vandenhoeck & Ruprecht, 1979). For Zwingli's theology, see G. W. Locher, *Zwingli's Thought* (Leiden: E. J. Brill, 1981), and W. P. Stephens, *The Theology of Huldrych Zwingli* (Oxford: Clarendon Press, 1986). On Zwingli's use of Scripture, see E. Nagel, *Zwinglis Stellung zur Schrift* (Freiberg i. B. and Leipzig: J. C. B. Mohr [Paul Siebeck], 1896), and E. Künzli, "Zwingli als Ausleger von Genesis und Exodus" (Th.D. diss., University of Zürich, 1951), and Stephens, *The Theology of Huldrych Zwingli,* pp. 51-79. Part of Künzli's dissertation is published in *Zwingliana* 9 (1950): 185-207, 253-307 as "Quellenproblem und mystischer Schriftsinn in Zwinglis Genesis- und Exoduskommentar."

that decisions would be made under its authority. Then in June 1525 the prophecy began, with its scholarly study of the Bible in the original languages. From it came the Zurich Bible and a series of biblical commentaries.

Scholars differ about whether Zwingli was a Reformer when he began his ministry in Zurich in 1519. Some see the decisive moment in his becoming a Reformer as his turning to Christ and Scripture in 1516. Others point to 1521 when he renounced his papal pension. All agree that from 1522 his writings manifest a Reformation faith. In the process of becoming a Reformer, the initial impact came from Zwingli's reading Erasmus and meeting with him in 1516. This was followed by his study of the fathers, especially Augustine. Both Erasmus and Augustine had an important influence both on his theology and on his understanding and use of the Bible.

Zwingli and Luther became Reformers independently of each other, although Zwingli read several of Luther's books. Already in 1523 potential differences between them can be seen in their writings. Later these began to be focused in the eucharistic controversy that developed in the 1520s. It was not, however, until 1527 that Zwingli engaged with Luther by name. Then in 1529 there was an attempt at reconciliation in the Marburg Colloquy. There was agreement on fourteen of the fifteen articles of doctrine, and on the Eucharist they agreed on five out of six points. However, on the crucial matter of the presence of Christ they could not agree, and as a result division between the Lutheran and Reformed traditions lasted for more than four centuries.

II. Seeberg and Gollwitzer on Zwingli and His Use of John 6

At the Marburg Colloquy the initial response of Oecolampadius and Zwingli to Luther's challenge was to point him to John 6 and in particular to John 6:63. Indeed, Zwingli later said that this passage was going to break Luther's neck.[2] Yet despite its importance, there have been few detailed examinations of Zwingli's use of it.[3]

---

2. Luther, *Das Marburger Gespräch* (WA 30/3:113.1-2, 123.27-28).

3. John 6:63 has been discussed incidentally in all the major studies of Zwingli on the Eucharist. See, e.g., W. Köhler, *Zwingli und Luther. Ihr Streit über das Abendmahl nach seinen politischen und religiösen Beziehungen*, vol. 1: *Die religiose und politische Entwicklung bis zum Marburger Religionsgespräch 1529* (Leipzig: Heinsius, 1924); vol. 2: *Vom Beginn der Marburger Verhandlungen 1529 bis zum Abschluss der Wittenberger Konkordie von 1536* (Gütersloh: Bertelsmann, 1953); S. N. Bosshard, *Zwingli-Erasmus-Cajetan* (Wiesbaden: Steiner, 1978); Stephens, *The Theology of Huldrych Zwingli*, pp. 218-59.

In an article in 1929 Erich Seeberg considered the difference between Zwingli and Luther.[4] He sees it as lying in the different ways Zwingli and Luther understood flesh and spirit. Unlike Luther, Zwingli regards body (or flesh) and spirit as opposites, so that the Spirit works only on our spirit. Seeberg holds that this opposition is expressed not only in the sacraments but also in other areas of Zwingli's theology. He is not concerned with the origins of Zwingli's position, although he mentions Erasmus and the humanists. He also refers in passing to an overemphasis of the Augustinian-Franciscan view in which the outward act ordained by God is not of itself accompanied by God's working spiritually. In Luther's and Zwingli's description of each other as sacramentarian and in Luther's word to Bucer at Marburg ("our spirit is different from yours"), Seeberg sees confirmation of his view that the difference between Luther and Zwingli has to do with their different understandings of flesh and Spirit.[5]

The discussion was taken further by Helmut Gollwitzer in an examination of John 6.[6] He views John 6:63 as a text that satisfied Zwingli's metaphysical presuppositions, that is, the opposition between the spiritual and the bodily. This metaphysical dualism determined the way Zwingli understood, for example, revelation, faith, the sacraments, and the presence of God.[7] It also determined the way he understood and used Scripture in the eucharistic controversy, with John 6:63 simply legitimating his position.[8] Ignoring the

---

4. E. Seeberg, "Der Gegensatz zwischen Zwingli, Schwenckfeld und Luther" in *Reinhold Seeberg Festschrift,* vol. 1: *Zur Theorie des Christentums* (Leipzig: Deichert/Scholl, 1929), pp. 43-80. In reference to Zwingli's use of John 6:63 he says, "Die Kardinalstelle, auf welche Zwingli seine Abendmahlsdoktrin nicht bloss in seinen Streitschriften, sondern auch in der Marburger Disputation gestützt hat, ist bekanntlich Joh. 6: 'Das Fleisch ist nichts nütze.' Das bedeutet aber nicht bloss eine exegetische Eigenwilligkeit, sondern dahinter verbirgt sich eine ganz bestimmte Anschauung vom Geist" (pp. 44-45). He comments on Zwingli's view of flesh and Spirit, "Der Grundgedanke also, der uns hier entgegentritt, ist die Entgegensetzung vom Fleisch und Geist; . . . Geist nur auf Geist wirkt, . . . Geist nur aus Geist entsteht, . . . Geist nur die Vernunft lebendig machen kann" (p. 45). Fritz Blanke offers some criticism of Seeberg in "Zu Zwinglis Vorrede an Luther in der Schrift 'Amica Exegesis' 1527," *Zwingliana* 5 (1930): 185-92.

5. Luther, *Das Marburger Gespräch* (WA 30/3:150.4-10).

6. H. Gollwitzer, "Zur Auslegung von Joh. 6 bei Luther und Zwingli," in *In Memoriam Ernst Lohmeyer,* ed. W. Schmauch (Stuttgart: Evangelisches Verlagswerk, 1951), pp. 143-68. Gestrich makes some criticisms of Gollwitzer in C. Gestrich, *Zwingli als Theologe. Glaube und Geist beim Zurcher Reformator* (Zürich: Zwingli Verlag, 1967), pp. 119-22.

7. "Nicht dass er in solchen Kategorien dachte, war das Verhängnis, wohl aber, dass sie ihn exklusiv beherrschten. . . ." Gollwitzer, "Auslegung," p. 156. See also p. 150.

8. "Ein Vergleich der zwischen Luther und Zwingli gewechselten Schriften zeigt den verschiedenen Ursprung ihrer Argumentation: Zwingli argumentiert von seinem Geist-Materie-

role of Erasmus and Augustine in shaping Zwingli's exegesis and theology, Gollwitzer interprets Zwingli in relation to the idealism manifested in the nineteenth century from Schleiermacher to Dilthey. He goes so far as to say that Socinianism is the logical consequence of Zwingli's understanding in relation to the sacraments.[9]

Gollwitzer certainly grasps one important factor in shaping Zwingli's thinking and is clearly aware of many important elements in his understanding of the sacraments. However, his presentation is distorted by not recognizing the seriousness of Zwingli's exegesis, by not appreciating all the other elements in his theology, and by not giving a proper place to some of the driving forces behind his position in the eucharistic controversy.

More recently two articles on Bucer have commented on Zwingli's use of John 6 in his controversy with Luther. In the first, Ian Hazlett offers a useful analysis of some of the points of difference between them.[10] In the second Gottfried Hammann has drawn on Gollwitzer.[11] He emphasizes the fundamental dualism between body and spirit[12] and in the light of this refers to eating bodily as "an ontological impossibility."[13]

It is time to look again at the Seeberg-Gollwitzer thesis to see whether it does justice to Zwingli's use of John 6:63. We shall need to determine

---

Dualism her, den er in Joh. 6:63 legitimiert fand, Luther dagegen argumentiert immer von der Offenbarung her." Gollwitzer, "Auslegung," p. 160. David Steinmetz is more careful in his judgment: "Zwingli's exegesis of this text depended, at least in part, on his dualistic understanding of human nature" (p. 257). See D. C. Steinmetz, "Scripture and the Lord's Supper in Luther's Theology," *Interpretation* 37 (1983): 253-65.

9. Gollwitzer, "Auslegung," pp. 158, 161-62.

10. W. I. P. Hazlett, "Zur Auslegung von Johannes 6 bei Bucer während der Abendmahlskontroverse," in *Bucer und seine Zeit*, ed. M. de Kroon and F. Krüger (Wiesbaden: Franz Steiner, 1976), pp. 74-87. There is also reference in his doctoral thesis, "The Development of Martin Bucer's Thinking on the Sacrament of the Lord's Supper in Its Historical and Theological Context 1523-1534" (Th.D. diss., University of Münster, 1975). On Zwingli's letter to Matthew Alber he writes, "In his letter, Zwingli makes it clear at the outset that his point of departure is John 6, and thus makes explicit what in Hoen and Carlstadt was only implicit." "Development," p. 99.

11. G. Hammann, "Zwischen Luther und Zwingli: Martin Bucers theologische Eigenständigkeit in Lichte seiner Auslegung von Johannes 6 im Abendmahlsstreit," in *Johannes-Studien*, ed. M. Rose (Zürich: Theologischer Verlag, 1991), pp. 109-35.

12. "Je mehr der Abendmahlsstreit an Bedeutung gewann, desto schärfer unterstrich Zwingli die Unvereinbarkeit von Geist und Materie. Mit immer mehr Nachdruck betont er, dass man Christus nur im Glauben, d.h. geistlich empfangen könne. . . . Für Zwingli stehen Geist und Fleisch ontologisch im Widerspruch und schliessen sich gegenseitig aus." Hammann, "Zwischen Luther und Zwingli," pp. 115-16.

13. Hammann, "Zwischen Luther und Zwingli," p. 117. Zwingli's concern is, of course, primarily soteriological.

whether it may not suffer by concentrating too much on his body-spirit dualism, by ignoring his stress on the sovereignty of God, and by disregarding the influence of Augustine, especially his tractates on John's Gospel.

The first extended treatment of John 6 is in *A Commentary on True and False Religion* in 1525. It is the exposition most frequently used by those who have written on Zwingli. It comes from the middle period in Zwingli's sacramental theology, when the symbolic view was most clearly expressed. It also comes from a work that shows Zwingli's humanism more than most others and where precisely in the discussion of the Eucharist he emphasizes the opposition between body and spirit. A more complete picture emerges if we begin with Zwingli's earlier works. In 1522 and 1523 we can see how John 6 was used in eucharistic and noneucharistic contexts, including the emphasis on God's sovereignty and initiative in John 6:44-45. In 1524 in the letter to Matthew Alber we have his first detailed exposition of the chapter, one in which John 6:63 is regarded as the final conclusive argument, not the heart of the discussion. After 1525 and until 1529 John 6 and in particular 6:63 were important elements in the eucharistic controversy, primarily (but not exclusively) with Luther and his supporters.

Like Luther, Zwingli does not regard John 6 as being about the Eucharist. But whereas Luther wishes to exclude it from any discussion of the Eucharist, Zwingli sees it as a chapter that overthrows rather than supports the views held in the church about bodily eating in the sacrament. He does this by an exposition that identifies his opponents' view with that of the Jews and that interprets Christ's reply in terms of spiritual eating with the emphasis on faith. In the light of John 6 and particularly 6:63, he also argues for a trope in the words "This is my body. . . ." He defends his interpretation and use of John 6:63 essentially in two ways: by faith and Scripture. Both are necessary: Scripture as God's Word, and faith for the proper interpretation of Scripture.

III. The Influence of Erasmus and Augustine

Few of Zwingli's writings from before 1522 survive, and none of them deals with John 6. They were, however, years that influenced Zwingli's exegesis and theology. Two fundamental influences were Erasmus and Augustine, and there is evidence of this in the marginal notes in his books.[14]

---

14. The notes have been published only in part and questions have been raised about the accuracy of what has been published. See Gäbler, *Huldrych Zwingli*, p. 35.

Erasmus was decisive in Zwingli's development as a Reformer and made a profound impact on his exegesis and theology, including his understanding of the Eucharist.[15] When Erasmus's *Paraphrase on John* is set alongside Zwingli's writings, there are important elements in common, but also notable differences. The Erasmian emphases on the dualism of body and spirit, on bread and wine as food for the soul, on the need for faith and eating in faith, and on moving from the outward to the spiritual, are evident in Zwingli, though Erasmus emphasizes much more than Zwingli the inward and spiritual. Yet there are striking differences. Faith in Erasmus is essentially faith in Christ; in one instance it is expressed specifically as faith in Christ as the Son of God, but for Zwingli it is primarily faith in Christ as the Son of God and in his having died for us. Flesh and blood are seen as referring to Christ's teaching, but not (as in Zwingli) to his saving death — indeed, there is only a passing reference to his death in Erasmus. Nor is what is said about flesh and blood understood as the words that are referred to in John 6:63b. Zwingli's strong antithesis in 6:63 is missing in Erasmus's comment that flesh taken by itself is helpless, and so is the emphasis on interpreting the word "eat" as believe. Moreover, Erasmus's comments on John 6:44 ("No one can come to me unless the Father who sent me draws him") are characteristically semi-Pelagian.[16]

In the fifth article in Erasmus's *Enchiridion*, a reference to John 6:63 is introduced after a statement about the gospel's having its flesh and its spirit, which is not characteristic of Zwingli. It is later put in a eucharistic context, with a reference to the need for spiritual eating, an emphasis that characterizes Zwingli as well. Yet — and this is unlike Zwingli's use — it is spoken of here in moral and ecclesial terms, with no reference to faith in Christ's death. The closeness of Zwingli to Erasmus is seen later in a reference to the uselessness of having Christ in the flesh and of the necessity for him to go away for the Spirit to come. As his bodily presence did not profit people to salvation in his earthly life, so we should not place our hope in anything material.[17]

The influence of Augustine on Zwingli's writings is evident both in his extended quotations from many of Augustine's works and in his use at many points of Augustine's exposition of John 6. In *A Friendly Exegesis* in

---

15. See, e.g., G. Krodel, "Die Abendmahlslehre des Erasmus von Rotterdam und seine Stellung am Anfang des Abendmahlsstreites der Reformation" (Th.D. diss., University of Erlangen, 1955).

16. Erasmus, *Paraphrase on John,* in LB 7:541-52; translated in CWE 46:75-90.

17. Erasmus, *Enchiridion* (LB 5:29-32; CWE 66:69-73).

1527, Zwingli spoke of his early indebtedness to Augustine and his tractates on John.[18] His marginal notes on the tractates were made either before he came to Zurich at the end of 1518 or in the first year or two there, and they show the impact of Augustine before Zwingli wrote on the Eucharist. In his marginal notes Zwingli comments that John speaks only of spiritual eating in John 6 but that Augustine speaks of bodily eating. He notes "believe and you have eaten" and "the flesh profits nothing." He also takes up other matters in the eucharistic controversy, such as that the Eucharist is a sign of unity and that the body of the Lord can be in one place.[19]

When Zwingli's writings are set alongside the tractates on John 6, the points of contact are numerous.[20] Zwingli understood John 6 as about the gospel, not about the Eucharist. He first used it as about the gospel, but he soon used it to expound the content of the Eucharist, and then he came to use it primarily to demonstrate that the Eucharist could not be about bodily eating. A central element for Zwingli in his interpretation was Augustine's view that eating in John 6 is believing.

He draws on Augustine's references to faith, for example, in 6:27-29. Yet he brings out more than Augustine that faith is in Christ as the Son of God (6:62) over against the Jews' view of him as only human (6:42), and in particular that faith in Christ is faith in his saving death. However, it is especially in his attack on bodily eating that Zwingli finds support in Augustine. Here he makes use of Augustine's speaking of eating with the heart and not the teeth, his holding that the matter at issue in 6:60-61 is the eating of the flesh, his reference to the ascension in 6:62, and his interpretation of 6:63 in terms of bodily flesh. Zwingli's argument that the flesh profits as slain, not as eaten, reflects Augustine's view that through the flesh Christ has accomplished our salvation. Augustine relates Rom. 5:5 to the Spirit in 6:63b, and Zwingli uses the same text in relation to 6:63, though for a different purpose. Augustine points out that in 6:64 Christ says that they did not believe, not that they did not understand. Zwingli does the same, though in a different way, as he is challenging Luther's interpretation of 6:63 in terms of fleshly understanding. Augustine expounds the communication of properties in 6:62, though in a slightly different way from Zwingli, who also uses *alloeosis* in other verses. There is an emphasis on

18. Zwingli, *Amica Exegesis* (ZSW 5:713.2–714.2).

19. Zwingli, *Randglossen zu Augustin* (ZSW 12:144.20-21, 34-35, 39–145.1, 23-25).

20. Augustine, *Tractates on John* (PL 35:1592-1621). For a discussion of Zwingli's use of the fathers, see G. Hoffmann, "Sententiae Patrum — Das patristische Argument in der Abendmahlskontroverse zwischen Oekolampad, Zwingli, Luther und Melanchthon" (Th.D. diss., University of Heidelberg, 1971).

God's role rather than the minister's in John 6:44-45, with a reference to 1 Cor. 3:7. Zwingli has a similar emphasis — indeed he stresses even more God's sovereignty. Alongside these points of contact, Zwingli also worked independently on the text, as he was discussing John 6 largely in terms of the controversy over bodily eating, first in relation to transubstantiation and the role of the Mass, and then in relation to Luther.

IV. Zwingli's Early Use of John 6

Zwingli's use of John 6:63 must be set in the context of the whole chapter, both because he expounded it several times in that context and because he used John 6 in writing about the Eucharist before he used 6:63. One verse that is important throughout his writings is 6:44. It characterizes his whole theology with its stress on the initiative of God in our salvation. God's initiative is expressed in Zwingli's doctrines of providence and election, and in his understanding of faith. In Zwingli, faith, in the sense of trust, always speaks first of God who gives it rather than of us who have it. It is, moreover, faith that Christ died for us.[21]

Part of Zwingli's argument in *The Clarity and Certainty of the Word of God* (1522) is that God's Word is clear and convincing. Among New Testament testimonies he uses to support his case are several verses from John, especially 6:44-45. These verses show that what we need is not human teachers, but God. It is through God's teaching of our hearts that we come to him, and not through human beings, however exalted they are. "Even if you hear the gospel of Jesus Christ from an apostle, you cannot act on it unless the heavenly Father teaches you by his Spirit and draws you." Zwingli then quotes 6:35, stating that in these words Christ is speaking of the food of teaching that is to be found in him. If someone has been fed in this way, he does not need to turn to anyone else to be fed.[22]

The discussion of John 6 in 1522 is not eucharistic. However, in *An Exposition of the Articles* in 1523 John 6 is used largely, though not wholly, in a eucharistic context.[23] In article 1, John 6:44 and 45 are used to insist that it

---

21. Zwingli, *Von Klarheit und Gewissheit des Wortes Gottes* (ZSW 1:373.36–374.9).

22. Zwingli, *Von Klarheit und Gewissheit des Wortes Gottes* (ZSW 1:366.18–369.11).

23. In some of the earlier articles the context is not eucharistic. There are references, e.g., to 6:40, 47, 51, 57, 58, and 63 in the context of the gospel, salvation, and faith. In article 7 he quotes 6:32 and then refers to the whole chapter as being about Christ as the word and food of the soul. Zwingli, *Auslegen und Gründe der Schlussreden* [hereafter *Auslegen*] (ZSW 2:54.4-7).

is divine teaching that we need and that without it we do not come to know Christ.[24] Later 6:44 is used to make it clear that faith is not a human activity, but that its origin is in God and its increase is dependent on him. The text is seen as a clear testimony against human merit and free will.[25]

For Zwingli the meaning of Scripture is to be determined by its author, God. This, he says, is clear from the word of Christ, "They shall all be taught of God" (6:45). He resists the idea that we need an arbitrator, in other words, the pope, if there is a disagreement in the understanding of Scripture. He allows that the Spirit might teach the pope. However he cannot bind the Spirit so that "if someone is pope he may not err," for "the wind blows where he wills."[26]

Zwingli's main discussion of John 6 is in his exposition of article 18 on the sacrifice of Christ and the Mass as a memorial of the sacrifice and not itself a sacrifice. Zwingli says that he will indicate the content of the holy food and does so by expounding John 6.[27] Jesus uses parables in John 6 to show that his Word is food for the soul and the one word of all Christ's words in which we find comfort is that he has given his body for our redemption and his blood for our cleansing. This is seen in 6:51, "The bread which I shall give you is my body."[28] (Later he interprets the Word of God by which we live in Matt. 4:4 in relation to John 6:51; then with an allusion to 6:44 he states that our believing in Christ's saving death comes from the Father who draws us.[29])

From 6:51 he turns to 6:53-55, which speak of those who eat his flesh and drink his blood as having eternal life, for his flesh and blood are truly food and drink. Eating and drinking his body and blood are understood as believing that Christ died for us, that his flesh and blood, slain and shed for us, have freed and cleansed us from sin. (In article 5 Zwingli has already referred to eating Christ as meaning believing in and relying on his word.[30]) He now offers in support the words that follow in 6:60-63 and that show that some of his disciples thought that Christ was referring to the bodily eating and drinking of his flesh and blood. Christ challenged this with the

---

24. Zwingli, *Auslegen* (ZSW 2:22.36–23.4, 24.1-17).

25. Zwingli, *Auslegen* (ZSW 2:181.24–184.26). In the preface Zwingli contrasts Spirit and flesh in the sense of the flesh as sinful (18.17-19; cf. 38.11). To be of the flesh is to be of the devil (259.10-11). Zwingli contrasts living carnally, i.e., according to human reason and strength, and living spiritually, i.e., being freed from them and being led by Spirit (80.30–81.5).

26. Zwingli, *Auslegen* (ZSW 2:109.24–111.6).

27. Zwingli, *Auslegen* (ZSW 2:141.14–144.13).

28. Cf. Zwingli, *Auslegen* (ZSW 2:407.21–408.2).

29. Zwingli, *De canone missae epichiresis* (ZSW 2:583.3-17).

30. Zwingli, *Auslegen* (ZSW 2:43.3-11).

words, "It is the Spirit who gives life; the flesh profits nothing. The words which I have spoken to you are spirit and life." Jesus also referred to the fact that some of them did not believe (6:64). If we believe, says Zwingli, that the giving of Christ's body and blood have redeemed us, then our soul is fed with the flesh of Christ. Such faith is given by the Holy Spirit.

Zwingli points out that Christ has given his body in edible form, the bread, to enable the simple to grasp his testament more easily. They are strengthened in their faith by a visible act. Just as in baptism dipping in water does not wash away sin unless the person being baptized believes in the gospel, so with the Eucharist the body of Christ does not profit those without faith; but the food strengthens those who have faith. Indeed, anyone who lacks faith should not communicate. In a passing reference Zwingli says he is not concerned about what the theologians have invented about the transformation of the bread and wine.

What is striking is how relatively undeveloped Zwingli's exposition of John 6 is in *An Exposition of the Articles*. Later he expounds the chapter in detail as providing arguments that rule out the idea of a bodily eating of Christ, but that is not present here. In article 7 he has already spoken of the whole of John 6 as being about Christ as the Word and as food for the soul, and that is simply expanded in article 18. The emphasis is on Christ as having given his body and blood for our salvation, with eating his flesh and drinking his blood meaning faith in Christ as having died for us. This faith is the work of the Spirit, and it can be strengthened with the Eucharist. There is a passing reference to the distinction between Christ's humanity and divinity in relation to 6:38. This distinction, an important one in Zwingli, is developed later.

The letter to Thomas Wyttenbach in June 1523 is a reply to an inquiry from him. It is concerned with the presence of Christ, whereas *An Exposition of the Articles* is concerned with the sacrifice of Christ. It is dominated by the role of faith. The key reference to John 6 is once again 6:51, in which the bread, which is food for the soul, is the faith that Christ was slain for us. Zwingli states quite simply that the Eucharist is eaten only where there is faith. Moreover, where people have faith in Christ's death for their salvation, their faith is strengthened.

The role of the sacrament is related to our senses, for our spirit, which is taught inwardly by the Spirit of God, is burdened by the body, and it is made more certain and joyful by the visible sign. Zwingli distinguishes the weak and the strong in their relationship to the sacrament. Referring to the bread and food of which Christ speaks in John 6, he writes: "If anyone eats this food in his heart with genuine faith . . . he is now eating the bread and drinking the blood, so that the simple mind may be rendered more assured and joyful by the testimony of the senses also." The weak should communicate frequently to strengthen their faith, and the strong will do so for spiritual delight. If people ate the bread, as Christ says in 6:51, that is, believed in his death for our salvation, they would not be anxious as to how it came about that they ate him who is at God's right hand.[31]

Then Zwingli turns to the practice of reserving the sacrament. He has already referred dismissively to transubstantiation, and now he rejects any notion of reservation, except in the human soul. He states that the Eucharist exists only in use and that Christ is either in heaven at the right hand of God or on earth in the believing heart. He is food for the soul, and is therefore to be eaten, not adored. Moreover, Christ gave the command to eat before saying that it was his body. However, Zwingli makes it clear that he is not teaching publicly all that he says in his letter, since the time is not ripe. But with those with whom he discusses it, he uses the analogy of flint, in which there is fire only when it is struck, and then it streams forth abundantly. "Thus Christ is not contained under the species of bread, and is eaten only at the moment when he is desired and sought there by faith, but in a wondrous manner which a person of faith does not anxiously investigate." He is critical of the adoration of the reserved sacrament as those who adore it adore bread. In any case, only God is to be adored, and not even Christ is to be adored insofar as he is a creature.[32]

In this letter it is again 6:51 that is important, while faith continues to be critical. There are references to Christ's humanity and to his being at the right hand of God. They will be developed, as will the relation of the sacraments to the senses.

In *The Canon of the Mass* (1523) our needing spiritual food is related to our soul's being spirit, as it is made in the image of God. This is supported by John 6:63, which says "the flesh profits nothing," but the emphasis is on the first half of the verse, "It is the Spirit who makes alive." The prayer is made for God's Word not to be taken away, so that we may be made alive by his Spirit.[33]

At the Second Disputation in October 1523, Schmid expresses a similar view to Zwingli's. In a discussion of the Mass he relates faith in Christ and his death for us to spiritual eating, with a reference to John 6:35 and 6:44. Before the Eucharist those who believe the preaching of Christ's death for us enjoy Christ's flesh and blood spiritually. They may then also enjoy

---

31. Zwingli, *Brief an Thomas Wyttenbach* (ZSW 8:85.7–87.1).
32. Zwingli, *Brief an Thomas Wyttenbach* (ZSW 8:87.1–88.19).
33. Zwingli, *De canone missae epichiresis* (ZSW 2:606.14-35).

them in the Eucharist visibly, with the strengthening of their faith and the increasing of their love.[34]

V. The Development of Zwingli's Interpretation of John 6 in 1524

1524 shows an interesting contrast between *A Proposal concerning Images and the Mass* and the letter to Matthew Alber. In the former he gives a five-point scriptural exposition of the Eucharist, in which — unlike the letter to Alber — there is no explicit reference to John 6. At first sight this is surprising given its prominence in his earlier writings, but Zwingli may have omitted reference to it since he did not regard the chapter as being about the Eucharist. He examines the accounts of the last supper in Matthew, Mark, Luke, and Paul, considers 1 Cor. 10:16-17 and John 1:18, and makes various passing references, but none to John 6.[35]

Zwingli read the letter of Cornelis Hoen in 1524, and the effects of it are to be seen in his letter to Alber in November. The most important insight for Zwingli was Hoen's understanding of "is" as "signifies." This was a permanent contribution to Zwingli's view of the eucharist.[36]

Hoen's letter has several references to John 6, but none of them adds to what Zwingli has already said about it. Nor does Hoen give a central place to the chapter. There is in his letter, as already in Zwingli, an emphasis on faith, which he sees as trust in Christ rather than assent and on the necessity in the sacrament for the recipient to have faith. Later Hoen refers to faith in transubstantiation, which is not saving faith, unlike faith in Christ and his death.[37] This is as yet only implicit in Zwingli, who makes a similar but more developed contrast in his letter to Alber. Hoen asserts that the whole religion of the pope would fall if the bodily presence of Christ were

---

34. *Die Akten der zweiten Disputation* (ZSW 2:737.27–738.34). Jud's comments on John 6:63 in the Second Disputation in October 1523 are typically Erasmian. He saw it as a weapon against images that fall away when we have the Spirit. Furthermore, the bodily presence of Christ was not effective; otherwise the Jews would have been saved. Moreover, Christ said that unless he went away, the Spirit would not come (696.4-12). The same ideas can be found in Zwingli.

35. Zwingli, *Vorschlag wegen der Bilder und der Messe* (ZSW 3:123.13–129.15).

36. The text of Hoen's letter is printed in ZSW 4:512-19. It is important to remember that Luther repudiated Hoen's views early in 1523 in *The Adoration of the Sacrament,* a year and a half before Zwingli read the letter.

37. Hoen, *Epistola christiana* (ZSW 4:512.18-30).

eliminated.[38] Again, Zwingli will make a similar point, but for him it is the bodily eating that is more important than bodily presence. It is not usually noted that there are several points where Zwingli does not follow Hoen, or where there is a difference of emphasis.

In his letter to Alber, Zwingli directs attention first to John 6, which now begins to have a dominant part in his eucharistic teaching. It contains the gist of the matter. He recognizes that it is not concerned with the Eucharist. For him, however, it disproves certain views of the Eucharist, and it is his first line of attack.[39]

Zwingli gives an extended exposition of the chapter. First, in an Erasmian way, he sees Christ as moving according to his custom, from the things of sense to inward spiritual things, from the eating of bodily food to the eating of the word, which he calls heavenly food. In accordance with Hebrew custom he refers to it sometimes as bread and sometimes as food. When the Jews thought he meant bodily food, such as the manna, he said, "I am the bread of life. Whoever comes to me [that is, believes in me] shall not hunger, and whoever believes in me shall never thirst" (6:35). The Jews could not understand how Christ could be the bread of life and come down from heaven, and said, "Is not this the son of Joseph?" (6:42) Jesus replied that this is not a matter of human understanding but of divine teaching and that no one believes that Christ came down from heaven and is food for the soul unless the Father draws and teaches him (6:44-45). He will become food for the soul by giving his flesh and dying for the world (6:51). The flesh of Christ, if eaten, could produce nothing but flesh (John 3:6). The Jews did not catch on that "eating me" means "believing in me," and asked, "How can this man give us his flesh to eat?" (6:52). Christ was speaking not of bodily eating that comforts only the body, but of spiritual eating. But if Christ is not in anyone bodily, why do we ask about eating the body? "His body is eaten when it is believed that it was slain for us. It is, therefore, faith and not eating of which Christ is speaking here."[40]

Zwingli then defends his interpretation that Christ speaks in John 6 of faith and not of the Eucharist, asserting that his interpretation is derived from Scripture rather than forced on it. He offers four arguments. The first two are based on John 6:27: "Do not labour for the food which perishes, but for the food which endures to eternal life, which the Son of Man will

---

38. Hoen, *Epistola christiana* (ZSW 4:517.1-5).
39. Zwingli, *Ad Matthaeum Alberum de coena dominica epistola* (ZSW 3:336.19–337.5). Zwingli's discussions in Zurich began with John 6.
40. Zwingli, *Ad Matthaeum Alberum* (ZSW 3:337.5–339.36).

give to you; for on him God the Father set his seal." Zwingli says that Christ gave no other food to make us happy than the gospel of his death. Third, "This is the work of God, that you believe in him whom he has sent" (6:29). The work through which we obtain the food is faith in Christ and not eating the body bodily. There would otherwise be two ways of salvation. Fourth, "The true bread is that which comes down from heaven, and gives life to the world" (6:33). The body of Christ did not come down from heaven. Moreover, Christ gives life to the world because he is God and not because he is flesh. He is life insofar as he is believed to be the Son of God and to have died according to the flesh he received from Mary.[41]

Zwingli then offers what he regards as a conclusive argument, though he indicates that there are many others. It is given by Christ in 6:63. He saw that the Jews could not turn their attention from his body, for they did not wish to trust in his death. He therefore said, "It is the Spirit who gives life; the flesh profits nothing." This for Zwingli is the decisive argument against those who believe that the bread is transformed into flesh. "Are we therefore to say that Christ gave what does not profit?" Christ then tells us what does profit us: "The words that I have spoken to you are spirit and life." Those words are: "Whoever eats my flesh and drinks my blood has eternal life" (6:54). It is by faith alone that we are justified (Rom. 5:1), faith that "Christ crucified is our redemption and salvation."[42]

Zwingli encourages Alber to do as he has done and to teach first and foremost that by "eat" Christ means "believe." To anyone who says, "Do you not believe that the body of Christ is eaten here?" the answer is, "The flesh profits nothing." To be a Christian is "to believe that Christ, the Son of God, suffered for us."[43]

The second part of the letter deals with what Zwingli regards as most difficult: the words "This is my body, which is given for you" (Luke 22:19). He rejects Carlstadt's view of the words, though he commends his sense of the importance of faith. He affirms that faith knows that salvation can come only through Christ and not through the sacramental eating of bread and wine. Those with faith see, therefore, that there must be a figure of speech in Christ's words.[44] Following Hoen, Zwingli argues that the word "is" means "signifies." In this he draws on the fathers as well as Scripture.

41. Zwingli, *Ad Matthaeum Alberum* (ZSW 3:339.37–340.25).
42. Zwingli, *Ad Matthaeum Alberum* (ZSW 3:340.26–341.2).
43. Zwingli, *Ad Matthaeum Alberum* (ZSW 3:341.28–342.10).
44. Zwingli, *Ad Matthaeum Alberum* (ZSW 3:342.11–347.12). Zwingli claimed that he had read little of Carlstadt, but Carlstadt's publications were one reason for Zwingli's writing (ZSW 3:335.14–336.17; cf. 8:275.23-24).

Zwingli says that he doubts whether people had ever thought that they ate Christ bodily, although they taught it. Toward the end he argues that the theologians advocating transubstantiation outdid the Jews in John 6, for they shrank away from bodily eating. Despite Christ's words in John 6:63, these theologians insist, "For we eat the body of Christ truly and bodily, as he lay in the manger, and as he hung on the cross." In some concluding comments he refers to Augustine's distinction in tractate 26 between sacramental and spiritual eating.[45]

A month later in a letter to Strasbourg, the importance of John 6:63 to Zwingli is clear. He supports the interpretation of "is" as "signifies" by reference to it and 2 Cor. 5:16. He also recommends an approach beginning with "no one has ever seen God" (John 1:18), followed by "the flesh profits nothing" and then 1 Corinthians 10. In addition, he uses the argument from faith, which enables us to grasp the true meaning of Scripture.[46]

VI. The Central Role of John 6 in Rejecting Bodily Eating

True and False Religion offers Zwingli's first extensive treatment of John 6. He expounds it, he says, because it has not been rightly understood by the great majority.[47] He identifies six arguments from it that show that in this chapter Christ understands through "bread" and "eat" nothing other than "the gospel" and "believe," because whoever believes that he was slain for us and trusts in him has eternal life. Therefore Christ was not speaking here of sacramental eating.[48] His exegesis shows how closely he has studied Augustine's tractates.

First, the food we are to labor for is faith in Christ; only with faith do we not hunger or thirst again (6:27-29).[49] Second, Christ is our salvation

---

45. Zwingli, *Ad Matthaeum Alberum* (ZSW 3:350.6–352.3). From this point John 6:63 has an increasing role in the interpretation of "This is my body. . . ."

46. ZSW 8:275.23–277.13.

47. Zwingli, *De vera et falsa religione commentarius* (hereafter *Commentarius*) (ZSW 3:715.37-39).

48. Zwingli, *Commentarius* (ZSW 3:776.22-26).

49. Typically, Zwingli interjects supporting arguments. Following Augustine, he adds that where Christ says "he who comes to me shall not hunger," he means "he who believes in me" as those present had come to him but did not believe in him. Zwingli, *Commentarius* (ZSW 3:777.22-28). Zwingli states later that in *True and False Religion* and *The Eucharist* he has used the fathers to support his reading that eating and drinking in John 6:56 means believing in Christ who died to save us and his view that John 6 is about the gospel, not the sacrament. Zwingli, *Eine klare Unterrichtung vom Nachtmahl Christi* (ZSW 4:810.16-24).

by virtue of the godhead that came down from heaven and not by virtue of the body born of Mary (6:51). Third, he is our salvation only by being slain for us. He could be slain only according to the flesh, but his flesh or humanity did not save us, for he could bring salvation only according to his divinity. However, by virtue of the communication of properties something is attributed to one nature that belongs to the whole Christ (6:52-55). Fourth, innumerable people eat and drink the body and blood of Christ sacramentally, but they are not in God, or God in them, except in the same way that he is in an elephant and a flea (6:56). Only those who believe in Christ abide in him, and they are those who are drawn by the Father (6:44). Eating and drinking mean believing in Christ's death for us. Fifth, the most explicit mark is "the flesh profits nothing." It profits greatly, by being slain — but not by being eaten. However, the Jews were disputing about eating, not about offering it as a sacrifice, so that Christ's words must refer not to that but to eating. Zwingli notes that those holding onto Christ's flesh deserted him. He uses Berengar's recantation in describing his opponents' view, which is like that of the Jews in John 6, who deserted Christ. They claim to know better than Christ, who says "the flesh profits nothing." Sixth, as the crown of what he said, Christ is the gospel and whoever believes in him is saved.[50]

After offering these reasons for interpreting John 6 as rejecting bodily eating, Zwingli uses the argument from faith. Like Luther, he sees faith as a principle for interpreting problematic texts. For Zwingli faith means that salvation comes from faith in Christ, with the implication — for him — that it therefore does not come from things of sense.[51] This was to be a major argument in the eucharistic controversy.

It is after this that Zwingli affirms the strong opposition between body and spirit, so that to talk of eating bodily flesh spiritually is to assert that what is body is spirit. He then explains that he is making use of the philosophers here against those who have made philosophy the mistress of God's word.[52] It should, of course, be noted that in *True and False Religion* Zwingli also opposes spirit and flesh, in which the Spirit is the Holy Spirit and flesh is the whole person as sinner.[53]

When Zwingli turns to the words "This is my body," he immediately

---

50. Zwingli, *Commentarius* (ZSW 3:775.37–784.30). Zwingli later refers to John 6:63 as a wall of bronze that opponents will not be able to shake, let alone break (785.40–786.1).

51. Zwingli, *Commentarius* (ZSW 3:785.1-8).

52. Zwingli, *Commentarius* (ZSW 3:787.2-17).

53. E.g., Zwingli, *Commentarius* (ZSW 3:657.36–658.13, 659.37–660.5, 692.21-22).

draws on "the flesh profits nothing" as the first and fundamental argument. Then, when he has used other arguments, he returns to it as sufficient to prove that "is" is used for "signifies."[54] He rejects the view that it should be interpreted by "This is my body." John 6:63 is clear, and what precedes and follows it cannot have an allegorical or symbolic meaning. Faith sees that the literal meaning is right; moreover, the senses also rebel against the idea that bodily flesh is being eaten.[55]

After arguing from John 6, Zwingli turns to the fathers, especially Augustine, in support of his interpretation. He has used the fathers before, in support of the Eucharist as a memorial of the sacrifice and in support of the idea of a figure of speech in the words "This is my body." Now he uses Augustine's comments in support of his view of 6:63 and bodily flesh. "If Christ has profited us much through his flesh, how does flesh profit nothing? But through the flesh the Spirit has accomplished something for our salvation. The flesh was a vessel; observe what it had, not what it was."[56] He quotes Augustine on 6:36 in support of his view that the body and blood do not mean something bodily. "He who does not abide in Christ . . . neither eats his flesh spiritually nor drinks his blood although he crushes carnally and visibly with his teeth the sacrament of the body and blood of Christ."[57] Augustine explains the absence of a reference to the Eucharist in the Johannine passion narrative by reference to what John has said elsewhere. Zwingli uses this as support to assert that the kind of eating necessary for the Eucharist is the same as has been described in John 6, that is, trusting in Christ as the pledge of salvation.[58]

Zwingli defends his quotations from the weightiest of the fathers not in order to support with human words what is clear in God's word but so that people can realize that he is not the first to put forward his view and that it has very strong support. He states that Augustine did not dare to tell the truth explicitly in his day. Zwingli says that he himself had also discussed his view for some years in private before publishing it.[59] The influence of Erasmus can also be seen, for example, in the way Zwingli portrays Christ as using parables to lead people to higher things and purposely going from outward and earthly things to inward and spiritual things.[60]

---

54. Zwingli, *Commentarius* (ZSW 3:791.9-12, 801.22-28).
55. Zwingli, *Commentarius* (ZSW 3:792.8-33).
56. Zwingli, *Commentarius* (ZSW 3:810.4-31).
57. Zwingli, *Commentarius* (ZSW 3:814.35–815.28).
58. Zwingli, *Commentarius* (ZSW 3:815.29-38).
59. Zwingli, *Commentarius* (ZSW 3:810.32–811.5, 816.1-9).
60. Zwingli, *Commentarius* (ZSW 3:698.5-12).

Other writings in 1525 underline the context of Zwingli's exegesis and mark his beginning to deal with objections to it. In *The Eucharist* (August) the context is an attack on idolatry, the fundamental contrast in his theology between trusting in God and anything else. Zwingli feels bound to support those opposed to idolatry and teach: what is seen cannot be adored, flesh profits nothing, and Christ's bodily flesh cannot be eaten.[61] He is being challenged by the interpretation of flesh as fleshly understanding and defends his understanding of flesh. He argues first from the context, where Christ dealt with the Jews' problem, which was eating flesh. In answer to the argument that where the word "flesh" is used by itself it means fleshly understanding, he quotes 1 Cor. 8:13, where it cannot have that meaning.[62]

Another challenge was to interpreting "eat" as "believe." That could make the verse say, "whoever believes that this bread is my flesh shall live for ever." Zwingli resists this use of the word "believe," which does not mean "trust" as in 6:47, but "having an opinion." He rejects it, moreover, as setting up two ways of salvation: trust in Christ and believing that the bread is the bodily flesh of Christ, which is what the Jews refused to believe. Zwingli also appeals to usage in taking "eat" as "believe." He has earlier made the point that the apostles did not teach that eating flesh brings salvation, whereas they did teach that faith brings it.[63]

VII. The Interpretation of John 6 in 1526

Zwingli and Luther do not write directly against each other till 1527. However, the differences between them become increasingly evident after 1523. As further challenges emerge, Zwingli develops his exegesis and seeks support in the fathers, although Oecolampadius soon becomes the authority on the fathers. To Bugenhagen in October 1525 he defends his interpretation of John 6:63 against Luther's interpretation that it means fleshly understanding, by appealing to the interpretation of Cyril, Augustine, and Chrysostom among the fathers, and Erasmus among recent expositors, as well as arguing, in the way we have already seen, from the context in John 6. He then argues — as Luther was later to argue against him — that his

---

61. Zwingli, *Subsidium sive coronis de eucharistia* (ZSW 4:461.31-34).
62. Zwingli, *Subsidium* (ZSW 4:494.8–495.9).
63. Zwingli, *Subsidium* (ZSW 4:492.17-19, 494.8–496.12). He deals with fleshly understanding in a letter to Oecolampadius (ZSW 8:318.18-24).

opponents must show that their interpretation was required in 6:63, not simply that it was possible.[64]

In 1526 Zwingli published *The Lord's Supper,* written in German to reach a wider audience. He understands the problem as lying in the misunderstanding of the words, "This is my body." He presents his case in four articles. John 6 is part of the second article. In it Zwingli seeks to show from Scripture and the creed that the words cannot mean what they are said to mean, while in the third article he shows what they do mean. The role of John 6 is, therefore, as before essentially negative. This negative role is natural. Against those who view John 6 as eucharistic, he insists that Christ "is not speaking of this sacrament but is preaching the gospel under the figure of eating his flesh and drinking his blood."[65] However, he relates it to the sacrament because people "have dragged the bodily flesh and blood into the sacrament," and we should seek the remedy in the situation where it first arose.[66] In 6:69 Peter said he believed in Christ, the Savior, the Son of the living God, not "we believe that we eat your flesh and blood."[67]

John 6:63 cannot be isolated from John 6 although it is in itself for Zwingli a decisive argument. For him it is by itself strong enough to prove that "This is my body" cannot be understood of bodily flesh. But he also uses it to put his opponents on the defensive, by demanding that they prove their view from Scripture.[68]

The exposition shows some developments on that in *True and False Religion.* First, the focus on faith is clearer since he makes 6:27-29 as a whole stand as a sign that everything Christ is about to say about eating and drinking is intended to lead his listeners to trust in him as the true nourishment of the soul.[69] Second, he understands "and" in 6:35 as a Hebrew way of explaining that "comes" means "believes."[70] Third, he explicitly relates 6:44 to 6:63 and points to the role of the Spirit in both, though in this period it is the words "the flesh profits nothing" that predominate.[71]

---

64. Zwingli, *Responsio ad epistolam Ioannis Bugenhagii* (ZSW 4:561.4–565.29, 566.21-28).

65. Zwingli, *Eine klare Unterrichtung vom Nachtmahl Christi* (ZSW 4:810.22-24).

66. Zwingli, *Eine klare Unterrichtung* (ZSW 4:825.15-24).

67. Zwingli, *Eine klare Unterrichtung* (ZSW 4:820.4-12). In a reply to Edlibach he identified his opponents with the Jews who said, "Give us this bread always" (John 6:34) and the Samaritan woman who said, "Give us this drink" (John 4:15). Zwingli, *Responsio brevis* (ZSW 5:350.17-27).

68. Zwingli, *Eine klare Unterrichtung* (ZSW 4:796.25-31, 823.12-17).

69. Zwingli, *Eine klare Unterrichtung* (ZSW 4:811.13–812.2).

70. Zwingli, *Eine klare Unterrichtung* (ZSW 4:813.7-9).

71. Zwingli, *Eine klare Unterrichtung* (ZSW 4:813.25-31, 815.3-7, and 819.5-15).

Fourth, he relates his argument about two opposed ways of salvation (eating or believing) to 6:47 and 54, where the parallel is clear, rather than to 6:27-29, as he did in the letter to Matthew Alber.[72] Fifth, the reference to the ascension in 6:62 begins to have a more important role, largely in the way Augustine uses it. The ascension will show those to whom Christ was speaking that he is Son of God, and it also will mean that they have not eaten him and that he cannot be eaten. It leads at once into a reference to the fact that it is the Spirit who gives life, a point that Zwingli will develop later.[73]

He deals with two objections: "flesh" in John 6:63 means fleshly understanding, and it would mean Christ's flesh only if it said "my flesh." He answers the first as before, arguing also that the fathers do not interpret "flesh" as fleshly understanding, as his opponents do, but as bodily eating — with spiritual eating as believing in Christ. To the second he says that the flesh is Christ's flesh, just as the Spirit must be Christ's Spirit, though he does not say "my Spirit."[74]

It is notable that the fathers, especially Augustine, now feature regularly, though as supports secondary to the biblical argument. He quotes the papal canons, for the sake of the papists, as he puts it, and not for true believers.[75] After the recantation of Berengar, he also notes that Gratian's quotation from Augustine, "What need of teeth and stomach?" conflicts with the former's "pressing with the teeth." Augustine's "Believe and thou hast eaten" makes it clear that "to feed on Christ is simply to trust in him." He emphasizes Augustine's words, "You will not eat the body which you see. . . ."[76]

In the eucharistic controversy Zwingli used two criteria: faith and Scripture. In a letter to Billican he notes that failure to collate passages of Scripture was a cause of heresy with Arius. He insists that John 6:55 must be related to 6:29 and 6:63.[77]

---

72. Zwingli, *Eine klare Unterrichtung* (ZSW 4:817.19-27). Cf. Zwingli, *Ad Matthaeum Alberum* (ZSW 3:340.1-18).

73. Zwingli, *Eine klare Unterrichtung* (ZSW 4:818.31–819.5). This view of John 6:47 is stressed later in the commentary on John. Zwingli, *Annotationes in evangelium Joannis* in HZW 6/1:713.30-37.

74. Zwingli, *Eine klare Unterrichtung* (ZSW 4:819.15-24, 823.18–825.6).

75. Zwingli, *Eine klare Unterrichtung* (ZSW 4:800.30–801.4, 820.13-22).

76. Zwingli, *Eine klare Unterrichtung* (ZSW 4:806.25–807.20, 820.30–823.17).

77. In a letter to the Nuremberg City Council in 1526, John 6:63 is one of Zwingli's three "invincible" passages, along with Luke 22:19 and Mark 16:19 (ZSW 8:640.4-15).

VIII. The Interpretation of John 6
in the Eucharistic Controversy

It was in the years 1527 to 1529 that Luther and Zwingli engaged directly in controversy over the Eucharist. The writings of Zwingli in this period up to the Marburg Colloquy can be treated together since there is no substantial difference between them.[78] Zwingli's attack is based on faith and Scripture: faith in Christ as the Son of God who has given his life for us, and Scripture as including the collation of passages of Scripture, the use of tropes, idiom, and analogy. Like Erasmus and the fathers, Zwingli uses the doctrine of accommodation. God in his goodness is said to accommodate himself to human ways of speech. This makes it absolutely necessary for the expositor to be familiar with tropes and figures. It is, however, faith that is our guide as to what words are to be interpreted as a trope.[79] He emphasises the need to have both faith and Scripture. Neither is sufficient in itself. Thus Scripture has to be interpreted under the direction of faith, and yet Scripture is the touchstone of what we say. We must keep to Scripture, following the example of Christ; but without faith we shall not understand Scripture aright.[80]

Of fundamental importance in Zwingli's appeal to Scripture is John's Gospel. If you take it away, "you take the sun from the world." It provided him with *alloeosis,* especially in John 6 and in particular 6:63.[81] *Alloeosis* (the sharing or interchange of properties) was one of the figures of speech Zwingli saw in Scripture. It throws light on John 6 as well as other New Testament passages. Zwingli claims that in not taking "This is my body" literally he was led by faith and Scripture, with John 6:63 as one of many examples from Scripture. He explicitly rejects Luther's charge that he had invented a meaning and then read it into Scripture. He adds that it was

---

78. The four main works against Luther are *A Friendly Exegesis (Amica Exegesis)* (ZSW 5:548-758) in February 1527, *A Friendly Answer (Freundliche Verglimpfung)* (ZSW 5:763-794) in March 1527, *Zwingli's Christian Reply (Dass diese Worte)* (ZSW 5:795-977) in June 1527, and *Two Replies to Luther's Book (Über D. Martin Luthers Buch)* (ZSW 6/2:1-248) in August 1528. The Bern Disputation, the Marburg Colloquy, and the commentary on John are all in the period 1527 to 1529.

79. Zwingli, *Amica Exegesis* (ZSW 5:729.20–752.20, esp. 752.12-15). When rejecting the Lutheran view of John 6:63, Zwingli argues directly and indirectly from the Bible. This can be seen in the use of arguments, inferences, witnesses, signs, documents, and probabilities (ZSW 5:611.1–612.34).

80. Zwingli, *Amica Exegesis* (ZSW 5:733.29–734.25) and *Freundliche Verglimpfung* (ZSW 5:772.24–775.3).

81. Zwingli, *Amica Exegesis* (ZSW 5:564.10-16).

only after being convinced by faith and Scripture that he received Hoen's letter, with its example of trope.[82]

John 6:63 is far from being the only text that Zwingli uses, yet it is always seen as decisive. It is the place where Christ cut the knot with an axe so sharp that there is no hope of putting body and eating together again.[83] If Christ's flesh does not profit by being eaten, it follows that Christ's body was not given to be eaten. Therefore the words "This is my body" must mean something other than that Christ gave us his body to eat.[84]

The emphasis is largely on the words "the flesh profits nothing," but on occasion Zwingli stresses the role of the Spirit as giving life. Faith cannot be strengthened except by the Spirit from whom it comes.[85] Zwingli relates the words "it is the Spirit who gives life" to other passages about the Spirit (John 14:26; Rom. 5:5; 8:11 and 15). It is not from bodily eating but from the Holy Spirit that we receive the assurance of sonship, as well as faith, love, and comfort. Everything that Luther ascribes to bodily eating is to be ascribed to the grace of God and the Spirit of God.[86] A similar point is made at the Bern Disputation in 1528, where John 14 to 18 are cited as evidence in support of John 6:63 that it is the Spirit who comforts the soul, not the bodily eating of Christ's body.[87]

Zwingli's interpretation of Spirit and flesh in 6:63 continued to be challenged by Luther and others. This led Zwingli to a series of defenses. He argues that his interpretation is supported by the fathers and all his contemporaries who have written on John, including Melanchthon, and even by Luther in his sermon on John 6:55.[88]

He allows that when "flesh" and "spirit" are used together, "flesh" can be used to refer to our flesh as the flesh of the old Adam. But then, however,

---

82. Zwingli, *Dass diese Worte* (ZSW 5:903.22–908.4).

83. Zwingli, *Amica Exegesis* (ZSW 5:616.9-13).

84. Zwingli, *Amica Exegesis* (ZSW 5:630.32–631.1).

85. Zwingli, *Amica Exegesis* (ZSW 5:625.4-9). The dualism of body and spirit is evident in his commentary on John in his comment on 6:63, but so are the initiative and grace of the Spirit in drawing us (John 6:44): "sed spiritus spiritum docet: spiritus inquam dei, miserum hominis spiritum dignatur ad se trahere. . . ." Zwingli, *Annotationes in evangelium Joannis* (HZW 6/1:717.47-48).

86. Zwingli, *Dass diese Worte* (ZSW 5:895.13-20, 897.7-11, 19-26, 898.18–899.11).

87. Zwingli, *Voten Zwinglis an der Berner Disputation* (hereafter *Voten Zwinglis*)(ZSW 6/1:336.19–337.3). In his comment on John 16:8, he relates John 6:63 to Christ's leaving the world and giving his Spirit, pointing out that it is not the flesh that convinces us of sin. Zwingli, *Annotationes in evangelium Joannis* (HZW 6/1:753.43–754.15).

88. Zwingli, *Amica Exegesis* (ZSW 5:609.23–611.5). For Luther, see *Sermon auf unsers Herrn Fronleichnamstag* (WA 12:582.29-33).

"spirit" does not refer to God but to our spirit touched by the Spirit of God, as in Galatians 5. However, in John 6:63, since the Spirit who gives life must be Christ's, so must the flesh be his, in order to make an antithesis.[89] Moreover, the use of the article with "spirit" makes it clear that the reference is to the Spirit.[90] Elsewhere Zwingli accuses Luther of being like Marcion in distorting Scripture. For though Luther's translation of the Greek included the article, yet in order to refer "flesh" to the old Adam and not to Christ's flesh he omitted the article.[91] In opposition to Luther, he points out that where "flesh" and "spirit" are used together, "flesh" does not always refer to the old Adam. As examples, he cites 1 Pet. 3:18 and 1 Tim. 3:16.[92]

Zwingli continues to defend his interpretation of John 6:63 as referring to Christ's flesh against Luther's interpretation. He makes his case in seven points in A Friendly Exegesis. The murmuring in 6:61 shows that they were dealing with the same subject as before, that is, eating, and the "this" could not refer to fleshly understanding, which had not been mentioned. The ascension in 6:62 shows that they do not believe that he is Son of God but think he is speaking of eating flesh, whereas with the ascension they believe that he is Son of God and that he spoke of faith in himself and not of eating with their teeth the flesh that is going to heaven. Then, after the argument from 6:63, he states that if Christ had been speaking of fleshly understanding he would have spoken of fleshly understanding and not of believing in 6:64. Furthermore, in 6:68 Peter speaks of believing and not of understanding. Finally, if Christ had been talking of fleshly understanding, he would have said that the flesh harms, rather than that it profits nothing.[93]

Zwingli continues to advance arguments based on the exegesis of particular verses in John 6, as well as making his case from the coherence with 6:63 of the verses before and after it. Thus in discussing John 6 with Burgauer at the Bern Disputation, Zwingli argues from Erasmus's Greek New Testament against the Vulgate that the "which" in 6:51 must not be omitted. It makes it clear that in both parts of the sentence Christ refers

---

89. Zwingli, *Dass diese Worte* (ZSW 5:967.25–969.10). Cf. Zwingli, *Über D. Martin Luthers Buch* (ZSW 6/2:190.3–191.10).

90. Zwingli, *Über D. Martin Luthers Buch* (ZSW 6/2:186.11-27).

91. Zwingli, *Dass diese Worte* (ZSW 5:808.6-10, 963.4–965.10). For Luther, see *Dass diese Wort Christi* (WA 23:195.33-37).

92. Zwingli, *Dass diese Worte* (ZSW 5:969.11-32).

93. Zwingli, *Amica Exegesis* (ZSW 5:606.4–609.22). Cf. Zwingli, *Dass diese Worte* (ZSW 5:965.11–967.24).

to his flesh given in death.[94] In 6:33 the bread that gives life is the divine nature, and it is that and not bodily eating that gives life.[95] The eating of the flesh that gives life in 6:53 must mean faith and not a bodily eating of the flesh or it would conflict with the frequent promise of salvation to faith.[96] In 6:62 Christ speaks of his ascension and hence of being absent, not of being present unseen. Moreover, without his going away, the Spirit will not come (John 16:7). This is related to 6:63, which makes it clear that it is the Spirit who gives life, not the flesh. It was equally true in Christ's earthly life that his bodily presence did not itself give people faith.[97]

In the collation of Scripture to help people understand "This is my body," John 6:63 is an important passage, but not the only one.[98] Underlying the collation of Scripture is the conviction that the Spirit, who is the author of Scripture, is one of agreement, and therefore the various passages will agree.[99] The knowledge of figures of speech is vital for the understanding of Scripture, as it is full of them. They include *alloeosis*. It is relevant in the exegesis of John 6, which is necessary to a sure understanding of 6:63. Thus "flesh" in 6:55 is not Christ's human nature but his divine nature, which has taken flesh in order to satisfy the righteousness of God. This is supported by 6:63, which says that it is the Spirit who gives life.[100]

In his neo-Platonic opposition between flesh and spirit, Zwingli differs from Luther, but not when the opposition is between the flesh as the old Adam and the Holy Spirit. It is presumably the latter view to which Zwingli refers when he says that no one has presented more purely and brightly than Luther the hostility between flesh and Spirit.[101]

---

94. Zwingli, *Voten Zwinglis* (ZSW 6/1:303.11–304.5).

95. Zwingli, *Voten Zwinglis* (ZSW 6/1:357.13–358.3).

96. Zwingli, *Amica Exegesis* (ZSW 5:591.18-25).

97. Zwingli, *Amica Exegesis* (ZSW 5:689.12–691.19) and *Über D. Martin Luthers Buch* (ZSW 6/2:207.12-25).

98. Zwingli, *Amica Exegesis* (ZSW 5:604.16-26).

99. Zwingli, *Amica Exegesis* (ZSW 5:735.21-23).

100. Zwingli, *Amica Exegesis* (ZSW 5:605.9-23). *Alloeosis* makes sense of flesh in John 6:51: "dicit: Carnem suam esse vere cibum, non quidem carnem puram intelligens, sed naturam potiorem qua carnem adsumpserat, ut ea perlitaret ac placaret aeternam iustitiam. Per alloeosim ergo de mortali natura loquitur, quum tamen de immortali et divina sentiat. . . . Nam ut deus et homo unus est Christus, ita fit, ut quum iuxta carnem caesus sit (Quis enim deum posset occidere?) ac mors eius nobis vita facta sit, ut propter naturarum unitionem et communicationem alteri nonnunquam tribuatur naturae, quod totius Christi est." Zwingli, *Annotationes in evangelium Joannis* (HZW 6/1:715.3-20).

101. Zwingli, *Amica Exegesis* (ZSW 5:723.3–724.3).

Zwingli must be set in the context of his theology, particularly his sense of the sovereignty of God and his attack on idolatry as consisting in the placing of faith in anything or anyone other than God or the origin of faith other than in God.[102] The sovereignty of God is expressed in other contexts, for example in relation to the word, by reference to 1 Cor. 3:6-7, where neither the planter nor the waterer is anything, but only God who gives the growth.[103] The Marburg Article on the outward word could apply equally to the Eucharist: the Holy Spirit "works through and with the outward word and creates faith, where and in whom he wills."[104] *The Providence of God*, referring to the same text ("Faith comes from hearing," Rom. 10:17), comments that Paul "attributes to the nearer and better known cause what belongs only to the Spirit, not to outward preaching, as the sacramentarians generally contend." He can refer to the word as an instrument that is used, but it is God who is the cause. He then characteristically refers to 6:44 and the work of the Spirit in drawing. The ineffectiveness of the word without the Spirit is seen in experience by the lack of faith in so many who hear the word.[105]

IX. John 6 in Zwingli's Writings after the Marburg Colloquy

It is striking that in Zwingli's writings in 1530-31 references to John 6 and John 6:63 are relatively few. In *An Account of the Faith* not five lines in some two hundred deal with 6:63. Zwingli advances texts to demonstrate that Christ's body is in heaven, and only then uses 6:63 to show that Christ's natural body is not eaten by the mouth.[106]

Two of Zwingli's works in this period are confessional statements, *An Account of the Faith* and *An Exposition of the Faith*. They are modeled on the Apostles' Creed. It is natural, therefore, that they offer a more positive presentation of his theology. His concern to give a positive expression to his views may have led to his giving less place to John 6, and in particular John 6:63. First, he does not regard the Eucharist as the subject of John 6, and therefore it would be less likely to be present in a positive statement

102. Zwingli, *Über D. Martin Luthers Buch* (ZSW 6/2:206.16–207.4).
103. Zwingli, *Über D. Martin Luthers Buch* (ZSW 6/2:100.1-5).
104. Zwingli, *Die Marburger Artikel* (ZSW 6/2:522.15-16).
105. Zwingli, *De providentia* (ZSW 6/3:186.12–187.7).
106. Zwingli, *Fidei ratio* (ZSW 6/2:809.12-16). His dualism is then evident when he insists that as the body cannot be fed by something spiritual, so the soul cannot be fed by something bodily (810.9).

of his understanding of the Eucharist. In this we can make a comparison with his account of the Eucharist in *A Proposal concerning Images and the Mass*, where he does not use John 6. Second, the main role of John 6 in Zwingli's writings is to deny the bodily eating of Christ. This negative role fits less well a positive presentation of the Eucharist. The term "sacramental eating" is now used positively, not for a merely outward eating of the sacrament but for an eating of it with faith.

In these years Zwingli expresses his view of the sacraments more positively by reference to the role of the senses, although it remains the Spirit who gives and increases faith. Whereas preaching appeals only to the sense of hearing, the sacraments appeal to all the senses. The role of the senses is clearest in *The Letter to the Princes of Germany* and *An Exposition of the Faith*. In the former he speaks of the whole Christ being presented as it were visibly *(sensibiliter)* to the senses. Furthermore, when the senses have presented to them what is most like that on which the mind is working, the assistance of the senses is not slight.[107] In the latter, the sixth virtue of the sacraments is that the sacraments aid and assist faith. It is through the senses that our faith is tempted. The sacraments point to salvation in Christ and are like a bridle, by which the senses, when they are on the point of running after their desires, are recalled and brought back to the service of the mind and of faith. However, Zwingli always insists that faith comes only from the Spirit and speaks of the sacraments as giving simply historical faith.[108]

His writings give the larger context in which his comments on John 6:63 are to be understood. In the first article of *An Exposition of the Faith* he states that those "who attribute to the creature what is the creator's alone" overthrow the first foundation of the faith.[109] In the article on the sacraments in *An Acccount of the Faith* he insists that if God's gifts were bound to the sacraments, we should be denying the freedom of the Spirit, who gives to whom he wills, and the free grace of God, whose giving — according to Isaiah and Jeremiah — is not related either to human merit or outward ceremonies.[110]

The glory and sovereignty of God are at the heart of Zwingli's theology. They may be expressed in a dualistic form of body and spirit, but the form does not determine these central convictions, and they stretch the

107. Zwingli, *De convitiis Eckii* (ZSW 6/3:260.3–261.3).
108. Zwingli, *Fidei expositio* (ZSW 6/5:158.12–159.9, 160.25-27).
109. Zwingli, *Fidei expositio* (ZSW 6/5:61.3-8).
110. Zwingli, *Fidei ratio* (ZSW 6/2:803.5–804.16, 805.23-29).

form from time to time. In *The Letter to the Princes of Germany* he replies to Eck's attacks on his views, but ignores his references to John 6:63. He rejects the doctrine that the sacraments convey the grace of God, since that would limit the freedom of the Spirit. However, it is consistent with the freedom of the Spirit for him to use the sacraments, without being bound by them.[111] The fathers are given a relatively large place in these works, and Zwingli could even go so far as to speak of Augustine as an arbitrator.[112]

His commentaries on Matthew and Luke and *The Death of Christ* and *The Resurrection and Ascension of Christ*, which come from this period, express the same essential position. The glory and sovereignty of God are fundamental, but as long as they are safeguarded he can speak positively of outward things. Thus he states that we are to direct our heart away from bodily things to Christ in heaven, and yet adds that faith can use bodily things — but not so that salvation is bound to them or given through them.[113] Zwingli affirms that, as with miracles, God sometimes uses and sometimes does not use outward things. He adds significantly that it is important to note the reason why he sometimes does not use them: that we may be aware of God's power.[114] Power, he insists, belongs to God, not to us, or any creature. When God is said to give people power (Luke 9:1), it means "that everywhere they will preach, he himself wills to work at the same time."[115]

After a reference to John 6:56, he declares that the sacraments are not bare symbols, but Christ, the eternal high priest, feeds believers.[116] He is not present bodily, and he is not eaten bodily. Yet if he is not present, Zwingli asserts, then it would not be the Lord's Supper.[117]

---

111. "Atque haec omnia dum fiunt, unus atque idem operatur spiritus, qui inspirando nunc citra instrumentum trahit, nunc cum instrumento, quo, quantum et quem vult." Zwingli, *De conviciis Eckii* (ZSW 6/3:271.10-12). It is notable that Zwingli refers first to the Spirit's acting without an instrument and then to his acting with one.

112. Zwingli, *De conviciis Eckii* (ZSW 6/3:270.15-17).

113. Zwingli, *Brevis commemoratio* (HZW 6/2:55.25-36). "Fides quidem, quae soli deo nititur, corporalibus rebus uti potest, sed non ut iis rebus salus alligetur, et per illa exhibeatur, sed ut fides ac caritas exerceatur" (55.34-36).

114. Zwingli, *Annotationes in evangelium Matthaei* (HZW 6/1:356.1-4). "Adhibet aliquando deus externa quaedam, ut caro nostra tranquilletur, quemadmodum in coena externum sacramentum sensibus exhibet divina sapientia. Aliquando vero non adhibet, ut videamus solam dei virtutem operari."

115. Zwingli, *Annotationes in evangelium Lucae* (HZW 6/1:609.5-20).

116. Zwingli, *Brevis commemoratio* (HZW 6/2:10.4-13). "Pii vero non solum symbola dentibus premunt, nec nuda habent symbola, sed ultra symbolorum manducationem quae ore corporis fit, intus in mentibus suis corpore et sanguine Christi per fidei manducationem pascuntur" (10.4-7).

117. For example, Zwingli, *Fidei expositio* (ZSW 6/5:90.14-15).

X. Conclusion

In 1525 Zwingli attacked rebaptism, saying that it would be a return to the blindness in which we once lived, seeking comfort for our souls in outward things.[118] This is the context in which we must understand Zwingli's view of bodily eating. It helps also to explain the dualism of body and spirit in Zwingli. However, it is his sense of the glory and sovereignty of God and not the dualism of body and spirit that is most fundamental in Zwingli's theology. It finds expression in his attack on idolatry, on putting faith in anything or anyone other than God, including bodily eating.

The two great influences on Zwingli were Erasmus and Augustine. This is evident in his exposition and use of John 6:63. In the understanding he brought to it, his debt to both of them is clear. Although his exposition of John 6 owed more to Augustine's tractates on John than it did to Erasmus's paraphrase and *Enchiridion*, yet he owed more to Erasmus in his scholarly methods. In his twofold approach in the eucharistic controversy (in terms of faith and Scripture), he is indebted to both of them.

The principle of faith, which is a fundamental principle of biblical interpretation, is found in Augustine's use of the translation of Isa. 7:9, "If you do not believe, you will not understand."[119] (There is a parallel to this in the distinction between the spirit as the meaning of a word and the letter.) The faith by which we understand Scripture is faith in Christ as the Son of God who died for us. This guides our understanding of a text, so that we know there is a trope if the literal interpretation of a passage conflicts with such faith. The principle of the glory of God is similar to that of faith. Where there are two contradictory passages of Scripture, then the one that ascribes glory to God is to be accepted.[120] Since the Spirit is the author of faith as well as of Scripture, the use of the principle of faith is one way in which the Spirit can be said to interpret Scripture.

The principle of faith or the glory of God rules out for Zwingli any interpretation that ascribes to us or to anything we can do (including bodily eating) what is to be ascribed to God alone. Such an interpretation calls in question, for example, the role of God in electing us to salvation, the necessity of Christ's death for our salvation, and the freedom of the Spirit

---

118. Zwingli, *Von der Taufe* (ZSW 4:284.8-9).

119. See Tractate 29 in Augustine, *Tractates on John* (PL 35:1592-1621). This is the translation of the Septuagint and Vulgate. Zwingli translates it according to the Hebrew in *Jesaja-Erklärungen* (ZSW 14:180.6-22).

120. This is present from the beginning in Zwingli. See, e.g., *Wer Ursache gebe zu Aufruhr* (ZSW 3:408.20-32).

in our salvation. In John 6:63, the clause "It is the Spirit who makes alive" expresses for Zwingli the divine initiative and freedom. The clause "the flesh profits nothing" does the same, though in a different way.[121]

Scripture is authoritative, since it is God's word and not a human word. In the way Zwingli interpreted it, his debt to Erasmus is evident, for example, in the use of the collation of Scripture, in the understanding of a verse in context, in the approach to figures of speech, and in his view of accommodation. So much of the debate on John 6:63 manifests these principles of interpretation, especially the first two. John 6:63 is constantly set in the context of John 6, and it is related to other passages, including typically Erasmian ones, such as John 16:7 and 2 Cor. 5:16. Yet when we allow his debt in the use of Scripture, it must be said that in the detailed exegesis of John 6 there are more evident parallels with Augustine's tractates than with Erasmus's paraphrases. For Zwingli Scripture, of which John 6:63 is an example, as well as faith will not tolerate bodily eating.[122]

Zwingli can appeal to experience, but only in support of Scripture, not when it conflicts.[123] The ineffectiveness of bodily eating is as true in our experience as it was in John 6. Zwingli can also appeal to canon law, though only for the sake of those who accept it.[124] He appeals occasionally to his contemporaries and to theologians in the past, such as Paschasius Radbertus,[125] but especially to the fathers. They are, however, only supports, for he does not hesitate to criticize even Augustine. Although Zwingli increasingly uses the fathers in support of his exegesis, what is ultimately determinative is Scripture as God's Word, over against all human words, and the glory of God.[126]

An examination of Zwingli's use of John 6 shows that there is truth in the Seeberg-Gollwitzer interpretation of Zwingli, but that it is at best a half-truth. There is in Zwingli an opposition between flesh and Spirit in terms of outward and inward, with the Spirit working inwardly on our

---

121. See, e.g., Zwingli, *Die beiden Predigten Zwinglis in Bern* (ZSW 6/1:476.9-22).

122. Zwingli, *Freundliche Verglimpfung* (ZSW 5:787.3–789.27).

123. Zwingli, *Ad Matthaeum Alberum* (ZSW 3:273.1–276.17).

124. F. Schmidt-Clausing contrasts Zwingli's and Luther's use of canon law with the words, "Luther hat's verbrannt, Zwingli hat's benutzt," in "Das Corpus Juris Canonici als reformatorisches Mittel Zwinglis," *Zeitschrift für Kirchengeschichte* 80 (1969): 21.

125. Zwingli, *Über D. Martin Luthers Buch* (ZSW 6/2:247.28–248.14).

126. "Haec ex gravissimis patrum attulimus, non quo rem per se manifestam et verbo dei firmam, humana velimus autoritate fulcire, sed quod imbecillioribus manifestum fiat nos non primos esse, qui hunc sensum proferamus, nec fortasse infirmissimum. Deum enim testor, quod eius solius gloriam iam annis aliquot rem hanc cum multis doctis clam contuli. . . ." Zwingli, *Commentarius* (ZSW 3:816.1-6).

spirit. This differs from Luther's characteristic use of the terms, although Zwingli like Luther can speak of the whole person as flesh and his understanding of the Spirit is not the spiritualist one that they emphasize. Ultimately the Seeberg-Gollwitzer view of Zwingli misinterprets him. It disregards the influence of Augustine alongside that of Erasmus. It ignores the serious and detailed attention that Zwingli gives to the exegesis and exposition of John 6, with particular reference to Augustine's tractates. It takes little or no account of the central place of the sovereignty of God in Zwingli's theology and in his interpretation of Scripture. Zwingli emphasizes the sovereignty of God in his use of John 6:44-45, and it is an important element in his understanding of John 6:63. It is true that his views are expressed in a Platonic manner (in some of the ways he opposes flesh and Spirit), but they are shaped fundamentally by his belief in the sovereignty of God and his concern to give glory to God.

PART III

CONTINUITY AND CHANGE IN MID-SIXTEENTH-CENTURY BIBLICAL INTERPRETATION

"The Spiritual Man Judges All Things": Calvin and the Exegetical Debates about Certainty in the Reformation

SUSAN E. SCHREINER

"**N**OTHING IS MORE miserable than uncertainty."[1] Luther's statement leads the historian to the very heart of sixteenth-century polemics. Armed with the question of certainty, the historian of the late Middle Ages and the Reformation can examine almost any subject: the Hussites, the Catholic polemicists, the Scripture principle, the Radical Reformers, theologies of justification, the sacramental controversies, and the rise of skepticism. Even late-medieval discussions about epistemology, optics, and semantics demonstrate the interest in certitude. Devotional and mystical writers from Julian of Norwich to Ignatius of Loyola reveal the continual preoccupation with this issue. Finally, in 1547 the Council of Trent had to address the problem of certainty dogmatically.

The multifaceted nature of this concern with certitude is clearly too vast a topic for one essay. However, by limiting the analysis to Luther, Zwingli, and Calvin, a coherent pattern emerges. These exegetes illustrate the major exegetical battles of the first- and second-generation Reformers. My ultimate focus is on Calvin's use of certainty as an exegetical and doctrinal test of the truth.[2] From the Reformers' perspective, the search for

---

1. *De servo arbitrio*, WA 18:604.33; LW 33:22.
2. The best general work on Calvin remains François Wendel, *Calvin: Origins and Development of His Religious Thought* (1963; reprint ed., Durham, N.C.: Labyrinth, 1987). The best studies on Calvin's exegesis are T. H. L. Parker, *Calvin's New Testament Commentaries* (Grand Rapids, Mich.: Eerdmans, 1971); idem, *Calvin's Old Testament Commentaries* (Edin-

certitude crystallized around two interrelated problems: the certainty of salvation and the certainty of authority. The former involves the claim to an inward, experiential, and subjective certainty of salvation. The latter concerns the attempt to legitimate this experience exegetically. To ground experiential certainty on the Bible necessitated the concomitant claim for the authoritative interpretation of Scripture; the experience justified by scriptural authority demanded a hermeneutical certitude.

All sixteenth-century polemics appealed to the Spirit as the agent of certainty. The Spirit sanctioned both the inward experience of salvation and the authoritative knowledge and exegesis of the believer. This reliance on the Spirit was itself justified biblically and gave rise to heated exegetical arguments. The following verses served Luther and Zwingli as the decisive exegetical vehicle for the dual claims to certitude:

> And because you are sons, God has sent the Spirit of his Son into our hearts, crying, "Abba Father!" (Gal. 4:6)

> . . . for you did not receive the spirit of slavery to fall back into fear, but you have received the spirit of sonship. When we cry "Abba Father!" it is the Spirit himself bearing witness to our spirit that we are children of God. (Rom. 8:15-16)

> The spiritual man judges all things but is himself judged by no one. (2 Cor. 2:15)

> No one can come to me unless the Father who sent me draws him. (John 6:44)

> Do not believe every spirit, but test the spirits to see whether they are of God. (1 John 4:1)

The sixteenth-century battle over certainty was fought on the terrain of exegetical arguments about the Spirit. This essay concentrates on how the Bible was used in this important theological debate at the core of the Reformation. One way of approaching this subject would be to trace the exegetical evolution of certain passages beginning with the patristic and medieval eras, note the changes rung by the Reformers, and suggest how this background informs and illuminates the controversy

burgh: T & T Clark, 1986); Alexandre Ganoczy and Stefan Sheld, *Die Hermeneutik Calvins. Geistesgeschichtliche Voraussetzungen und Grundzüge* (Wiesbaden: Franz Steiner, 1983); David Steinmetz, *Calvin in Context* (New York and Oxford: Oxford University Press, 1995).

about certitude in the Reformation. I do not wish to treat these passages so developmentally. My intent is to locate the reader within the sixteenth century and allow him or her to experience the exegetical firestorm this debate ignited. But the people of the sixteenth century learned in the hardest way that, like fire, the Spirit blows where it wills. They learned that not all appeals to the Spirit were equally successful or persuasive. The experiential, affective language of the Spirit was dramatically effective in defense of the certainty of salvation. However, when this language was transferred to the issue of authority, the vocabulary about spiritual certainty tended to collapse in on itself.[3] The last section of this essay seeks to place Calvin in the midst of these debates and to determine how he negotiated inherited problems about the use of the Spirit in the problem of certitude.

The fully polemical nature of these exegetical discussions becomes clear only when placed in their sixteenth-century context. The Reformers fought on a twofold front, namely, against Catholicism and against the different strands of the Radical Reformation. As the sacramental controversies show, the "magisterial" Reformers also argued vehemently with one another. Defense of the subjective certainty of salvation was aimed primarily against Catholic theologies of justification. The struggle for the certainty of authority was aimed at all the disputants of the era.

3. On the issue of authority see David V. N. Bagchi, *Luther's Earliest Opponents, Catholic Controversialists, 1518-1525* (Minneapolis: Fortress, 1991); S. H. Hendrix, *Luther and the Papacy: Stages in a Reformation Conflict* (Philadelphia: Fortress, 1981); Rupert E. Davies, *The Problem of Authority in the Continental Reformers: A Study in Luther, Zwingli and Calvin* (London: Epworth, 1946); G. R. Evans, *Problems of Authority in the Reformation* (Cambridge: Cambridge University Press, 1992); Kenneth Hagen, *Foundations of Theology in the Continental Reformation: Questions of Authority* (Marquette: Marquette University, 1974); Mark U. Edwards, *Luther and the False Brethren* (Stanford: Stanford University Press, 1975). On the certainty of salvation see Walther von Loewenich, *Luther's Theology of the Cross,* trans. from the 5th German edition (1967) by Herbert J. A. Bouman (Minneapolis: Augsburg, 1976); Paul Althaus, *The Theology of Martin Luther,* trans. Robert C. Schultz (Philadelphia: Fortress, 1966); Karl Heim, *Das Gewissheitsproblem in der systematischen Theologie bis zu Schleiermacher* (Leipzig, 1911); Ralf Hoburg, *Seligkeit und Heilsgewissheit: Hermeneutik und Schriftauslegung bei Huldrych Zwingli bis 1522* (Stuttgart: Calwer, 1994); Robert W. A. Letham, "Saving Faith and Assurance in Reformed Theology: Zwingli to the Synod of Dort," 2 vols. (Ph.D. thesis, University of Aberdeen, 1979); idem, "Faith and Assurance in Early Calvinism: A Model of Continuity and Diversity," in *Later Calvinism, International Perspectives,* ed. W. Fred Graham (Kirksville, Mo.: Sixteenth Century Journal Publishers, 1994); Steven E. Ozment, *The Reformation in the Cities:. The Appeal of Protestantism to Sixteenth-Century Germany and Switzerland* (New Haven: Yale University Press, 1975), pp. 12, 26; Randall C. Zachman, *The Assurance of Faith* (Minneapolis: Fortress, 1993).

Medieval discussions about justification had involved complex analyses about the role of grace, the abilities of the *viator* in sin and in grace, the extent of free will, the possibility of congruous and condign merits, and the nature of predestination. Regardless of their differences, medieval theologians agreed that the Christian could not attain the final, subjective certitude of salvation. The necessity for attaining holiness meant that, in the absence of a special revelation, any claim to the final certitude of salvation was the sin of pride or presumption. The definitive text that reinforced the ultimate uncertainty of salvation was Eccl. 9:1: "No man knows whether he is worthy of love or hatred." This was the position reaffirmed at the Council of Trent: the Christian may quite rightly experience fear and apprehension concerning grace "since no one can know with the certainty of faith, which cannot be subject to error, that he has obtained the grace of God."[4]

Nonetheless, medieval theologians did not deny all forms of certainty. The believer could be assured of an objective certainty that none of the elect would die in mortal sin, even if the *viator* could have only a conjectural certainty that he was in a state of grace or one of the elect. Two men most decisive in Luther's development, Gabriel Biel and John Staupitz, both discussed the various forms of certitude.[5] According to Biel, the light of truth, delight in good works, and peace of the conscience might provide conjectural certitude. But such signs might also be tricks of the devil. Furthermore, no final certainty of perseverance was possible. Staupitz took greater care to clarify the forms of conjectural certitude. The *viator* could safely look to the merciful nature of God as Father, the love evident in the atonement, the internal change wrought by grace, the objective effect of the sacraments, and the struggles of temptation. Still, these signs were only conjectural; the Christian had no subjective certainty as to whether "he was worthy of love or hatred."

Despite their many differences, the Reformers agreed that saving faith was not a faith formed by love that enabled the *viator* to earn merits. Nor was justification a process whereby one progressed toward the holiness necessary to meet the justice of God.[6] In place of the *viator* status we find

4. Session VI, 1545, Ch. IX. See also A. Stakemeier, *Das Konzil von Trient über die Heilsgewissheit* (Heidelberg: F. H. Kerle, 1947).

5. In the following section I am dependent on David Curtis Steinmetz, *Misericordia Dei* (Leiden: E. J. Brill, 1968), pp. 91-92, 122-30; and Heiko A. Oberman, *The Harvest of Medieval Theology* (repr., Durham, N.C.: Labyrinth, 1983), pp. 217-20.

6. Heiko A. Oberman, "'Justitia Christi' and 'Iustitia Dei': Luther and the Scholastic Doctrines of Justification," in *The Dawn of the Reformation* (Edinburgh: T & T Clark, 1986), pp. 104-25.

the new Reformation doctrine of certitude. Moving far beyond notions of objective and conjectural certainty, Luther, Zwingli, and Calvin defended the individual's subjective certainty of salvation. They did so by equating faith with certitude. One might even say that, for the Reformers, justifying faith was not a faith formed by love but a trust or faith formed by certainty.

I. Luther and Zwingli on the Search for Certitude

The relationship between faith and certainty moved Luther and Zwingli into the precarious realm of the experiential. Repeatedly they were drawn to the experiential, affective language of interiority and immediacy in order to explain the nature of faith as the sure knowledge of justification. Luther spoke of a "feeling," "tasting," "sweetening," or "experiencing" that takes place in the "heart" of the believer.[7] Luther's description of an affective interior feeling of salvation was anchored in a biblical appeal to the Spirit; the work of the Holy Spirit was the creation of an *experience*. No one, Luther explained,

> can correctly understand God or his Word unless he has received such understanding immediately from the Holy Spirit. But no one can receive it from the Holy Spirit without experiencing, proving, and feeling it. In such experience, the Holy Spirit instructs us as in his own school.[8]

Zwingli also appealed to the experience of the Spirit. While he and Luther dramatically clashed on the means used by the Spirit to illumine and comfort the soul, this controversy did not create any significant difference in their respective views of the effect of the Spirit on faith. Like Luther, Zwingli spoke of a "feeling," an "experience," and the "certainty" of salvation.[9] Zwingli's emphasis on John 6:44 and 6:63 may have intensified his

---

7. See Luther, *Operationes in Psalmos*, WA 5:285.29-30, 387.40-45; *Von den guten Werken*, WA 6:217.25-27; *Das Magnificat*, WA 7:546.25.30, 548.4-11; *De servo arbitrio*, WA 18:605.34; 782.9-11; *Annotationes in Ecclesiasten*, WA 20:161.18-20; *In epistolam S. Pauli ad Galatas Commentarius*, WA 40/1:228.33-40, 523.30.32, 524.32-34; *Das XIV und XV Capitel S. Johannis gepredigt und ausgelegt*, WA 45:475.4-7, 507.30-36, 588.25, 590.24-28, 594.29-33; 599.9-15, 624.6-7; *Auslegung des ersten und zweiten Kapitels Johannis*, WA 46:718.30-32. On the complex nature of experience see Loewenich, *Luther's Theology of the Cross*, pp. 77-88, 93-101.

8. Luther, *Das Magnificat*, WA 7:546.24-29; LW 21:299.

9. Zwingli, *De vera et falsa religione commentarius*, ZSW 3:761.4-19, 782.6-10, 821.30-32 (LWZ 3:183, 208, 254); *De providentia Dei*, ZSW 6/3:169.21, 171.15-18, 176.21-177.4, 179.17-19, 180.13-15 (LWZ 2:193-95, 196, 199); *Fidei ratio*, ZSW 6/2:800.30-35 (LWZ 2:43-44).

sense of the immediacy of the Spirit. Thus Zwingli spoke of an "inward drawing" of the Spirit, a "feeling" of freedom in the inmost heart, a feeling of "trust," "rest," and "security."[10] Zwingli's believer experienced the certainty of faith directly from the Spirit "in the veins of his soul."[11] Indeed, the baptism of the Holy Spirit produced an "inward flooding"[12] of the Spirit that gave certainty to the soul.

When focusing on the certitude of faith, both men turned to the aforementioned biblical passages depicting the immediacy of the Spirit in order to describe the certainty of faith. For Luther, the primary locus of the immediacy and certainty of salvation was Paul's accounts of how believers are impelled to cry "Abba Father!" In these verses Luther found language about the divine Spirit directly touching the human spirit so that the believer receives the "spirit of sonship" and feels himself to be the child of God. Commenting on Gal. 4:6, Luther incorporates both Rom. 8:16 and Eccl. 9:1:

> We have this innate evil in us that we are in doubt about the favor of God toward us and we cannot believe with certainty that we are pleasing to God. . . . Meanwhile, however, the Holy Spirit is helping us in our weakness and interceding for us with sighs too deep for words [Rom. 8:26] and he is bearing witness with our spirit that we are children of God [Rom. 8:16]. . . . To prove and support this wicked error [the papacy] used the statement of Solomon in Ecclesiastes 9:1, "The righteous and the wise and their deeds are in the hand of God; whether it is love or hatred man does not know." . . . The chief point of all Scripture is that we should not doubt. . . . Let us thank God, therefore, that we have been delivered from this monster of uncertainty and now we can believe with certainty that the Holy Spirit is crying and issuing a sigh too deep for words in our hearts. . . . Now that the plague of uncertainty, with which the entire Church of the pope is infected, is driven away, let us believe with certainty that God is favorably disposed to us.[13]

Hesitant to talk explicitly about predestination, Luther often refers only to the inner certainty of being in a state of grace. However, John 6:44

10. Zwingli, *De vera et falsa religione*, ZSW 3:670.34, 671.4-7, 694.12-19, 715.30-34, 760.17-34, 784.25-30 (LWZ 3:93-94, 122, 146, 182, 211); *Fidei ratio*, ZSW 6/2:800.30-34 (LWZ 2:43-44); *De providentia*, ZSW 6/3:177.11, 180.9 (LWZ 2:196, 199).

11. Zwingli, *De providentia Dei*, ZSW 6/3:180.13-15 (LWZ:199).

12. Zwingli, *De vera et falsa religione*, ZSW 3:764.25-26, 766.2 (LWZ 3:187, 189).

13. Luther, *In epistolam S. Pauli ad Galatas commentarius (1535)*, WA 40/1:580.10-12, 581.23-25, 587.29-588.12, 589.1-5, 591.27-28.

and 14:9 allow him to go further and affirm the certitude of election. Indeed, commenting on Gen. 26:9, Luther states that Christ "came into the world to make us certain," and that God revealed himself so that "you may know whether you are predestined or not." He makes clear that John 6:44 and 14:9 anchor the revelation and certitude of predestination not in the hidden God but in the God revealed in Christ. Hence the hiddenness of God should not deter us from the certitude of election: "Therefore we should rather impress these statements on our hearts, such as John 6:44, 'No one can come to me unless the Father draw him.' Through whom? Through Me. 'He who sees Me also sees the Father'" (cf. John 14:9). Going beyond the objective certainty of election, Luther argues that the unrevealed God becomes the revealed God and sends the Son through whom one gains the certainty of election: "For 'he who sees Me,' says Christ, 'also sees the Father himself' (cf. John 14:9). If you listen to Him, are baptized in His name, and love His Word, then you are surely predestined and certain of your salvation."[14]

Unlike Luther, Zwingli was only too happy to discuss predestination. Indeed, his defense of certitude has its starting point in the doctrine of God's immutable election. His argument differs from Luther's primarily because of his insistence that one finds certainty by contemplating election directly. His biblical text for proving the certitude of election is almost always John 6:44. This verse was of central importance because it both demonstrates predestination and supports Zwingli's underlying theological anthropology. Fundamental to Zwingli's reliance on passages about the Spirit was his conviction that the human spirit can be taught immediately by the divine Spirit; John 6:63 implies that external means and teachers are not necessary.[15] This immediacy between Spirit and spirit produces certitude. For Zwingli, the reference to "drawing" and the statement that the "flesh profits nothing" both demonstrate this direct connection between the divine and the human, that is, the connection between God's election and the human certitude of faith.

The key to Zwingli's doctrine of certitude is his belief that election precedes faith. Using John 6:44, Zwingli affirms that true faith is never within human power; as Gal. 5:22 proves, the very existence of faith is due to the inner presence of the divine Spirit. Reasoning backward, Zwingli

---

14. Luther, *Vorlesungen über 1. Mose*, WA 43:457.32-462.27; LW 5:42-49. This discussion is Luther's most complete statement about the certainty of salvation or predestination.

15. Zwingli, *De vera et falsa religione*, ZSW 3:782.6-7 (LWZ 3:207); *Von Klarheit Gewissheit des Wortes Gottes*, ZSW 1:365.14-366.4, 366.19-367.5, 370.27-371.6.

argues that "Faith is the sign of election," or "faith is given to those who have been elected and ordained to eternal life, but so that election precedes and faith follows election." Zwingli could then maintain that since faith is a sign of election, the experience of faith is the proof of the certainty of election: "Be assured that he who believes has been elected by the Father and predestined and called. He believes, therefore, because he has been elected and predestined to eternal salvation. . . ."[16] Zwingli consistently attributes this certainty to the work of the Spirit:

> He, then, who is thus protected by the shield of faith knows that he is elect of God by the very security based on his faith. And this is the pledge by which the Spirit binds our soul to Himself. . . . And he who has not this certainty so that he feels it stand forth dauntless and immoveable in the veins of the soul, as it were, . . . should pray daily "Thy kingdom come," and "Lord, increase our faith."

Zwingli concludes that neither sin nor death can shake this inner certitude, for "their election is such that it is not only known to God but also to the elect themselves."[17]

A. The Problem of Authority

If the controversy between the Reformers and their Catholic opponents had been limited to issues of justification and the certainty of salvation, arguments about authority might not have taken the problematic turn that came to characterize sixteenth-century polemics. But as the pneumatic language of certainty was transferred to the realm of authority, Reformation arguments followed a critical and disturbing trajectory. One of the most fascinating features of this crisis is that disputes about authority were propelled along this new course by the use of the same theological-heuristic principles, many of the same texts, and much of the same vocabulary marshaled earlier in the debates about the certainty of salvation. However, when used to buttress a claim for authority, the recourse to pneumatic texts led the Reformers along a line that ultimately missed its mark.

---

16. Zwingli, *De providentia Dei*, ZSW 6/3:178.9-10 (LWZ 2:79-80). See also *De providentia Dei*, ZSW 6/3:178.22-184.17; *In catabaptistarum strophas elenchus*, ZSW 6/1:178.6-7 (see *Refutation of the Tricks of the Baptists*, in *Ulrich Zwingli: Selected Works* [Philadelphia: University of Pennsylvania Press, 1901, 1972], pp. 237-43).

17. Zwingli, *De providentia Dei*, ZSW 6/3:180.8.21 (LWZ 2:199-200).

The issue of authority encompassed diverse issues and included all religious parties of the era. Catholic controversialists attacked Luther on this issue as early as 1518, and the 1525 Peasants' War seemed to prove their point.[18] The eruption of sacramental and spiritualist debates only exacerbated the problem. The crisis of authority clearly reflected theological, social, and political dimensions. However, in the pages that follow, we will continue to examine only the exegetical nature of the debates and focus on the way in which the appeal to the Spirit fueled a specifically hermeneutical crisis of authority. In short, the following discussion analyzes the decline of what Steinmetz has called the "exegetical optimism" of early Protestantism.[19]

The problem within Protestantism surfaced as early as 1522, when the Zwickau prophets emerged, protesting infant baptism, claiming to have been called directly by God, and declaring that their teachings were inspired by the Holy Spirit. This episode presaged things to come as various radical groups claimed their interpretation of Scripture as authoritative, developed different hermeneutical principles, published books, and took part in biblical colloquies and disputations. Controversies about baptism, the Eucharist, tradition, and ecclesiology threw into doubt the ideal of a purely biblical theology. All the warring parties appealed to the guidance of the Spirit in their scriptural interpretation. Claims to an immediate inner experience of the "Spirit," "inner word," or "Wisdom of God" became common claims for the certainty of authority.[20] Despite their complexity and variety, the views of the Radical Reformers about the relationship between Word and Spirit became an intrinsic and essential part of the overarching and deepening crisis of certitude and authority.

The Reformers were acutely aware of the problems created by these disputes internal to Protestantism. Luther frequently observed that all the world claimed to have Christ, Baptism, Sacrament, and Holy Scripture. Luther also knew that the problem revolved around the Spirit, complaining that all he ever heard was "Geist! Geist! Geist!" Referring to the Catholics, Anabaptists, and ancient Montanists, Luther said, "Their one boast is of nothing but the Spirit. . . . Our whole quarrel with all these factions revolves

18. Bagchi, *Luther's Earliest Opponents,* pp. 98, 168, 178, 250.
19. David C. Steinmetz, *Luther in Context* (Bloomington: Indiana University Press, 1986), p. 96.
20. George Huntston Williams, *The Radical Reformation,* 3rd ed. (Kirksville, Mo.: Sixteenth-Century Journal Publishers, 1992), pp. 1247-55; Steven E. Ozment, *Mysticism and Dissent: Religious Ideology and Social Protest in the Sixteenth Century* (New Haven: Yale University Press, 1973).

around their claim that they have the Holy Spirit and therefore should be believed."[21]

The challenge for both Luther and Zwingli was to establish a hermeneutical certitude that distinguished them from all their opponents (including one another). To address this unwanted problem, they combined verses interpreted as the subjective certitude of salvation with biblical references to the authority of "spiritual judgments" such as 1 John 4:1, 1 Cor. 2:14-15, and 2 Cor. 2:11-13. The connection between verses about salvation and verses about judgments was decisive. Only because the believer had experienced the inward "drawing" of election or the cry of "Abba Father!" could he go on to make authoritative decisions. For Luther and Zwingli, the authoritative text was 2 Cor. 2:15: "The spiritual man judges all things." Luther moves effortlessly between the two forms of certitude. He begins his discussion of Gal. 4:6 by first vindicating the right of the faithful to judge. Commenting on the words, "God has sent the Spirit of his Son into your hearts," Luther argues that the believer has been re-created with a new judgment, new sensation, and new drives. Such changes

> are the gift and accomplishment of the Holy Spirit, who comes with the preached Word, purifies our hearts by faith and produces spiritual motivation in us. Therefore, there is the greatest possible difference between us and the enemies and perverters of the Word. We . . . are able to declare and judge with certainty, on the basis of the Word, about the will of God toward us, about all laws and doctrines, about our lives and those of others. On the other hand, the papists and the fanatical spirits are unable to judge with certainty about anything.[22]

Throughout his writings Luther asserts the right of the "spiritual man" to make judgments. The believer can judge the wickedness and the idolatry of the world. The "spiritual man" has the authority to judge the purity of doctrine, especially the nature of faith and works. Consequently, Luther's believer could safely judge all forms of heresy and unbelief, including those of the Turks, Jews, Faber, Eck, Oecolampadius, and Zwingli.[23] Of course,

---

21. Luther, *Das XIV und XV Kapitel S. Johannis*, WA 45:622.16-22, 716.25-34 (LW 24:176-77, 280). See also Regin Prenter, *Spiritus Creator*, trans. John M. Jensen (Philadelphia: Muhlenberg, 1953).

22. Luther, *In epistolam S. Pauli ad Galatas commentarius* (1535), WA 40/1:572.20-29 (LW 26:375).

23. See Luther, *An den Christlichen Adel deutscher Nation von des christlichen Standes Besserung*, WA 6:412.20-31; *De captivitate Babylonica ecclesiae praeludium*, 561.3-18; *Deuteronomion Mosi cum annotationibus*, WA 14:670.7-19; *Annotationes in priorem epistolam ad*

Zwingli also believed in the authority of his own spiritual judgments, and he, too, cited 1 Cor. 2:15:

> Again I know for certain that God teaches me, because I have experienced the fact of it. . . . Hear the words of Paul [1 Cor. 2:15], "But the natural man receives not the things of the Spirit of God: for they are foolishness unto him. Neither can he know them, because they are spiritually discerned. But he that is spiritual judges all things, yet he himself is judged by no one. . . . The spiritual man judges all things, that is, he sees at once whether the doctrine is of God or not. But he is judged by none, that is, even if he is judged . . . he will not let himself be torn or turned aside.[24]

The dilemma is obvious. With everyone appealing to the same text, the sixteenth-century quest for certitude took on the nature of an intense hermeneutical crisis. This crisis was intensified greatly by the constant appeals to the Spirit. By their very nature, such appeals were based on experience; just as believers experienced the certainty of salvation, so, too, they experienced the illumination of Scripture by the Spirit. The Spirit gave birth to a new perception. Experience authorized judgment, and, once again, the Spirit became the agent of certainty. But experiential authority is notoriously and intrinsically problematic since it is virtually impossible to judge true from false experience. The application of passages about the Spirit to bolster one's interpretation of the "objective" clarity of Scripture only transferred the affective language of salvation to the realm of authority. The anguished and heated question was not simply "Where is the church?" but, more precisely, "Where is the Spirit?"

Luther and Zwingli tried valiantly to avoid the dangers caused by the experiential and omnipresent claims to the Spirit. Despite their many differences, however, both men finally had recourse to the objective clarity of Scripture. They exhorted readers to come to the Word with an open mind and not to impose their own thoughts on the text.[25] But regardless of their

---

Timotheum, WA 26:108.20-109.11; *In Esaiam prophetam enarraciones,* WA 31/2:452.31-453.3; *Predigt über Johannis 7:16-18,* WA 33:365.5-366.34; *In epistolam S. Pauli ad Galatas Commentarius,* WA 40/1:603.14-31, 40/2:111.20-31, 40/2:174.14-34; *Contra asinos Parisienses Lovaniensesque,* WA 54:448.3-31. For an early interpretation of 1 Cor. 2:15 see Luther, *Dictata super Psalterium,* WA 4:353.17-18.

24. Zwingli, *Von Klarheit und Gewissenheit des Wortes Gottes,* ZSW 1:379.19-380.25 (LCC 24:90-91). See also *Adversus Hieronymum Emserum antibolon,* ZSW 3:260.4-5 (LWZ 3:373); *De vera et falsa religione,* ZSW 3:672.29-673.17, 678.24 (LWZ 3:96, 102).

25. Zwingli, *Die Predigten über Ev. Joh. VI–VIII,* WA 33:363.4-366.11; *Von Klarheit und Gewissheit Wortes Gottes,* ZSW 1:359.33-360.20, 376.13-377.10 (LCC 24:74-75, 88-89).

attempts to argue from the certainty of an objectively clear Scripture, we are always recalled to the astute observation of George Williams that "the vagaries [about the relationship of Word and Spirit] should not obscure from view the fact that a large element in the spiritualism of the Radical Reformation goes back to Luther himself and, to a lesser extent, Zwingli."[26] Moreover, the fact that Luther and Zwingli could not themselves agree on the interpretation of eucharistic passages recalls us to the caustic but penetrating insight of John Eck:

> By this example, taken from the modern heretics [who reject any other judge than Scripture] is shown how the Lutherans and Oecolampadians and Zwinglians fight over the sacrament of the Eucharist, as to whether here is truly and spiritually the body and blood of Christ, or only a figure and sign. Who among them will be judge? Who will ever bring them into harmony? Scripture or the Church? (Apart from these no other judge can be provided.) It is not indeed upon Scripture, which each contends to be the judge, that they lay their foundation — all the while in the self-same words of Scripture — and thus they do not admit Scripture as judge against their own doctrine but they make themselves judges over Scripture. Accordingly, the Church will be the necessary judge. . . .[27]

The sacramental controversies posed a seemingly insurmountable challenge to the exegetical optimism of the Reformers. Nonetheless, the difficulties with conflicting interpretations, arguments from experience, the use of affective, experiential language, and the opposing appeals to the Spirit met additional challenges *within* the theologies of Luther and Zwingli. By continuing to focus on exegesis we discover that Luther and Zwingli held theological-exegetical principles, internal to their thought, that undermined their claims for a certitude of authority. For Luther that principle was demonology; for Zwingli the issue was ecclesiology.

---

26. Williams, *The Radical Reformation*, pp. 1248-49. Ever since the work of Joseph Lortz, many Luther scholars have tried to defend Luther against the charge of subjectivism. For examples of this debate and a defense of Luther's objectivity that is not reflected in this paper see Joseph Lortz, *The Reformation in Germany*, 2 vols., trans. Ronald Walls (London: Darton, Longman & Todd, 1968), 1:184, 451, 455; Michael Baylor, *Action and Person* (Leiden: E. J. Brill, 1977), p. 267; B. A. Gerrish, *Continuing the Reformation* (Chicago: University of Chicago Press, 1993), pp. 38-56; Prenter, *Spiritus Creator*, pp. 205-53.

27. Johannes Eck, *Enchiridion locorum communium adversus Lutherum et alios hostes ecclesiae* (1525-43), ed. P. Fraenkel, Corpus Catholicorum, 34 (Münster, 1979), pp. 81-82; John Eck, *Enchiridion of Commonplaces*, trans. Ford Lewis Battles (Grand Rapids: Baker, 1979), p. 48.

B. Luther and the Threat of the Demonic

Scholars such as Oberman and Edwards have demonstrated the relationship between Luther's theology, apocalypticism, and demonology.[28] Living at the end time, Luther believed the devil was intensifying his activity through the Jews, Turks, Rome, and the "fanatics." Luther passionately asserted that all his opponents were "bewitched" and inspired by Satan. Continually he charged Müntzer, Carlstadt, the Sacramentarians, the Anabaptists, and Rome with being under the devil's spell and control. Once again the issue was connected to pneumatology; just as the Spirit enlightened the believer, Satan deceived and blinded his followers. Luther thought that although his opponents honestly believed they were inspired by the Spirit, in reality they were being deluded by the devil: Satan puts on a "most beautiful appearance," "captivates," "dazzles," and "blinds," so that those who are in error "cannot escape even though one were to present the truth to them so clearly and directly that they could almost touch it."[29] Maintaining that his doctrine was "true, pure, certain, and divine," Luther condemned those who differed from him by saying that they were "sent from the devil and . . . with the utmost confidence we pronounce them anathema."[30]

But Luther did not restrict his demonology to polemics. He went on to make Satan central to the already heated exegetical arguments about the certainty of authority. In so doing he further compounded the crisis of authority both in his polemics and in terms of the internal coherence of his thought. Luther intensified the exegetical reliance on the Spirit by turning to 2 Cor. 11:14 to explain exactly *how* Satan worked: "for even the devil transforms himself into an angel of light." Luther's preoccupation with this verse escalates the problem of authority in his thought because at times he leads the reader so far into the realm of Satanic deception, delusion, and unreality that even the life of the believer threatens to become a series of chaotic mirages. In short, the use of 2 Cor. 11:14 endangers Luther's certitude of authority based on his claim that the "spiritual man judges all things."

28. Heiko A. Oberman, *Luther: Man between God and the Devil*, trans. Eileen Walliser-Schwarzbart (New Haven: Yale University Press, 1989); Mark U. Edwards, *Luther and the False Brethren* (Stanford: Stanford University Press, 1975); idem, *Luther's Last Battles, Politics and Polemics, 1531-1546* (Ithaca: Cornell University Press, 1983), pp. 97-115.

29. Luther, *Vier tröstliche Psalmen an die Königin zu Ungaren (1526)*, WA 19:599.4-14.

30. Luther, *In epistolam S. Pauli ad Galatas commentarius (1535)*, WA 40/1:122.30-123.6, cited by Edwards, *Luther and the False Brethren*, p. 123.

Luther believed that Satan's effectiveness depended upon hiddenness. Scholars have long recognized the importance of *divine* hiddenness in Luther's theology.[31] However, an equally important counterpart to the hiddenness of God is the hiddenness of Satan. Like God, Luther's devil also hides under a contrary appearance, that is, under the appearance of holiness, knowledge, truth, and piety. Satan transforms himself into the likeness of Christ: "the devils can clothe and adorn themselves with Christ's name in such a way that one could swear a thousand oaths that it is truly Christ himself, although in reality it is the archenemy and the true Archantichrist."[32] Satan quotes Scripture "under the name and guise of Christ," and teaches "God, Christ, the Holy Spirit, and Christendom."[33] The devil "insinuates himself into our hearts, not as one who is evil and false but as one who is good and the best, as an angel of light."[34] Satan blinds heretics with theories that appear brilliant so that the heretic truly believes he is always illumined by the Holy Spirit. Hence Luther warns against accepting inspiration uncritically because it may not be from the Spirit but from Satan transformed into an angel of light.[35]

Most importantly, this "white devil"[36] can produce his own kind of certainty. According to Luther, the devil hides by disguising himself as an angel of light in order to "blind" and "bewitch" the mind. In Luther's judg-

---

31. Hellmut Bandt, *Luthers Lehre vom verborgenen Gott: Eine Untersuchung zu dem offenbarungsgeschichtlichen Ansatz seiner Theologie* (Berlin: Evangelische Verlagsanstalt, 1958); John Dillenberger, *God Hidden and Revealed: The Interpretation of Luther's Deus Absconditus and Its Significance for Religious Thought* (Philadelphia: Muhlenberg, 1935); Fritz Blanke, *Der verborgene Gott bei Luther* (Berlin: Furche, 1928); Heinrich Bornkamm, "Der verborgene und der offenbare Gott," *Theologische Rundschau*, n.s. 16 (1944): 38-52; Brian Gerrish, "'To the Unknown God,' Luther and Calvin on the Hiddenness of God," in *The Old Protestantism and the New* (Chicago: University of Chicago Press, 1982), pp. 131-49; Egil Grislis, "Martin Luther's View of the Hidden God: The Problem of the *Deus Absconditus* in Luther's Treatise *De Servo Arbitrio*," *McCormick Quarterly* 21 (1967): 81-94.

32. Luther, *Das XIV und XV Kapitel S. Johannis*, WA 45:475.4-10 (LW 24:16).

33. Luther, *Das XIV und XV Kapitel S. Johannis*, WA 45:503.2-11 (LW 24:46).

34. Luther, *Vorlesung über den 1. Brief des Johannis 1527*, WA 20:649.25-27 (LW 30:241-42).

35. Luther, *Vorlesung über 1. Mose*, WA 42:668.1-6, 43:416.14-19, 31-38 (LW 3:167, 4:389). See also WA 42:667.28-42 (LW 3:167). In his exposition of Psalm 68 (WA 3:407-8; LW 3:348-49), Luther tries to delineate ways in which one can distinguish between divine and diabolical inspiration. However, to my knowledge these criteria play no real role in his other discussions of this problem or in his citations of 2 Cor. 11:14. Cf. John L. Thompson, "Patriarchs, Polygamy, and Private Resistance: John Calvin and Others on Breaking God's Rules," *Sixteenth Century Journal* 25/1 (Spring 1994): 21-26.

36. Luther, *In epistolam S. Pauli ad Galatas commentarius (1535)*, WA 40/1:96.10 (LW 26:4).

ment, the Catholic and radical opponents did not *refuse* to understand but, rather, they were *unable* to do so. They were incapable of recognizing the truth because they were "under a spell," in a "dream" or "stupor." Luther believed his opponents were locked into a world of Satanic deception that seemed all too real. This "bewitchment of the spirit" was the demonic transformation that produces an experientially real but delusional certitude. For Luther, the devil convinces us that his opinions are certain and "truly godly":

> Nowadays [the ancient serpent] is showing his ability to do this in the fanatics, the Anabaptists, and the Sacramentarians. With his tricks, he has so bewitched their minds that they are embracing lies, errors, and horrible darkness as the most certain truths and the clearest light. . . . [The devil] works internally with plausible opinions and ideas about doctrine, by which, as I have said, he so dements the hearts of men that they would swear that their most vain and wicked dreams are the most certain truth.[37]

In Luther's view, the devil creates a reality that is an indistinguishable mirror-image of the truth. The hiddenness of God and the hiddenness of Satan are locked into a deadly contest between the real and the counterfeit. The individual is immersed in a delusion that appears more real than the truth. Consequently, in Luther's frequent use of 2 Cor. 11:14 the world becomes a nightmare of mimicry, illusions, and deceptions that skillfully masquerade as reality. Evil parodies the good so authentically that claims to the certitude of authority fall into a demonic perceptual chaos that the objective clarity of Scripture cannot penetrate. The hiddenness of God confronts the hiddenness of Satan so that the world becomes a tragic shadow play where the line between deception and reality, bewitchment and sight, truth and lies, threatens to disappear.

Luther's doctrine of the certainty of faith, based primarily on Rom. 8:15 and Gal. 4:6, removes the anxiety and doubt about salvation. But this anxiety seems, in turn, to be replaced by the burden of "testing the spirits" (1 John 4:1), a burden that lies heavily on one surrounded by competing and conflicting claims to illumination by the Spirit. Not surprisingly, 1 John 4:1 takes on an urgency in Luther's thought that indicates the depth of the authority crisis.[38] Thus he warns that "Christ does not give you the right

---

37. Luther, *In epistolam S. Pauli ad Galatus commentarius (1535)*, WA 40/1:316.26-29–317.1-20 (LW 26:192).

38. Luther, *Ein Brief an die Fürsten zu Sachen von dem aufrührischen Geist*, WA 15:213.19-22 (LW 40:52); *Die Predigten über Ev. Joh. VI–VIII*, WA 33:275.26-276.21 (LW

to run to and fro in search of the Spirit, to lose yourself in reverie and say, 'I have this by the inspiration of the Spirit.' Actually, it may be the devil who inspired you."[39] To "test the spirits" was to plunge the believer into the battlefield between the Spirit, "who does not deceive," and Satan, who deceives all too well by "transforming himself into an angel of light." The believer needed a powerful spiritual discernment that could safely distinguish between the two opponents.

Luther's answer to the dilemma caused by his frequent use of 2 Cor. 11:14 reflects again the exegetical optimism that originally underlay his assertion of a hermeneutical certitude: the Holy Spirit cannot be divorced from the clarity of the Word. On the surface, evil and good look alike. But God commands us to "test the spirits" by the external perspicuity of Scripture:

> By it we judge the spirits and doctrines of all men, also with the greatest certainty. . . . We spoke of this earlier as the external clarity of Scripture. We hold that all spirits should be proved in the sight of the church by the judgment of Scripture.

The reader may recall and compare Ignatius's famous thirteenth rule when noting the urgency Luther felt to "test the Spirits" not by the pope or institutional authority but by Scripture only: "But if I am to test a spirit, I must have the Word of God. The latter is to be the rule or touchstone or Lydian stone by which I can tell black from white and evil from good."[40]

C. Zwingli and the Elusive Magisterium

In the face of growing controversy with Catholics, Lutherans and Anabaptists, Zwingli also had recourse to several exegetical principles in order to establish hermeneutical authority. Renouncing one's own thoughts and desires, the reader must be subject to Scripture. Rather than seeking support

---

23:174); *Dass diese Wort Christi "Das ist mein Leib" noch fest stehen 1527*, WA 23:283.12-14 (LW 37:159); *In epistolam S. Pauli ad Galatus commentarius (1535)*, WA 40/1:511.33-34 (LW 26:331); *Auslegung des ersten und zweiten Kapitels Johannis in Predigten 1537 und 1538*, WA 46:593.34-594.2 (LW 22:67-68).

39. Luther, *Die Predigten über Ev. Joh. VI-VIII*, WA 33:273.39 (LW 23:173).

40. Luther, *De servo Arbitrio*, WA 18:653.22-27 (LW 33:28); *Die Predigten über Ev. Joh. VI–VIII*, WA 33:276.3-7 (LW 23:174, 229-233); cf. WA 33:356-366. Ignatius's words were, "If we wish to proceed securely in all things, we must hold fast to the following principle: What seems to me white, I will believe black if the hierarchical Church so defines."

for his own views, the Christian must be *theodidacti,* that is, "taught of God" rather than by any human authorities.[41] But the objective clarity of Scripture was obviously insufficient; all parties in the debate quoted the Bible. In response to conflicting interpretations, Zwingli emphasizes that the Spirit must teach the meaning of Scripture. The Spirit inspired Scripture, and the Spirit must illuminate the words and the mind in order that the believer may know with certainty the meaning of the text. Moreover, the "spiritual man" must "try the spirits" in order to ascertain which meaning tends most to the glory of God. Most often, however, the direct teaching of God or the Spirit is sufficient to "test the spirits."[42]

There are, or course, important differences between Luther and Zwingli on the interpretation and use of Scripture. The most familiar issue involves the complexities regarding the relationship of Word and Spirit. For our purposes, however, the most important discrepancies occur in the realms of demonology and ecclesiology. In Zwingli's writings, passages about spiritual judgments are not suffused with a demonology that threatens to undercut certainty. But Zwingli's struggle for the hermeneutical certitude of authority must confront his emphasis on the church of the elect. Zwingli creates a tension within his own thought by combining 1 Cor. 2:15 and 1 John 4:2-3, not with 2 Cor. 11:14 but with John 6:44 ("No one can come to me unless the Father who sent me draws him") and John 10:3-5 ("the sheep hear his voice, and he calls his own sheep by name . . . and the sheep follow him, for they know his voice. A stranger they will not follow . . . for they do not know the voice of strangers").

We have seen that Zwingli interprets the directness or immediacy between the divine and human spirit as the guarantee for the subjective certainty of salvation. This same theology of immediacy also functions as the basis for certitude in the realm of authority. Just as believers know they are elect because of the inner drawing of the Spirit, so, too, the elect church bears authority because it is taught directly by God. In his *Reply to Emser* and the *Account of the Faith,* Zwingli explains the three meanings of the term "ecclesia." The "church" may refer to the mixed body of the faithful

41. Zwingli, *Von Klarheit und Gewissenheit des Wortes Gottes,* ZSW 1:366.18-23, 377.29 (LCC 24:79, 89); *De vera et falsa religione commentarius,* ZSW 3:642.35-37, 9 (LWZ 3:59); *De providentia Dei,* ZSW 6/3:189.8 (LWZ 2:205).

42. Zwingli, *Adversus Hieronymum Emserum antibolon,* ZSW 3:260.5-9, 264.5-7 (LWZ 3:377); *De vera et falsa religione commentarius,* ZSW 3:673.7-8, 678.24 (LWZ 3:96, 102); *In catabaptistarum stropphas elenchus,* ZSW 5:195.12 (*Refutation of the Tricks of the Baptists,* p. 257); cf. *Von Klarheit und Gewissenheit des Wortes Gottes,* ZSW 1:370.12-374.31 (LCC 24:82-83).

and the unfaithful. The term may also refer to the local church such as the Church of Rome. The word "church" may also denote the universal elect church that comes together only on the last day.[43] The tension in Zwingli's thought arises when he identifies the church that cannot err with this latter elect church. Arguing that this church cannot err because it rests on God's Word alone, Zwingli adds, "It is the Lord's flock, the sheep that hear no one's voice save its shepherd's."

> Whence, however, have the sheep such discerning knowledge of Christ that they accept no one else's voice for his? From the fact that they are known only by God [Gal. 4:9]; from the fact that the father draws them (for no one comes to Christ except him whom the father draws [Jn. 6:44]); from the fact that they all are taught by God [Jn. 6:45]; . . . those sheep do not err who know the voice of their shepherd so well, . . . and not of any shepherd whatsoever but only of the one who enters in by the door.[44]

In his *Account of the Faith* (1530), Zwingli clearly states that this elect church "does not err in regard to truth, namely, in those fundamental matters of faith upon which everything depends."[45] Zwingli makes his crucial exegetical move when he equates this elect church with the one in Eph. 5:27, that is, with the church "without spot or wrinkle."[46] This spotless and infallible church is not identical to the mixed church or the local church. Nor is this church identified with an institution or hierarchy. The problem is not the existence of the elect church but, rather, its knowability. While Zwingli insists that the believer knows he is individually elect, nonetheless, that believer cannot judge who else might be elect. The church without spot or wrinkle that cannot err is known only to God.[47]

The problem of identifying Eph. 5:27 with the authority of the elect church is clear. Zwingli is thereby attributing infallibility and authority to the invisible church — indeed, a church knowable only to God. How can an invisible church exercise interpretive authority of any kind? Again, John

43. Zwingli, *Adversus Hieronymum Emserum antibolon,* ZSW 3:252.23-269.6 (LWZ 3:366-382); *Fidei Ratio,* ZSW 6/2:800.16-803.5 (LWZ 2:43-45).

44. Zwingli, *Adversus Hieronymum Emserum antibolon,* ZSW 3:259.8-17 (LWZ 3:372).

45. Zwingli, *Fidei Ratio,* ZSW 6/2:802.5-8 (LWZ 2:45).

46. Zwingli, *Adversus Hieronymum Emserum antibolon,* ZSW 3:254.25-255.21, 256.9 (LWZ 3:368); *Fidei Ratio,* ZSW 6/2:800.19 (LWZ 2:43).

47. Zwingli, *Adversus Hieronymum Emserum antibolon,* ZSW 3:256.9 (LWZ 3:369); *Fidei Ratio,* ZSW 6/2:800.16-201.8 (LWZ 2:43). See also W. P. Stephens, *The Theology of Huldrych Zwingli* (Oxford: Clarendon Press, 1986), pp. 260-70.

Eck quickly sensed this danger in Zwingli's ecclesiology. In rebuttal, Eck insisted that Eph. 5:27 refers to the authoritative Catholic church that is undergoing sanctification.[48] This church is knowable in its hierarchy, its history, its representative councils, and the pope. Detecting the issue of authority as the Achilles' heel of the Reformers, Eck makes abundantly clear that "Holy Mother Church" has the necessary and knowable means of settling exegetical controversies. While the Reformers claim the mantle of 2 Cor. 2:15 and appeal to the spiritual man who judges all things, Eck brands them with Judg. 17:6/21:25, "In those days there was not a king in Israel, but each man did what seemed good to him."[49]

II. Calvin and the Search for Certainty

By the mid-sixteenth century these claims to certainty, especially the certainty of salvation, had become commonplace among the Reformers. The appeal of the Reformation doctrine of certitude is clear in the debates about justification at the 1541 Colloquy of Regensburg and in the popularity of such texts as the *Beneficio di Cristo*. As a second-generation Reformer, Calvin inherited these forceful but often problematic claims to certitude based on the certitude of the Spirit. Like Luther and Zwingli, Calvin understood the nature of faith as carrying within it the individual certainty of salvation. But when trying to establish the certainty of authority, Calvin exhibits an exegetical restraint that tries to avoid the dangers of "spiritualism." However, instead of claiming the Spirit and Word as the only sources of authority, we will see that for Calvin the very experience of certainty becomes a way to decide between disputed doctrines.

In order to argue these issues exegetically Calvin turned primarily to the following verses:

"Abba, Father!" (Gal. 4:6 and Rom. 8:14-16)

He has put his seal upon us and given us his Spirit in our hearts as a guarantee." (2 Cor. 1:22)

In him you also . . . were sealed with the promise of the Holy Spirit which is the guarantee of your inheritance. . . . (Eph. 1:13-14)

---

48. Eck, *Enchiridion,* p. 18 (p. 7 in Battles's translation).
49. Eck, *Enchiridion,* p. 54 (p. 31 in Battles's translation).

If the Spirit who raised Jesus from the dead dwells in you he . . . will give life to your mortal bodies also through his Spirit which dwells in you. (Rom. 8:11)

And you, being a wild olive, were engrafted in among them, and became a partaker with them of the root. . . . (Rom. 11:17)

Examine yourselves, whether you be in the faith; prove your own selves. Do you not know with regard to your own selves that Jesus Christ is in you, unless, indeed, you are reprobate? (2 Cor. 13:5)

Calvin's teaching on the *certitudo fidei* has the same aim as the theologies of certainty in Luther and Zwingli. The cry "Abba, Father" stems from the fully experienced, inner certainty of adoption. With his insistence that faith pertains to both the mind and the heart, Calvin uses the familiar affective language of experience to describe the nature of faith. We again find the vocabulary of "feeling," "tasting," "experiencing," and "inwardness." Uneasy doubting is replaced by the "feeling of full assurance" that cannot happen "without our truly feeling its sweetness and experiencing it in ourselves." The cry of "Abba, Father!" is possible only for the elect who have experienced confidence and have "tasted" the Spirit of adoption.[50] Calvin argues that "faith is not content with a doubtful or changeable opinion . . . but requires a full and fixed certainty such as men are wont to have from things experienced and proved."[51] Replying to the Council of Trent, Calvin argues that one should "attend to the antithesis between faith and doubt, plainly intimating that faith is destroyed as soon as certainty is taken away."[52]

Calvin voices other crucial views in agreement with Luther and Zwingli. Like these predecessors, Calvin assumes that the Spirit is the agent of certainty. The *testimonium internum Spiritus Sancti* is the inner teacher who illumines the mind or heart and "seals" the certainty and confidence that enables the believer to call God "Father." Commenting on Eph. 1:13-14, Calvin explains the twofold operation of the Spirit as the beginning of faith in knowledge and the completion of faith as a "firm and steady conviction, which admits of no opposing doubt."[53] The certainty of salvation that

---

50. Calvin, *Inst.* 3.1.3, 2.11-12, 15-16, 34, 37, 39; OS 4:3, 21-23, 25-27, 45, 47, 49.

51. Calvin, *Inst.* 3.2.15; OS 4:20-21, 25-26, 45.

52. Calvin, *Acta Synodi Tridentinae cum antidoto,* CO 7:456; John Calvin, *Selections from His Writings,* ed. John Dillenberger (Missoula: Scholars, 1975), p. 173.

53. Calvin, Comm. on Eph. 1:13, in *Opera exegetica* (Geneva: Droz, 1992), 16:166-67; *Inst.* 3.1.3-4, 3.2.2, 11-12, 16, 35-36, 39; OS 4:3-6, 10, 21-23, 26-27, 46-47, 49. On Calvin's understanding of faith, including the certainty of faith, see Heribert Schützeichel, *Die*

believers experience of their own salvation originates not from human perception "but from the sealing of the Spirit who imparts to their consciences such certainty as to remove all doubt."[54]

Finally, Calvin also argues that "election is the cause of faith."[55] However, predestination does not play the central role in the defense of certainty that it did for Zwingli. Calvin's main purpose is not to reason backward from election to the certainty of salvation. His purpose in stressing that "no one comes to Christ unless the Father draws him" is, rather, to demonstrate that faith does not depend on human powers.

Nonetheless, important differences do exist between Calvin's discussions of certainty and those of Luther and Zwingli. Themes often subordinate or only implicit in the former thinkers become for Calvin the exegetical basis for defending the certitude of salvation. In particular Calvin stresses biblical references to the believer's union with Christ, a union effected by the Spirit. Romans 8:11; 11:17 and 1 John 3:24; 4:13 serve to explain how the certainty of faith rests upon the believer's oneness with Christ. The fact that believers are "engrafted into Christ" means that they "know that he abides in us from the Spirit whom he has given us" (1 John 3:24). Furthermore, "we know that we abide in him and he in us because he has given us of his Spirit." This spiritual oneness enables the believer to stop viewing Christ "afar off" or "outside" oneself and to "inwardly embrace" the promise of mercy.[56]

For Calvin, the ever-increasing unity between Christ and the believer disproves the theory that the Christian should properly alternate between hope and fear.[57] Scriptural verses denoting the "abiding" or "indwelling" of the Spirit describe the inward certitude of faith. The more the "engrafting" or "indwelling" grows, the more certain the believer becomes of salvation. In Calvin's thought, the notion of growth and progress applies not only to

---

Glaubenstheologie Calvins (Münich: Max Hueber, 1972). See also David Foxgrover, " 'Temporary Faith' and the Certainty of Salvation," *CTJ* 15/2 (November 1980): 220-32; Wilhelm-Albert Hauk, *Die Erwählten Prädestination und Heilsgewissheit nach Calvin* (Gütersloh: C. Bertelsmann, 1950); W. Stuermann, *Calvin's Concept of Faith* (Tulsa: University of Tulsa, 1952).

54. CO 51:153.

55. Calvin, *Comm. on Acts* 13:48, CO 48:314.

56. Calvin, *Inst.* 3.1.1, 3.2.24, 39; OS 4:1, 34-35, 49.

57. The biblical references to "fear" or "fear and trembling" obviously gave Calvin trouble and forced him to address them directly: see *Inst.* 3.2.22-23. These sections are concluded by *Inst.* 3.24 with the fact that the certainty of faith rests upon oneness with Christ. In this latter section Calvin argues against those who "so set the conscience between hope and fear that it alternates between one and another intermittently and by turns." This view was perfectly acceptable in medieval theology but is now attributed by Calvin to Satan, who tries to destroy the certainty of faith. Cf. 3.2.27; OS 4:37.

sanctification but also to certitude. The Christian gradually becomes more capable of conquering the deadly temptation of doubt. This temptation to question one's salvation is Satanic and must be battled by the shield of faith. For Calvin, the preeminent model of that victorious faith is David, whose certitude was never completely defeated by doubt.[58]

Calvin wants David's certainty to be the example for all Christians; the ordinary believer does not need a "special revelation" to rest in the certainty of salvation. The union with Christ that produces such certitude is an experience common to all the faithful. Against Catholic critics, Calvin denies that the certainty of God's will is a prideful or presumptuous claim. Citing an array of biblical passages, Calvin asserts that "Unless one knows that Christ dwells in him, he is reprobate."[59]

Turning to Calvin's defense of his own exegetical and doctrinal authority, we can discern a certain shift from Luther and Zwingli, a reserve that appears to reflect the past difficulties posed by claiming the Spirit as the source of certitude. This is not to say that Calvin renounces the Spirit as the agent of certainty in debates about authority. As did many Reformers, Calvin argues that the "inviolable bond" between Word and Spirit results in certitude: "For as God alone is a fit witness of himself in his Word, so also the Word will not find acceptance in men's hearts before it is sealed by the inward testimony of the Spirit."[60] Here again, the discussion of scriptural authority is framed in terms of inward certainty.

Moreover, as did his predecessors, Calvin insisted that the Spirit be always anchored in the Word. He perceived the dangers of spiritualism not only in the Libertines but also in Catholicism; both groups claimed the guidance of the Spirit but had forsaken the Word. According to Calvin, the Quintinists believed Scripture was a "dead and killing letter" so that "they abandon [Scripture] in order to come to the life-giving spirit." But in the process they "stroll amid the clouds" and fail to understand that "God does not promise his apostles a spirit that will create new doctrines for them; rather the Spirit only confirms them in the gospel which was preached to them."[61] In Calvin's view both the Catholics and the Libertines tore apart that "inviolable bond" between Scripture and the Spirit. As did the "Anabaptists," Sadoleto "boasted" of the Spirit

---

58. Calvin, *Inst.* 3.2.17-21; OS 4:27-32.

59. Calvin, *Inst.* 3.2.15, 39-40; OS 4:25-26, 49-50. On Calvin's interpretation of Eccl. 9:1, see *Inst.* 3.2.28, 38; OS 4:38-39, 47-48.

60. Calvin, *Inst.* 1.7.4; OS 3:68-70.

61. Calvin, *Contre la secte phantastique et furieuse des Libertins qui se nomment spirituelz,* CO 7:175.

without the Word.[62] When Sadoleto asserted that the church "had always and everywhere been directed by the one Spirit of Christ," Calvin answered that the church is "bound together by the one *doctrine* and Spirit of Christ."[63]

Calvin's theology of Word and Spirit has been thoroughly analyzed by Reformation scholars.[64] However, the problem goes deeper than the authority of the Word, the recognition of that authority by the Spirit, or the bond between Word and Spirit. *Institutes* 1.6-9 refers only to the authority of Scripture. There is no discussion there of the interpretation of Scripture or the dilemma posed by conflicting interpretations of biblical passages. If we seek his views about the authority to interpret, we must look not to Book 1 of the *Institutes* but to *Institutes* 4.8-9. Remarkably, Calvin does *not* cite 1 Cor. 2:15 there as an authority to judge the true meaning of Scripture. Admittedly, when confronted with 1 Cor. 2:15 in his commentary on Corinthians, Calvin does repeat the familiar assertion that only the "spiritual man" can really "distinguish between truth and falsehood, between the teaching of God and the inventions of man, and he is deluded very little."[65] However, even in this passage he is reticent to attribute too much power to spiritual discernment.

Nor did Calvin appeal to the spiritual and invisible church of the elect. Neither John 6:44 or Eph. 5:27 directs authority to the perfected church known only to God. Against what he considered to be the Anabaptist illusion of a perfect church in the world, Calvin cites Eph. 5:27 as referring to the mixed body of the visible church.[66] Stressing the visible church, Calvin argues that we are commanded to keep communion and to revere "the whole multitude of men spread over the earth who profess to worship one God and Christ." This church, which contains hypocrites,

62. Compare Calvin, *Inst.* 1.9.1; OS 3:170-71, and *Responsio ad Sadoleti epistolam,* CO 5:391-93. Calvin compares the pope to the "Anabaptists" whom Calvin often depicts as spiritualizers.

63. Calvin, *Responsio ad Sadoleti epistolam,* CO 5:394.

64. A few authorities include H. Jackson Fortsman, *Word and Spirit: Calvin's Doctrine of Biblical Authority* (Stanford: Stanford University Press, 1962). Fortsman includes an analysis of previous literature. See also Hermann Noltensmeier, *Reformatorische Einheit: Das Schriftverständnis bei Luther und Calvin* (Graz-Köln: Hermann Böhlaus Nachfolger, 1935); Werner Krusche, *Das Wirken des Heiligen Geistes nach Calvin* (Göttingen: Vandenhoeck and Ruprecht, 1957), pp. 161-84.

65. Calvin, *Comm. on 1 Cor.* 2:15, CO 49:345.

66. Calvin, *Briefe instruction pour armer tous bons fideles contre les erreurs de la secte commune des Anabaptistes,* CO 7:67. Calvin argues that Eph. 5:26-27 must be joined to Matt. 13:24, 25, and 29 in order to understand the nature of the earthly church. Cf. *Inst.* 4.1.10, 13; OS 5:14-15. Also see Calvin's use of Eph. 5:26-27 against the notion of the infallibiity of the church: *Inst.* 4.8.12; OS 5:14-15, 17.

is visibly known by the pure preaching of the Word and proper admin-istration of the sacraments, and it is this church with whom we must stay in unity. Avoiding what he considered the errors of men such as Zwingli, Calvin tried to anchor certainty in the visibility of the church: "Just as we must believe, therefore, that the former church, invisible to us, is visible to the eyes of God alone, so we are commanded to revere and keep communion with the latter, which is called 'church' in respect to men."[67]

The interpretation of Scripture, moreover, is an ecclesial event, in that when Calvin confronts the problem of conflicting interpretations he can only fall back on "a synod of bishops" where the controversy can be ex-amined. Invoking Christ's Spirit, this synod is to bring forth a definition derived from and tested by Scripture.[68] The argument may well seem in-sufficient or circular. This is because Calvin's desire to resist tyrannical institutional authority as well as unrestrained spiritualism left him with no option but a continuing confidence in the ultimate clarity of Scripture and the persuasive power of good exegesis.

A closer examination, however, reveals that in several crucial contro-versies Calvin himself uses another criterion than the authority of Scripture, namely, certitude itself. Having determined that faith entails certainty, Cal-vin argues in such a way that the test of doctrine is not only Scripture but inner certitude. In other words, if a doctrine renders one uncertain, then that doctrine is, by definition, wrong. Several examples will demonstrate this mode of argumentation.

In the *Institutes* 1.6-9 Calvin refutes the Catholic position that Scrip-ture derives its authority from the church. Although he cites a number of biblical passages, Calvin's fundamental concern is the need for the con-science to rest in certainty. Calvin concludes that the Catholic position must be incorrect because it leaves the conscience in doubt:

> Yet if this is so, what will happen to miserable consciences seeking firm assurance of eternal life if all promises of it consist in and depend solely on the judgment of men? Will they cease to vacillate and tremble when they receive such an answer?[69]

---

67. Calvin, *Inst.* 4.1.7; OS 5:12. Cf. *Inst.* 4.1.4, 8-11; OS 5:7, 12-15.

68. Calvin, *Inst.* 4.9.13; OS 5:161-62. Ironically this advice comes just after Calvin has examined the fallibility of councils.

69. Calvin, *Inst.* 1.7.1; OS 3.65-66. See also Heiko A. Oberman, "'Quo Vadis Petre?' Tradition from Irenaeus to *Humani Generis*," in *The Dawn of the Reformation* (Grand Rapids: Eerdmans, 1992), pp. 269-96.

Augustine cannot serve his opponents because "he wants the certainty of the godly to rest upon a far different foundation." The "certainty that piety requires" comes not from the authority of the church but only from the Spirit and the self-authenticating power of Scripture.[70]

Calvin thus argues here *from* (rather than *for*) certainty in this debate about faith and justification. The scholastic doctrine of penance is said to be wrong because it can never grant full certainty:

> Unless this knowledge [of the forgiveness of sins] remains clear and sure, the conscience can have no rest at all, no peace with God, no assurance or security; but it continuously trembles, wavers, tosses, is tormented and vexed, shakes, hates, and flees the sight of God.[71]

The "facere" doctrine — that is, the Ockhamist notion that God requires us to do *(facere)* only what lies within us — is incorrect because "If they say that we must do what is in us, we are always brought back to the same point. For when will anyone dare assure himself that he has applied all his powers to lament his sins?" So, too, the Catholic doctrine that the sinner must perform satisfaction for sins is dismissed by Calvin not only because it is unbiblical but, finally, because it renders the believer uncertain:

> But if it is a question of quieting the conscience, what will this quieting be if a man hears that sins are redeemed by satisfactions? When can he at length be certain of the measure of that satisfaction? Then he will always doubt whether he has a merciful God; he will always be troubled and always tremble.[72]

The teaching that one can have only a "conjectural" certitude and the belief that one's knowledge of perseverance must remain in suspense are both wrong because they contradict the certainty of faith.[73]

This test of certitude also dominated Calvin's controversy with the

---

70. Calvin, *Inst.* 1.7.3-4; OS 3:67-70.

71. Calvin, *Inst.* 3.4.2; cf. 3.4.17; OS 4:87-88; 104-5.

72. Calvin, *Inst.* 3.4.27; OS 4:116-17. The same argument is made for dismissing absolution in *Inst.* 3.4.21: "Why, then, do they say that they absolve by the authority given to them, when their absolution is uncertain. . . . Now I hold that it is either nothing or so uncertain that it ought to be considered nothing . . ." (OS 4:109-10).

73. Calvin, *Inst.* 3.2.38; OS 4:38 (regarding Eccl. 9:1) and *Inst.* 3.2.39-40; OS 4:49-50 (regarding the necessity for a "special revelation"). See also *Iohannis Calvini commentarius in Epistolam Pauli ad Romanos,* ed. T. H. L. Parker (Leiden: E. J. Brill, 1981), p. 171.14-22.

Lutheran pastor Andreas Osiander. Both Calvin and Osiander emphasized the unity of Christ with the believer. Calvin found himself in the awkward position of having to distinguish his own view of the indwelling of Christ from Osiander's doctrine of essential righteousness. After making his theological and exegetical arguments, Calvin harnesses all of his resources to prove the decisive point: Osiander had to be wrong because his doctrine destroyed the certainty of salvation. By confusing justification and regeneration, Osiander's teaching of essential righteousness required a perfection not available to the believer in this life. Experience shows that traces of sin always remain, traces that would throw one into uncertainty if an essential righteousness were required. Osiander, therefore, failed the test of certitude:

> No portion of righteousness sets our consciences at peace until it has been determined that we are pleasing to God, because we are entirely righteous before him. From this it follows that the doctrine of justification is perverted and utterly overthrown when doubt is thrust into men's minds, when the assurance of salvation is shaken and the free and fearless calling upon God suffers hindrance — nay, when peace and tranquillity with spiritual joy are not established. . . . Assuredly, he will hang uncertainly, wavering to this side and to that, for he will not be allowed to assume in himself as much righteousness as he needs for assurance.[74]

Calvin applies the same argument to Osiander, the Anabaptists, the "schoolmen," and any other party that requires works: the illusion of perfectionism must be avoided at all costs.[75] This theological principle, however, has as its final authority the test of certitude. To be sure, Calvin cites numerous biblical passages, but so do all of his opponents. Calvin argues against alternate interpretations not simply on the basis of "Scripture alone" but ultimately because his opponents fail the test of certainty. Fundamentally Calvin insists that the demand for perfection or any human righteousness must be wrong because it nullifies one's subjective certitude of salvation. Thus, by making certitude itself the test of doctrinal or exegetical authority, Calvin believes he can argue with hermeneutical confidence regarding the truth of doctrine and the meaning of Scripture.

---

74. Calvin, *Inst.* 3.11.11; OS 4:66-67. Cf. *Inst.* 3.13.3-4; OS 4:217-19.
75. Calvin, *Inst.* 3.2.14; OS 4:24-25.

III. Conclusion

David Steinmetz has written that the Bible was,

> in the fullest sense of the term, a sixteenth-century book. It influenced European attitudes toward war and peace, the structure of civil government and the family, the process of human growth and development, theories of child-rearing and education, as well as attitudes toward economic relations and policies of taxation. The Bible was appealed to by people who loved the Church and who hated it. . . . The Bible was on the lips of religious martyrs — Roman Catholic, Protestant, and Anabaptist — and on the lips of their executioners. In the judgment of sixteenth-century Europeans, the Bible was worth both the dying and the killing for.[76]

This essay has shown that some of the most pitched battles in the Reformation centered on scriptural passages concerning certitude. Indeed, it can be argued that certainty was the fundamental theological locus of the sixteenth century. That "the Bible was on the lips of martyrs — Roman Catholic, Protestant, and Anabaptist — and on the lips of their executioners," is nowhere more evident than in an examination of the anguished search for certitude.

---

76. David C. Steinmetz, *Luther in Context* (Bloomington: Indiana University Press, 1986), pp. 44-45.

· 10 ·

Wolfgang Musculus's Commentary on John: Tradition and Innovation in the Story of the Woman Taken in Adultery

CRAIG S. FARMER

ALTHOUGH WOLFGANG MUSCULUS (1497-1563) was one of hundreds of second-generation Protestant Reformers working to consolidate and advance the reform of the church in mid-sixteenth-century Europe, he distinguished himself as one of the few whose published theological and exegetical writings exerted an influence long after his death. That is not to say that Musculus is well known among Reformation historians. Few textbooks include even a passing reference to Musculus, and specialized studies have been remarkably rare. If he is remembered, it is usually for his massive work in systematic theology, the *Loci Communes Sacrae Theologiae*, first published in 1560.[1] Among his contemporaries, however, Musculus's reputation rested primarily on his work as a commentator on Scripture. Over a period spanning nearly twenty years, Musculus produced ten commentaries treating fifteen biblical books. All of his commentaries went through

---

1. *Loci Communes in usus Sacrae Theologiae candidatorum parati* (Basel: Johann Herwagen, 1560). A new edition was produced in 1561, and thereafter followed printings in 1563, 1564, 1573, and 1599. The work was published in English in 1563 and 1578, in French in 1577, and portions were translated into German in 1618. It is ironic that Musculus has been extolled as a systematician, since the *Loci Communes* were culled from his commentaries and were written in the service of exegesis. For a bibliography of Musculus's writings, including the various printings, see Paul Romane-Musculus, "Catalogue des œuvres imprimées du théologien Wolfgang Musculus," *Revue d'Histoire et de Philosophie Religieuses* 43 (1963): 260-78.

multiple printings, giving evidence of a wide readership that continued well into the seventeenth century.[2]

Musculus's commentaries were produced in the course of an active career as a leading Reformer in the cities of Augsburg and Berne. His career was launched by the Strasbourg Reformers, who quickly recognized Musculus's abilities when he arrived in the city in 1527 after fifteen years as a Benedictine monk in his native Lorraine. Martin Bucer eventually procured a preaching position for Musculus in the free imperial city of Augsburg in 1531, and the young Reformer quickly rose to prominence. When Catholic services were outlawed by the city council in 1537, Musculus assumed the prestigious preaching post at the cathedral church of Augsburg, a position that he held until his expulsion from the city in 1548 for refusing to accept the terms of the Interim. The following year he took an appointment in Berne, succeeding Simon Sulzer as a professor in the "Hohe Schule." He served as an ecclesiastical adviser and helped to mediate in the incessant disputes between Calvin and the Bernese clergy. But until his death in 1563, Musculus worked primarily as a scholar and teacher preparing other young men for ministry. It was during these years that he published the great bulk of his exegetical writings.[3]

The extent of Musculus's influence as a commentator is well attested by his contemporaries. The Reformed theologian Martin Micron informed Musculus that the commentary on Genesis had been very useful to the Protestants of East Frisia. Felix Cruciger, pastor at Secymin and superintendent of the Reformed churches in Little Poland, sent word that

---

2. Musculus authored commentaries on Matthew (1540), John (1545), the Psalms (1550), the Decalogue (1553), Genesis (1554), Romans (1555), Isaiah (1557), 1 and 2 Corinthians (1559), Galatians and Ephesians (1561), and Philippians, Colossians, 1 and 2 Thessalonians, and 1 Timothy (1564). Musculus's John commentary was published in in two installments, in 1545 and 1547. The complete work was reprinted in 1553, 1554, 1564, 1580, and 1618.

3. The most important source for Musculus's biography is the work written by his son, Abraham Musculus, "Historia Vitae et Obitus Clarissimi Theologi D. Wolfgangi Musculi Dusani, S. Litterarum apud Bernates professoris, per Abrahamum Musculum Filium, pietatis ergo scripta," in ΣΥΝΟΨΙΣ *festalium concionum, authore D. Wolfgango Musculo Dusano. Eiusdem vita, obitus, erudita carmina* (Basel: Conrad Waldkirch, 1595). This is the primary source for two nineteenth-century biographies: Ludwig Grote, *Wolfgang Musculus, ein biographischer Versuch* (Hamburg: Rauhes Haus, 1855), and Wilhelm Theodor Streuber, "Wolfgang Musculus oder Müslin. Ein Lebensbild aus der Reformationszeit. Aus dem handschriftlichen Nachlasse des verstorbenen Dr. Wilhelm Theodor Streuber," in *Berner Taschenbuch auf das Jahr 1860* (Berne, 1860), pp. 1-79. A brief but excellent recent study is that of Rudolf Dellsperger, "Wolfgang Musculus (1497-1563)," in *Die Augsburger Kirchenordunung von 1537 und ihr Umfeld,* ed. Reinhard Schwarz (Gütersloh: Gerd Mohn, 1988), pp. 91-110.

Musculus's "lucubrations on the New Testament" had found a wide and receptive audience among the Protestants there.[4] The Genevan Reformer Guillaume Farel wrote to Johann Haller in Berne that many were eager to get their hands on Musculus's new Psalms commentary.[5] John Calvin, in the preface to his own Psalms commentary, ranked Musculus's interpretation of the Psalms with Bucer's, and noted that Musculus "by his diligence and industry has earned no small praise in the judgment of good men."[6] For many years after his death, Musculus's exegesis continued to elicit praise from distinguished admirers. The French Oratorian Richard Simon (1638-1712), arguably the greatest biblical scholar of his age, praised Musculus as a man who understood the proper way to interpret Scripture.[7]

How did Musculus interpret the biblical text? What were the features of his exegesis that earned him such respect in the sixteenth and seventeenth centuries? The genius of Musculus's exegetical work lies in his ability to bring together the best of old and new in the interpretation of Scripture. His commentaries reflect a significant debt to patristic and medieval scholarship both in method and content, yet they also incorporate the new currents of sound biblical scholarship in their careful consideration of linguistic and grammatical problems and in their attention to the doctrinal *loci* of particular concern in the sixteenth century. Musculus's exhaustive approach resulted in commentaries that are among the most prolix of any in the sixteenth century. However, he preserves the utility of his commentaries as reference tools by the careful arrangement of various levels of exposition that allow the reader to locate desired information quickly.

In seeking to introduce Musculus as an exegete, the balance of this essay will focus on his commentary on the Fourth Gospel, looking first of all at the method he adopts. Then, in order to highlight the characteristics of

---

4. The letters from Micron and Cruciger survive in the collection of the Zofingen Stadtbibliothek (PA 15A). The letter from Micron is also printed in J. H. Gerretsen, *Micronius. Zijn leven, zijn geschriften, zijn geesterichting* (Nijmegen: H. Ten Hoet, 1895), pp. ix-xi of the appendix.

5. Farel to Haller, March 1551 (CO 14:80 [#1466]): "Saluta quaeso pium Musculum. Nondum audimus istius psalmos absolutos, quos non puaci optant."

6. Calvin, *In Librum Psalmorum Commentarius* (CO 31:13): "Nec vero de Wolphgangi Musculi commentariis, si iam tunc in lucem prodiissent, tacere fas fuisset quando et hic sedulitate et industria non parum laudis bonorum iudicio meritus est."

7. Richard Simon, *Histoire Critique du Vieux Testament* (Rotterdam, 1685; repr. ed., Frankfurt: Minerva, 1967), pp. 438-39: "On peut dire que cet Auteur a connu la veritable manière d'expliquer l'Écriture." In particular, Simon praises Musculus's Psalms commentary for its careful attention to patristic scholarship. Musculus, he claims, showed more respect for antiquity than most Protestant authors.

Musculus's exegesis, we will focus on the story of the woman taken in adultery (John 8:1-11), a text that serves well to display not only Musculus's debt to his predecessors but also his willingness to explore new exegetical terrain.

I. Musculus's Method

In his commentary on John, Musculus takes the reader through various stages of exposition. He first quotes several verses of the text and offers a general summary, occasionally noting textual difficulties in the passage. He then quotes the text again, phrase by phrase, presenting a more detailed explanation of the text. Finally, he quotes these phrases still once more, enumerating various "observations" *(observationes* or *notanda)*. This organizational scheme, adopted by Musculus in many of his commentaries, may owe its inspiration to Martin Bucer, his mentor and teacher. Bucer had divided the sections of his 1528 John commentary into *paraphrasis, annotationes,* and *observationes* — a tripartite division mirrored in Musculus even though the section titles "paraphrase" and "annotations" are not used.

The basic text for Musculus's commentary is the Latin translation of Erasmus, first published in 1519 to accompany the second edition of his Greek New Testament. However, Musculus clearly has his eye on the Greek text of John's Gospel because he occasionally opts for the reading of the Vulgate or for his own translation when he judges Erasmus to have gone astray.[8] Most of his alterations of the Erasmus translation are rooted in questions of style based on Musculus's analysis of Greek grammar and sentence structure. Usually, he draws no attention to these changes, tacitly introducing his corrections without indicating the issue at stake. Occasionally, however, Musculus explains his disapproval. At John 6:39, for example, he argues that Erasmus is "more concerned with the structure of Latin discourse than with expressing the mind of the Lord's words."[9] A particular

8. Four significant editions of the Greek New Testament were available to Musculus as he worked on his John commentary: the 1516 and 1527 Erasmus editions, the 1522 Complutensian edition, and the 1534 edition of Colinaeus. T. H. L. Parker, *Calvin's New Testament Commentaries* (Grand Rapids: Eerdmans, 1971), pp. 93-123, gives a helpful analysis of the different editions of the Greek New Testament that were published in the first half of the sixteenth century.

9. Musculus, *Commentariorum in evangelistam Ioannem, Heptas prima* (Basel: Bartholomäus Westheimer, 1545), p. 288. The second volume is entitled *Commentariorum in evangelistam Ioannem, Heptas altera, item tertia et postrema in eundem* (Basel: Johann Herwagen, 1547). Both volumes hereafter cited as *In Ioannem.*

nuance of the Greek is retained in the awkward, though literal, Vulgate translation of this verse. Therefore, Musculus argues, "it is better that we read simply as the words are in the Vulgate edition."[10] There are also other instances where Musculus voices his polite yet firm disagreement with Erasmus's Latin (occasionally even when Erasmus and the Vulgate agree), but these disagreements are rooted not in a reactionary disposition but in the humanist principle of returning to the original sources.

Musculus also makes frequent use of Erasmus's *Annotationes in Novum Testamentum* for evaluating text-critical problems and difficulties in lexicography, grammar, and syntax. In fact, at several of the places where Musculus corrects Erasmus's Latin translation, he is clearly basing his changes on information gleaned from the *Annotationes*.[11] The very fact that Musculus offers linguistic and text-critical analysis shows the influence of humanist biblical studies on his method of interpreting John. Although some of his technical discussions are not based directly on the work of Erasmus, his method of glossing Greek words and expressions with several Latin counterparts owes its inspiration to humanist ideals of biblical scholarship.[12] Musculus also goes beyond Erasmus by his repeated suggestions that John's Greek veils an underlying Hebraism. Strange expressions and grammatical constructions often can be explained, he argues, by examining the particularities of Hebrew grammar and idiom that lie behind the Greek.[13] The *Annotationes* never provides the direct inspiration for these arguments, for Erasmus examines Hebrew only when discussing the etymology of loanwords, or when comparing John's Old Testament quotations with the original. Yet Musculus's study of latent Hebraisms certainly reflects the spirit of the *Annotationes* in an area where he held a technical advantage over Erasmus, who never mastered Hebrew.

Musculus's technical linguistic studies are impressive, but they constitute a small part of his overall work as a commentator on John. The great bulk of his exegesis is devoted to the sections of *observationes*, where, having explained the literal meaning of the text, he seeks to draw the spirit out of the letter. In

---

10. Musculus, *In Ioannem*, 1:288: "satius est ut simpliciter sicut verba habent, cum vulgata aeditione legamus."

11. In each of the following places Musculus rejects the translation of Erasmus for another rendering given in the *Annotationes*: John 4:6, 4:27, 5:45, 8:23, and 10:24.

12. See, e.g., his argument concerning the meaning of the verb σώζεσθαι at John 10:9. Erasmus does not gloss the word in the *Annotationes*. Yet Musculus offers, in Erasmian fashion, a lengthy explanation of the word's meaning, supported by quotations from Virgil.

13. See, e.g., his comments on John 1:17, 2:11, 6:50, 9:37, 15:9, 15:25, and 20:1 (*In Ioannem*, 1:27-28, 62-63, 304; 2:263, 350, 360, 443).

his comments on John 5:39 ("you search the scriptures . . ."), Musculus argues that the interpretation of the Bible requires a special kind of "searching" *(scrutatio)* such as that mentioned by Jesus. This searching takes place "whenever the very words of scripture are inspected more deeply beyond the sense of the letter, so that the sense of the spirit may be drawn out, a thing which should be done in parables, allegories, metaphors, and mystical figures."[14] However, when the expositor is dealing with a text that is not transparently parabolic or allegorical, it is still appropriate, according to Musculus, to use a "threefold kind of searching" *(scrutationem triplicis generis)*. First, Scripture must be read christologically: every biblical text should be examined more deeply in order to see how it relates to and reveals Christ. Second, Scripture should be interpreted morally, a method useful to establish a zeal for piety and good works. Finally, there is a third type of searching that nurtures hope, a type of exposition he finds described at Rom. 15:4.[15]

Musculus's remarks on the threefold levels of "searching" closely approximate the standard medieval categories of the three spiritual senses: allegory, tropology, and anagogy.[16] Moreover, in his sections of "observations," it is not difficult to find examples of spiritual exegesis that conform to the medieval pattern. Despite his warnings in other places regarding the excesses of medieval allegorization, Musculus makes selective use of the exegetical tradition in re-presenting, and occasionally reinterpreting, standard allegorical readings of the Fourth Gospel.[17] However, in his "observations" the moral or tropological exegesis is the overwhelming mode of interpretation. In terms of the sheer quantity and scope of his moral exegesis, Musculus has few rivals, for he discovers latent ethical principles in even the most seemingly innocuous details of the biblical text.

In his voluminous "observations" Musculus also frequently allows the words and events of the text to trigger discussions of topics only tangentially related to the gospel narrative, much as Bucer did in his John commentary.

---

14. Musculus, *In Ioannem*, 1:208: "quando ipsa scripturae verba ultra literae sensum penitius introspiciuntur, ut sensus spiritus eruatur, id quod in parabolis, allegoriis, metaphoris & figuris mysticis est faciendum."

15. Musculus, *In Ioannem*, 1:208.

16. In his interpretation of the feeding of the five thousand (John 6:1-13), Musculus devotes an entire section of his comments to the anagogical signficance of the feeding miracle (a section entitled *De anagogico historiae huius sensu;* see *In Ioannem*, 1:236. Musculus rarely used the term "allegory" for his exegesis, preferring labels such as "mystical meaning," "mysterious meaning," or "image."

17. See Craig S. Farmer, "Wolfgang Musculus and the Allegory of Malchus's Ear," *WTJ* 56 (1994): 285-301.

But the extent to which Musculus allows his exegesis to blossom into topical essays is an important and distinctive feature of his method of interpreting the Fourth Gospel. The story of the raising of Lazarus (John 11:1-44), for example, occasions a lengthy discussion of bodily illness, the mutual love of siblings, hospitality, burial customs, and the practice of viewing the dead.[18] Indeed, Musculus's topical observations occasionally grow to such proportions that they resemble separate treatises, complete with titles and subdivisions.[19] It is clear that the words of the biblical text had an extraordinarily suggestive power for Musculus.

II. Musculus's Exegesis

In the course of centuries of exposition, an exegetical agenda emerged that embodied the interpretative problems facing a commentator on John as well as the possible solutions to those problems. Musculus's exegesis thus reflects not only his response to the words of the biblical text itself but also to the words of the commentators who precede him. Although Musculus rarely identifies the commentators with whom he is interacting, a comparison of Musculus with his exegetical forebears demonstrates the pervasive influence of traditional ideas.

With respect to the story of the woman taken in adultery, one of the thorniest traditional questions is that of the authenticity of the story itself. Latin commentators since Augustine had interpreted the text, which was included in the Vulgate.[20] But Latins also had to reckon with the disturbing silence of the Greek exegetical tradition on the story. And, in addition to this text-critical issue, three other sets of interpretive problems are reflected in the tradition. First, there are problems associated with the accusation of adultery. Why is the accused woman brought to Jesus? And why is her partner in crime (the adulterer) not also brought? Second, there are problems associated with Jesus' response to the scribes and Pharisees. The meaning of his puzzling

---

18. Musculus, *In Ioannem*, 2:223-25, 236-37, 244-46.

19. In his interpretation of the wine miracle at Cana (John 2:1-11), Musculus offers an extended discussion of marriage that he divides into six sections entitled "observations concernings weddings," "what marriage is," "its source, that is, its author," "how it is honorable," "how it is useful," and "how it is necessary" (*In Ioannem*, 1:55-57).

20. The story appears in some Old Latin texts of the Gospels. Its authenticity was defended by Jerome in *Contra Pelagium* 2.17 (PL 23:495-590), and by Augustine in *De coniugiis adulterinis* 2.7 (PL 40:451-86). No earlier Western father mentions the text, and no Eastern father cites it before the tenth century.

gestures (bending down, writing in the dirt) cries out for explanation. And his verbal response — "let him who is without sin among you first throw a stone" — seems untenable in a world requiring order and discipline. Third, there are problems associated with Jesus' forgiveness of the woman. Why does he forgive an adulteress who expresses no sorrow and offers no confession? And why does Jesus pardon the woman in a way that seems to violate proper penitential practice? We will look at these issues in turn.

A. *Textual Difficulties*

Musculus begins his exposition of John 8 by noting that the story is not found in all the ancient Greek codices, nor is it treated by all ancient commentators on the Gospel.[21] By making this observation, Musculus is simply reflecting the long-standing awareness (since Augustine and Jerome) of the division between Eastern and Western Christianity regarding the authenticity of the story. Medieval commentators were equally familiar with the textual problems; they could hardly fail to notice that Chrysostom and other Greek expositors had simply passed over the story in their commentaries on John. Although not all medieval scholars addressed the matter in their exegesis, some commentators offered various explanations for the disagreement regarding the status of the story. The thirteenth-century commentators Bonaventure and Hugh of St. Cher both observed that the Greeks considered the story apocryphal, noting its glaring omission in Chrysostom's exposition of the Gospel. Both conceded that the story was not found in all the ancient manuscripts, and both suggested that John himself may have added the story at a later time. Hugh condemned the supposition that someone other than the Evangelist could have been so rash as to import the story into the Gospel narrative. For both Hugh and Bonaventure, the antidote for the troubling omission of the text in the Greek tradition was amply supplied by a consideration of its distinguished use in the Latin tradition. "Since the Holy Latins expound it and since it is read in the Latin Church," wrote Hugh, "we also will expound it." Similarly, Bonaventure reassured his readers that Augustine and "our expositors" (*expositores nostri*) considered the story worthy of exposition.[22]

---

21. Musculus, *In Ioannem*, 2:6.

22. Bonaventure, *Doctoris Seraphici S. Bonaventurae . . . opera omnia* 6: *Commentarius in Evangelium Ioannis* (Florence: Quaracchi, 1893), p. 355; Hugh of St. Cher, *Opera Omnia in Vniversvm Vetvs & Novvm Testamentvm* 6: *In Evangelia secundum Matthaeum, Marcum, Lucam, & Ioannem* (Cologne: Johannes Gymnicus, 1621), fol. 336^v.

Unlike the medieval commentators, Musculus makes no effort to defend the Johannine authorship of the adulteress narrative. In fact, he repeats information from Erasmus's *Annotationes* that the story, according to Eusebius, was imported from the apocryphal Hebrews gospel. Erasmus had argued that although the story is apocryphal it nevertheless may relate an authentic event in the life of Jesus.[23] Musculus, however, like the medieval commentators, simply declares his willingness to follow those interpreters who have treated the text. Musculus offers no judgment as to whether the story is true or not, but clearly he has lost little sleep over the issue: "we are not very worried here," he concludes.[24]

B. On the Double Standard

For most commentators the first major problem of the narrative centers on why the woman is brought to Jesus. The Gospel itself indicates that the scribes and Pharisees were testing Jesus in order to be able to accuse him. But the question remains: What sort of test or temptation *(tentatio)* was introduced here? The standard exegetical response, rooted in Augustine and reflected throughout the medieval commentary tradition, is that the woman's accusers were attempting to trap Jesus in an inescapable dilemma. Jesus was caught on the twin horns of his reverence for the law and his teaching of mercy toward sinners. If he gave his approval to the stoning, he would lose face with the people who had come to expect gentleness and mercy from Jesus. If, on the other hand, he pardoned the woman, his enemies would have just cause to accuse him of violating a clear Mosaic precept.[25]

Musculus describes the test in terms that echo traditional exegesis. But he heightens the dramatic quality of the confrontation by paraphrasing the Pharisees' speech. These accusers, feigning sympathy for the woman, were saying in effect:

> This penalty [of stoning] seems more severe than the nature of the sin requires. We are touched, in fact, by a feeling of pity for this wretched woman, but we do not dare rashly to break the law given by Moses. . . . You, therefore, since you are such a great teacher, considered among the

23. Anne Reeve (ed.), *Erasmus' Annotations on the New Testament: The Gospels* (London: Duckworth, 1986), pp. 245-46.

24. Musculus, *In Ioannem*, 2:6.

25. Augustine, *Tractates on the Gospel of John*, 33.4 (FC 88:53-54).

people so much more excellent than all others, so that what you teach is considered indubitable oracles, tell us in keeping with your intelligence and authority how the matter appears to you.[26]

Although the Pharisees and scribes were intent on trapping Jesus between justice and mercy, they mask their malice, attempting to soften *(emollirent)* him with respectful speech. Throughout his commentary, Musculus shows great skill as a paraphrast, not simply to add occasional color to his exposition, but to re-create imaginatively (in ways reminiscent of Luther) the mood and tone of the dialogue in the Gospel narrative.

The accusation of adultery provides Musculus with ample material for a number of observations regarding the nature of hypocrisy, rules for proper legal proceedings, and the nature of testing or temptation *(tentatio)*. His lengthiest discussion, however, centers on the subject of adultery itself, and is prompted by a troubling question. If the woman was caught in the very act of adultery, as the text declares, then why was the adulterer not also seized and accused together with the adulteress? For in a case of adultery, Musculus argues, the law clearly prescribes the death penalty for the woman and the man.[27]

Other than Musculus, few sixteenth-century commentators on John voice concern over the apparent double standard in accusing only the woman.[28] But Musculus is clearly taking up a question much discussed in late medieval exegesis, for both Nicholas of Lyra and Denis the Carthusian offered various theories to account for the absence of the guilty man. It is possible, they suggested, that the accusers hoped to raise the suspicion in the minds of the gathered crowd that one of Jesus' disciples had committed the offense. It is also possible that the man simply escaped from their hands or bribed his way out of trouble. Denis, however, favored the theory that they brought the woman and not the man in order to support their strategy of enticing Jesus to violate the law. Moved by a sense of compassion, judges often make more allowances for guilty women than for guilty men since in women "weakness is greater, carnality

---

26. Musculus, *In Ioannem*, 2:6: "quasi dicerent, uidetur haec poena seuerior esse quam delicti qualitas exigat. Tangimur quidem miserae huius commiseratione, uerum non audemus temere legem a Moise datam infringere. . . . Tu ergo cum tantus doctor, ac reliquis omnibus ita excellentior apud populum habeare, ut quae doces pro indubitatis oraculis habeantur, edic nobis pro intelligentia & autoritate tua, quid tibi uideatur."

27. Musculus, *In Ioannem*, 2:7, citing Deut. 22:22 and Lev. 20:10.

28. The matter is not addressed — here, at least — by Melanchthon, Bucer, Bullinger, Oecolampadius, Calvin, Erasmus, Major, or Broickwy von Königstein.

stronger, and intellect more feeble" *(fragilitas major, carnalitas fortior, intellectus debilior).*[29]

In the absence of textual evidence, Musculus argues that no definite theory can account for the absence of the adulterer. "Nothing can be asserted with certainty," he writes, "whether or not they arrested the adulterer together with the woman. And if they arrested him, why they did not also bring him." However, Musculus repeats Denis's suggestion that by bringing a woman, and not a man, they hoped to create a pitiful scene that would evoke Jesus' compassion. Yet regardless of whether the Pharisees actually held to a double standard, Musculus thinks the text implicitly condemns the unequal application of law to men and women. Railing against the corruption of his own age, he notes that "while male adulterers and fornicators are left alone, women alone are chastised, especially if the men are of some reputation, means, or distinguished family." In effect, Musculus argues, the weak are punished while the strong are allowed to sin with impunity. This perverse justice is intolerable, for "the law of God does not approve this inequality."[30]

Musculus then develops his discussion of the double standard into a lengthy discussion of adultery. Primarily he wants to refute two unbiblical ideas ingrained in the culture of his time. First, he attacks the notion that adultery is committed by a man only when he has relations with a married woman other than his wife, but not when with a prostitute or a single, unattached woman. Those who think in this way, Musculus argues, have not carefully considered the proper order of marriage, "the fetters of which bind the man no less than the woman." The Apostle Paul prescribes "an equal law" *(parem legem)* for both partners in marriage; neither husbands nor wives rule over their own bodies, but each has surrendered this power to the other. Therefore, Musculus argues that a married man who surrenders his body to another woman, be she single, married, or a prostitute, has certainly committed an "adulteration of the legitimate marriage bed" *(legitimi thori adulteratio).* Second, Musculus attacks the opinion that a married woman sins more grievously in committing adultery than a married man, because she takes the risk of bearing an illegitimate child. While Musculus concedes that it is more harmful *(nocentior)* for a married

29. Nicholas of Lyra, *Biblia Sacra cvm Glossis, Interlineari & Ordinaria, Nicolai Lyrani Postilla & Moralitatibus, Burgensis Additionibus, & Thoringi Replicis,* 6 vols. (Lyons: Antoine Vincent, 1545), 5:210ᵛ; Denis the Carthusian, *Opera omnia,* vol. 12: *Enarratio in Lucam (X-XIII), et Johannem* (Monstrolii: S. M. De Pratis, 1901), pp. 423-24.

30. Musculus, *In Ioannem,* 2:7: "hanc inaequalitatem lex Dei non approbat."

woman to commit adultery because she threatens to "corrupt the conjugal offspring" *(coniugalem sobolem viciat)*, she commits no more treachery than a married man who "has an affair with some unattached woman" *(cum libera quapiam rem habeat)*. A husband who commits adultery "adulterates the trust given to his wife and also transfers offspring outside of the marriage bed to another." Therefore, Musculus argues that Christians must reject the conventional practice of holding women to a higher standard than men.

> Wherefore, I think their opinion should be avoided, who attribute the crime of adultery to a married woman alone. . . . For apart from the fact that this opinion is wrong, it is also most pernicious. Therefore, let it be considered adultery among us whenever an outsider, married or un-married, is allowed in by either spouse, husband or wife, for carnal intercourse.[31]

Musculus's topical digression on the subject of adultery is one of the most typical features of his exegesis. Certainly, other sixteenth-century commentators use the commentary genre in order to discuss theological "common places." But in Musculus's exegetical asides we frequently find the most interesting and innovative elements of his commentary. Few sixteenth-century commentators use John 8 as a springboard for a treatment of adultery. In fact, prior to Musculus, I have found only two sixteenth-century exegetes who do so in this context, both Roman Catholics: John Major and Antonius Broickwy von Königstein. Major addressed the very question that concerns Musculus, "whether an adulteress sins more gravely than an adulterer" *(an moecha gravius peccet quam moechus)*.[32] However, Musculus's entire discussion of the subject likely takes its cue from the medieval commentators who address the problem of the apparent double standard.

---

31. Musculus, *In Ioannem*, 2:8: "Quapropter cauendam censeo illorum sententiam, qui adulterii facinus soli mulieri coniugatae tribuunt. . . . Praeterquam enim quod erronea est haec sententia, simul etiam perniciosissima est. Sit ergo nobis adulterium, quoties a coniuge, siue marito siue uxore, ad copulam carnis aliena persona, qualis illa sit, admittitur."

32. Broickwy, *Antonii Broickwy a Koningstein, viri doctissimi, & observantiae regularis, Novimagensis Gardiani, eruditissimarum in quatuor Evangelia enarrationum . . .* (Cologne: P. Quentel, 1539), fol. 236ᵛ; John Major, *In quatuor Evangelia expositiones luculente et disquisitiones et disputationes contra hereticos plurime . . .* (Paris: Josse Bade, 1529), fol. 286ᵛ. Major argues that in some cases a man actually may sin more grievously than a woman. A priest, e.g., sins more than a young maiden of humble means. Normally, however, because of the risk of illegitimate offspring, the woman's crime is greater than that of the man.

C. The Meaning of Jesus' Writing

When Musculus turns his attention to Jesus' enigmatic response to the woman's accusers, he offers several possible solutions to the gestural riddle that has puzzled commentators for centuries. The text seems to cry out for explanation since Jesus writes something both before and after he pronounces his judgment ("let him who is without sin . . ."). The strangeness of the act has clearly bothered many commentators. Bonaventure, for example, argued that it would be "a childish act" (factum puerile) unless Jesus intended to convey something more mysterious and profound by the deed.[33] And, in fact, commentators from the ancient and medieval periods sought to explain the deeper significance of Jesus' writing in the dirt on two basic levels. First, why did Jesus do this? And second, what did he write?

In his sermons on John, Augustine answered the "why" by arguing that Jesus was visually demonstrating his authorship of the law, written by the finger of God (Exod. 31:18).[34] This explanation, popular throughout the Middle Ages, was elaborated early in the twelfth century by Rupert of Deutz to account for Jesus' repetition of writing. When the original tablets of the law were broken, new tablets were inscribed by the power of the Holy Spirit; this double action is dramatically reenacted by Jesus, who signifies that his authorship of the law makes him a greater authority than Moses.[35] One of the earliest explanations of what Jesus wrote was given by Jerome, who stated quite simply that Jesus wrote the accusers' names in the earth as a visual reference to Jer. 17:13: "Those who turn away from you shall be written in the earth."[36] Ambrose made a similar suggestion, and the notion that Jesus wrote words of judgment, echoing Jeremiah, finds its way into most medieval commentaries.[37]

---

33. Bonaventure, *Commentarius in Evangelium Ioannis*, p. 356. This is perhaps an allusion to Augustine's remark in *Contra Faustum* 22.25 that pagans had accused Jesus of childishness for writing on the ground (NPNF 4:282; PL 42:417).

34. Augustine, *Tractates*, 33.5 (FC 88:55).

35. Rupert of Deutz, *Commentaria in Evangelium Sancti Iohannis* (CCSL 9:421-22); Bonaventure, *Commentarius in Evangelium Ioannis*, p. 356; Hugh, *In Evangelia secundum Ioannem*, fols. 336ᵛ-37ʳ; Thomas Aquinas, *Opera omnia*, 10: *Commentum in Matthaeum et Joannem Evangelistas* (Parma: P. Fiaccadori, 1860; repr. ed., New York: Musurgia, 1949), p. 442; *Catena aurea: Commentary on the Four Gospels Collected out of the Works of the Fathers*, 4 (Oxford: J. H. Parker, 1845), p. 282.

36. Jerome, *Contra Pelagium* 2.17 (NPNF 6:469).

37. Ambrose, *Ep.* 26 (PL 16:1089). Usually the passage from Jeremiah is conjoined with Luke 10:20, "Rejoice and exult that your names are written in heaven."

While the patristic opinions are repeated by most subsequent commentators, speculative theories regarding the riddle of Jesus' gestures proliferate at a geometric rate in the medieval commentaries. Hugh of St. Cher, for example, recited no fewer than seven opinions as to why Jesus wrote on the ground, and six opinions as to what he wrote. Many of the medieval theories are simply variations on the older patristic arguments, but there are also new interpretations.

One of the most popular medieval theories, rooted in Alcuin's exegesis, argues that Jesus wrote with his finger on the ground in order to demonstrate that no one should rush to condemn the sins of others, but that every admonition should be accompanied by discretion. The finger, which by its joints displays flexibility, signifies the wisdom of discretion. This moral interpretation, seen in such standard exegetical manuals as the *Ordinary Gloss* and the *Catena aurea*, finds its way into the commentaries of Bonaventure, Hugh of St. Cher, and Thomas Aquinas.[38] Another moral interpretation emerges from the observation that Jesus wrote the second time in order to give his accusers, who were embarrassed and confused by Jesus' verbal response, the opportunity to make a graceful exit. By averting his gaze, Jesus rejects the all-too-human tendency to gloat in the face of a defeated enemy. Implicitly, Jesus also teaches that those who admonish the sins of others should afterward humbly examine their own consciences.[39]

Medieval commentators were not hesitant to venture new ideas regarding the substance of what Jesus wrote on the ground. Several suggested that he simply wrote the sentence that he was about to pronounce, "Let him who is without sin. . . ." Others argued that he wrote the sins of the accusers. And many suggested various quotations from Scripture that would have been apropos. But one of the most interesting new suggestions is that Jesus sketched some sort of mystical figure that translated itself so that each of the accusers saw in the drawing a representation of his own particular sins. This notion of a pictorial display that acted as a kind of visual *glossolalia* was proposed by Hugh of St. Cher, Nicholas of Lyra, and Denis the Carthusian. Hugh explicitly connected the self-translating power of the figure to the account of the

---

38. The interpretation is attributed to Alcuin in Aquinas's *Catena aurea*, 4.282. See also *Glossa ordinaria*, PL 114:389; Bonaventure, *Commentarius in Evangelium Ioannis*, p. 356; Hugh, *In Evangelia secundum Ioannem*, fol. 336ᵛ; Thomas, *Commentum in Joannem*, p. 442.

39. *Glossa ordinaria*, PL 114:389-90; *Catena aurea*, p. 283; Thomas, *Commentum in Joannem*, p. 442; Hugh, *In Evangelia secundum Ioannem*, fol. 337ʳ; Denis, *Enarratio*, p. 424.

apostles' tongue-speaking in Acts. Nicholas noted that by using such a figure, Jesus was able to convict each individual accuser without publicizing individual sins to the crowd.[40]

Turning to Musculus, we find him reluctant to join the chorus of speculation regarding the riddle of Jesus' writing. Since the Evangelist is silent, the matter, he argues, "is not to be curiously investigated" *(nec curiose inuestigandum esse)*. Yet Musculus can hardly restrain his own curiosity, and he concedes that he would not reject a "modest conjecture" *(moderatam coniecturam non reiecerim)*. In fact, Musculus trots out several modest conjectures, many of which clearly echo the ideas of previous commentators! Jesus may have written the sentence he was about to pronounce. He may have written down the sins of the accusers or something else that "would beat them back" *(eos reuerbaret)*. He may have written (the second time) in order to allow them to beat a hasty retreat with a modicum of dignity. Musculus also offers two quite contradictory explanations as to why Jesus wrote on the ground. It may be that Jesus was taking into account their shame, and so he modestly *(per modestiam)* writes the sentence that he reluctantly pronounced publicly when pressed by their interrogation. Or it may be that Jesus was feigning hesitation in order to incite the fury of his enemies. Whatever the case, Musculus concludes, "nothing can be asserted with certainty on either question, as to what and why he wrote on the ground."[41]

Although Musculus expresses uncertainty regarding the traditional explanations for Jesus' writing, he makes two moral observations designed to refute false interpretations of the text. Once again, it is here that Musculus demonstrates his ability to develop moral discussions of weighty spiritual matters from the details — often seemingly innocuous details — of the Scripture text. First, he notes that some have disparaged the written word of Scripture, because Jesus authored no books. Musculus concedes that John 8 is in fact the only text that recounts that Jesus wrote anything at all. But he ridicules the foolish interpreters (he does not name names) who depreciate the written word on the basis of a strict imitation piety. How would they know, he asks, whether or not Jesus wrote anything unless they had the witness of the sacred Scriptures? Not everything done or not done by Christ should be taken as a rule of imitation. Otherwise, Musculus argues, Christians could not in good conscience take wives, have children, or produce books.[42]

40. Hugh, *In Evangelia secundum Ioannem,* fol. 337ʳ; Lyra, *Postilla,* 5:210ᵛ, Denis, *Enarratio,* p. 424.

41. Musculus, *In Ioannem,* 2:10-11.

42. Musculus, *In Ioannem,* 2:10-11.

Second, Musculus argues against those who see in Jesus' mysterious scribblings a basis for using "magical characters" *(magicos characteres)* in combating demonic forces. Here Musculus may be reacting against the medieval speculations about Jesus having drawn a mystical figure.[43] Musculus assures the reader that Christ never made use of magical incantations or divinizations since Scripture expressly condemns such activity.[44]

In his final observation on Jesus' writing, Musculus expresses appreciation for the allegorical signification of the gesture. The act of writing depicts "beautifully" *(pulchre)* the activity of the Holy Spirit who functions as the finger of God inscribing "hearts of flesh" *(corda carnea)* in the process of regeneration.[45] Musculus, however, was certainly not the first exegete to unleash the symbolic potency of things such as dirt (suggesting malleability or fertility) and Jesus' finger (suggesting divine power). Augustine, for example, suggested that by writing on the fertile soil of the earth Jesus signified the fruitfulness that he, as the divine author of the law, desires in the lives of the faithful — an interpretation repeated and developed by Alcuin, Thomas, Bonaventure, and Hugh of St. Cher.[46] Musculus's interpretation, however, more closely approximates the allegory of Rupert of Deutz, who suggested that Jesus wrote in the earth to signify the "scripture of new grace" *(novae gratiae Scripturam)* that is inscribed upon the heart by the power of God's Spirit.[47]

D. Jesus' Response to the Pharisees and the Woman

Turning to the verbal response of Christ, "let him who is without sin among you first throw a stone at her" (John 8:7), we find that Musculus joins a chorus of previous commentators who extol the wisdom of Christ, who in one brief statement cuts the Gordian knot of the Pharisees' legal challenge. "Oh, response of Wisdom!" wrote Augustine, for Jesus maintains justice without abandoning gentleness and mercy. Most medieval commentators echoed this refrain, many (Thomas, Hugh, and Lyra) citing the very words

43. This interpretation was still current in the sixteenth century, for the Catholic commentators John Major (*In quatuor Evangelia expositiones*, fol. 237ʳ) and Broickwy (*In quatuor Evangelia enarrationum*, fol. 286ᵛ) both argue for a mystic figure that reflected the accusers' sins.

44. Musculus, *In Ioannem*, 2:11, citing Lev. 19:20.

45. Musculus, *In Ioannem*, 2:11.

46. Augustine, *Tractates*, 33.5 (FC 88:55).

47. Rupert, *Commentaria in Evangelium Sancti Iohannis* (CCSL 9:422).

of Augustine, who paraphrased Jesus' statement: "Let the woman who has sinned be punished, but not by sinners; let the Law be fulfilled, but not by transgressors of the Law."[48] Musculus, too, marvels at the "wonderful response" *(admirabilem responsionem)*, which eludes the intended snare while exposing the hypocrisy of the woman's accusers. Musculus unpacks the psychological force of Jesus' words very effectively by placing a speech in Jesus' mouth:

> "I grant the sin of the woman. I grant even the law teaching that such [as she] should be stoned. You seek and press for my response. I know what you are doing. But now you listen. I do not prohibit you from obeying the law of God, but I remind you of this: The same law of God abominates not only sins of this kind, but also all others; it condemns not only an adulteress, but also other sinners of whatever kind. Therefore, I do not say if *all* but rather if only *one* of you is free of sin, let him come forward and in the presence of all let him first cast a stone at this adulteress. It is not my duty to pronounce sentence against the sin of this woman and to overlook your sins, as if she alone has done wrong while you are righteous. . . . Wherefore, before judging concerning the sins of others, you should first explore your own consciences."[49]

Although Musculus praises the genius of Jesus' words to the woman's accusers, he is clearly worried about the practical implications of those words for judicial proceedings in general. He concedes that Jesus' words seem to suggest a kind of juridical Donatism that would call into question the validity of judgments rendered by magistrates themselves guilty of sin.

The problem is compounded by the fact that Musculus agrees with Erasmus's argument in the *Annotationes* that the Greek word ἀναμάρτητος" *(sine peccato* in the Vulgate) denotes not only one who has not sinned but one who is incapable of sin *(ne possit peccare)*. Such a prerequisite seems highly unreasonable, Musculus complains, barring all mortals from admin-

---

48. Augustine, *Tractates*, 33.5 (FC 88:55-56).

49. Musculus, *In Ioannem*, 2:10: "Audio mulieris peccatum, audio legem etiam praecipientem, ut tales lapidentur. Quaeritis & urgetis quid ego respondeam. Scio quid agatis. Sed audite uicissim. Non prohibeo, quo minus legi Dei obtemperetis: sed huius uos admoneo, legem Dei hanceandem non solum huius generis peccata, sed cuncta etiam alia detestari: nec adulteram modo, sed quosuis etiam alios peccatores damnare. Proinde non dico, si omnes, sed si unus inter uos est qui immunis sit a peccato, prodeat ille, & coram omnibus primus lapidem in adulteram hanc iaciat. Mei muneris non est, contra mulieris huius peccatam sententiam dicere, & ad uestra conniuere: quasi illa sola deliquerit, uos uero iusti sitis. . . . Quapropter conscientias uestras prius exploretis, quam de aliorum peccatis iudicetis."

istering legal correction. It would have been "more tolerable" *(tolerabilius)* if Jesus "had taught that an adulterer could not condemn an adulteress or adulterer, or that it was not fitting for a murderer to punish a murderer, or a blasphemer to punish a blasphemer." But as it is, Jesus seems to abolish completely the magisterial function of legal correction and discipline. Only angels sent from heaven, it would seem, can possibly fulfill the strict prerequisite for administering the "use of the sword" *(usum gladii)* in human affairs.[50]

In expressing these concerns, Musculus follows a long line of medieval commentators who struggled with the troubling implications of Jesus' words. Rupert of Deutz, for example, argued that Jesus in no way denies the validity of "legitimate judgment" *(iudicium legitimum)*, but accuses the woman's accusers of criminal behavior that disqualifies their suitability as prosecutorial witnesses. In any legitimate legal examination both accusers and witnesses should be free of crime *(sine crimine esse)*.[51] However, for most medieval commentators Rupert's solution does not go far enough in explaining the degree of sinlessness required. Must a judge, asks Hugh of St. Cher, be entirely free of sin before hearing a case? No, he answered, for Jesus requires only that the accusers be free of any notorious crime. Bonaventure argued similarly that if an accuser is a notorious sinner guilty of mortal sin or of the same sin as the accused, then he sins doubly, "by a sin of scandal and a sin of contempt" *(peccato scandali et contemptus)*. A secret sinner does not sin by accusing another, although he is guilty of a sin of contempt. For Thomas, a judge who publicly flaunts his sin *(publice in peccato existens)* sins by causing a scandal *(scandalizando)*. A secret sinner, however, may legitimately pass sentence as a minister of the law. If, however, the judge accuses another "by his own impulse" *(proprio motu)* apart from the duties of his office, then he sins in making an accusation. Denis simply glossed "without sin" to mean "without mortal sin," for no one, he wrote, is free of venial sins, "except perhaps for a moment" *(nisi forte ad horulam)*. And venial sins do not disqualify anyone from judging or correcting the sins of others.[52]

We see, then, that when Musculus takes up the subject of magisterial authority, he is continuing a long-standing medieval discussion of the

---

50. Musculus, *In Ioannem*, 2:11-12.

51. Rupert, *Commentaria in Evangelium Sancti Iohannis* (CCSL 9:424).

52. Hugh, *In Evangelia secundum Ioannem*, fol. 337[r]; Bonaventure, *Commentarius in Evangelium Ioannis*, pp. 356-57; Thomas, *Commentum in Joannem*, p. 442; Denis, *Enarratio*, p. 423.

requirements for juridical office. But Musculus is also preceded by earlier sixteenth-century commentators on John. Philip Melanchthon, who authored the first Protestant John commentary in 1523, provided a lengthy discussion of the subject of magisterial authority, arguing that the "chief topic" of the story of the adulteress is what it teaches "concerning the distinction of offices" *(de discrimine ministeriorum)*.[53] The early Reformed commentators, including Johannes Oecolampadius, Heinrich Bullinger, and Martin Bucer, also highlighted the subject as of principal importance.

All these commentators were eager to demonstrate that Jesus' words do not invalidate the exercise of magisterial authority. Although Jesus is certainly the legitimate judge of the whole world, his mission as God incarnate was not to condemn but to save sinners. Therefore, Christ teaches by his words that it was not his business to render judgment concerning matters that pertained to the judicial inquiry of the civil magistrate. The accusers, Melanchthon argued, should have taken the adulteress to the judges who were entrusted with capital cases; Jesus had nothing to do with deciding bodily punishments since he came as a minister of the gospel, not as a minister of the law. Oecolampadius wrote that the accusers were trying to force Jesus "to administer an office not his own" *(ut alieno officio fungeretur)*. He teaches by example that we should not seize an office not entrusted to us.[54]

For these sixteenth-century commentators, Jesus' words ("whoever is without sin . . .") must not be applied to the magistracy; and both Melanchthon and Oecolampadius quickly pointed out that the Anabaptists, by so doing, have erroneously interpreted the text. Oecolampadius reassured his readers that Jesus is not talking about a requirement for magistrates, but is rebuking those who rashly accuse others of sin. "The world," he writes, "cannot exist without the magistracy, just as we cannot live without food and drink and other things."[55] Therefore, the sentence of a judge — even an ungodly one — should be regarded as valid because he judges "not as a private person, but as a public person."[56] Bucer argued that "the public good is advanced to the greatest possible degree" when magistrates exercise

---

53. Melanchthon, *Annotationes in Evangelion Ioannis*, CR 14:171.

54. Melanchthon, *Annotationes*, CR 14:170; Oecolampadius, *Annotationes . . . in Evangelium Iohannis* (Basel: Bebel & Cratander, 1533), fol. 166[r].

55. Possibly echoing Melanchthon, who writes, "it is granted to the pious in this bodily life to make use of lawful civil ordinances, just as they make use of light, air, food and drink, and similar things necessary for bodily life" (*Annotationes*, CR 14:171).

56. Oecolampadius, *Annotationes in Evangelium Iohannis*, fol. 166[v]: "non ut priuata persona, sed ut publica."

the sword entrusted to them by God. Since adultery is a capital crime according to divine law, the pious should regard the punishment of adulteresses as both "necessary and salutary."[57] Oecolampadius and Bullinger both made the suggestion, startling to us, that Jesus would not have questioned the stoning of the woman if she had already been sentenced by the legitimate authorities. He would have forgiven her sin, Bullinger argued, but he would not have interfered with her execution just as he did not interfere with the execution of the thief he pardoned on the cross.[58]

Like his fellow Reformers, Musculus wants to limit the force of Jesus' verbal response in order to avoid undermining magisterial authority. The response, he argues, does not prescribe a "general rule" (*generalem regulam*), but is aimed solely at exposing the hypocrisy of the scribes and Pharisees who were motivated not by a sincere zeal for justice but by a grotesque desire for blood. By a careful examination of Jesus' language, Musculus attempts to demonstrate exegetically that the response must be limited to its original audience and not drawn into a universal prescription. Jesus does not say "let him who is free of sin" (*qui immunis est a peccato*), but "let him *among you* who is free of sin" (*qui uestrum immunis est a peccato*). The words were not directed generally to the citizens of Jerusalem, nor even to all the scribes and Pharisees, but were specifically addressed to those scribes and Pharisees who persisted in their interrogation of Jesus. "Therefore," Musculus concludes, "this statement of Christ should not be forced to serve an end for which it was not intended."[59] Certainly, Jesus rebukes the hypocrisy of the scribes and Pharisees, but he does not question the legitimacy of the magisterial office, nor does he signify that adultery ought to go unpunished among Christians. Like Oecolampadius and Bullinger, Musculus argues that if the woman had been equitably tried and convicted by the legitimate authorities, Jesus would not have permitted her to go free, but "would have said something entirely different."[60]

---

57. Bucer, *Opera Latina* 2: *Enarratio in Evangelion Iohannis*, ed. Irena Backus (Leiden: E. J. Brill, 1988), p. 312. John Major agrees that Jesus does not call into question the legitimacy of stoning for adultery. However, Major thinks that the punishment is harsh, and he is pleased that most kingdoms no longer regard adultery as a capital offense. He notes that the Portuguese and Spaniards continue to execute adulteresses in his own day (*In quatuor Evangelia expositiones*, fol. 287[r]).

58. Oecolampadius, *Annotationes in Evangelium Iohannis*, fol. 167[v]; Bullinger, *In Divinum Iesu Christi Dominis nostri Euangelium secundum Ioannem, Commentariorum libri X* (Zurich: C. Froschauer, 1543), fol. 98[v].

59. Musculus, *In Ioannem*, 2:12: "Non debet itaque aliorsum haec Christi sententia rapi, quam quo destinata est.

60. Musculus, *In Ioannem*, 2:18: "omnino aliud dicturum fuisse."

Although Musculus denies that Jesus establishes a technical prerequisite of sinlessness, he is quick to argue that the spirit of the words does in fact teach a moral lesson for those "who manage the administration of judgment" *(qui iudicii administrationem gerunt)*. By reminding such magistrates of their own proclivity to sin, Jesus teaches that sentences of judgment and punishment should be seasoned "with sympathy" *(commiseratione)* for the accused. Certainly, a magistrate should not excuse the crimes of his subjects in order to avoid hypocrisy, for that would simply neglect the duty entrusted to him by God. Yet by remembering the common nature he shares with the accused, a magistrate will avoid rash and hasty judgments, and will seek to amend his own life by personal repentance. In fact, Musculus argues, all Christians would do well to remember Jesus' words so that fraternal correction might be conducted with sober moderation.[61]

E. Pardoning the Woman

We come now to the final part of the story, in which Jesus pronounces his absolution of the errant woman with the words: "Neither do I condemn you. Go and sin no more" (John 8:11). In the history of exegesis, commentators since Augustine celebrated these words as expressing the marvelous mercy and gentleness of Jesus. Not only does Jesus freely pardon the woman but he also warns her against future sin, thus demonstrating that the grace of Christ never provides a license for gratifying the desires of the flesh. As Augustine wrote (words that are quoted in Hugh of St. Cher and in both the *Catena* and commentary of Thomas Aquinas), Jesus did not say, "Go, live as you will. Be without anxiety as regards my liberation. However much you sin, I shall free you from all the punishment of Gehenna and the tortures of Hell."[62]

Musculus also emphasizes the dual character of Jesus' words of absolution. By the word "go" *(vade)*, Jesus expresses gentle compassion toward the sinful woman, offering her "free absolution and remission [of sin]" *(liberam absolutionem & dimissionem)*. But this free absolution is conjoined with the warning to avoid future sin, thus teaching the nature of true repentance. There is nothing in Musculus's remarks here that does not reflect traditional exegesis. However, he does raise a question regarding Jesus' pardoning of the woman that is not treated by most sixteenth-century

61. Musculus, *In Ioannem*, 2:12-13.
62. Augustine, *Tractates*, 33.6 (FC 88:57).

commentators, namely, "why he imposed no satisfaction on this woman for her sins."[63] By addressing this topic, Musculus demonstrates once again his willingness to dialogue with medieval commentators who were concerned to explain Jesus' apparent violation of penitential practice.

One can easily see why medieval commentators were concerned. The text offers no evidence of the woman's contrition and gives no indication that she ever confesses her sin to Jesus. Moreover, when Jesus absolves the woman of her guilt, he prescribes no works of satisfaction — that is, no temporal punishment that would enable her to complete the penitential process. Thomas suggested that Jesus remitted both her guilt and punishment by filling her with "sufficient contrition" *(sufficientem contritionem)*. Yet Jesus' act is a clear case of a *non imitandum,* for no one may presume to absolve a sinner "apart from confession and imposing punishment" *(absque confessione et poenae inflictione).* As Lord, Jesus was able to confer the effect of the sacrament without using the sacramental protocols.[64] Bonaventure and Hugh of St. Cher similarly argued that Jesus imposed no penance because of his power and authority as Lord of the sacraments. Hugh, however, suggested that Jesus may have prescribed the woman's penance when he wrote in the ground the second time.[65] Lyra and Denis echoed Thomas by suggesting that Jesus poured "so much contrition" *(tantam contritionem)* into the woman that she was released from her guilt and her punishment; or perhaps Jesus foresaw how contrite she would be and therefore justly excused her from works of satisfaction. Both Lyra and Denis, however, warned priests against presuming to imitate Christ here. Denis wrote, "that form of absolving must not be taken for imitation, but satisfaction must be imposed on the one who confesses."[66]

In the sixteenth century, few commentators addressed the topic of penitential practice that so preoccupied medieval scholars. The Catholic theologian John Major made a brief allusion to the traditional problem by asserting that the woman "merited" release from a prescribed penalty because of her "reverent shame" *(verecundia).*[67] It would seem, therefore, that Musculus, by discussing penance in his comments on John 8:11, takes yet another cue from medieval exegesis. Still, it should come as no surprise that he wants to challenge the terms that defined the medieval discussion.

---

63. Musculus, *In Ioannem,* 2:19.

64. Thomas, *Commentum in Joannem,* pp. 442-43.

65. Bonaventure, *Commentarius in Evangelium Ioannis,* p. 357; Hugh, *In Evangelia secundum Ioannem,* fol. 337ᵛ.

66. Lyra, *Postilla,* 5:210ᵛ; Denis, *Enarratio,* pp. 425-26.

67. Major, *In quatuor Evangelia expositiones,* fol. 286ᵛ.

Jesus did impose satisfaction, Musculus argues, but not the kind of satisfaction that the "papists" require of confessing penitents. Jesus demanded simply that the woman sin no more, and this is the only satisfaction that is ever required of the penitent. Those who impose penalties and works in the confessional booth "are more addicted to human statutes than to true repentance." To perform works of satisfaction may satisfy mortals, but God is satisfied only by true repentance that changes our lives. Jesus' words, according to Musculus, confirm the wisdom of the German proverb, *Nit meer thun / ist ein rechte busz* — "To do it no more is a true penance."[68]

III. Conclusion

Earlier in this essay I argued that the distinctive characteristics of Musculus's exegesis are discernible only when viewed in the context of the exegetical tradition. By a comparative study of his comments on one short pericope, the story of the woman taken in adultery, I have attempted to show the complex set of relationships that underlie the composition of biblical commentary. The famous Reformation slogan *scriptura sola* — frequently mischaracterized by modern scholars — certainly does not mean that Musculus, or other Reformation biblical scholars, had committed themselves to interpret Scripture armed only with their intellects and the guidance of the Holy Spirit. In fact, Musculus's Johannine exegesis demonstrates that he is not commenting on the Gospel text alone, but is also conversing with previous interpreters of the Fourth Gospel. Although he seldom cites all the sources that inform his discussion, comparative analysis reveals the strong and pervasive influence of the antecedent exegetical tradition.

What is the nature of this influence? Most importantly, the exegetical tradition establishes for Musculus a field of interpretive problems that define the general contours of his exegesis. The first task of the commentator is to know the kinds of questions that one must ask of the text. For Musculus, these questions are not simply snatched out of the air as they occur to him in isolated moments of inspiration; rather, they emerge in the context of his dialogue with previous commentators. Musculus's interpretation of the story of the adulteress thus revolves around certain central questions: Why was the adulteress brought to Jesus without her partner in crime? What and why does Jesus write on the ground? Does Jesus establish

---

68. Musculus, *In Ioannem*, 2:19.

a criterion of sinlessness in any act of judgment, implicitly calling into question magisterial duties? And why does Jesus absolve the woman without imposing works of satisfaction? These questions are not simply my organizational rubrics for presenting Musculus's exegesis, but are in fact the questions that emerged in the centuries of Johannine interpretation preceding Musculus.

The exegetical tradition also establishes a field of possible solutions to the interpretive problems of the text of Scripture. This level of influence is also important in evaluating Musculus's exegesis, for we find him frequently weighing various interpretive solutions in the course of his exposition. However, Musculus's commentary is far from being a mere catena of patristic and medieval citations. For example, Musculus knows from the tradition that Jesus' mysterious act of writing in the dirt suggests an allegorical reading, but the allegory he proposes does not correspond exactly to any previous interpretation I have seen. Also, in evaluating the content and reasons for Jesus' writing, he displays a fondness for several of the older and more figurative explanations, but he refuses to build on any foundation except that of moral exposition — equally venerable, to be sure, but far less speculative.

In his development of moral themes, Musculus shows remarkable ingenuity and skill. Here, we find him venturing into areas explored by few other commentators, such as his discussion of adultery and his warnings against the dangers of magic. In both of these instances, he takes his cue from topics in older exegesis (the absence of the adulterer, and the mystical drawing), but goes far beyond the traditional tropological arguments. In these moralizing excursions, Musculus comments not only on the Bible and the exegetical tradition but also on his own times. He does not know, for instance, if the adulteress of John 8 was a victim of a double standard, but he does know that women suffer under a double standard in the sixteenth century, and he sees in the story of the adulteress an appropriate occasion to warn Christians of their equal responsibilities to marital fidelity.

Finally, although Musculus's commentary on John displays a significant debt to traditional exegesis, albeit with a creative reworking of traditional themes, it also displays his familiarity with the most recent critical scholarship of the early sixteenth century. It is significant that Erasmus is the only sixteenth-century author that Musculus cites by name in his entire commentary on John. Not only does he make critical use of Erasmus's translation, but he peppers his commentary with discussions of textual difficulties, problems of translation, and the meaning of the underlying Greek, in ways that should have made Erasmus himself proud.

In the sixteenth and seventeenth centuries, Musculus was justly famous for his commentaries on Scripture. Twentieth-century commentators would do well to include him in their own studies of the biblical texts. There are, in fact, certain indications of a new climate in biblical studies that may resurrect the history of exegesis as a living tradition. New Testament scholar Ulrich Luz has recently noted that in his reading of the classical commentaries on the Gospels — he mentions Origen, Aquinas, Denis the Carthusian, Musculus, Calvin, and others — he was impressed that these exegetes "really *understood* something about the meaning of the texts."[69] It says something, I believe, about the hubris of twentieth-century biblical studies that scholars are only now beginning to recognize (with a certain degree of astonishment) that many "precritical" exegetes were highly skilled, indeed even critical interpreters of Scripture. As scholarship in general begins to question some of the central tenets of modernism, one can only hope that we may be moving into an era in which the voices of "precritical" biblical scholars will be recovered and included in the ongoing conversation regarding the meaning of the Scriptures. Those who read and interpret the Bible today owe a debt — whether acknowledged or not — to the interpretive work of our own forebears, among whom one must number Wolfgang Musculus.[70]

---

69. Ulrich Luz, *Matthew in History: Interpretation, Influence, and Effects* (Minneapolis: Fortress, 1994), p. 4.

70. I would like to thank Edwin R. Tait, a recent graduate of Milligan College, who served as research assistant for this essay.

· 11 ·

Heinrich Bullinger's Exegetical Method: The Model for Calvin?

JOEL E. KOK

Heinrich Bullinger wrote his commentary on Romans for the sake of the inexperienced and moderately educated.[1] His dedication to simplicity for this purpose won him a wide and appreciative readership.[2] Notable among those who recognized and agreed with this judgment of Bullinger's virtue as a biblical commentator was John Calvin. In the dedicatory preface to his own commentary on Romans, Calvin includes Bullinger, along with Philip Melanchthon and Martin Bucer, in his select list of interpreters of Romans "who have done the most significant work."[3] According to Calvin, "Bullinger expounded doctrine with an ease of expression, and for this he has been widely commended."[4]

Calvin's praise for Bullinger's commentary on Romans seems ambiguous, however, when one compares it to his remarks about Melanch-

---

1. "Scripserunt illi eruditis, ego rudibus et mediocribus." Heinrich Bullinger, *In Sanctissimam Pauli ad Romanos Epistolam* (Zurich: Christopher Froschouer, 1533), p. 4, hereafter cited as Bullinger, *Comm. Rom.*, with chapter, verse, and page.

2. Carl Pestalozzi, *Heinrich Bullinger: Leben und ausgewälte Schriften* (Elberfeld: R. L. Friderichs, 1858), pp. 305-9.

3. "De iis qui praecipuam operam navarunt, dicam quod sentio." John Calvin, *Iohannis Calvini Commentarius in Epistolam Pauli ad Romanos,* ed. Thomas H. L. Parker (Leiden: E. J. Brill, 1981), p. 2, hereafter cited as Calvin, *Comm. Rom.,* with chapter, verse, and page; translation here is that of Ross Mackenzie (CNTC 8:2).

4. Calvin, *Comm. Rom.,* p. 2 (CNTC 8:2): "habuit enim coniunctam cum doctrina facilitatem."

241

thon's and Bucer's works. Calvin commends Bullinger more briefly and faintly than these other two commentators. In addition, he passes over Bullinger in silence when he goes on to offer thoughtful critiques of his other two evangelical predecessors.[5] Regarding this omission, T. H. L. Parker observes, "whether his silence on Bullinger implies approval we cannot tell."[6] Given Bullinger's place in the Reformed tradition, the question merits further investigation.

Within the Reformed tradition, Bullinger is a significant yet overshadowed figure.[7] From one side, he is overshadowed by Huldrych Zwingli, whom he succeeded as lead pastor in Zurich after Zwingli's death in the Battle of Kappel in 1531. From another side, he is overshadowed by Calvin, who surpassed Bullinger with respect to theological leadership in the Reformed church. Still, Bullinger's prodigious output of publications during his forty-four years of labor in Zurich was vastly influential — not only in Switzerland but also internationally.[8] His emphasis on the biblical idea of covenant distinguished his theology from Calvin's and continues to be discussed today as possibly representing "the other Reformed tradition."[9] However, by means of the Zurich Consensus of 1549, Bullinger and Calvin "were able to unite the Zwinglian and Calvinist factions in the Reformed church on the question of the Lord's Supper."[10] Bullinger and Calvin, then,

---

5. Calvin, *Comm. Rom.*, pp. 2-3 (CNTC 8:2-3).

6. T. H. L. Parker, *Commentaries on the Epistle to the Romans 1532-1542* (Edinburgh: T. & T. Clark, 1986), p. 74.

7. For a view of Bullinger in the context of the Swiss Reformation, which includes a summary of Bullinger research and references to the ongoing project to produce a critical edition of his works, see Fritz Büsser, *Wurzeln der Reformation in Zürich: Zum 500. Geburtstag des Reformators Huldrych Zwingli* (Leiden: E. J. Brill, 1985), pp. 106-98. For an overview of Bullinger's life and work, Pestalozzi's *Heinrich Bullinger: Leben und ausgewälte Schriften* (see n. 2, above) has not yet been replaced. For a more recent overview of Bullinger's life and work, see Fritz Blanke and Immanuel Leuschner, *Heinrich Bullinger: Vater der reformierten Kirche* (Zürich: Theologischer Verlag, 1990). For a brief but very helpful essay on Bullinger's life and thought see David C. Steinmetz, "Heinrich Bullinger (1504-1575): Covenant and the Continuity of Salvation History," in *Reformers in the Wings*, (repr. ed., Grand Rapids: Baker, 1981), pp. 133-42.

8. Büsser, *Reformation in Zürich*, pp. 164-69; see also Blanke and Leuschner, *Heinrich Bullinger*, pp. 225-31.

9. J. Wayne Baker, *Heinrich Bullinger and the Covenant: The Other Reformed Tradition* (Athens, Ohio: Ohio University Press, 1980), p. 165.

10. Steinmetz, "Heinrich Bullinger," p. 140. For a careful discussion of the Zurich Consensus, see Timothy George, "John Calvin and the Agreement of Zurich (1549)," in *John Calvin and the Church: A Prism of Reform*, ed. Timothy George (Louisville, Ky.: Westminster/John Knox, 1990), pp. 42-58.

combine theological differences with confessional unity. For this reason, comparing their works promises to yield significant insight with respect to the development of the Reformed theological and exegetical tradition.

A good way to carry out this investigation is to compare Bullinger's and Calvin's commentaries on Romans. These commentaries were major publications for both men, and Calvin's references to Bullinger's work reveal that he examined it respectfully in composing his own work. On the basis of Calvin's comments, Fritz Büsser has made a case for "Bullinger as Calvin's model in biblical exposition."[11] According to Büsser, "among Calvin's contemporaries there were none who had dealt so extensively with exegetical work as Bullinger."[12] This makes Bullinger important for Calvin "in a twofold way, both practically and theoretically."[13] While noting parallels between the two commentaries on Romans, Büsser also notes some differences — the most important of which involves the natural revelation of God to the pagans.[14] Büsser seems to favor Bullinger's perspective with respect to this issue, and he also praises Bullinger for achieving greater clarity of thought in his commentary than did Calvin.[15]

Büsser's opinion regarding Bullinger's importance and strength as a commentator stands in contrast to Parker's view on this matter. According to Parker, "Bullinger must be regarded as a commentator whose theory and intentions surpassed his performance, even when he had faithfully put his methods into practice."[16] Parker asserts further that Bullinger falls short of Calvin in theological penetration of Paul's thought.[17] He concludes that "when Calvin commended him, it must surely have been for his theory rather than his practice."[18] The conflicting opinions of Büsser and Parker on the question of Bullinger's influence on Calvin provide the starting point for the present comparison of these Reformers' commentaries on Romans.[19]

11. Fritz Büsser, "Bullinger as Calvin's Model in Biblical Exposition: An Examination of Calvin's Preface to the Epistle to the Romans," in *In Honor of John Calvin, 1509-1564: Papers from the 1986 International Calvin Symposium*, ed. E. J. Furcha (Montreal: Faculty of Religious Studies, McGill University, 1987), pp. 64-95.

12. Büsser, "Bullinger as Calvin's Model," p. 70.

13. Büsser, "Bullinger as Calvin's Model," p. 70.

14. Büsser, "Bullinger as Calvin's Model," pp. 85-87.

15. Büsser, "Bullinger as Calvin's Model," p. 87.

16. Parker, *Commentaries on Romans*, p. 15.

17. Parker, *Commentaries on Romans*, p. 22.

18. Parker, *Commentaries on Romans*, p. 22.

19. Reference should be made at this point to Susi Hausammann, *Römerbriefauslegung zwischen Humanismus und Reformation: Eine Studie zu Heinrich Bullingers Römerbriefvorle-*

I. Calvin's Implicit Judgment on Bullinger's Commentary

As he explains in his preface, Bullinger's dedication to simplicity in his commentary is based in part on the model for writing that he finds in Paul's Epistle to the Romans itself.[20] According to Bullinger, although Paul's subject matter is serious, his style is clear rather than obscure.[21] From this perspective, Bullinger criticizes those who needlessly complicate or even forsake the genuine meaning of Scripture by imposing multiple meanings on the text.[22] Bullinger positions his method of exegesis, which recognizes the nature of biblical rhetoric, in the tradition of Jerome and Augustine.[23] However, an even more important model is Paul himself, who wrote clearly and intelligibly.[24] Paul was also exemplary for Bullinger in the acknowledgment of his debt to both the learned and the simple.[25] Thus, Bullinger calls on a biblical model for his emphasis on such qualities as clarity and simplicity.

All of this comports very well with Calvin's ideal for exegetes, which was "to unfold the mind of the writer whom he has undertaken to expound."[26] In his well-known comment to Grynaeus, Calvin recalls their agreement "that lucid brevity constituted the particular virtue of an interpreter."[27] Bullinger's commentary is both lucid and brief, and in this and other ways parallels between Bullinger's and Calvin's methods and styles

---

sung von 1525 (Zürich: Zwingli Verlag, 1970). While this thorough book is helpful as a general background to the present study, it is not directly relevant to its conclusions. Hausammann examines Bullinger's 1525 interpretation of Romans, while this study explores his 1533 effort. Naturally enough, Hausammann does not include Calvin, who was not yet on the Reformation scene, in her comparison. Her point is to prove that Bullinger "im wesentlichen Luther- und Melanchthonschüler war" (p. 317).

20. Bullinger, *Comm. Rom.,* fol. 2^v: "Equidem Epistola Pauli ad Romanos locupletissimum huius rei testimonium est. Cum enim Christianorum schola, ea nihil unquam habuerit melius, nihil tersius, simplicius quoque et purius nihil; quippe qua omnis Evangelii virtus, non tam copiose quam perspicue exposita sit."

21. Bullinger, *Comm. Rom.,* fol. 7^r: "Dictio autem vel stilus huius epistolae convenit rebus. Nam gravis est, non utique obscurum, sed decorus et maiestatis plenus, a qua perspicuitatem nemo unquam separavit."

22. Bullinger, *Comm. Rom.,* fols. 3^r-4^v.

23. Bullinger, *Comm. Rom.,* fol. 4^v.

24. Bullinger, *Comm. Rom.,* fol. 7^r: "Perspicue ergo et solide scribit Apostolus modo."

25. Bullinger, *Comm. Rom.,* fol. 3^r: "Quin potius certissimum est Apostolum Paulum sermonis characterem ecclesiis attemperasse, ut debitor erat eruditorum et rudium; ipsum itaque docte et clare, sed suo more et idiomate scripsisse."

26. Calvin, *Comm. Rom.,* p. 1 (CNTC 8:1): "Et sane quum hoc sit prope unicum illius officii, mentem scriptoris, quem explicandum sumpsit, patefacere."

27. Calvin, *Comm. Rom.,* p. 1 (CNTC 8:1).

are undeniable.[28] These parallels, however, do not mean that Bullinger was Calvin's model since it is equally probable that they shared a common debt to earlier examples and common ideals.[29] Comparing their attitudes toward Erasmus is instructive with respect to how Bullinger and Calvin can differ in their attitude toward a common possible model for their exegetical standards.

Bullinger relies often on Erasmus for guidance, and his references to the humanist scholar are uniformly positive and often highly complementary.[30] Even in his comments on Rom. 3:24, a key passage for the Reformation doctrine of justification, Bullinger makes explicit and grateful use of Erasmus's grammatical insights for the sake of his own evangelical interpretation.[31] In addition, Bullinger's stated purpose for his commentary, the promotion of humble piety among ordinary believers,[32] echoes Erasmus's well-known desire that farmers, weavers, and "even the lowliest women read the Gospels and the Pauline Epistles."[33] Indeed, with its critique of obscurantism and its emphasis on simple piety, Bullinger's commentary on Romans can be seen as an evangelical response to the plea Erasmus makes in the *Paraclesis:* "What we desire is that nothing may stand forth with greater certainty than the truth itself, whose expression is the more powerful, the simpler it is."[34]

28. Having sketched Bullinger's hermeneutical principles, John H. Leith states, "this would seem to be a fair summary of Calvin's own hermeneutical principles." John H. Leith, "Calvin's Doctrine of the Proclamation of the Word and Its Significance for Today," in George (ed.), *John Calvin and the Church,* pp. 214-15.

29. On the difficulties of proving influence, see David C. Steinmetz, *Luther and Staupitz: An Essay in the Intellectual Origins of the Protestant Reformation* (Durham, N.C.: Duke University Press, 1980), pp. 7-8. On Calvin's use of the Bible and the church fathers as models, see Richard C. Gamble, "*Brevitas et Facilitas:* Toward an Understanding of Calvin's Hermeneutic," *WTJ* 47 (1987): 153-65.

30. Bullinger, *Comm. Rom.* 1:1, 1:30, 1:31, 3:24, and 3:31 (fols. 7^v, 32^{r-v}, 54^v, and 60^v). In the last example listed, Bullinger states, "Eleganter et breviter (ut omnia alias) Erasmus hanc responsionem istis exposuit."

31. Bullinger, *Comm. Rom.* 3:24, fol. 54^v: "Erasmus per comparationem ac subiectionem haec sic concinnavit bellissime."

32. Bullinger, *Comm. Rom.* 16:25-27, fol. 184^r: "Iam vero te appello, amice Lector, atque oro, ut haec nostra cum iudicio legas, lectaque boni consulas. Si aspera et incompta est orationis nostrae phrasis, memineris me noluisse eloquentiam ostentare, utpote qui ex tempore intra certos dies scripserim haec omnia Pietatem apud te magnificare atque ad hanc te volui pellicere."

33. Desiderius Erasmus, "The *Paraclesis,*" in *Desiderius Erasmus: Christian Humanism and the Reformation, Selected Writings,* ed. John C. Olin (Gloucester, Mass.: Peter Smith, 1973), p. 97.

34. Erasmus, "The *Paraclesis,*" p. 94.

Calvin, too, refers to Erasmus frequently, and these explicit references are no doubt only part of a more extended dialogue with the humanist scholar.[35] However, Calvin corrects Erasmus more often than Bullinger does, and his tone is often negative.[36] It is also worth noting that, in contrast to Bullinger, Calvin does not refer to Erasmus in commenting on Rom. 3:24 but instead makes use of a causal scheme to explicate this key passage on justification.[37] In contrast to Bullinger, Calvin is eager to supplement and correct Erasmus theologically and to indicate where the humanist fails in "sufficiently expressing the mind of the apostle."[38]

The significance of this difference between Bullinger and Calvin regarding Erasmus should not be exaggerated. Calvin certainly shares both Bullinger's critique of obscurantism and his interest in promoting humble piety among even the lowly.[39] This accounts for their shared dedication to clarity and brevity, for which they are both indebted to Erasmus, among others. However, Calvin claims that, in light of what his predecessors have done, the particular contribution of his commentary on Romans comes from "using a different kind of writing."[40] His difference from Bullinger in this respect would seem to be less emphasis on simplicity and greater attention to protecting less learned readers from a confusing variety of interpretations.[41] While Bullinger emphasizes simplicity for the sake of clarifying matters for the inexperienced among his readership, Calvin adds

35. Calvin, *Comm. Rom.* 1:14, 2:8, 4:20, 4:21, and 6:11 (pp. 24, 42, 96, 98, and 127).

36. Calvin, *Comm. Rom.* 4:20, 4:21, 5:14, 6:11, and 6:17 (pp. 96, 98, 112, 127, and 132).

37. Calvin, *Comm. Rom.* 3:24, p. 72 (CNTC 8:75): "Nullus est forte in tota Scriptura insignior locus ad vim istius iustitiae illustrandum. Ostendit enim Dei misericordiam, causam esse efficientem: Christum cum suo sanguine, esse materiam: formalem, seu instrumentalem, esse fidem e verbo conceptam: finalem porro, Divinae et iustitiae et bonitatis gloriam."

38. Calvin, *Comm. Rom.* 8:19 (CNTC 8:172): "Retinui autem Pauli verba, quia mihi audacior quam par sit, visa est Erasmi versio, Donec palam fiant filii Dei: neque tamen satis exprimere Apostoli mentem." For further information on Bullinger's and Calvin's relationships to Erasmus in their commentaries, see T. H. L. Parker, *Calvin's New Testament Commentaries* (Grand Rapids: Eerdmans, 1971), pp. 37-41 and 62-67.

39. This comes out in Calvin's criticism of Bucer. Calvin, *Comm. Rom.*, p. 2 (CNTC 8:3): "Bucerus et prolixior est quam ab hominibus aliis occupationibus districtis raptim legi; et sublimior quam ab humilibus et non valde attentis intelligi facile queat."

40. Calvin, *Comm. Rom.*, p. 2 (CNTC 8:3): "De me nihil praedicare audeo, nisi quod iudicavi non inutilem fore hanc operam; ad quam suscipiendam nulla me unquam alio ratio, quam publicum Ecclesiae bonum induxisset. Ad haec, sperebam fore ut in diverso scribendi genere nulla aemulationis invidia premerer, quae mihi in primis timenda erat."

41. Calvin, *Comm. Rom.*, p. 3 (CNTC 8:3): "Verum quia illi non raro inter se variant, atque ea res multam praebet difficultatem lectoribus parum acutis, dum haesitant cuius sententiae potius debeant assentiri."

a corrective note to this emphasis on clarification. In a revealing statement, he explains why he has "relieved them [his more simple readers] of the trouble of making a judgment. Their own judgment, I believed, is somewhat erratic."[42] Thus, Calvin's explicit praise of Bullinger for expounding doctrine in an accessible way is mixed with an implicit determination to provide a fuller and more precise doctrinal exposition in his own work.[43] In a remark that applies at least in part to Bullinger, Calvin, while expressing respect for and even a certain amount of latitude regarding the expository efforts of his predecessors, asserts with equal emphasis that "in the teachings of religion, in which God has particularly desired that the minds of his people should be in agreement, we are to take less liberty."[44] Calvin's differences from Bullinger with respect to theological and philosophical issues, which will be explored in the next two sections of this essay, lend evidence to the view that this remark, while not aimed primarily at Bullinger, does apply to him in certain respects.[45]

II. Theological Differences in the Two Commentaries

Bullinger and Calvin exhibit different, though not contradictory, tendencies not only in the method and style but also in the theological and exegetical content of their commentaries. One way this comes out is in the way the two evangelical allies oppose what they view as false religion. While united in their exposition and defense of justification by faith and in their opposition to common enemies, they concentrate their attacks on different battle

---

42. Calvin, *Comm. Rom.*, p. 3 (CNTC 8:3): "Putavi hunc quoque laborem non poenitendum fore, si optimam interpretationem indicando, sublevarem eos a iudicandi molestia, quibus non satis firmum est a seipsis iudicium."

43. This is not to say that Calvin is more doctrinal than Bullinger in the sense of imposing a doctrinal framework on the text. Both Bullinger and Calvin reflect a traditional consensus that good biblical exegesis will always reflect and support orthodox church teachings. The point here is that Calvin shows more concern than Bullinger does for imparting detailed and precise doctrinal understanding.

44. Calvin, *Comm. Rom.*, p. 4 (CNTC 8:4): "sed sola necessitate coacti, nec aliud quaerentes quam prodesse, a superiorum sententiis discedamus: deinde ut id fiat in Scripturae expositione: in religionis autem dogmatibus, in quibus praecipue voluit Dominus consentaneas esse suorum mentes, minus sumatur libertatis."

45. Calvin's remark also applies, e.g., to Martin Bucer, whom Calvin praises highly but also criticizes sharply — most of his theological criticisms being implicit. See Joel Edward Kok, "The Influence of Martin Bucer on John Calvin's Interpretation of Romans: A Comparative Case Study" (Ph.D. diss., Duke University, 1993).

fronts. This difference in polemic against confessional foes is related to further differences with respect to both certain exegetical details and their common struggle to understand the inscrutable God they meet in Romans.

The chief confessional foe for both Bullinger and Calvin is Roman Catholicism. In his attacks on Roman Catholicism, however, Bullinger directs most of his criticism against externalism, which he often associates with monasticism.[46] Therefore, according to Bullinger, at Rom. 2:1 Paul is exposing as sinners "the hypocrites and monks of the Gentiles."[47] Calvin certainly opposes externalism and probably agreed with Bullinger's association of externalism with monasticism.[48] However, Calvin does not bother to denounce monks at Rom. 2:1. Instead, he observes that "sin properly belongs to the mind."[49] This diagnosis leads Calvin to pay more attention to the doctrines of the papists than to their externalism or abuses. Thus at Rom. 5:1-2, while Bullinger takes the opportunity to attack ceremonialism and papal teachings on the intercession of the saints,[50] Calvin takes up the dogmatic issues of moral conjecture and final perseverance and argues that this passage "demolishes the two most troublesome doctrines of the sophists."[51]

Bullinger's and Calvin's remarks on Rom. 1:18-32 are consistent with their respective tendencies of fighting externalism as opposed to doctrinal error. For Bullinger, Paul in this passage condemns false religion as a sin consisting of two parts: superstition and the public wickedness that follows from false religion.[52] For Calvin, Paul's references here to impiety and unrighteousness are simply two ways to express the one sinful way people offend God — that is, by dishonoring him.[53] Bullinger goes on at Rom. 1:23 to

46. Bullinger, *Comm. Rom.* 1:26-27, 4:4-5, 6:9-11, 12:2, and 12:9-13 (fols. 29^v, 63^{r-v}, 86^r, 145^v–146^v, and 151^r). Fritz Blanke's observation that Bullinger learned Reformation biblical interpretation while living in a monastic community is relevant here. Fritz Blanke, *Der junge Bullinger, 1504-1531* (Zurich: Zwingli-Verlag, 1942), p. 65.

47. Bullinger, *Comm. Rom.* 2:1, fol. 35^r: "Hos ergo hypocritas et Gentium monachos hoc loce protrahit Paulus, et peccatores esse probat."

48. Calvin, *Comm. Rom.* 2:25-29, pp. 52-54 (CNTC 8:54-57).

49. Calvin, *Comm. Rom.* 2:1, p. 38 (CNTC 8:40): "Et agere dicit, quia non recto sint animo: quandoquidem peccatum proprie animi est."

50. Bullinger, *Comm. Rom.* 5:1, fol. 73^r.

51. Calvin, *Comm. Rom.* 5:2, p. 103 (CNTC 8:105). Moral conjecture is a late medieval teaching that believers, by relying on signs of grace, can have knowledge, though not certain knowledge, that they are in a state of grace. See Heiko Augustinus Oberman, *The Harvest of Medieval Theology: Gabriel Biel and Late Medieval Nominalism* (repr. ed., Durham, N.C.: Labyrinth, 1983), pp. 217-20.

52. Bullinger, *Comm. Rom.* 1:18, fol. 17^r.

53. Calvin, *Comm. Rom.* 1:18, p. 28 (CNTC 8:30).

engage in a lengthy polemic against idolatry, in which he equates papal teachings on the saints with pagan superstition.[54] Then, temporarily abandoning his ideal of brevity (which indicates how important the issue is to him), he offers an extended argument against the use of images in worship.[55] Once again, Calvin would certainly agree with Bullinger in connecting Roman Catholicism to pagan superstition and in opposing the use of images in worship, but the reader would have to consult the *Institutes* to learn this.[56] Calvin's emphasis in his commentary is different. At Rom. 1:23 Calvin does not concentrate on the worship of saints or any other contemporary abuse. Instead, he faults idolators for fashioning "a fictitious new God."[57] For Calvin, the use of images is "a sure proof that their ideas of God are gross and illogical."[58] While Bullinger directs his fire primarily against the use of external images, Calvin concentrates his attack on false mental images of God.

One other difference between Bullinger and Calvin in their interpretation of Rom. 1:18-32 is their divergence in perspective regarding Paul's talk (in Rom. 1:24, 26, and 28) of God "giving over" *(tradidit)* the unrighteous to the consequences of their own sins. In dealing with this word, Bullinger emphasizes that it neither relieves human beings of their guilt nor implicates God in sin.[59] For Bullinger, God's "giving over" is God's just judgment taking the form of permitting sinners to walk in the darkness of their own ways.[60] This is a scriptural form of speaking,[61] and, therefore, readers err if they interpret Paul's words too simply in terms of divine causality.[62] While Calvin agrees with Bullinger with respect to exempting God from sin,[63] he is not willing to soften *tradidit* into mere permission but, instead, argues that God

---

54. Bullinger, *Comm. Rom.* 1:23, fol. 23^r.

55. Bullinger, *Comm. Rom.* 1:23, fols. 23^v–26^r.

56. John Calvin, *Institutes of the Christian Religion*, trans. and annot. Ford Lewis Battles (Grand Rapids: The H. H. Meeter Center for Calvin Studies/Eerdmans, 1975), pp. 20-21. This is Calvin's 1536 explication of the second commandment. Battles notes Calvin's continuity with Zwingli here.

57. Calvin, *Comm. Rom.* 1:23, p. 32 (CNTC 8:33): "longe abfuit quin verum Deum agnoscerent: sed factitium et novum Deum."

58. Calvin, *Comm. Rom.* 1:23, p. 32 (CNTC 8:34).

59. Bullinger, *Comm. Rom.* 1:24, fol. 26^v.

60. Bullinger, *Comm. Rom.* 1:24, fols. 26^v–27^r: "Hinc iusto iudicio tradit nos nobis ipsis, id est, permittit nos nostro iudicio ut viis nostris ingrediamur, tunc vero ambulamus in tenebris."

61. Bullinger, *Comm. Rom.* 1:24, fol. 27^r.

62. Bullinger, *Comm. Rom.* 1:24, fol. 27^v: "Ideoque probe pensitandum quod Apostolus hoc loco non simpliciter dicit, Deus tradit eos in concupiscentias, sed cum conditione et suppacta caussa."

63. Calvin, *Comm. Rom.* 1:24, p. 34 (CNTC 8:35): "Tantum id excipiamus, peccati causam a Deo non provenire: cuius radices in peccatore ipso perpetuo resident."

directs the fall of sinners into their own folly.[64] Calvin also speaks of Satan's involvement in this process,[65] thereby raising a subject that Bullinger does not mention.

Similar patterns emerge in Bullinger's and Calvin's comments on Romans 9. While upholding the idea of election against any idea of merit,[66] Bullinger seems more troubled than Calvin is by the question of God's justice with respect to hardening sinners and reprobation. Bullinger finds refuge in Isaiah 55, which contrasts God's ways with our ways and therefore renders certain arguments concerning fairness inapplicable.[67] While he does not attempt, in dealing with Rom. 9:18, to reduce the offense of the word "harden" by reading it passively, that is, as denoting permission, he deals with the word only briefly and speaks of God using Pharaoh's own tyranny and obstinacy for the glory of his own name.[68] Calvin, while also recognizing the limits of human understanding with respect to God's pre-destination,[69] speaks more often and more freely than Bullinger does re-garding God's secret will in election and reprobation.[70] Not surprisingly, Calvin makes it a point to argue that God's hardening signifies not only God's permission but also the action of God's wrath.[71] With respect to both Rom. 1:18-32 and Rom. 9:6-29, then, we can conclude that Bullinger is more guarded than Calvin is with respect to the inscrutability of God. While both attempt to bow humbly before the truth of revelation, Calvin is more insistent regarding God's propensity to speak words through Paul that are

---

64. Calvin, *Comm. Rom.* 1:24, p. 33 (CNTC 8:35): "De modo quo Deus hominem in vitium tradit, . . . non sinendo tantum et connivendo, illum permittere hominem prolabi: sed iusto iudicio dispensare."

65. Calvin, *Comm. Rom.* 1:24, p. 34 (CNTC 8:35): "Ut tum a propria concupiscentia, tum a diabolo in eiusmodi rabiem exagitetur."

66. Bullinger, *Comm. Rom.* 9:10-13, fol. 121ʳ: "Elegit autem quos vult: imo quos velit et sibi eligere proposuerit, hoc exemplo demonstravit, nempe Gentes. Proinde certa est Vocatio Gentium, qua etiam constat salutem solius esse gratiae et nullius meriti."

67. Bullinger, *Comm. Rom.* 9:14, fol. 121ᵛ: Having stated an objection to God's justice in election, Bullinger admits "apud homines quidem valeret argumentatio: verum consilium domini non est sicut consilium nostrum, neque viae eius ut viae nostrae."

68. Bullinger, *Comm. Rom.* 9:18, fol. 122ᵛ: "At quis est qui Deum huius gratia iniusticiae accuset, maxime si inscrutabilia Dei expendamus consilia? Nam eius tyrannide et obstinatia ad gloriam nominis sui usus est."

69. Calvin, *Comm. Rom.* 9:14-18, p. 204 (CNTC 8:202): "Est enim praedestinatio Dei, vere labyrinthus, unde hominis ingenium nullo modo se explicare queat."

70. Calvin, *Comm. Rom.* 9:7, 9:11, 9:14, 9:17, 9:18, and 9:22 (pp. 200, 201-2, 206, 208, 209, and 213).

71. Calvin, *Comm. Rom.* 9:18, p. 209 (CNTC 8:207): "Caeterum Indurandi verbum, quum Deo in Scripturis tribuitur, non solum permissionem sed Divinae quoque irae actionem."

shocking to hear.[72] Bullinger's greater defensiveness with respect to the secret will of God and his quicker resort to the limits of human understanding connect him to a long exegetical tradition, reflected also in Erasmus and Melanchthon, that struggles to understand God's inscrutable ways in this passage.[73] In contrast to Bullinger, and to most other interpreters of Romans 9, Calvin has a more "severely antiapologetic stance."[74]

III. Differences regarding Pagan Philosophy

The conversation partners in Bullinger's and Calvin's commentaries include not only Christian exegetes and theologians but also pagan poets and philosophers. In this aspect of their dialogue, Bullinger and Calvin again combine many agreements with some differences in emphasis. Both contrast biblical revelation to pagan philosphy while also making use of pagan writers for the sake of explicating certain passages and concepts. Bullinger, however, discerns greater continuity than Calvin does between Christian revelation and pagan writings.[75] This difference in perspective on pagan literature has important interpretive consequences.

Not surprisingly, these differences in emphasis emerge most clearly in how Bullinger and Calvin comment on Rom. 1:18-32.[76] For Bullinger, Paul's general point in this passage is "that all Gentiles are sinners."[77] While noting that the Gentiles perverted true religion with their superstitions,[78] Bullinger

72. Calvin, *Comm. Rom.* 9:27, p. 216 (CNTC 8:214-15): "Horrendum enim auditu est, quod ex infinita multitudine exiguus tantum numerus salutem consequetur."

73. See John B. Payne, "Erasmus on Romans 9:6-24," in *The Bible in the Sixteenth Century*, ed. David C. Steinmetz (Durham: Duke University Press, 1990), pp. 119-35.

74. David C. Steinmetz, "Calvin among the Thomists," in *Calvin in Context* (New York and Oxford: Oxford University Press, 1995), p. 151.

75. John T. McNeill, at LCC 20:82 n. 1, following Henri Strohl, notes that John Sturm, Bucer, and Zwingli apply the designation *divus* to pagan writers. It is important to note further that Calvin does not follow his fellow Reformers in this practice. Bullinger is closer to them than Calvin in this regard. "The universal note present in Zwingli's understanding of the covenant is also present in Bullinger." Steinmetz, "Heinrich Bullinger," p. 138.

76. For a thorough comparative treatment of Calvin's discussion of this passage, see David C. Steinmetz, "Calvin and the Natural Knowledge of God," in *Via Augustini: Augustine in the Later Middle Ages, Renaissance and Reformation*, ed. H. A. Oberman et al. (Leiden: E. J. Brill, 1991), 142-56.

77. Bullinger, *Comm. Rom.* 1:18, fol. 16ᵛ: As a sectional heading, Bullinger states, "quod omnes gentes sint peccatores."

78. Bullinger, *Comm. Rom.* 1:18, fol.17ʳ: "Gentes ergo veram religionem sua superstitione adulterarunt."

also argues that "we see an uncommon knowledge of God and divine things, by no means entirely disagreeable to people of faith, in certain Gentiles."[79] Out of many possible examples, Bullinger selects Seneca as an example of this.[80] Bullinger also argues that there are gradations in both true and false religion.[81] Related to this is Bullinger's further observation, gleaned in part from Erasmus and Cicero, that the Gentiles, even while acknowledging many gods, nevertheless believed in one maker of all things.[82]

Calvin is more emphatic than Bullinger in arguing that, according to Paul, outside the gospel all are damned.[83] He acknowledges a degree of knowledge of God among the pagans[84] but does not follow Bullinger in emphasizing possible positive qualities of that knowledge. Instead, he makes it a point to criticize even Plato.[85] Rather than referring to Erasmus or Cicero for further information regarding Gentile religion, Calvin refers his readers to Lactantius, Eusebius, and Augustine for a further description of "these abominable practices."[86]

Such a difference in attitude explains, at least in part, why, in comparison with Calvin, "we also find in Bullinger by far more quotations from classical antiquity and from the humanists."[87] Bullinger, at Rom. 6:21, argues that the Scriptures and pagan writers agree regarding the intrinsic desirability of virtue both in this life and the life to come.[88] Calvin does not echo this notion, but, instead, observes that only the light of the Lord can open our eyes to our misery, the awareness of which is a fundamental principle of Christian philosophy.[89]

---

79. Bullinger, *Comm. Rom.* 1:20, fol. 18[r]: "Videmus item non vulgarem Dei rerumque divinarum cognitionem in quibusdam Gentilibus non omnino pessimae fidei hominibus fuisse."

80. Bullinger, *Comm. Rom.* 1:20, fol. 18[r].

81. Bullinger, *Comm. Rom.* 1:21, fols. 18[v]–19[r]: "Istis autem didicimus quibus gradibus et incrementis crescat vera religio. . . . Contra vero iisdem pene incrementis assurgit humana impietas."

82. Bullinger, *Comm. Rom.* 1:22-23, fols. 18[v]–19[r]. See also Büsser, "Bullinger as Calvin's Model," p. 87.

83. Calvin, *Comm. Rom.* 1:18, p. 28 (CNTC 8:29): "ex comparatione contrariorum argumentatur, quo probet iustitiam nonnisi per Evangelium conferri vel obtingere, nam extra hoc, omnes damnatos ostendit."

84. Calvin, *Comm. Rom.* 1:21, p. 30 (CNTC 8:32).

85. Calvin, *Comm. Rom.* 1:23, p. 32 (CNTC 8:34).

86. Calvin, *Comm. Rom.* 1:23, p. 32 (CNTC 8:34).

87. Büsser, "Bullinger as Calvin's Model," p. 83.

88. Bullinger, *Comm. Rom.* 6:21, fol. 91[r]: "Virtutes autem per se quidem pulchrae et appetibiles, . . . Quod si quis similes ex Sacris, ex Seneca quoque, et aliis scriptoribus sententias congerat hunc locum mire illustrabit."

89. Calvin, *Comm. Rom.* 6:21, p. 135 (CNTC 8:135).

In commenting on Romans 7, Bullinger focuses his discussion on the law and notes the agreement of Cicero, Plato, and Moses regarding the origin of the law.[90] Calvin, on the other hand, gives more attention than Bullinger does to human nature in commenting on Romans 7 and makes a point of contrasting philosophy and the Scriptures regarding this topic.[91] In his introduction to Romans 12–15, Bullinger follows Melanchthon and the philosophers in dividing moral precepts into private and public or political categories, with Romans 12 describing the former and Romans 13 the latter.[92] Calvin, on the other hand, rejects the private-public distinction in his comments on Romans 12:19 and focuses instead on the internal state of the believer.[93] While Calvin never rejects philosophy per se, he is more determined than Bullinger is to distinguish the transforming message of the gospel from even the most splendid teachings of the pagans.[94] He explains this concern more fully in a 1556 addition to his commentary, in which he criticizes Origen and especially Erasmus for allowing a philosophical and secular mentality to weaken their view of human corruption and, therefore, almost destroy the grace of Christ.[95] Bullinger certainly does not want to deny human corruption or minimize grace, but he seems more receptive than Calvin is to the possibility of finding the grace of Christ outside the visible people of God.

IV. Conclusion

Comparing Bullinger's and Calvin's commentaries on Romans has yielded not dramatic but consistent results. While they agree on exegetical standards

90. Bullinger, *Comm. Rom.* 7:7, fols. 93ᵛ–94ʳ.

91. Calvin, *Comm. Rom.* 7:14, p. 146 (CNTC 8:146): "Nunc proprius committere inter se Legem et hominis naturam incipit, ut clarius intelligatur unde mortis vitium emergat." Calvin, *Comm. Rom.,* 7:15, p. 149 (CNTC 8:149): "Et sane talis est apud Philosophos descriptio humani ingenii. Verum Scriptura longe altius philosophatur."

92. Bullinger, *Comm. Rom.* 12:1, fol. 145ʳ.

93. Calvin, *Comm. Rom.* 12:19, p. 279 (CNTC 8:277).

94. Calvin, *Comm. Rom.* 12:1, p. 264 (CNTC 8:262): "Atque hoc praecipuum est Evangelii et Philosophiae discrimen. Quanvis enim splendide et cum magna ingenii laude Philosophi de moribus disserant, quicquid tamen ornatus refulget in eorum praeceptis, perinde est ac praeclara superficies aedificii sine fundamento: quia omissis principiis mutilam doctrinam non secus ac corpus capite truncatum proponunt."

95. Calvin, *Comm. Rom.* 5:14, p. 112 (CNTC 8:114): Speaking of Origen, Calvin states, "philosophice profaneque disputat de humani generis corruptelis, et gratiam Christi non modo enervat, sed totam fere delet. Quo minus excusabilis est Erasmus, qui in excusando tam crasso delirio nimium laborat."

such as clarity and brevity, Bullinger's emphasis on simple explanation differs from Calvin's emphasis on doctrinal precision and correction. While they agree in upholding their evangelical teaching on justification against Roman Catholic opposition, Bullinger's emphasis on externalism and image worship differs from Calvin's emphasis on doctrinal error and conceptual idolatry. While they agree that God alone saves sinners through Christ alone, Bullinger is more defensive than Calvin is regarding predestination and reprobation and more hopeful regarding the possible salvation of noble pagans. The common theme for these various differences in emphasis is the way in which Bullinger and Calvin perceive how the clarity of the gospel presents itself to the attentive mind. For Bullinger, the gospel is clear because God is sheer light, and if we simply overcome our apathy and ignorance, we can easily see this.[96] Calvin, too, finds the human race asleep in their sins, but he also gives more attention to our delusions and false ideas, from which the gospel must cast us down.[97] Bullinger emphasizes the gospel overcoming our dullness; Calvin emphasizes the gospel subduing our stubborn errors.[98]

For all these reasons, it is claiming too much to say, with Büsser, that Bullinger is Calvin's model. It is more accurate to see Bullinger and Calvin as sharing important exegetical standards and theological positions, with Calvin seeking to improve on the effort of his evangelical ally by offering a more doctrinally precise commentary. Calvin's independence with respect to Bullinger, however, does not detract from Bullinger's commentary on Romans. Bullinger may be, as Parker argues, less theologically penetrating than Calvin. Still, as an exemplary scholar has stated, "Bullinger is less important for his originality than for his wisdom. He was the humane and compassionate *pastor pastorum,* whose learning and gifts were modestly put at the service of others."[99]

96. Bullinger, *Comm. Rom.,* fol. 2^r: "Nam fieri non potest ut ex ipso deo, qui veritas et limpidissima lux est aliquid proficiscatur obscuri. Obscuritas enim omnis et divinarum rerum difficultas e nobis, hoc est ex socordia nostra, deinde ex idiomatum et schematum neglectu, postremo ex non observatio orationis contextu enascitur."

97. Calvin, *Comm. Rom.,* p. 5 (CNTC 8:5): "Verum quia homines suis vitiis indormiunt et blandiuntur, et falsa iustitiae opinione se deludunt, ut se indigere fidei iustitia non putent, nisi iam omni confidentia deiecti."

98. Compare Calvin's description of his own conversion experience in the introduction to his commentary on the Psalms. CO 31:21: "Ac primo quidem, quum superstitionibus papatus magis pertinaciter addictus essem, quam ut facile esset e tam profundo luto me extrahi, animum meum, qui pro aetate nimis obduruerat, subita conversione ad docilitatem subegit."

99. Steinmetz, "Heinrich Bullinger," p. 142.

· 12 ·

The Survival of Allegorical Argumentation in Peter Martyr Vermigli's Old Testament Exegesis

JOHN L. THOMPSON

B Y THE TIME the continental Reformers became aware of Peter Martyr Vermigli, he had already spent half of his adult life in the service of the Roman Catholic Church, pursuing a career shaped equally by his vow as an Augustinian Canon, his interests in Aristotle and Aquinas, and a fascination with Scripture that led him to undertake the mastery of Hebrew with a Jewish physician. Born in Florence in 1499, it was only in 1537 (in Naples) that Vermigli was exposed to the writings of Reformers such as Zwingli, Bucer, and Melanchthon. Over the next four years, Vermigli's Reformed theological sympathies became increasingly apparent, and in 1542 he fled Italy for Zurich. Shortly thereafter, he succeeded the late Wolfgang Capito as a professor of theology in Strasbourg. Vermigli prospered there, leaving to teach at Oxford only in 1547, when the Augsburg Interim placed Strasbourg in Lutheran hands. Vermigli's stay at Oxford was itself ended in 1553 by the accession of Mary; he returned to Strasbourg for a few years, then moved to Zurich in 1556, where he remained until his death.[1]

1. Vermigli's career is nicely sketched by David C. Steinmetz in "Peter Martyr Vermigli (1499-1562): The Eucharistic Sacrifice," in idem, *Reformers in the Wings* (Philadelphia: Fortress, 1971), pp. 151-61. Recent biographical studies of Vermigli include Marvin W. Anderson, *Peter Martyr, A Reformer in Exile (1542-1562): A Chronology of Biblical Writings in England and Europe* (Nieuwkoop: B. de Graaf, 1975); Philip McNair, *Peter Martyr in Italy: An Anatomy of Apostasy* (Oxford: Clarendon Press, 1967), who also contributed a brief

Vermigli's literary output was varied, but virtually all his writings (with the notable exception of his commentary on Aristotle's *Ethics*) emerged in the course of his exposition of Scripture. He lectured on many books of the Bible, from which were published commentaries on 1 Corinthians, Romans, Judges, the books of Samuel and Kings, Genesis, and Lamentations, though only the first three appeared during his lifetime. His other best-known works also derived from his work as an expositor. In particular, two of his polemical treatises — on the Eucharist and on clerical celibacy — were provoked by attacks on his early commentary on 1 Corinthians. But even his lengthy work of "systematic" theology, first published in 1576 as the *Loci Communes*, was merely a posthumous gathering of the many excursuses on theological topics ("common places") that punctuated his commentaries.[2]

As an author of commentaries and as an interpreter of Scripture, Vermigli is not much of an innovator, but he does follow some distinctive patterns. The format of his commentaries, wherein he preferred to alternate verse-by-verse comments with common places, is one such distinctive. Such excursuses in Vermigli may be few but long, as the extensive common places on justification and predestination in his Romans commentary, or many but short: the Judges commentary contains 130 common places! Such a format, modeled early in the course of the Reformation by Martin Bucer and others, was by no means merely a handy organizational scheme. To the contrary, such "excursuses" grew out of a widespread and considered view that Christian doctrines ought to emerge from the soil of Scripture itself. What better way to acknowledge this, then, than to discuss a given doctrine

biographical essay to the first volume of The Peter Martyr Library (see following note); and Mariano Di Gangi, *Peter Martyr Vermigli, 1499-1562: Renaissance Man, Reformation Master* (Lanham, Md.: University Press of America, 1993). Josiah Simler's early life of Vermigli is reprinted in English in *The Life, Early Letters and Eucharistic Writings of Peter Martyr*, ed. J. C. McLelland and G. E. Duffield (Abingdon, Oxford: Sutton Courtenay Press, 1989), pp. 22-94. Students venturing into the field for the first time should be aware that Vermigli is with equal frequency designated simply as "Martyr."

2. Interest in Vermigli has experienced an awakening in the last thirty years or so, and the recent bibliography of works by and about Vermigli renders superfluous any further bibliographical references here. See *A Bibliography of the Works of Peter Martyr Vermigli*, ed. John Patrick Donnelly, S.J., and Robert M. Kingdon (Kirksville, Mo.: Sixteenth Century Journal Publishers, 1990); the volume includes a register of Vermigli's correspondence by Marvin W. Anderson. Our understanding of Vermigli will only be increased by the appearance of The Peter Martyr Library, an ongoing project to translate his works into English, edited by John Patrick Donnelly and Joseph C. McLelland, and co-published by Thomas Jefferson University Press and Sixteenth Century Journal Publishers. As of this writing, three volumes have appeared.

at its taproot?[3] Even though Calvin's well-known "lucid brevity" led him to avoid interrupting his commentaries with such excursuses, he did not really omit common places so much as gather them all together in a single place — namely, in his *Institutes*.[4] To be sure, Vermigli was apparently content to leave his common places in the contexts where they arose, whence they were later gathered by Robert Masson and organized after the pattern of Calvin's *Institutes*.

If Vermigli's commentaries therefore seem more prolix than, say, Calvin's, the impression is only deepened by another contrast that might be drawn. Specifically, Vermigli's commentaries — in particular, the commentaries on Judges and Genesis, which lie at the heart of this study — are concerned not only to explicate the text of Scripture but also to recapitulate the views of Vermigli's exegetical forebears. Unlike the model set forth in Nicholas of Lyra's *Postils* or even in the *Ordinary Gloss*, Reformed and Lutheran commentaries often refused to chronicle exegetical debates, though they were at times just as free in plagiarizing their predecessors. Students of the history of exegesis will often benefit, therefore, from the details Vermigli provides. Indeed, the wealth of particulars often includes a summary of rabbinic argumentation as well as the sort of references to canon and Roman law for which one looks to Calvin in vain, despite his much-touted legal training.

The distinctive aspect of Vermigli's exegesis that will most concern the balance of this study pertains less to his use of the rabbis or lawyers, however, than to his patristic debts. It also pertains to Vermigli's position as a Protestant Reformer and exegete schooled first of all as a medieval Catholic and as an Augustinian in particular. What I wish to sketch is the unexpected tendency in Vermigli to take recourse to allegorical modes of argumentation and exegesis in texts where his Protestant colleagues had mostly set such arguments aside. For the purpose of tracing this peculiarity, I have selected three passages from Vermigli's commentary on Genesis and one from Judges. The passages chosen share no particular theme, yet they are all instances in which Vermigli is clearly aware of the views of his contemporaries and yet follows his own, singular path — a path, it will appear, often trod by Augustine and Ambrose before him. Following a

---

3. On the relationship between common places in commentaries and in theological systems, see Richard A. Muller, *Post-Reformation Reformed Dogmatics*, Vol. 2: *Holy Scripture: The Cognitive Foundation of Theology* (Grand Rapids: Baker, 1993), p. 527.

4. See "John Calvin to the Reader (1559)" (OS 3:6.27-28; LCC 21:5), where Calvin says that in light of what he has written in the *Institutes*, he has "no need . . . to digress into commonplaces" in his commentaries.

survey of these four passages — in which Vermigli addresses (in part) the image of God, Abraham's treatment of Hagar, Jacob's dubious husbandry of Laban's sheep, and Jephthah's vow — I will offer some suggestions about how Vermigli's apparent dissent from the interpretations of his fellow Protestants may have been aided by the example of Zwingli, whose enthusiasm for figurative exegesis Vermigli may well have refined and modeled for later generations.

I. Allegories and Types in Vermigli: Four Cases

A. Genesis 1:27 and the Image of God

There are many traditional controversies surrounding the creation of human beings in the image of God, including what constitutes that image and whether (or how) it survived the Fall. One of the lesser controversies, however, was whether the image of God somehow bore a figurative meaning. The best-known suggestion was coined by Augustine, who located the image of God in the trinitarian structure of the human mind. That is to say, God's existence as Father, Son, and Spirit is imaged in the mind's existence and activity as memory, intellect, and will.[5] Most Protestant commentators on Genesis are familiar with this triadic interpretation, and while there is a degree of admiration for Augustine's cleverness, most (including Vermigli) find it insufficient.[6]

Another figurative reading of the image of God — one less well-known — derives from Augustine, Ambrose, Origen, and ultimately from Philo. This figurative reading finds in the *imago Dei* an image not of the Trinity but of male and female, even as Gen. 1:27 reads, "in the image of God he created them; male and female. . . ." For Ambrose, the image of God resides in the human mind, which is made up of a "higher" part (reason) and a "lower" part (the senses and their appetites). These parts correspond to the typical attributes of male and female, respectively.[7] Augustine later refined this allegory, arguing that while the lower part of the mind is concerned with managing our bodily or domestic concerns,

---

5. Augustine, *De trinitate* 10.

6. For Vermigli, see *(inter alia)* his *Comm. 1 Cor.* 11:7, fol. 286[r]. Calvin argues similarly: "a definition of the image of God ought to rest on a firmer basis than such subtleties"; see his *Comm. Gen.* 1:26 (CO 23:26; CTS 1:93). Luther dismisses Augustine here as simply "not . . . very useful"; see his *Comm. Gen.* 1:26 (WA 42:45; LW 1:60-61).

7. Ambrose, *De paradiso* 2.11 and 15.73 (PL 14:295, 329; FC 42:294, 351).

the higher part of the mind is concerned with contemplating eternal truth, and therefore that part more truly images God. Augustine's allegory is developed largely to deal with the puzzling statement in 1 Cor. 11:7, where many read St. Paul as implying that women do not bear the image of God. Augustine is actually trying to get Paul off the hook by imputing to him this allegory: both women and men bear the image of God, but only in the upper, rational ("male") part of their minds.[8]

Although Augustine's gender-based allegory of the image of God was commonly appropriated by medieval commentators, who freely juxtaposed it with his trinitarian speculations, the allegory virtually disappears in the Reformation. And this is the point to which we have been building: of some eighteen commentators from the early to mid-sixteenth century whom I have examined, only one acknowledges this interpretation: Vermigli.[9] Attributing the allegory explicitly both to Ambrose and to Augustine, he does not develop it at any length but seems satisfied to use it in traditional fashion, as an illustration of how our minds are tempted by our "lower" appetites. Nonetheless, Vermigli adds, this allegorical opinion is "not to be overlooked."[10] The same allegory is recounted at length also in Vermigli's commentary on 1 Cor. 11:7, where he cites Augustine to the effect that "we are called men when we contemplate God, . . . but we are called women when we care for earthly things."[11] And, again, although he concludes by warning his readers not to base their interpretations on allegories,[12] it is surely the case that Vermigli has furnished these details not to dismiss the allegory but precisely because he likes it.

---

8. Augustine, *De trinitate* 12.7.12 (CSEL 50:367; NPNF 3:160). The most careful discussion of Augustine on this point is Kari Elisabeth Børresen, "Imago Dei, privilège masculin? Interprétation Augustinienne et Pseudo-Augustinienne de *Gen* 1,27 et *1 Cor* 11,7," *Augustinianum* 25 (1985): 213-34.

9. On this question I have consulted commentaries not only on Genesis but also on the crucial passage in 1 Cor. 11:7. My basis for comparison draws on Lutherans (Brenz, Luther, and Melanchthon), the Reformed (Bucer, Bullinger, Calvin, Capito, Musculus, Oecolampadius, Pellican, and Zwingli), and Roman Catholics (Cajetan, Catharinus, Erasmus, Jean de Gaigny, Claude Guillaud, Lefèvre d'Etaples, and Titelmans), as well as many of their patristic and medieval predecessors.

10. Vermigli, *Comm. Gen.* 3:15 (fol. 16ʳ): "Nec est prætereundum. . . ."

11. Vermigli, *Comm. 1 Cor.* 11:7 (fol. 286ᵛ), paraphrasing Augustine, *De trinitate* 12.7.10.

12. Vermigli, *Comm. 1 Cor.* 11:7 (fol. 286ᵛ): "Sed allegoricis interpretationibus non est innitendum."

B. Genesis 21:14 and Hagar's Exile

The complicated and poignant story of how Abraham received a son by his polygamous union with Hagar — and of Hagar and Ishmael's subsequent banishment in the wake of Isaac's birth — generated a fair amount of discomfort among the commentators. In particular, there has always been a great deal of curiosity about exactly what it was that Ishmael (or his mother) did that provoked Sarah to such indignation. But only in the late Middle Ages, when Christian interpreters began to discover rabbinic readings of this story, did they also begin to ponder whether Abraham himself committed a second serious sin (that is, in addition to his polygamy) by driving his concubine and her son into the desert with woefully inadequate supplies. Traditional exegesis had an arsenal of strategies for excusing or ameliorating the misdeeds of the patriarchs. The excuse that trumped all others, of course, was to assert that what appears to be an evil act was actually done by special divine command in the service of some (possibly inscrutable) divine plan. Unfortunately, evidence for such special commands was often far from explicit in the text of Scripture. In the face of such scriptural silences, interpreters had to resort to other strategies, such as arguing that a given misdeed was to be read as an allegory of something more edifying (Origen), or asserting that the deed was done "prophetically," that is, to establish the basis for a later typological fulfillment (Augustine).[13]

In the Reformation, the allegorical excuse — as with allegorical exegesis in general — falls into widespread disfavor. Typological exegesis, however, insofar as it appears to look to a specific, historical fulfillment, was not so uniformly cast aside. Most traditionally messianic texts retained their cogency, as did the various passages of the Old Testament cited in the New. But in cases involving apparent immorality on the part of Old Testament heroes, few sixteenth-century commentators invoked allegorical or typological excuses; if they excused these heroes or at all ameliorated their deeds, they usually did so on the grounds of more naturalistic arguments, appealing variously to extenuating circumstances, good intentions, differing customs, or the excuse of "necessity." By and large, the Reformers prefer to read the silence of Scripture as embodying or concealing only those argu-

---

13. For example, where Origen interpreted Abraham's polygamy as an allegory of taking "multiple virtues," Augustine excused Abraham by arguing that he was obliged to provide for St. Paul's typology in Galatians 4. See Origen, *Hom. Gen.* 6.3 and 11.1 (PG 12:197-98, 221; FC 71:126, 168); and Augustine, *Contra Faustum* 4.2 (PL 40:218-19; NPNF[1] 4:162).

ments that would have been licit also for their own readers. Rather than portray God as everywhere granting special permission — an exegetical strategy with potentially dire and anarchistic implications — they were far more comfortable finding the men and women of the Old Testament guided by the principles of natural law and equity.

With respect to Abraham's sudden eviction of Hagar and Ishmael, then, most Reformers believed he was acting in obedience to the command of God recorded in verses 12 and 13. Nonetheless, they do not thereby minimize the austerity of Abraham's provisioning of his concubine and son, and many continue to debate whether Abraham was inhumane in the way he treated them. Such is the general question entertained by Cajetan, Luther, Calvin, Zwingli, Pellican, and Musculus. But in grappling with the problem, Vermigli is again unique. He begins by observing how the "Hebrews" explain Abraham's harshness as serving a "prophetic" purpose, in that Abraham's asperity toward Ishmael foreshadowed how the Ishmaelites would later deny water to the Israelites as they were taken into captivity.[14] Had he endorsed this view, Vermigli even then would have stood out, but — more remarkably still — he instead substitutes an allegorical (not typological!) excuse. "If we wish to adopt [the Hebrews'] opinion, let us say that those things which arise from the flesh are to be treated in this way, namely, that by utterly removing hidden things the flesh may be mortified."[15] In other words, Abraham's severity models the rigor with which *we* should "banish" sinful impulses. Obviously, Vermigli's argument bears even less connection with historical or literal exegesis than the rabbinic typology he has copied. Not only does his argument stand alone among his contemporaries, but there is also only a rather distant precedent for his allegory here.[16] Admittedly, he goes on to offer two more explanations, one suggesting that Abraham might have given the exiles more than the text mentions, the other simply asserting that Hagar and Ishmael deserved such severity. Nonetheless, this cobbling together of three explanations discloses how deeply uncomfortable Vermigli is, both with Abraham's deed and with the silence of the text. When push comes to shove, however, he remains willing to place at least one leg of his tripod on an allegorical base — despite the warning he himself had uttered earlier.

14. Vermigli could have gleaned this interpretation from Rashi's comments on Genesis 21.

15. Vermigli, *Comm. Gen.* 21:14 (fol. 84^r).

16. Cf. Ambrose, *De Abraham* 2.73 (PL 14:515), where Ambrose obviously depends on Philo.

C. Genesis 30:25-43 and Laban's Sheep

The ploy by which Jacob succeeded in outwitting his father-in-law and returned to Canaan a wealthy man has traditionally occasioned quite a bit of comment. Many commentators puzzled over whether his quasi-genetic manipulation of Laban's sheep was to be accounted a miracle sent by God, or whether Jacob simply was exceptionally learned in natural science. The answer to that question bears, further, on an ethical matter, for if Jacob's experiments in sheep breeding were divinely directed, there can be no doubt but that his behavior was faultless. But if the project was undertaken on his own initiative, his deception of Laban may well require some explanation. The latter problem surfaced very early. Josephus, for example, omits from the story any reference to Jacob's manipulations.[17] Augustine explicitly denies any fraud on Jacob's part, insisting that he acted as a prophet and by a special revelation.[18] Jerome had earlier defended Jacob as having "preserved justice and equity" by practicing "a new art," and later medieval commentators such as Lyra and Denis merely combined these two solutions.[19] The passage was allegorized by other writers, including Ambrose, Gregory, Isidore, Raban Maur, and Rupert of Deutz, but the question of Jacob's morality never disappeared.[20]

Sixteenth-century commentators essentially follow Lyra and Denis. Luther, for example, adduces three arguments, excusing Jacob's deed on the grounds of his natural rights (namely, to provide for his family), special divine permission, and his extreme need. Nonetheless, Luther remains con-

---

17. Josephus, *Antiquities* 1.19.8-9, §§309-11, 320-21 (LCL Josephus 4:148-55).

18. Augustine, *Quaest. Hept.* 1.93 on Gen. 30:33 (CCSL 33:35; PL 34:572).

19. Jerome, *Quaest. Gen.* 30:41-42 (PL 23:985).

20. Ambrose allegorized Jacob's sheep as the flock of virtues that he tended "for Christ" (*De Iacob et vita beata* 2.4.19-20 and *De fuga saeculi* 4.22-23 [PL 14:651-52, 609; FC 65:156-57, 298]), probably drawing on a similar allegory found at several places in Philo. Isidore took the notion of "Christ's flock" a step further: Jacob's variegated sheep correspond not to his virtues but to the diverse nations represented in the flock of Christ (*Quaest. Gen.* 25.33, PL 83:264). For Rupert, putting peeled rods before the sheep corresponds to holding up "the lives and teachings of the ancient fathers" before the people as examples, albeit sometimes with the "bark" of their literal deeds peeled away. To this point he has merely abridged Gregory the Great, who made the same argument in general terms in his *Moralia in Job* 21.1 (CCSL 143A:1063-64), but Rupert's interest is more specific: the "bark" to be discarded is Jacob's polygamy, whereas Jacob's sheep breeding is actually defended with an allusion to Luke 10:7 — "a laborer deserves to be paid" (*De trinitate* 7.36-39 on Genesis, PL 167:480-83). Surprisingly, Augustine seems to have offered no allegorical interpretation here. See also Raban Maur, *Comm. Gen.* 3.18 on 30:37-39 (PL 107:605).

cerned lest someone imitate Jacob![21] Similar arguments are cited by Zwingli, Pellican, Musculus, and Calvin. Most of what Vermigli says also runs along these lines. Like many of his contemporaries, he is much interested in the question of fetal influences, calling to the bar the usual authorities on this question (Quintilian and Hippocrates, who were cited early on by Jerome and Augustine, respectively) and dismissing the more recent claims of Avicenna and Pomponazzi.[22] Further, he analyzes with care the continuum between natural causes and the miraculous, concluding that the same providence works in both. But when he comes to address the question of the propriety of Jacob's deed, Vermigli does not see much of an ethical problem. After considering the relative market value of strong sheep with variegated wool versus weaker sheep with wool of a single color, he concludes that "all things were thus distributed justly and with utility," since Jacob's sheep needed to be especially fit for the long journey to Canaan. Yet his next remark seems a throwback to a still earlier time:

> But if all these things seem less than appropriate, let us recognize that (these other arguments notwithstanding) in the allegorical reading, the sheep of Jacob — that is, of Christ — are fittingly of diverse colors, because pious, Christian people truly become "all things to everyone," just as Paul said to the Corinthians [in 1 Cor. 9:20-23. . . .[23]

Vermigli's application of St. Paul here might be read as developing a traditional allegorical reading of the text, possibly building on that of Isidore (n. 20, above), though the most exact precedent actually derives from Zwingli, as we will discuss below. In any case, Vermigli does not hesitate to use this allegory to ameliorate Jacob's dubious dealings with Laban. But in

21. Luther, *Comm. Gen.* 30:40-43 (WA 43:694-95; LW 5:385-86), reading in part: "This example will not have to be imitated by anyone except in a similar situation. . . . You should by no means follow it unless you are like Jacob in all respects and all circumstances in a similar situation impel you."

22. Like many of his predecessors and contemporaries, Vermigli was a strong believer in the power of a mother's mind to affect her fetus, but he is unusual in extrapolating this theory to explain justification by faith. In essence, if the mind "lays hold of and receives" Christ and his promises, the mind is itself changed and induces a change in all the habits and affections of the whole person. See Vermigli, *Comm. Gen.* 30:33 (fol. 125^v).

23. Vermigli, *Comm. Gen.* 30:33 (fol. 126^v): "Omnia itaque, vt vides, & iuste & vtiliter sunt distributa. Quod si ista omnia minus videntur apposite dici, illis semotis, in Allegorico sensu cognoscamus, Iacobi, id est, Christi oues commode esse diuersorum colorum, quia vere pij & Christiani omnibus omnia fiunt, vt Paulus ad Corinth. dicebat, Iudæis Iudæus, absque lege his qui sine lege erant, non sui aut carnis, lucri vel quæstus gratia, sed vt Christo homines addicerentur, &c."

adopting such a strategy, he isolates himself from virtually all of his fellow Reformers, save Zwingli.

D. Judges 11:29-40 and Jephthah's Vow

A final illustration of how a commitment to the literal sense of scripture did not provoke Vermigli to discard allegoresis from his exegetical toolbox may be drawn from the tragic story of Jephthah's rash vow and his subsequent sacrifice of his daughter. While the tale provoked a host of incidental comments, it was Augustine's lengthy response in his *Questions on the Heptateuch* that dominated the discussion for fully a thousand years. Augustine devotes nearly equal space, first, to the ethical issue raised by a literal reading and, then, to Jephthah's typological significance. His findings may be sorted out under three headings. First of all, he argues that Jephthah's rash vow is to be utterly condemned — and all the more so, given Augustine's belief that Jephthah really meant to sacrifice not his daughter but his wife! — *unless*, of course, he acted by a special divine command. In fact, Augustine is disinclined to think that Jephthah did have such a dispensation. Second, in Jephthah one may discern a striking prefiguration of Christ, who was similarly disowned by his brethren, associated with outcasts, acted for the deliverance of Israel, and (eventually) will "offer up" to God his "virgin daughter," that is, the church. A third heading actually combines the other two, and may well be Augustine's preferred conclusion. However heinous Jephthah's deed may have been, it is quite possible (Augustine suggests) that God allowed it — indeed, provided for it! — both to show the horrible consequences of vowing human life and to bequeath to Israel a riveting type of the Messiah who was to come.[24]

Augustine was copied and imitated by the majority of medieval interpreters; the *Ordinary Gloss* on the chapter consists of nothing but Augustine, augmented by a short excerpt from Isidore. Augustine's voice thus drowned out almost all others, until a radically different interpretation propounded by two medieval rabbis gradually became known to Christian scholars. Joseph and David Kimhi, a father and son of the late twelfth and early thirteenth century, argued that Jephthah actually made a twofold vow, wherein he would sacrifice whatever first met him on return from victory if it were fit to be so offered; otherwise, "it will be the LORD's" (Judg. 11:31),

---

24. These three motifs appear in Augustine's *Quaest. Hept.* 7.49.6, 14-15, 26 (CCSL 33:361, 365-66, 372).

that is, perpetually consecrated to God for divine service but by no means killed. Yet this clever argument was exceedingly slow to disseminate. Curiously, although the fourteenth-century *Postils* of Lyra contend that the daughter was not sacrificed, Lyra mentions neither the Kimhis nor the crucial grammatical details of their argument. It is not until the publication of the rabbinic Bibles in the Renaissance — and, in particular, Sebastian Münster's Latin account of the argument in his *Biblica Hebraica* of 1534-35 — that the view begins to gather momentum, as well as controversy. Suffice it to say, despite the endorsement of Conrad Pellican, Vermigli's immediate predecessor as professor of Hebrew at Zurich, the interpretation continued to be contested both in general and by Vermigli in particular.[25]

As expected, Vermigli offers both verse-by-verse comments on Judges 11 a separate common place on Jephthah's vow. What impresses the reader of these pages is Vermigli's determination both to lay to rest what he sees as a spurious rabbinic argument and to prosecute to the fullest his belief that Jephthah's deed can in no way be excused — despite the contrary arguments of Augustine and Ambrose. But Vermigli's remarkable momentum finally fails when he collides with the traditional and irrefutable argument from silence: What if Jephthah was acting in obedience to some inscrutable divine command? Vermigli has no reply but to admit this possibility as an equal, if less desirable, explanation.

> If it be asked whether he sinned in doing this, one may answer in two ways. First, given that he was human, he may well have sinned, even as many of the ancients fell. Secondly, it might be said that he did this by the impulse of the Holy Spirit, not as though God would have others imitate this act, but so that people would thereby understand that Christ would one day die for their salvation. Everyone is free to choose either of these answers. I, however, think it likely that he fell.[26]

Once Vermigli has at all countenanced (however grudgingly) those who would excuse Jephthah, it is amazing to see him so instinctively link the excuse based on special dispensation to Augustine's typological rationale. In other words, however more likely it may be that Jephthah's vow consti-

---

25. Commentators of the early to mid-sixteenth century who show some awareness of the argument for the daughter's survival (whether from Lyra or from a more direct report such as that of Münster) and who argue against it include Luther, Cajetan, and Vermigli. Bucer and Calvin affirm that the daughter was killed, but do not mention the opposing view. Those who endorse the argument include Vatablus, Clarius, Pellican, and Brenz.

26. Vermigli, *Comm. Judges* 11, "De voto Iephtæ" (fol. 141[r], ET fol. 196[r]).

tuted a fall into sin, once that explanation is preempted, Vermigli is quick to find the harsh providence behind Jephthah's fall cushioned by an equally providential — but tremendously more comforting — lesson of the Christ to come. And for a fourth time among sixteenth-century commentators Vermigli's interpretation represents a minority of one.

II. On the Significance and Sources of Vermigli's Allegoresis

The preceding four examples from Vermigli's commentaries are by no means the only instances of allegorical or typological exegesis in his Old Testament commentaries. But however much Vermigli's views stand out from those of his Protestant colleagues in these four particular instances, it would be misleading to generalize his uniqueness. To be sure, Protestant Reformers did try to minimize allegorical exegesis, as did a handful of sixteenth-century Roman Catholic commentators (of whom Cajetan is only one example). But a categorical elimination of allegory and typology was simply impossible, for Scripture itself offers numerous allegories and typologies which therefore bear the stamp of canonical authority; and other venerable types and figures were widely believed to be implied in Scripture, even if not quite explicit.[27] Even the purest exponents of literal exegesis — Calvin, for example — acknowledged such scriptural precedents. The notion that the Protestant commitment to *sola scriptura* entailed a wholesale rejection of figurative exegesis is a stereotype that still endures among the untutored but that has been amply refuted many times.[28] By the same token, in railing against the abuses of allegory (Origen is a favorite target), the Reformers themselves inadvertently cultivated this very stereotype. One of the worst offenders may be Zwingli, whose comments on Genesis extol how his own "straightforward" treatment of the literal sense avoids "inept alle-

---

27. The much-discussed messianic exegesis of the Psalms is a classic case. Another example may be drawn from the attempts to account for the more unexpected members of Christ's genealogy; thus, Christ's descent from Perez (Matt. 1:3; Luke 4:33), Judah's son by his adulterous union with Tamar, is read into Genesis 38 as a factor ameliorating Tamar's conduct by Pellican, Vermigli, and Musculus.

28. T. H. L. Parker, e.g., calls attention to how Bullinger's *Ratio studiorum* of 1527 reiterates (rather than omits) the traditional rule for allegoresis; see *Calvin's New Testament Commentaries* (Grand Rapids: Eerdmans, 1971), p. 40. The enduring diversity of later Reformed exegesis is compactly illustrated by Muller, *Post-Reformation Reformed Dogmatics*, 2:500. The use of allegorical exegesis among earlier Protestants (here including Musculus, Cruciger, Oecolampadius, and Pellican) is nicely documented by Craig S. Farmer, "Wolfgang Musculus and the Allegory of Malchus's Ear," *WTJ* 56 (1994): 285-301, esp. 299.

gories" that "obscure the history" — and yet no early Protestant commentary on Genesis is as filled with allegories and typologies as his own.[29]

Zwingli simply corroborates, then, that it is not a question of whether figurative exegesis survived the Reformation, but rather a question of through whom, and in what degree, and to what end such exegesis survived. The last part of this question may be dispatched first. By and large, allegories and typologies are embraced and employed by Protestants for two very traditional reasons: First, such figurative exegesis is a way of recognizing that a text may bear on contemporary readers in ways that transcend the apparent literal sense of its words. It has been aptly observed that while many humanist exegetes denigrated allegorical interpretation, they often arrived at similar conclusions and applications by the more "modern" way of rhetorical analysis.[30] Second, figurative exegesis is also exceedingly useful for explaining the difficult and (arguably) unedifying parts of Scripture, a rationale that is clearly at work not only in Vermigli's treatments of Abraham, Jacob, and Jephthah's daughter, but also throughout Zwingli's commentary on Genesis.

The first two parts of our question about figurative exegesis in early Protestant exegesis (that is, "through whom" and "in what degree") would require a more comprehensive study than can be offered here. But here again, Zwingli's distinctive exegesis and the role of his writings in precipitating Vermigli's break with Catholicism make him a useful foil for considering not only Vermigli's role in preserving figurative exegesis but also some critical differences in their respective allegoresis. There are two points of contact between Vermigli and Zwingli to consider. First, we know from Simler's account that while Vermigli was in Naples (1537-40), he read two of Zwingli's works in particular.[31] Although neither of these was the commentary on Genesis, Simler records that Vermigli "profited much" from reading Zwingli, as well as Bucer on the Psalms and Gospels and "some books" of Erasmus. A second point of contact — for the moment only

---

29. See Zwingli, *Comm. Gen.* 1:28 (ZSW 13:14.23-24). Zwingli's figurative exegesis is examined in great detail by Edwin Künzli, "Quellenproblem und mystischer Schriftsinn in Zwinglis Genesis- und Exoduskommentar," *Zwingliana* 9 (1950-51): 185-207, 253-307; cf. idem, "Zwingli als Ausleger des Alten Testament," in ZSW 14:871-99.

30. See the conclusions of Richard A. Muller, "The Hermeneutic of Promise and Fulfillment in Calvin's Exegesis of the Old Testament Prophecies of the Kingdom," in *The Bible in the Sixteenth Century,* ed. David C. Steinmetz (Durham, N.C.: Duke University Press, 1990), pp. 81-82.

31. Specifically, he read Zwingli's *Of True and False Religion* and his treatise on the providence of God; see p. 42 in the McLelland-Duffield volume (n. 1, above), and McNair, *Peter Martyr in Italy,* p. 149.

hypothetical — is Vermigli's possible use of Zwingli for his allegorical interpretation of Jacob's sheep breeding. Although Zwingli's allegory is far longer and more varied than Vermigli's allegorical "afterthought," and despite Vermigli's divergence from Zwingli with respect to the other two texts we examined from Genesis, Vermigli's appeal to 1 Cor. 9:20-23 (quoted above at n. 23) is fully anticipated in Zwingli.[32] Moreover, while there are a number of variations on the allegorical meaning of Genesis 30, a connection between Jacob's variegated sheep and becoming "all things to all people" is not drawn by Ambrose, Augustine, Gregory, Isidore, the *Gloss*, Lyra, or Denis — nor by any other commentator known to me. Indeed, if anyone is to be credited with an original development of the earlier allegoresis of this text, Zwingli is the far better candidate, for Vermigli's brief sentence seems at best a hasty abridgement of Zwingli's longer and richer account. Still, this remains but a single parallel between the two, and the question of Vermigli's use of Zwingli merits further study.[33]

32. See Zwingli, *Comm. Gen.* 30:40 (ZSW 13:198.26-35): "Varii coloris grex typum gerit ecclesiae Christi, quae, cum corpus unum sit, varia tamen membra habet, varia item dona, iis uti convenit ad corporis totius utilitatem. Quod ut fiat commodius, Prothaei esse debemus et hac versutia uti, qua usus est Jacob; non ut simus inconstantes, ut quovis vento circumferamur, ut fluctuemus; non ut proximum vafricie aut calliditate circumveniamus; non ut nostra quaeramus, sed ut fiamus omnia omnibus et occasioni nos adcommodemus, ut Paulus se fecisse testatur."

33. Accordingly, it is possible that Vermigli coined the allegory independently, against which it may be observed that Vermigli's figurative exegesis usually draws on established tradition. One avenue of inquiry derives from the possibility that Vermigli may have owned Zwingli's 1545 *Opera* (see Alexandre Ganoczy, *La Bibliotheque de l'Académie de Calvin: Le Catalogue de 1572 et ses Enseignments* [Geneva: Droz, 1969], pp. 16, 87, who does not find any mark of ownership on the set), wherein his annotations on Genesis were reprinted as pp. 4a-86a of volume three. Vermigli's lectures on Genesis (published posthumously, in 1569), however, were delivered during his first Strasbourg period (1542-47), so Zwingli's 1545 *Opera* may not even be relevant. Vermigli might have used Zwingli's commentary in its 1527 edition, of course, but there is no external corroboration for this. Indeed, if Vermigli used any Reformed commentary on Genesis in the 1540s, one might expect him to have consulted not Zwingli but another Zuricher and Hebraist, Conrad Pellican (whom he met in 1542), especially in view of Zwingli's mixed reputation. That is to say, while Bullinger wrote in 1527 that Zwingli was the foremost of "our" Old Testament interpreters, a decade later Calvin was less than enthusiastic about Zwingli's commentary on Isaiah: "[he] supplies an apt and ready exposition, but he often takes too much liberty and strays far from the Prophet's meaning." (Both comments are recorded in Parker, *Calvin's New Testament Commentaries*, pp. 40, 88.) Still, Vermigli's enduring respect for Zwingli is registered in the closing lines of his Judges commentary (fol. 208[r], ET fol. 288[v]), where Luther, Zwingli, Oecolampadius, and Melanchthon are described as "heroes" who, like the judges, were raised up by God to proclaim the gospel. On Vermigli's appreciation for Zwingli, see also the contrasting pair of observations by John Patrick Donnelly, *Calvinism and Scholasticism in Vermigli's Doctrine of Man and Grace* (Leiden: E. J. Brill, 1976), p. 39 and p. 118 n. 64.

Even if there is not an exact correspondence between Zwingli and Vermigli on every pericope of Genesis, in their general attitude toward allegoresis they still might seem to be birds of a feather. But there are contrasts to be drawn here, too. Overall, Zwingli resorts to allegory and typology more quickly, more confidently, and, I think, less critically than Vermigli does. Specifically, whereas Zwingli's allegorical and typological arguments verge on evading the historical difficulties, Vermigli's arguments tend more self-consciously to supplement the historical sense — to ameliorate the difficulties, maybe, but not simply to dodge them. Vermigli's rather trite allegory on the banishment of Hagar (as figuring our own fleshly desires) actually bears this out, insofar as it stands as but one of three possible explanations, all worded carefully in the subjunctive. He seems to know that his allegory skates on thin ice! But the impression that Vermigli is more concerned than Zwingli to protect Scripture's literal and historical significance emerges also from another pair of quotations. The first is from Zwingli, addressing how the whole episode of Jacob's "industriousness" against Laban is directed from above:

> Thus one should attend not only to the literal history, but also to divine providence. . . . For those things which seem to us to be done by human scheming are effected by the providence of God. God promised Jacob, when he went to Mesopotamia, that he was going to make him rich. God now brings this to pass for him, at the same time that Jacob was putting his ingenuity and industry to good use. In addition, all these things were done by them as a figure, written down for our instruction (lest anyone should seek to shield his avarice or cupidity from this story, or take occasion from what Jacob did to cheat or defraud someone).[34]

In other words, Zwingli would be alarmed were he to see Jacob's behavior replicated in one of his fellow citizens, but Jacob is nonetheless excused by his typological status. (Vermigli, one may recall, argued that the distribution of sheep was, in fact, equitable.)

Now notice what Vermigli says about Lot's incest with his daughters:

> Those who wish to protect at any cost the misdeeds of the patriarchs say that these things are to be excused because they were prophecies of types and shadows of things to come. Therefore they think that nothing is to be sought here beyond what is signified, but not whether things happened

---

34. Zwingli, *Comm. Gen.* 30:40 (ZSW 13:198.18-26).

lawfully or not. We, however, freely embrace the signs, types, and shadows, but not so as to neglect the history.[35]

Here Vermigli tips his hand. A commitment to the literal and historical sense of the text does not mean forsaking allegory or typology, but it does demand that figurative exegesis yield to historical concerns. Zwingli, for the record, had fully exonerated Lot's daughters of incest (though he rebuked Lot for his drunkenness) and went on to find in the daughters' sons a lesson — really, a mild allegory — of how some who seem to belong to the people of God are really persecutors in disguise.[36] Is Zwingli the target of Vermigli's rebuke, quoted above? It is hard to say. Zwingli is as aggressive as any in excusing Lot's daughters, but the role of allegory here is rather under-developed in comparison with its place in some of the patristic writers who are explicit in fashioning from allegory not an excuse but merely an ame-lioration of the scandal. Still, the rebuke serves as one more measure of the distance between Zwingli and Vermigli as allegorists.

There are, of course, other contrasts to note between Zwingli and Vermigli. The former's Genesis commentary falls far short of Vermigli's command of rabbinic literature, canon and Roman law, and patristic ex-egesis.[37] At the same time, Zwingli and Vermigli seem to share a commit-ment to allegorical and typological exegesis that (regardless of how one resolves the question of dependence) is both independent and considered. Moreover, it is a commitment that is sustained at a level that sets these two apart from most of their fellow Reformers. Like many of their contem-poraries, Zwingli and Vermigli drank deeply at the well of Erasmus, yet neither felt obliged to repudiate Erasmus's high regard for allegorical ex-egesis, nor did either see any conflict between a tempered application of allegory and the evangelical agenda of the Reformation.[38] To be sure, be-cause of Vermigli's greater display of erudition, as well as for more circum-

35. Vermigli, *Comm. Gen.* 19:31 (fol. 78ᵛ). The closest Calvin comes to a typological appeal is his admiration for the explanation of Jacob's lie as a figure of how we are blessed not in ourselves, but in Christ; see *Serm. Gen.* 27:11-29 (CO 58:173-74). The figure is probably taken from Ambrose, but Calvin does not thereby fashion this figure into an excuse for Jacob.

36. Zwingli, *Comm. Gen.* 19:31 (ZSW 13:126-27).

37. In his survey of Zwingli's Genesis and Exodus commentaries, Künzli found a combined total of seventeen explicit patristic references (almost all to Augustine and Jerome), fifteen classical references, and nine references to Jewish sources (Josephus, Onkelos, David Kimhi); see "Quellenproblem und mystischer Schriftsinn," p. 197.

38. On Erasmus's deliberate juxtaposition of literal and allegorical exegesis, see Manfred Hoffmann, *Rhetoric and Theology: The Hermeneutic of Erasmus* (Toronto: University of Toronto Press, 1994), esp. pp. 95-133.

stantial reasons — namely, he lived longer than Zwingli and traveled and taught more widely — the commentaries of Vermigli proved more influential, particularly in England, where many have ranked him second only to Calvin.[39] But it is not implausible that Zwingli's exegesis was read by Vermigli as a warrant for his own efforts at preserving the best of traditional allegorical and typological exegesis. Precisely here, however, his continuity with Zwingli is matched by a marked contrast with Calvin, and if anyone offered the English Reformers and their heirs a bridge between patristic allegoresis and the Reformed love for the letter, it may well have been no one more than Peter Martyr Vermigli. Accordingly, perhaps also in his exegesis, as well as in his sacramental theology, one may conclude of Vermigli that "he was more important to his generation as a mediator than as an innovator."[40]

39. These often-repeated testimonies are helpfully measured by Donnelly in a chapter entitled "The Influence of Martyr's Thought," in *Calvinism and Scholasticism in Vermigli's Doctrine of Man and Grace*, pp. 170-96.

40. Steinmetz, "Peter Martyr Vermigli," p. 161. Research for this essay was made possible by a grant from the Pew Evangelical Scholars Program. My colleagues at Fuller Seminary (Charlie Scalise, Mel Robeck, and Daryl Fisher-Ogden) provided helpful editorial advice; Heinzpeter Stucki of the Institut für Schweizerische Reformationsgeschichte at the University of Zurich kindly verified a Zwingli reference; and Pat Donnelly of Marquette University prevented me from misleading my readers on at least two important points.

· 13 ·

Remembering the Sabbath Day:
Ursinus's Exposition of Exodus 20:8-11

LYLE D. BIERMA

Zacharias Ursinus (1534-83) does not rank among the leading biblical exegetes of the sixteenth century. During his career as docent at the St. Elizabeth Gymnasium in Breslau (1558-60), professor at the theological seminary (1561-77) and university (1562-68) in Heidelberg, and lecturer at the Reformed academy in Neustadt (1578-83), he taught mainly in the areas of catechetics, *loci communes,* and dialectics, and published mostly dogmatic, catechetical, apologetic, and polemical works.[1] His colleague Franciscus Junius once described him as "the most learned of theologians and most theological of the learned,"[2] but his reputation rested more on his work as a systematic theologian than as an exegete.

That is not to say, however, that he ignored the field of exegesis altogether. As rector, administrator, and sometimes sole teacher at the Sapience College (seminary) in Heidelberg, he was involved in the homiletical training of hundreds of pastors for the Palatinate churches. Following his exile from Heidelberg, he spent the remaining five years of his life at

---

1. For an overview of Ursinus's life and writings, see Karl Sudhoff, *C. Olevianus und Z. Ursinus: Leben und ausgewählte Schriften,* vol. 8 of *Leben und ausgewählte Schriften der Väter und Begründer der reformirten Kirche* (Elberfeld: Friderichs, 1857); G. Bouwmeester, *Zacharias Ursinus en de Heidelbergse Catechismus* (The Hague: Willem de Zwijgerstichting, 1954); and Derk Visser, *Zacharias Ursinus: The Reluctant Reformer — His Life and Times* (New York: United Church, 1983).

2. "Theologorum doctissimum et Doctorum theologotaton," as quoted in Bouwmeester, *Zacharias Ursinus,* p. 53.

the Neustadt Casimirianum lecturing on, among other things, the first twenty-one chapters of Isaiah. These Isaiah lectures, along with a commentary on John 1:1-15, several textual analyses and sermon outlines for students, and a few miscellaneous treatises, compose an entire volume of what Quirinus Reuter called "Exegetica" in his collection of Ursinus's works published in 1612.[3]

Perhaps Ursinus's most significant exegetical contribution, however, can be found in a place so familiar that it is easily overlooked: his commentaries on the Decalogue (Exod. 20:1-17) and the Lord's Prayer (Matt. 6:9-13) in the Heidelberg Catechism and, in much greater depth, in his subsequent lectures on the catechism. These commentaries, which helped to shape Reformed preaching and piety for generations to come, deserve to be studied not just as catechesis but also, because they deal firsthand with the biblical text, as exegesis. They provide insight both into Ursinus's exegetical method and, when they are examined in their broader context, into his place in the development of Protestant biblical interpretation in the mid-sixteenth century.

Because one cannot do justice to these commentaries in a single essay, I shall limit my analysis to Ursinus's exegesis of Exod. 20:8-11, the Fourth (or, for Roman Catholics and Lutherans, the Third) Commandment on Sabbath observance. This is an ideal passage on which to observe an exegete at work, first, because it requires that the commentator wrestle with some central issues in biblical interpretation. More than any other section of the Decalogue, the Fourth Commandment is fraught with hermeneutical difficulties. Why, for example, is this the only one of the commandments that was neither repeated in the New Testament nor literally kept by the early Christian church? How could the seventh-day Sabbath be abolished when it was based on a pattern of work and rest established at creation by God himself? Does this commandment have any bearing on the Christian observance of the Lord's Day, which the apostolic church adopted in place of the Jewish Sabbath? How one answers these particular questions reveals something of how he or she approaches the more fundamental hermeneutical issues that underlie them: the range of meanings allowed by the text, the continuities and discontinuities between the Old and New Testaments, and the dividing line between a permanent divine order of creation and the arguably transitory Mosaic moral law.

3. *D. Zacharias Ursini . . . opera theologica,* ed. Quirinus Reuter (Heidelberg: Johannis Lancellot, 1612), vol. 3.

This particular text is also of interest, however, insofar as studies of Ursinus's place in the history of interpretation of the Fourth Commandment have not agreed on whether his approach is essentially "Calvinist" or "scholastic." Most of those who have compared Ursinus's exposition of Exod. 20:8-11 (at least in its catechetical forms) with that of Calvin see not only little difference between them but also a dependence of the former upon the latter. According to Lang, Ursinus's treatment of the commandment in his *Catechesis maior* (1561 or 1562) follows very closely Calvin's Genevan Catechism of 1545, though in abbreviated form.[4] Hessey saw no real difference either between the Heidelberg Catechism and Calvin,[5] and Kuyper, Solberg, and Primus all identified Calvin as the actual source of the view expressed in the Heidelberg Catechism.[6] Finally, some who have examined Ursinus's more detailed catechetical lectures have also noticed parallels to Calvin there. Bacchiocchi, for example, found in both theologians an unresolved tension between the Sabbath as a permanent creation ordinance and as a temporary Old Testament ceremony,[7] and Gaffin detected "no real progression or difference of thought . . . between Calvin and Ursinus" in how they viewed the relation of the Fourth Commandment to the Lord's Day.[8]

A few scholars, however, have argued that there are significant differences between Ursinus and Calvin in their exegesis of Exod. 20:8-11 and, indeed, that Ursinus was returning to the same scholastic interpretation of this text that Calvin and Luther had condemned. Fairbairn, for example, maintained that the major Reformers of the sixteenth century were essentially unified in their interpretation of the Fourth Commandment but were divided on the crucial question of how the commandment is binding upon believers today: Does it require that we set aside only an

4. August Lang, *Der Heidelberger Katechismus und vier verwandte Katechismen* (Leipzig: Deichert, 1907), p. lxxii.

5. James Hessey, *Sunday: Its Origin, History, and Present Obligation* (London: Murray, 1889), p. 170.

6. Abraham Kuyper, *Tractaat van den Sabbath* (Amsterdam: Wormser, 1890), p. 60; Winton U. Solberg, *Redeem the Time: The Puritan Sabbath in Early America* (Cambridge: Harvard University Press, 1977), p. 20; John H. Primus, "Calvin and the Puritan Sabbath: A Comparative Study," in *Exploring the Heritage of John Calvin: Essays in Honor of John Bratt,* ed. David E. Holwerda (Grand Rapids: Baker, 1976), pp. 41, 74-75.

7. Samuel Bacchiocchi, "Remembering the Sabbath: The Creation-Sabbath in Jewish and Christian History," in *The Sabbath in Jewish and Christian Traditions,* ed. Tamara Eskenazi et al. (New York: Crossroad, 1991), p. 84.

8. Richard B. Gaffin, "Calvin and the Sabbath" (Th.M. thesis, Westminster Theological Seminary, 1962), p. 180; see also p. 177.

unspecified time for rest and worship (Luther, Calvin et al.) or one day in every seven (Bucer, Vermigli, Beza, Ursinus et al.)?[9] Bauckham regarded this difference as just one indication that the medieval Sabbatarian tradition with which Luther and Calvin had broken was "later readmitted to Protestant theology by the back door."[10] This trend toward Sabbatarianism, which "fell back on the scholastic position of a weekly day of rest for worship as the natural law content of the Sabbath commandment," could be detected in the Reformed tradition already in Zwingli, Bullinger, Bucer, and Vermigli, but it was even more pronounced in the Heidelberg theologians Ursinus, Junius, and Zanchius.[11] In addition, Parker found "widespread use" among second- and third-generation Reformers (including Ursinus) of "the Thomistic distinction between the moral and ceremonial parts of the sabbath precept," a scholastic interpretation that Calvin, for one, had rejected.[12]

An examination of Ursinus's commentary on Exod. 20:8-11 seems particularly appropriate, therefore, given the hermeneutical challenges of the passage and the lack of consensus on his interpretation of it. However, in order to place Ursinus's exposition in the same historical context that others have viewed it, I shall first summarize briefly the interpretations of the two commentators with whom Ursinus is often compared: Thomas Aquinas, in whom the medieval view came to its most definitive and influential expression,[13] and John Calvin. In all three cases we shall pay special attention to their use of the moral-ceremonial distinction alluded to above and to their understanding of the relationship of the Fourth Commandment both to the creation order and to the New Testament Lord's Day.

---

9. Patrick Fairbairn, The *Typology of Scripture*, 2 vols. (New York: Funk & Wagnalls, 1900), 2:451.

10. Richard J. Bauckham, "Sabbath and Sunday in the Protestant Tradition," in *From Sabbath to Lord's Day: A Biblical, Historical, and Theological Investigation*, ed. D. A. Carson (Grand Rapids: Zondervan, 1982), p. 312.

11. Bauckham, "Sabbath and Sunday in the Protestant Tradition," pp. 318, 319-20.

12. Kenneth L. Parker, *The English Sabbath: A Study of Doctrine and Discipline from the Reformation to the Civil War* (Cambridge: Cambridge University Press, 1988), pp. 32, 20.

13. Bauckham, "Sabbath and Sunday in the Medieval Church in the West," in *From Sabbath to Lord's Day*, p. 305; Parker, *The English Sabbath*, p. 20; and J. L. Koole et al., "The Relationship between Sabbath and Sunday," in *Acts of Reformed Ecumenical Synod, Cape Town 1976* (Grand Rapids: Reformed Ecumenical Synod Secretariat, 1976), p. 214. For an overview of the medieval interpretation of the Fourth Commandment, see Hugo B. Visser, *De Geschiedenis van den Sabbatsstrijd onder de Gereformeerden in de Zeventiende Eeuw* (Utrecht: Kemink en Zoon, 1939), pp. 24-30.

I. Aquinas

A. The Moral-Ceremonial Distinction

In approaching the Sabbath commandment, Aquinas employs the standard medieval fourfold exegesis — but with a special twist. The commandment in its literal sense, he says, is partly moral and partly ceremonial: moral insofar as it obligates people to set aside time in their lives to concentrate on the things of God, and ceremonial in that it designates a specific time, the seventh day of the week, for devotion to the things of God. The cere-monial seventh-day rest also had allegorical, moral (tropological), and anagogical senses, however, signifying respectively the seventh-day repose of Christ in the grave, our desisting from sin and resting in God, and our eternal rest in the enjoyment of God in heaven. The moral aspect of the commandment is permanent, but the ceremonial aspect was fulfilled at the coming of Christ, whose work made possible the spiritual rest prefigured by the Old Testament Sabbath.[14]

B. The Creation Order

Aquinas relates the moral dimension of the Fourth Commandment to natural law and connects the (literal) ceremonial dimension to God's sancti-fication of the seventh day at creation. As with all the moral precepts of the Decalogue, the setting aside of time for the worship of God is an obligation to which all people of all times are bound by natural law and can discover by natural reason; we can no more ignore our natural need for spiritual nourishment than our natural need for bodily sustenance or sleep.[15] Because our reason is sometimes confused by sin or does not always fully apprehend these precepts, however, they have been restated for us in the Ten Commandments.[16]

For Aquinas the seventh-day rest established by God at creation was not a permanent ordinance but the pattern for Israel to follow in remem-bering God's work of creation. The observance of the seventh day in the Old Testament commemorated the first and greatest of God's benefits in

---

14. Thomas Aquinas, *Summa Theologiae* [hereafter *ST*] 1^a-2^{ae}.100.3, 100.5, 102.4; 2^a-2^{ae}.122.4 (Blackfriars ed. 29:67, 79, 177; 41:305).

15. Aquinas, *ST* 1^a-2^{ae}.100.1, 100.3; 2^a-2^{ae}.122.4 (Blackfriars ed. 29:57-61, 67; 41:305).

16. Aquinas, *ST* 1^a-2^{ae}.99.2, 100.11 (Blackfriars ed. 29:37, 105).

the past, the creation itself, for Israel was instructed to sanctify that day not simply because God had rested but because God had rested from his work of creation ("Remember the Sabbath day . . . *for* in six days the LORD made the heavens and the earth . . ." [emphasis added]).[17]

C. The Lord's Day

Aquinas has very little to say about the shift from the Jewish Sabbath to the Christian Lord's Day. Whether for him one day in seven still had to be observed in the new dispensation or whether the day of worship had to be Sunday is not clear.[18] He simply states that, like the other Old Testament ceremonies, the seventh-day Sabbath has been replaced by a new ceremony, the Lord's Day, which commemorates "the new creature begun in the resurrection of Christ"[19] and which is observed now according to ecclesiastical decision and Christian custom, not according to the precept of the law.[20]

II. Calvin

A. The Moral-Ceremonial Distinction

As early as his first edition of the *Institutes* in 1536, Calvin vehemently rejected the distinction between the moral and ceremonial aspects of the Sabbath commandment, regarding it as nothing more than "the nonsense of the sophists [medieval scholastics]." The reason he attacks this distinction so harshly is that he understands it to refer simply to the difference between the observance of the seventh day of the week (ceremonial part) and the observance of one day a week (moral part), a difference so slight that it has led the Roman church into "crass and carnal sabbatarian superstition."[21] However, Calvin has misrepresented the scholastic tradition here. For example, Aquinas, who along with Albertus Magnus intro-

17. Aquinas, *ST* 1^a-2^{ae}.100.5 (Blackfriars ed. 29:77, 79).
18. See Bauckham, "Sabbath and Sunday in the Medieval Church," p. 306; Parker, *The English Sabbath*, p. 20.
19. Aquinas, *ST* 1^a-2^{ae}.103.3 (Blackfriars ed. 29:245).
20. Aquinas, *ST* 2^a-2^{ae}.122.4 (Blackfriars ed. 41:309).
21. John Calvin, *Institutes of the Christian Religion (1536 edition)*, ed. Ford Lewis Battles (rev. ed., Grand Rapids: Eerdmans, 1986), p. 24. Cf. also *Inst.* (1559) 2.8.34. All subsequent references to the *Institutes* are to the 1559 edition unless otherwise indicated.

duced the moral-ceremonial distinction into the medieval discussion of this passage, defines the moral part of the commandment not as the observance of one day in seven but, as we have seen, as the setting aside of time in one's life for the worship of God. Furthermore, Aquinas regards the tropological sense of the ceremonial aspect of the commandment as our resting from sin and in God. What is striking is that Calvin uses precisely these same distinctions but not always in the same terms. He, too, differentiates "the ceremonial part of the commandment," which was abolished at the coming of Christ, from those things that "are equally applicable to every age," including the regular public worship of God.[22] This sounds very much like the moral aspect of Aquinas's literal interpretation of the commandment. Calvin also distinguishes "the ceremonies and the outward rite" from "the *truth* of the precept" that the outward rite prefigured, namely, a spiritual rest from sin that we enjoy in part in this life but reach in full measure only in eternity.[23] These are what Aquinas identifies as the tropological and anagogical senses of the ceremonial part of the commandment. All his protestations aside, Calvin has actually repudiated only the terminology, not the substance, of the medieval moral-ceremonial distinction.[24]

B. The Creation Order

Like Aquinas, Calvin grounds the Fourth Commandment in natural law but only as one part of the whole Decalogue, which provides a "clearer witness" to what is obscured in natural law by human sin. He declares that "the inward law . . . asserts the very same things that are to be learned from the two Tables," but he is not specific about what those "same things" are in relation to the sanctification of the Sabbath.[25]

22. *Inst.* 2.8.31, 32.

23. *Inst.* (1536), p. 23, italics added. Cf. also *Inst.* (1559) 2.8.31.

24. Others have reached the same conclusion. Cf. Bacchiocchi, "Remembering the Sabbath," pp. 83-84: "[Calvin was] reproposing a new version of Aquinas's distinction between the moral and ceremonial aspects of the Sabbath"; Koole, "The Relationship between Sabbath and Sunday," p. 215: "We are of the conviction that essentially [Calvin] merely adopted the groundplan developed in the *Summa* by Thomas"; John H. Primus, *Holy Time: Moderate Puritanism and the Sabbath* (Macon, Ga.: Mercer University Press, 1989), p. 122 n. 5: "Calvin consistently uses the ceremonial category, distinguishing that aspect of the commandment from those aspects that are 'perpetual' in it. This would appear to be tantamount to the ceremonial-moral distinction."

25. Calvin, *Inst.* 2.8.1.

He is more forthcoming in his treatment of the relationship of the Fourth Commandment to God's seventh-day rest at creation. In fact, in his commentary on Gen. 2:3 he appears to teach that the Fourth Commandment reflects a universal creation ordinance of one day of rest in every seven when he states that "God dedicated every seventh day to rest, that his own example might be a perpetual rule," and that "inasmuch as [the Sabbath] was commanded to men from the beginning that they might employ themselves in the worship of God, it is right that it should continue to the end of the world."[26] This, however, seems to contradict his position both in the *Institutes*, where he criticizes any contemporary "fixing of one day in seven,"[27] and in his commentary on Exod. 20:8, where he describes seventh-day observance before the giving of the law as a "well-known and received custom" rooted in the example of God at creation and instituted after the Fall.[28] Gaffin offers the best solution to this apparent inconsistency by suggesting that the phrase "every seventh day" *(septimum quenque diem)* in the Genesis commentary refers not to the "one in seven" principle but to the seventh day of the week, and that "Sabbath" refers not to a weekly day of rest for worship but to the *principle* of regular rest for worship. In other words, God's dedication of the seventh day to rest was, for Calvin, a time-bound application of a timeless principle.[29] This is likely the principle that Calvin also believed to be contained in natural law. In any case, unlike Aquinas, Calvin sees the reflection of a creation ordinance in the Fourth Commandment, but only in the essence of the precept (rest for worship), not in the particular historical form it was given sometime after creation and again at Sinai (six days of labor, one day of rest).

26. See Calvin, *Commentaries on . . . Genesis* 2:3 (CTS 1:106-7; CO 23:33-34). Hereafter cited as *Comm. Gen.*

27. Calvin, *Inst.* 2.8.34.

28. *Commentaries on the Last Four Books of Moses* on Exod. 20:8 (CTS 2:439-40; CO 24:580-81).

29. Gaffin, "Calvin and the Sabbath," pp. 96-100, 102, 105, 109. Less successful attempts at reconciling this apparent discrepancy in Calvin are found in Kuyper, *Tractaat van den Sabbath*, p. 83, and Praamsma, "Calvijn over de Sabbath," *Church and Nation* 6 (Nov. 28, 1961): 92, both of whom maintain that the Genesis commentary (1554) reflects Calvin's mature position and that he did not incorporate this altered view into the last edition of the *Institutes* (1559). Primus ("Calvin and the Puritan Sabbath," pp. 64-65) offers a more plausible solution when he suggests that God's dedication of "every seventh day" to rest refers, for Calvin, to a *minimal* requirement for worship. Primus, however, understands "every seventh day" in the Genesis commentary to mean one day in every seven. The context seems to support Gaffin's contention that Calvin is talking here about the seventh day of the week.

C. The Lord's Day

Calvin maintains that after the coming of Christ, the Fourth Commandment no longer required one day of rest in every seven. He refuses to "cling to the number 'seven' so as to bind the church in subjection to it," and he will not "condemn churches that have other solemn days for their meetings, provided there be no superstition."[30] For "the peace of the Christian fellowship," the early church selected the Lord's Day for rest and worship — a most appropriate choice because the promise of true rest foreshadowed by the ancient Sabbath was fulfilled by the resurrection of Christ on the first day of the week.[31] But "the fixing of one day in seven," as the church did in medieval times, is a reversion to the "shadow rite" of the Jewish dispensation.[32] Now that Christ has brought these shadows to an end, the church is not bound to that ancient rhythm; whether we observe one day a week or two is a matter of Christian freedom.[33] Ideally, we should gather for worship every day, but knowing our weakness, God is content if we allow him the one day a week freely chosen by the apostolic church.[34]

III. Ursinus

A. The Moral-Ceremonial Distinction

Ursinus's best-known commentary on the Fourth Commandment is found in the third section (entitled "Gratitude") of the Heidelberg Catechism, a document to which he was likely the primary contributor. He also composed two catechetical works prior to the Heidelberg Catechism, however, the 323-question *Summa Theologiae* (1561 or 1562), sometimes called the *Catechesis maior,* and a 108-question *Catechesis minor* (1562). The precise dating, sequence, and original purposes of these earlier catechisms are still debated,[35] but both served

30. Calvin, *Inst.* 2.8.34.

31. Calvin, *Inst.* 2.8.33, 34. For Aquinas on this same point, see n. 19 above.

32. Calvin, *Inst.* 2.8.34.

33. *The sermons of M. Iohn Calvin upon the fifth booke of Moses called Deuteronomie* on 5:12-14, trans. Arthur Golding (London: Middleton, 1583), p. 205.

34. Calvin, *Sermons upon Deuteronomie* 5:12-14, pp. 203-4, 207.

35. On this debate, see Erdmann Sturm, *Der junge Zacharias Ursinus: Sein Weg vom Philippismus zum Calvinismus* (Neukirchen-Vluyn: Neukirchener, 1972), pp. 241-43, 246-48. In the following discussion, the Heidelberg Catechism will be abbreviated as HC; *Catechesis maior* as *Cat. maior;* and *Catechesis minor* as *Cat. minor.*

to some degree as sources for the Heidelberg Catechism (1563), the smaller catechism more so than the larger. In the *Cat. maior* Ursinus treats the Fourth Commandment in six questions and answers; in the *Cat. minor* and the HC he does so in a single question and answer apiece. The key question in the *Cat. maior* and its counterparts reads as follows:

Cat. maior 186

Q. What does [the Fourth Commandment] require?

A. That a certain time, free from hindering activities, be set for the public ministry of the church in which the true doctrine of God is taught and learned, the sacraments are properly administered and received, and public prayer and confession are made to God; that obedience and honor be given to this ministry, and that everyone in his own place earnestly desire to maintain it.[36]

Cat. minor 89

Q. What is required of us by the Fourth Commandment?

A. First, that the ministry of the church be maintained and cultivated; that the church meet at the appointed times to learn about the Word of God, to receive the sacraments according to the divine institution, to call on God together with public prayers, and to bring offerings of mercy, while all unnecessary hindrances to these are removed. And second, that throughout our whole life we think on and practice the things we have learned on these days, that is, by resting from all our evil works and by presenting our members to God as instruments of righteousness.

HC 103

Q. What is God's will in the Fourth Commandment?

A. First, that the gospel ministry and education for it be maintained, and that, especially on the festive day of rest, I regularly attend the assembly of God's people to learn what God's Word teaches, to participate in the sacraments, to pray to God publicly, and to bring Christian offerings for the poor. Second, that every day of my life I rest from my evil works, let the

---

36. For the Latin text of *Cat. maior* 185-90 and *Cat. maior* 89, see Lang, *Der Heidelberger Katechismus*, pp. 178-79, 215. I have followed an unpublished English translation by John Medendorp and Fred H. Klooster.

Lord work in me through his Spirit, and so begin already in this life the eternal Sabbath.[37]

Apart from a few differences of detail, the three questions and answers above are remarkably similar. All three understand the basic requirements of the Fourth Commandment to be, first, the maintenance of the ministry of the church by meeting together for instruction in the Word, participation in the sacraments, and public prayer; and, second, rest from our evil works. The most important similarity, however, is in Ursinus's understanding of the relevance of the commandment beyond Old Testament times. Is the Sabbath injunction still valid for the Christian community, which since the coming of Christ has ceased to sanctify the seventh day? Yes and no, he implies. The very way he phrases the questions in all three catechisms suggests the former. He does not ask, "What *did* this commandment require when it was given to Israel?" but rather "What *does* it require?" *(Cat. maior)*, "What *is* enjoined upon *us* in the Fourth Commandment?" *(Cat. minor)*, and "What *is* God's will in the Fourth Commandment?" (HC) The answers, too, make clear that living according to this commandment is something that "we" *(Cat. minor)* and "I" (HC) must do. It was not just ancient Israel that had to set aside a day in order to be reminded to rest from their sins and to devote themselves to the consideration of the works of God *(Cat. maior* 189); "we," too, must observe a certain time for the ministry of the church *(Cat. maior* 188, 190). And yet, he goes on to say in the *Cat. maior,* we are not bound to this commandment in every respect. The observance of the *seventh* day was a temporary measure, a Mosaic ceremony abolished by Christ at his coming *(Cat. maior* 190). To the best of our ability we must observe the time *(Cat. maior)* or times *(Cat. minor)* for ministry established by the church, especially "the festive day of rest" (HC), but we must not consider them "part of the worship of God" *(Cat. maior* 190), that is, times of worship to which we are absolutely bound by God's law.

In these first attempts at explaining the Fourth Commandment, then, it is clear that Ursinus is working with the substance, at least, of the distinction that we have already encountered in Aquinas and Calvin: a permanently valid moral aspect of the commandment and a temporary ceremonial aspect. Setting aside time for worship (Aquinas's moral part of the literal sense) and resting from evil works (Aquinas's tropological sense) still

---

37. For the German text of the HC, see Lang, *Der Heidelberger Katechismus,* pp. 42-43. I have followed the English translation in *Ecumenical Creeds and Reformed Confessions* (Grand Rapids: CRC Publications, 1987), p. 59.

apply to the Christian community even though the particular day on which Israel was instructed to rest and worship is no longer in force.

In his more detailed exposition of the Sabbath commandment in his lectures on the HC,[38] Ursinus not only moves beyond the substance of the moral-ceremonial distinction to adopt the terms themselves but also makes far more extensive use of the distinction than had either Aquinas or Calvin. He ascribes this double meaning, for example, not simply to the Sabbath commandment but also to the imitation of God's resting,[39] to works done on the Sabbath,[40] and even to the word Sabbath itself. The ceremonial or external Sabbath is a specific time set apart for rest or abstention from daily labor and for the public worship of God. The moral, internal, or spiritual Sabbath, on the other hand, is a zeal for the knowledge of God and his works, for avoiding sin, and for worshiping God in confession and obedience. This spiritual rest was signified already in God's rest on the seventh day at creation and later in the Old Testament ceremonial Sabbath Day (Ezek. 20:12). Though present in the converted only in incipient form in

---

38. Ursinus's lectures on the Sabbath commandment appeared in print in several different versions, all published after his death. His *Summa religionis christianae*, an incomplete set of loci lectures delivered at Heidelberg University sometime before he relinquished his chair in dogmatics to Zanchius in 1568, was first published in *Volumen Tractationum theologicarum* (Neustadt, 1584). *Doctrinae christianae compendium* (Geneva, Leiden, 1584; Cambridge, 1585; London, 1586) and *Explicationum catecheticarum* (Neustadt, 1585; Cambridge, 1587) were early versions of Ursinus's commentary on the HC based on student lecture notes. David Pareus, Ursinus's former student, spent a lifetime revising and publishing a number of editions of Ursinus's HC commentary under three different titles: *Explicationum catecheticarum*, which appeared in at least six editions from 1591 to 1608 and was also included as *Explicationes catecheseos* in the first volume of Reuter's *Ursini . . . opera theologica* (Heidelberg, 1612); *Corpus doctrinae orthodoxae* (1612, 1616); and *Corpus doctrinae Christianae* (1621, 1623, 1634, 1651). According to T. D. Smid ("Bibliographische Opmerkingen over de *Explicationes catecheticae* van Zacharias Ursinus," *Gereformeerd Theologisch Tijdschrift* 41 [1940]: 241), the editions of 1634 and 1651 are without a doubt the most reliable. My citations are taken from *Corpus doctrinae Christianae* (Hannover, 1634; hereafter cited as *Corp. doct.*). For the English translation, I have followed G. W. Williard's *The Commentary of Dr. Zacharias Ursinus on the Heidelberg Catechism* (1851; repr. Grand Rapids: Eerdmans, 1954), although I have made some corrections based on the Latin text. Citations from the first loci lectures (hereafter cited as *Sum. relig.*) are taken from the 1587 Neustadt edition of *Volumen Tractationum theologicarum*.

39. "Imitatio autem quietis suae ad quam Deus suo exemplo hortatur, duplex est: Ceremonialis sive significans, & moralis sive spiritualis, sive significata" (*Sum. relig.*, p. 326). Cf. also *Corp. doct.*, p. 591.

40. "Est autem duplex quietis divinae imitatio: caeremonialis & moralis. . . . Sic & opera nostra, a quibus cessare iubemur, duplicia sunt" (*Corp. doct.*, p. 591). Cf. also *Sum. relig.*, p. 326.

this life, it is a perpetual and continual Sabbath that we shall enjoy perfectly in the life to come, when we shall be fully released from all the miseries and cares of this world and praise and glorify God in perpetuity (Isa. 66:23).[41]

Corresponding to this twofold sense of the Sabbath is a twofold sense of Sabbath keeping. He divides the commandment into a "moral and perpetual part" (keeping the *Sabbath* holy) and a "ceremonial and temporary part" (keeping the *seventh day* holy). The moral and perpetual aspect of the Fourth Commandment is really a call to keep the moral Sabbath: God binds all people — from the beginning of the world to the end — to worship him and to refrain from sin (cf. *Cat. minor* 89 and HC 103). The former is consistent with God's intention that the church's ministry and communal worship be perpetually maintained so that he may be publicly praised, the faith and piety of the elect confirmed, agreement in doctrine and worship preserved, and the church visibly distinguished from the rest of humanity. The last point follows both from the example of God, who rested from all his labors after his work of creation, and from the typology of the Old Testament ceremonial Sabbath.[42]

The ceremonial and temporary aspect of the commandment was an injunction to observe the Old Testament ceremonial Sabbath, that is, to observe the Mosaic form of worship and to rest from daily labor on the seventh day of the week.[43] The temporary nature of the commandment is suggested in passages like Exod. 31:13 and Ezek. 20:12, which speak of the Sabbath as a "sign" between God and the Israelites that reminds them that it is the Lord who sanctifies them. Ursinus takes this to mean that the Sabbath of the seventh day commanded at Sinai was given to Israel as a "sacrament or type of the sanctification of the church by the Messiah who was to come."[44] To those who believed, God would grant pardon for sin and acceptance into his favor based on the finished work of the promised Messiah.[45] Like other ceremonies and types, however, this dimension of the Sabbath was fulfilled and abolished at the advent of the Messiah.[46] The Sabbath must still be kept holy but not necessarily on the seventh day (Col. 2:16).[47] Public worship must still be maintained (Ursinus cites, among other

41. Ursinus, *Corp. doct.*, pp. 592-93.
42. Ursinus, *Corp. doct.*, pp. 588-89, 591-92, 594.
43. Ursinus, *Corp. doct.*, pp. 589, 593.
44. Ursinus, *Corp. doct.*, p. 589. Cf. also Ursinus, *Corp. doct.*, p. 594.
45. Ursinus, *Corp. doct.*, p. 594.
46. Ursinus, *Corp. doct.*, pp. 589, 594.
47. Ursinus, *Corp. doct.*, p. 595.

texts, Acts 2:42, 13:15, 17:2, 20:7, and 1 Tim. 4:13), but not according to the Levitical pattern.[48]

In both his catechisms and his commentary, then, Ursinus makes widespread use of the moral-ceremonial distinction found in the medieval tradition and in Calvin. However, in his treatment of the moral element he does change Calvin's emphasis in one important way. For Calvin the "foreshadowing of spiritual rest occupied the chief place in the Sabbath" in the Old Testament,[49] and meditation upon that everlasting Sabbath is still the primary focus of the commandment today.[50] The church's ministry and public worship serve only to provide a context in which regular communal meditation on the works of God can take place.[51] Ursinus, however, reverses this priority. In the *Cat. maior* he refers only to the public ministry of the church as the requirement of the Fourth Commandment (*Cat. maior* 186); spiritual rest is mentioned in passing in a later question on the seventh day in the Old Testament (*Cat. maior* 189).[52] In the *Cat. minor* and HC, rest from wickedness is placed among the requirements of the commandment but in second place after the ministry of the church. Finally, in his later lectures Ursinus describes preservation of public worship and ministry as the "end of the precept" *(finis praecepti)*[53] and devotes considerably more space to it than to spiritual rest.

B. The Creation Order

Like Aquinas and Calvin, Ursinus regards the Fourth Commandment (in the sense of the moral obligation to set aside time for the worship of God) as part of the natural law engraved on the human mind at creation, obscured at the Fall, and later renewed in the Decalogue.[54] But what is the

---

48. Ursinus, *Corp. doct.,* pp. 598, 599.

49. Calvin, *Inst.* 2.8.29.

50. Calvin, *Inst.* 2.8.34.

51. Calvin, *Inst.* 2.8.34. Cf. "The Catechism of the Church of Geneva" (1545), in LCC 22:112, where Calvin lists "to symbolize spiritual rest" ahead of "the preservation of ecclesiastical polity" in his reasons for the Fourth Commandment and seems to suggest that the latter is a means by which true Sabbath rest is furthered.

52. "Igitur huius diei consecratione [Deus] voluit admonere populum suum, ut et ipsi a suis operibus, videlicet a peccatis desisterent . . ." (in Lang, *Der Heidelberger Katechismus,* p. 179).

53. *Corp. doct.,* p. 588. Later in the work (p. 597), Ursinus also lists "Publica celebratio Dei in ecclesia" as the first of eight "causa finales." Spiritual rest is mentioned third.

54. "*Obiect. 5.* Leges ante lapsum a Deo latae, non sunt typi beneficiorum Messiae, & omnes homines obligant: tunc enim nondum erat data promissio de Messia: & una eademque erat totius generis humani, in primis parentibus conditio. Sabbatum septimi diei institutum

connection, then, between the Fourth Commandment and the divine rest at creation? In his exposition of Exod. 20:11 Ursinus points out that the *ratio* or rationale for the commandment ("For in six days the LORD made the heavens and the earth . . . but he rested on the seventh day . . .") pertains, strictly speaking, only to the matter of the seventh day, which is the ceremonial or temporary part of the commandment.[55] That does not mean, however, that God's resting on the seventh day was only of passing significance. From the beginning of time this particular day was designated by God to excite us to a remembrance of his creative work[56] (cf. Aquinas) and to signify that people should, according to his example, rest from their works, especially from sin.[57] Indeed, if the human race had not fallen into sin, the ceremonial seventh day would never have changed; it became mutable only at Sinai, when the creation precept was reiterated but with an added sacramental or typological element that would be fulfilled at the advent of the Messiah.[58]

Thus far Ursinus has followed Calvin's argument quite closely. He deviates from Calvin, however, when he goes on to insist that there is something of the Old Testament *ceremonial* Sabbath that remains in effect today. The moral Sabbath, of course, continued into the new dispensation, but so also did what Ursinus calls "the general principle of the ceremonial Sabbath" *(genus sabbati caeremonialis),* one day of rest in every seven. The ceremonial Sabbath was annulled *in specie* (as seventh-day rest) but not *in genere* (as a weekly day of rest). The latter is a pattern rooted in the rhythm of God's creative work and rest and is as binding today as it was in the Old Testament.[59]

---

est a Deo ante lapsum generis humani. Ergo est universale & perpetuum. *Resp. per distinctionem Maioris,* quae vera est de legibus moralibus, quarum notitiae naturales menti humanae sunt impressae in creatione, non autem caeremonia septimi diei . . ." (*Corp. doct.,* pp. 595-96). For Ursinus's view of the relationship between natural law and the Decalogue as a whole, see pp. 521, 523.

55. *Corp. doct.,* p. 589.

56. Ursinus, *Corp. doct.,* p. 597.

57. Ursinus, *Corp. doct.,* pp. 589, 591-92, 594.

58. Ursinus, *Sum. relig.,* p. 322.

59. "Quamvis autem abrogatum sit in novo testamento sabbatum caeremoniale, morale tamen durat adhuc, & ad nos pertinet, ipsumque adeo genus sabbati caeremonialis, nempe tribuendum esse certum aliquod tempus ministerio. . . . alligati sumus sabbato moraliter, & caeremonialiter in genere, sed non in specie . . ." (*Corp. doct.,* pp. 594-95). Ursinus's position is obscured in Williard's English translation (*Commentary,* p. 563) by Williard's failure to translate Ursinus's reference to the binding "general principle of the ceremonial sabbath."

C. The Lord's Day

It is with this last distinction in mind that Ursinus deals with the New Testament church's adoption of the Lord's Day as "the festive day of rest" (HC). Not surprisingly, he again disagrees with Calvin. Since both the moral Sabbath (worship of God and rest from sin) and the ceremonial Sabbath "in general" were still in force, the church was obliged (contra Calvin) to set aside one day of the week for rest and public worship.[60] But since the Messiah had come, she was no longer bound to the seventh-day Sabbath of the old dispensation. Christ had conferred upon her the liberty to choose any one of the seven days of the week. When the apostolic church eventually selected Sunday as its Sabbath, it was because that was the day of Christ's resurrection, not because she was under any divine legal obligation to do so. For us who live after Pentecost, then, "it is necessary to have some day *(aliquem diem)* on which the church is instructed and the sacraments are administered, but we are not bound to any particular day *(certo diei)*."[61]

IV. Conclusions

As we have seen, past attempts to relate Ursinus's exegesis of Exod. 20:8-11 to its broader medieval and Reformation context have concluded either that he was largely dependent on Calvin or that he was returning to the same scholastic interpretation of this passage that Calvin had rejected. This lack of scholarly consensus can be explained in part by the fact that there are both continuities and discontinuities between Ursinus's and Calvin's explanations of the Fourth Commandment. It can certainly be argued that in composing Questions 185-90 of the *Cat. maior,* Ursinus relied to some degree upon the text of the Genevan Catechism, which he was translating into German at about the same time.[62] To the extent that the *Cat. maior* served as a source for

60. *Corp. doct.*, p. 594. Williard, *Commentary*, p. 563, translates part of this passage as ". . . there is now just as much necessity for a certain time to be set apart in the Christian church. . . ." Ursinus, however, uses the word "day" *(diem)*, not "time."

61. Ursinus, *Corp. doct.*, p. 595.

62. The Genevan Catechism is echoed, sometimes nearly verbatim, in Ursinus's references to preaching, prayer, and sacraments as the essence of public worship (*Cat. maior* 186), to human weakness as the reason that God designated a time for meditation on divine things (Q/A 188), to rest from labor for servants (Q/A 188), to the relation of the seventh day in the Old Testament to spiritual rest from sin and meditation upon the works of God (Q/A 189), and to the abolition of the seventh-day Sabbath as a Mosaic ceremony (Q/A 190); cf. Calvin, "Catechism of Geneva," LCC 22:111-13.

the HC, whether directly or indirectly (through the *Cat. minor*), Calvin's voice can also be heard in HC 103. And in Ursinus's commentary on the HC one can indeed find a number of parallels to Calvin's treatment of the Fourth Commandment in his catechisms, *Institutes,* commentaries, and sermons.[63] Nevertheless, in the course of this study we have discovered several deviations from Calvin as well: Ursinus's use of the language, not just the substance, of the medieval moral-ceremonial distinction; his different ordering of the twofold moral element of the Sabbath commandment; and his insistence upon a "one in seven" principle that is rooted in creation and extends into the New Testament age.

These differences remind us that Ursinus was not slavishly dependent on Calvin. But they also suggest that Calvin was not the only, and perhaps not even the primary, commentator Ursinus was reading. The long-standing tendency to compare Ursinus almost exclusively with Calvin is unfortunate, for it overlooks the fact that Ursinus received most of his theological training and developed some of his closest friendships not in Geneva but in Wittenberg and Zurich. He studied and boarded with Melanchthon for seven years in Wittenberg (1550-57), where he became a lifelong friend and supporter of his mentor. He also spent time in Zurich with Bullinger and Vermigli in 1558 during a tour of Reformation cities (including Geneva), and again in 1560-61 after he had left his teaching post in Breslau. Among Zurich's "pious, great, and learned men," as Ursinus described them, it was Vermigli who seems to have made the greatest impression on him and who may, in fact, have recommended him for the post in Heidelberg after Vermigli himself had turned it down.[64] It is hardly surprising, then, that

---

63. For example, the Sabbath's becoming a sacrament or type of sanctification at Sinai (Calvin, *Inst.* 2.8.29; *Comm. Gen.* 2:3 [CTS 1:106-7; CO 23:33]; *Commentaries on . . . Ezekiel* 20:13-14 [CTS 2:302, 311; CO 40:485, 492]; *John Calvin's Sermons on the Ten Commandments,* trans. Benjamin W. Farley [Grand Rapids: Baker, 1980], pp. 119, 120; Ursinus, *Sum. Relig.,* p. 322; *Corp. doct.,* pp. 589, 594). Other examples include the ceremony of Sabbath keeping as a distinguishing characteristic of God's covenant people (Calvin, *Sermons upon Deuteronomie* 5:13-15, p. 207; Ursinus, *Corp. doct.,* pp. 588, 591, 597); God's rest on the seventh day as a model for our rest from sin and meditation on his works (Calvin, "Catechism of Geneva," LCC 22:112; Ursinus, *Corp. doct.,* pp. 589, 591-92, 594); spiritual rest defined as God's working in us by the Holy Spirit (Calvin, "Catechism of Geneva," LCC 22:112; Ursinus, HC 103); and the church's selection of Sunday as the day of rest for the sake of good order (Calvin, *Inst.* 2.8.33; Ursinus, *Corp. doct.,* p. 593).

64. Fred H. Klooster, *The Heidelberg Catechism: Origin and History* (Grand Rapids: Calvin Theological Seminary, 1982), pp. 124, 127. According to Visser (*Zacharias Ursinus,* p. 106), it was Hubert Languet, not Vermigli, who recommended Ursinus for the post in Heidelberg.

Sturm (among others) has detected the impact of Melanchthon and the Zurich theologians on Ursinus's early theology, even as he was making the transition from Philippism to Calvinism.[65]

What Sturm discovered in other areas of Ursinus's theology may well be true also of his treatment of the Fourth Commandment. Ursinus's stress on the ministry and worship of the church as the heart of the Sabbath commandment is reminiscent of both Melanchthon's and Bullinger's approach,[66] as is his claim that seventh-day rest was instituted from the very beginning of the world.[67] We also find already in Melanchthon the language of "moral" and "ceremonial" elements in the Fourth Commandment,[68] the scholastic form of objections and replies,[69] and the catalogues of commanded and forbidden works on the Sabbath.[70] Vermigli had earlier employed the distinction between the general/perpetual and specific/temporary dimensions of the ceremonial Sabbath and had identified the former with the "one day in seven" principle.[71] Finally, Ursinus's organization of the material on the Fourth Commandment in his commentary on the HC,

---

65. Sturm, *Der junge Zacharias Ursinus,* passim (esp. pp. 1-3). See also Lang, *Der Heidelberger Katechismus,* pp. lxiv-civ; Gustav A. Benrath, "Die Eigenart der Pfälzischen Reformation und die Vorgeschichte des Heidelberger Katechismus," *Heidelberger Jahrbücher* 7 (1963): 24-26; Lyle D. Bierma, *The Doctrine of the Sacraments in the Heidelberg Catechism: Melanchthonian, Calvinist or Zwinglian?* Studies in Reformed Theology and History (Princeton: Princeton Theological Seminary, forthcoming). Cf. a similar conclusion by Richard A. Muller, *Christ and the Decree: Christology and Predestination in Reformed Theology from Calvin to Perkins* (Durham, N.C.: Labyrinth, 1986), p. 124, regarding Ursinus's mature theology: "In the years between 1563 and 1577 Ursinus . . . produced a synthesis of Reformed theology with the established scholastic method, related in its central motifs not only to the thought of Calvin but also to the theology of Bullinger, Vermigli, [and] Musculus, and to that of Luther, Melanchthon, and Bucer."

66. See *Melanchthon on Christian Doctrine: Loci Communes 1555,* trans. and ed. Clyde L. Manschreck (New York: Oxford University Press, 1965), pp. 95-96; and *The Decades of Henry Bullinger* 2.4, ed. Thomas Harding, 4 vols. (1849-52; repr., New York: Johnson, 1968), 1:254-61.

67. Ursinus, *Corp. doct.,* p. 594; Melanchthon, *Loci Communes 1555,* p. 96; Bullinger, *Decades* 3.5 (2:162).

68. Melanchthon, *Loci Communes 1555,* p. 97; and *Explicatio Symboli Niceni* (CR 23:417).

69. Ursinus, *Corp. doct.,* pp. 595-96; Melanchthon, *Explicatio Symboli Niceni* (CR 23:416-17).

70. Ursinus, *Corp. doct.,* pp. 597-601; Melanchthon, *Catechesis Puerlis* (CRO 23:133-34).

71. "Prout autem in aliis ceremoniis aliquid est perpetuum & aeternum & aliquid mutabile ac temporarium. . . . Ita quod unus dies certus in hebdomada cultui divino mancipetur, stabile ac firmum est: an vero hic vel alius constituatur, temporarium est ac mutabile." Peter Martyr Vermigli, *Loci Communes* 2.7.3 (London: John Kyngston, 1576), p. 272.

his discussion of daily, monthly, and yearly Sabbaths in the Old Testament, and his addition of almsgiving in the *Cat. minor* and HC as a fourth element of public worship all appear to bear the stamp of Bullinger.[72] None of these features, it should be pointed out, can be found in Calvin. To be sure, these parallels do not necessarily entail Ursinus's reliance on Melanchthon, Vermigli, or Bullinger, but the fact that he had such close ties to them and that their influence has also been detected elsewhere in his theology suggests at least some direct dependence.

Ursinus's differences with Calvin do not, however, represent the recrudescence of a scholastic position that Calvin had repudiated — at least if that scholastic position is defined as "the Thomistic distinction between the moral and ceremonial parts of the sabbath precept" (Parker)[73] or as "a weekly day of rest for worship as the natural law content of the Sabbath commandment" (Bauckham).[74] Parker is correct to the extent that Calvin spurns and Ursinus adopts the *language* of this Thomistic distinction, but he fails to recognize that Calvin makes frequent use of its substance and that this distinction is employed in some form by almost every Protestant interpreter in the sixteenth century. Bauckham's thesis is also inaccurate. In the first place, although Calvin is not as clear as Aquinas or Ursinus in explaining the connection between the Decalogue and natural law, he does not, as Bauckham contends, limit that connection to the second table of the law. For Calvin "the inward law . . . asserts the very same things that are to be learned from the *two* Tables."[75] Furthermore, all of the figures we have examined hold that the natural law content of the Fourth Commandment is the setting aside of *some* time for the worship of God, not specifically a weekly day of rest. Ursinus's and Vermigli's principle of "one day in seven" is related only to the ceremonial, not the moral (natural law), dimension of the commandment.

The conclusions of past research on Ursinus's exposition of Exod. 20:8-11, therefore, require some revision. There is a certain continuity of interpretation between Calvin and Ursinus, but Ursinus also appears to draw upon and synthesize a variety of other sources, making an original

---

72. Ursinus, *Corp. doct.,* pp. 592, 593, 600; Bullinger, *Decades* 2.4 (1:254-55, 261), 3.5 (2:161-67).

73. Parker, *The English Sabbath,* p. 20.

74. Bauckham, "Sabbath and Sunday in the Protestant Tradition," p. 318.

75. *Inst.* (1559) 2.8.1 (emphasis added). According to Hesselink, Calvin's position that the Decalogue is a clearer witness to natural law is "only a variant of that taken earlier by Thomas Aquinas and Martin Luther." I. John Hesselink, *Calvin's Concept of the Law* (Allison Park, Pa.: Pickwick, 1992), p. 51.

contribution to the discussion of this passage by greatly expanding the use of the moral-ceremonial distinction. There are also medieval scholastic elements in his exegesis of the Sabbath commandment, but most of these can be found in Calvin as well and are actually part of a general approach to this text that Reformation commentators inherited from the Middle Ages and adopted on a wide scale. In short, Ursinus's perspective on the Fourth Commandment can be considered both "Calvinist" and "scholastic," as long as one does not overlook his debt also to Melanchthon and the Zurich theologians. His interpretation of this passage is thus yet another place in his thought where the paths from Wittenberg, Zurich, and Geneva converge.

• 14 •

Holy Harlotry: Jerome Zanchi and the Exegetical History of Gomer (Hosea 1–3)

JOHN L. FARTHING

I. Hosea, Gomer, and Feminist Hermeneutics

Thanks in large part to the work of feminist critics, biblical texts that contribute to the subordination and oppression of women have risen to the forefront of concern not only for exegetes but also for historians of exegesis. In the spirit of Phyllis Trible's *Texts of Terror* (1984), feminist exegetes such as Elisabeth Schussler Fiorenza, T. Drorah Setel, Alice L. Laffey, Renita J. Weems, and Alice Ogden Bellis have highlighted the need to take seriously the part played by oppressive biblical texts in subverting rather than supporting the dignity of women. The feminist critique is one factor that has heightened concerns about the history of the interpretation of canonical materials that are offensive or embarrassing or, indeed, scandalous. Of recent studies in the history of exegesis, some of the most illuminating have focused on the interpretive history of morally problematic texts.[1]

---

1. Especially noteworthy is the work of David C. Steinmetz. See "Luther and the Drunkenness of Noah," in his *Luther in Context* (Bloomington: Indiana University Press, 1986), pp. 98-111; and "Luther and Tamar," *Lutheran Theological Seminary Bulletin* 73 (Winter 1993): 3-15. Also important are John L. Thompson's recent studies in the history of the interpretation of texts dealing with polygamy and other immoralities attributed to the Old Testament patriarchs: see his "The Immoralities of the Patriarchs in the History of Exegesis: A Reappraisal of Calvin's Position," *CTJ* 26 (1991): 9-46; and "Patriarchs, Polygamy, and Private Resistance: John Calvin and Others on Breaking God's Rules," *SCJ* 25/1 (1994): 3-27.

Among biblical materials that seem to cry out for a fresh examination in light of feminist criticism, none is more shocking or disturbing than the account of the union between the harlot Gomer and the prophet Hosea: God commands the prophet to marry "a woman of harlotry" (Hos. 1:2) and to father children by her. The point of the Gomer episode is finally a happy one: the underlying theme of Hosea 1–3 is God's unshakable fidelity, even to a religiously promiscuous people. The medium in which that message is conveyed, however, involves numerous elements that are troubling to consciences sensitized to the oppressive potential of words and images. In Hosea 1–3 a man is clearly a type of divine judgment and mercy, while a woman typifies human treachery and faithlessness. The analogy is clear: Hosea is to Gomer as Yahweh is to Israel. Feminist critics have argued that the effect of this analogy is to reinforce problematic stereotypes about the relation between the masculine and the feminine.[2] The masculine Yahweh/Hosea personifies all that is positive (righteousness and fidelity), while the feminine Israel/Gomer embodies all that is negative (sin and faithlessness).[3] Yahweh/Hosea takes the initiative; Israel/Gomer remains a passive recipient.[4] Even more damningly, Renita Weems has drawn attention to the part played by the threat of physical coercion and violence in Hosea 2.[5] But perhaps the most offensive feature

2. Alice Laffey indicts Hosea 1–3 for perpetuating "a patriarchal prejudice" in personifying faithlessness as feminine. See Laffey, *An Introduction to the Old Testament: A Feminist Perspective* (Philadelphia: Fortress Press, 1988), p. 153.

3. Laffey, *Introduction to the Old Testament,* p. 178: ". . . faithless Israel and still more faithless Judah are portrayed in female terms. . . . No one could better symbolize the sin of Yahweh's people. And yet, to portray Yahweh as male while portraying faithless Israel and faithless Judah as females was unjustly to relegate the female sex to an inferior status from which it has not yet recovered."

4. T. Drorah Setel: "Prophets and Pornography: Female Sexual Imagery in Hosea," in Letty M. Russell (ed.), *Feminist Interpretation of the Bible* (Philadelphia: Westminster, 1985), p. 92: "The sexes of Gomer and Hosea and their respective behavior are not a random representation but a reflection and reinforcement of cultural perceptions. Hence, Hosea's metaphor has both theological and social meaning. With regard to theological understanding, it indicates that God has the authority of possession and control over Israel that a husband has over a wife. The reverse of the representation is a view of human males as being analogous to Yahweh, while women are comparable to the people, who, by definition, are subservient to Yahweh's will." Cf. Mary Joan Winn Leith, "Verse and Reverse: The Transformation of the Woman, Israel, in Hosea 1–3," in Peggy L. Day (ed.), *Gender and Difference in Ancient Israel* (Minneapolis: Fortress, 1989), p. 108 n. 50; Alice Ogden Bellis, *Helpmates, Harlots, and Heroes: Women's Stories in the Hebrew Bible* (Louisville, Ky.: Westminster/John Knox, 1994), pp. 180-81.

5. Renita J. Weems, "Gomer: Victim of Violence or Victim of Metaphor?" *Semeia* 47 (1989): 94-98.

of the text is the way in which both Gomer and her children are simply used to serve the rhetorical strategy of the male author, who speaks in behalf of a masculine deity. That is what underlies Alice Laffey's mordant critique of the feminine imagery of Hosea 1–3 (along with that of Jeremiah 16 and Ezekiel 24): "This symbolism has been one of the most damaging to women in the entire Old Testament. More perhaps than any other, it has served to legitimate sexual discrimination. Its implications continue to permeate much Christian theology."[6]

It would be naive to expect the treatment of Gomer in sixteenth-century exegesis to reflect the specific concerns of recent feminist criticism. Yet it would be surprising if such a provocative story about the marriage of a prophet to a prostitute — and a marriage divinely arranged, at that — failed to stimulate comments bearing on issues of gender. This essay will outline some of the uses of feminine and sexual language in the Hosea commentary of the "Protestant Thomist," Jerome Zanchi (1516-90),[7] an Italian-born Reformer who taught theology at Strasbourg, Heidelberg, and Neustadt an der Haardt.[8] That discussion will provide a basis for assessing Zanchi's way of treating the elements of subordination, dependency, and threatened violence that feminist critics have found objectionable in the Gomer episode. Insofar as Gomer provides one feminine model of the human relationship to God, the issues that are addressed in Zanchi's comments on Hosea 1–3 may illuminate the connections between biblical sexual imagery and a Reformed theological vision.[9]

6. Laffey, *Introduction to the Old Testament*, p. 169.

7. Zanchi's work at Strasbourg spanned the decade between April 1553 and November 1563. It was while at Strasbourg that Zanchi lectured on the Old Testament. His lectures on Hosea, which began in 1558, formed the basis for a commentary on Hosea, published posthumously (Neustadt, 1600), later to comprise the fifth volume in the *Operum theolicorum D. Hieronymi Zanchii, I-VII* (Geneva: Stephanus Gamonetus [vols. 1-4, 7-8] and Matthaeus Berjon [vols. 5-6], 1605); hereafter cited as *Opera*.

8. Unfortunately, no comprehensive account of Zanchi's place in the Reformed tradition has yet been written. For a summary of Zanchi's life and work (with bibliography), see John L. Farthing, "Girolamo Zanchi," in Donald K. McKim (ed.), *Encyclopedia of the Reformed Faith* (Louisville: Westminster/John Knox, 1992), p. 412. For a fuller discussion of Zanchi's career, see C. J. Burchill, "Girolamo Zanchi: Portrait of a Reformed Theologian and His Work," *SCJ* 15/2 (1984): 185-207; and Joseph N. Tylenda, "Girolamo Zanchi and John Calvin: A Study in Discipleship as Seen Through Their Correspondence," *CTJ* 10 (1975): 101-41.

9. In the writing and revision of this essay, Rachel Wagner, Dennis Fox, and R. Scott Clark made bibliographical suggestions that proved invaluable; Jane Harris, my colleague at Hendrix College, pointed me toward several important works of feminist biblical criticism; and I owe a debt of gratitude, finally, to Sara Cole, who helped me gain access to important materials from the Duke Divinity School Library.

II. Between *Historia* and *Allegoria:* An Exegetical History of Gomer

One feature of Zanchi's commentary that makes his work a remarkably fertile field for the historian of exegesis is his detailed survey of four schools of thought regarding the character of the Gomer texts. Given the scandalous implications of God's command in Hos. 1:2, it is not surprising that the exegetical tradition betrays considerable anxiety about the implications of a literal or historical interpretation of this text. Early in his discussion of the Gomer materials, Zanchi notes that while it is beyond controversy *(dubium non est)* that Hosea received (either in a dream or in a waking vision[10]) a divine mandate to marry Gomer, there is considerable disagreement among commentators about the proper way of understanding how Hosea was to fulfill that command. Assuming that the command (1:2) was given in a dream or in a vision, did Hosea's act of obedience (1:3) take place merely in the prophet's imagination *(in visione tantum)* or was it fulfilled in actual historical reality *(reapse impleta)* as well?[11]

Regarding the degree to which the prophet's union with the harlot should be regarded as a historical fact, Zanchi sketches four alternatives.[12] The first way of understanding Hosea's marriage to Gomer might be called the literal/historical view. Zanchi attributes this interpretation to Irenaeus[13] and Augustine,[14] who argued that the account of Homer's union with Gomer is a narrative of actual events in space and time *(hanc fuisse veram et certam historiam).* An examination of the original texts cited by Zanchi makes it clear that he has read Irenaeus and Augustine carefully. He faithfully cites the evidence and examples that they deploy in support of a literal rendering of the text. Irenaeus sees a parallel to Hosea's marriage with Gomer in the union between Moses and the Ethiopian woman (Num. 12:1), who was thereby incorporated into Israel. In a similar way, Gomer was incorporated into the people of God through her union with the prophet, in keeping with Paul's dictum that a faithless wife is sanctified by her husband's faithfulness (1 Cor. 7:14). Augustine argues that the historical fact of Hosea's marriage to Gomer was a type of Christ's union with a

---

10. Zanchi, *In Hoseam* 1:2 (*Opera* 5:6): ". . . vel in somnis loquens ei sine spectro, vel in visione, id est in spectro aliquo ei apparens. Hi enim sunt duo modi ordinarii in quo Deus solet Prophetis sua mysteria revelare et eos spiritu prophetico afflare."

11. Zanchi, *In Hoseam* 1:3 (*Opera* 5:7).

12. Zanchi, *In Hoseam* 1:3 (*Opera* 5:7-9).

13. Cf. Irenaeus, *Against Heresies* 4.20.12 in ANF 1:492.

14. Cf. Augustine, *Against Faustus* 22.80, 89 in NPNF 4:304, 308-9.

church made up of people who had been idolatrous Gentiles; the prophet's action was not scandalous, however, since by the time of his union with Gomer she had ceased to be promiscuous *(fornicaria)*. Zanchi notes that Jerome's position, on the other hand, is not entirely clear: in his *Preface on Hosea to Pammachius,* he seems to regard the Gomer episode as taking place only within Hosea's imagination,[15] but his comments on the phrase "children of harlotry" *(Ac filios fornicationum)* in Hos. 1:2, suggests that the Gomer episode should be taken literally (although he does not condemn the opposite opinion).[16] Zanchi's readings of Irenaeus, Augustine, and Jerome reveal a thoroughness and a sensitivity to nuance that suggest anything but a careless or superficial approach. Clearly he is both competent and careful in handling the patristic sources.[17] Perhaps it is the weight of these patristic authorities that prompts Zanchi to give a careful presentation of arguments favoring the literal/historical view. Zanchi notes that one of the most compelling of these is related to the requirements of prophetic rhetoric: a merely imaginative fulfillment *(in visione tantum)* would be deficient in symbolic and expressive power.[18] Advocates of the literal view argue that if the point of the union between Hosea and Gomer was to make a statement to the people of Israel about their condition before God, any obedience that took place only within the prophet's subjectivity would not have been well adapted to that end. The proper names assigned to the harlot and her children suggest that we are dealing with historical personalities: the names of the children (Lo-ruhamma, Lo-ammi, and Jezreel) could not have been mere fictions if they were to function as visible signs conveying the prophetic message.[19]

---

15. Zanchi, *In Hoseam* 1:3 (*Opera* 5:8): "Hieronymus in praefatione in Hoseam ad Pammachium videtur negare hoc fuisse vere factum et veram historia, sed simplicem fuisse visionem." Cf. Jerome, *Commentariorum in Osee Prophetam Libri III: Ad Pammachium Prologus,* in CCSL 76:1-5; NPNF[2] 6:501.

16. Zanchi, *In Hoseam* 1:3 (*Opera* 5:8): "At vero in commentario exponens verba illa, Ac filios fornicationum, non omnino damnat priorem sententiam, sed ita tamen admittere videtur historiam, ut factum Prophetae typum esse velit matrimonii inter Christum et Ecclesiam." Cf. Jerome, *In Osee* 1.2, in CCSL 76:8-9. For Jerome's reading of Hos. 1:3-4 as a prophetic reference to Christ and the church, see CCSL 76:10.

17. An example of Zanchi's sensitive reading of the fathers is seen in his assessment of the ambiguity of Jerome's position: "Meo iudicio Hieronymus sensit hanc fuisse simplicem visionem, sicut in praefatione apparet, sed tamen posse defendi fuisse historiam. Sic enim in commentariis quasi per concessionem ait: Nec culpandus, inquit, Propheta ut interim sequamur historiam." Zanchi, *In Hoseam* 1:3 (*Opera* 5:8).

18. Zanchi, *In Hoseam* 1:3 (*Opera* 5:7).

19. Zanchi, *In Hoseam* 1:3 (*Opera* 5:7).

The literal view, of course, is subject to a number of substantial criticisms, as Zanchi is quick to note. Although he summarizes both the objections and possible responses to them, it soon becomes clear that he is persuaded by the arguments against the literal view. The Levitical prohibition against a priest being married to a harlot (Lev. 21:7) would certainly apply to a prophet as well. Hence a literal reading suggests that God commanded Hosea to transgress divine law. That would put God in the position of commanding what is shameful and wicked: a literal fulfillment of the command to marry a prostitute[20] would make Hosea "one body" with her, "which the Holy Spirit condemns through the Apostle" Paul (1 Cor. 6:16).[21] The literal/historical interpretation, therefore, would make God the author of sin.

To this objection, Zanchi notes the standard nominalist response (although he does not explicitly advocate this voluntarist theory):

> God is above the law, for his will is itself the rule of all equity and justice. Something is honorable, fair, good, and just, therefore, because God wills and commands it; he does not command it because it is just and honorable. Hence, just as he did not command iniquity when he ordered Abraham to kill his son . . . , so he did not command something unrighteous or shameful when he ordered the Prophet to "Go, take a wife of harlotry."[22]

The analogies between Hosea/Christ, on the one hand, and Gomer/church,[23] on the other, effectively refute the objection that sexual contact with a harlot would have had a polluting effect on the prophet. Christ is not made impure by contact with sinners (with whom he enters into a spiritual marriage); on the contrary, the church is made holy by her spiritual intercourse with Christ.[24] Accordingly, Jerome and Irenaeus cite 1 Cor. 7:14 to show that Hosea was not contaminated by his union with Gomer; on the contrary, she was purified by her union with him.[25] Finally,

---

20. The Hebrew of Hos. 1:2 suggests a promiscuous woman but not necessarily one who exchanges her favors for money; see Setel, "Prophets and Pornography," p. 91. Zanchi, however, understands the "wife of harlotry" as a reference to prostitution: his polemical use of phrases such as "meretrix Romana" or "cultum meretricium" (or his reference to Rome as "mater et lena nostra") depends on his identification of Gomer as a prostitute.

21. Zanchi, *In Hoseam* 1:3 (*Opera* 5:7).

22. Zanchi, *In Hoseam* 1:3 (*Opera* 5:7).

23. In Zanchi's exegesis, Gomer represents Israel, or more precisely the "Ecclesia Israelitica."

24. Cf. John L. Farthing, "*De coniugio spirituali:* Jerome Zanchi on Ephesians 5.22-33," *SCJ* 24/3 (Fall 1993): 621-52.

25. Zanchi, *In Hoseam* 1:3 (*Opera* 5:7).

critics of the literal/historical view protest against its implication that God commanded children to be conceived and born under dishonorable circumstances.[26] The defenders of the historicity of the Hosea/Gomer affair can deal with that objection, Zanchi claims, by rendering the imperative *(suscipe)* not as "beget" but rather as "adopt": then the objection evaporates, since this reading implies that the prophet was commanded not to beget children shamefully but simply to adopt the children of fornication whom Gomer brought with her to her marriage with Hosea.[27]

The second option, which might be called the visionary/imaginative view, Zanchi identifies as that of most rabbinic commentators and many (unnamed) Christian exegetes.[28] In this interpretation, the entire affair — God's command as well as Hosea's acts of obedience — took place not in space and time but strictly within the prophetic imagination. The reasoning that leads to a purely visionary view of Hosea 1–3 begins by noting the absurdities that a literal exegesis inevitably entails. Primary among these is that a literal fulfillment would have brought the prophet into contempt in the eyes of the Israelites. In that case, God's own command would have subverted the possibility that Hosea's message would be received with faith and obedience. A literal union with Gomer would have undermined the dignity of the prophetic office and thus destroyed the prophet's effectiveness.[29] By destroying his own prophet's credibility, God would be at cross-purposes with himself. But that is absurd.[30]

---

26. Zanchi, *In Hoseam* 1:3 (*Opera* 5:7): "Accedit etiam illud malum quod gignit filios fornicationum seu ex fornicatione. Sic enim ait textus, Et filios fornicationum scilicet suscipe."

27. Zanchi, *In Hoseam* 1:3 (Opera 5:7): "Non est iussus Propheta gignere filios ex fornicatione, sed illos qui iam nati erant ex fornicatione sibi in filios una cum matre accipere et eos in timore instituere. Hoc autem nec impium nec turpe est."

28. Zanchi, *In Hoseam* 1:3 (*Opera* 5:8): "Altera sententia est omnium fere Hebraeorum, quam etiam plerique ex nostris doctissimi viri amplectuntur. Ea est totum hoc contingisse Prophetae in visione et ita verba sunt intelligenda, ET ABIIT, scilicet in visione eadem in qua etiam Dominum alloquentem se audiverat; et accepit, id est, Visus est sibi abiisse et duxisse in uxorem scortum quoddam, cui etiam videbatur nomen esse Gomer et filia esse videbatur cuiusdam, qui appelaretur Diblaiim; visus est sibi congredi cum ea Gomer, et ex ea liberos tres suscepisse, ut sequitur."

29. Zanchi, *In Hoseam* 1:3 (Opera 5:8): "nempe Prophetam hoc facto suum ministerium poluisse et in contemtum apud Israelitas adduxisse, et huiusmodi contemtus autorem fuisse Deum, qui tam absurdam mandarit Prophetae."

30. Cf. Calvin, *Comm. Hos.* 1:2 (CO 42:203): "Certe non esset talis licentia in doctore tolerabilis. Videmus quid Paulus in episcopo requirat: nec dubium est quin hoc etiam olim locum habuerit in prophetis, ut scilicet domus illorum castae essent et purae ab omni macula et sinistra nota. Poterat igitur hoc exponere prophetam omnium ludibrio, si lupanar ingressus scortum sibi sumpsisset. . . ."

According to this second school of thought, Paul's dictum (1 Tim. 3:2) that a bishop must be blameless *(Oportet autem Episcopum . . . esse irreprehensibilem)*, combined with the canon law condemning unions of priests or teachers of the church with prostitutes, makes it clear that a literal or historical reading of Hos. 1:3 *(Et abiit, et accepit Gomer filiam Diblaiim)* is out of the question. Advocates of the visionary view of the text are not swayed by the fact that specific names are assigned to the harlot and her three children, since in prophetic literature fictional names are often used to convey spiritual meanings.[31] In contrast to Irenaeus and Augustine, proponents of the imaginative view of the text insist that the symbolic power of the Hosea/Gomer story is not diminished by its nonhistorical character.

> Even if it was not an actual fact *(res gesta)*, still it was a sign to the Israelites, for by the command of the Lord the Prophet related this vision to the Israelites, so that in the reciting of this vision, they should see what he expressed in words as clearly as if he had also written them on a tablet, namely, that Israel had committed fornication against her Lord.[32]

Zanchi cites Isaiah 20 and Ezekiel 4 as examples of vivid typology *(hypotyposis)*, in which events are recounted that seem at first glance *(primo aspectu)* to be historical happenings but turn out to be entirely visionary or imaginative in character.[33] Thus no compelling reason requires a literal reading of Hos. 1:3: "this is purely visionary, not historical. Therefore, just as the Lord's command to the Prophet took place in a dream or in a vision, so also the Prophet's obedience to that command was fulfilled within the vision."[34]

31. Zanchi, *In Hoseam* 1:3 (*Opera* 5:8): "Nomina enim sunt fictitia, ad significandum id quod postea disertis verbis explicat Propheta. Neque hic novum est in Scripturis, praesertim in Prophetis, ut in Ezech. de Haola et Haohba et in Apoc. de multis."

32. Zanchi, *In Hoseam* 1:3 (*Opera* 5:8): "Etiamsi non fuit res gesta, fuit tamen signum Israelitis, quia visionem hanc ex mandato Domini Propheta recitavit Israelitis, ut in ea visione recitata, tanquam in tabella quadam, viderent id quod etiam disertis verbis expressit: Israelem fornicatum esse a Domino."

33. Zanchi, *In Hoseam* 1:3 (*Opera* 5:8): "Sicut ergo illa nemo ait fuisse reipsa impleta, quia vel impossibilia sunt vel turpia, ita hoc quod refert Hoseas de se, quia per se turpe est, non debemus dicere fuisse historiam sed visionem."

34. Zanchi, *In Hoseam* 1:3 (*Opera* 5:8): "His et aliis rationibus adducuntur permulti viri doctissimi, ut sententiam Hebraeorum sequantur hanc fuisse meram visionem, non historiam. Itaque, sicut mandatum Domini fuit factum prophetae in somno vel in visione, sic etiam obedientiam Prophetae fuisse in visione completam."

Although Zanchi does not identify his source for the third position, it looks very much like the solution embraced by both Luther and Calvin.[35] According to this interpretation, which may be designated the nominal/rhetorical view, Hosea did not actually marry a harlot, nor did he beget (or adopt) children of fornication. Instead, to dramatize God's indictment of Israel's infidelity, God commands the prophet to call his wife a harlot and his children illegitimate. Thus the episode is a rhetorical device whose only historical element is the naming of Gomer and her children in a way that would convey God's message to Israel. In reality Gomer is an honest wife and the children are entirely legitimate, but the prophet designates them otherwise for rhetorical effect.[36] The assigning of names is the only historical element in the story: Hosea really did call his chaste wife a harlot, and he really did call his legitimate children illegitimate and name them Lo-ruhamma, Lo-ammi, and Jezreel, in order to make his message dramatic and compelling. Luther links this interpretation to a theology of the cross, pondering the abuse and persecution that such names must have aroused for Hosea and his godly family.[37] Zanchi, however, considers such exegesis insufficiently rooted in the clear words of the text: "For according to this interpretation we shall be forced to interpret the words 'Take a wife of harlotry' as 'call your wife a harlot and your children the offspring of harlotry. . . .'"[38] Such an interpretation strikes Zanchi as

---

35. Luther *Comm. Hosea* 1:3, WA 13:3: "Non ergo intellige quod fornicatio adhaeserit uxori, id est: non accipe active set intellige uxorem sic passam se nominari et pueros et virum propter populum et adversus populum, *ich heiss eine hure und mein man ein hurenbube dovon dass ir huren und buben seitt*." Cf. Calvin, *Comm. Hosea* 1:3, CO 42:204-5: "Videmus ergo nunc quomodo intelligi debeant simpliciter prophetae verba. Induit enim personam antequam in medium prodeat, et sub hoc habitu populum alloquitur, quod Deus iusserit eum ducere scortum in uxorem, et gignere ex ea liberos adulterinos. Non fuit hac de causa contemptibile eius ministerium: sciebant enim omnes eum probe et frugaliter semper vixisse: sciebant omnes domum eius exemptam esse omni opprobrio: sed in sua persona hic proposuit quasi vivam imaginem publicae turpitudinis."

36. Zanchi, *In Hoseam* 1:3 (*Opera* 5:8): "Cum vellet [Dominus], inquam, ut Propheta hoc indicaret populo, non solum verbis sed etiam symbolo aliquo, vellet autem ut hoc symbolum ostenderet in seipso, idcirco Dominum iusisse Prophetae ut et suam honestam alioqui mulierem hoc infami nomine, scorti scilicet, et eius liberos, honestos alioqui et legitimos, hoc infami nomine spuriorum vocaret, et se hoc facere iussu Domini testaretur in hunc fidem, ut Israelitae ipsi intellegerent se reapse tales esse coram Deo quales divinitus audiebant appelari honestam Prophetae uxorem et legitimos eius filios. . . ."

37. Luther, *Comm. Hosea* 1:3, WA 13:3: "En quantam crucem propter dei verbum sunt passi istis probosis nominibus."

38. Zanchi, *In Hoseam* 1:3 (*Opera* 5:8-9): "Haec expositio mihi non displiceret nisi verbis ipsis Prophetae vim quandam inferri viderem. Iuxta enim hanc interpretationem cogemur sic verba interpretari: Accipe uxorem fornicationum, id est, voca uxorem tuam fornicariam et filios tuos filios ex scortatione natos. . . ."

arbitrary to the point of misusing Scripture: he insists on taking the language of the text more seriously, more soberly, than that.

A final exegetical option is the allegorical/metaphorical view, which Zanchi describes in terms that tip his hand: "The fourth interpretation," he says, "seems to me the simplest."[39] This position — half-sister to the visionary/imaginative view — Zanchi attributes to "Jonathas Chaldaeus," or *Targum Jonathan*,[40] which reads the Gomer episode as pure allegory and identifies Gomer as an allegorical representation of the Israelite church.[41] Departing from his usual procedure, Zanchi does not go into great detail in outlining the strengths and weaknesses of this fourth view. Perhaps that is because those matters will be addressed in the articulation of his own position (a variant of the visionary/imaginative view), which in turn has much in common with the fourth interpretation.[42]

When Zanchi begins drawing the contours of his own opinion, he goes out of his way to indicate a reverence for the patristic authors and, accordingly, a certain caution or reluctance in rejecting the literal/historical interpretation: "As for me, I dare not, I cannot, condemn the first opinion, which is that of the Fathers and especially of Irenaeus and Augustine."[43] Yet he admits a preference for the visionary hypothesis.[44] In Zanchi's opinion, therefore, Hosea's message to Israel is this:

> Hear, O Israel, what the Lord commanded me to tell you. The Lord appeared to me in a vision and commanded me to take to myself a harlot, have sexual intercourse with her, and beget children of fornication, so that I might be for you a kind of mirror in which you may contemplate the public shamefulness and fornication of this land. And so it seemed in the vision that I took a certain notorious harlot by the name of Gomer, daughter of Diblaim . . . and that I performed with

39. Zanchi, *In Hoseam* 1:3 (*Opera* 5:9).

40. "Jonathas Chaldaeus" is a reference to the *Targum Jonathan*, an Aramaic paraphrase of the prophets (ascribed to Jonathan ben Uzziel). See Bleddyn J. Roberts, "The Old Testament: Manuscripts, Text, and Versions," in *CHB* 2:24. The text of the *Targum Jonathan* is published in A. Sperber, *The Bible in Aramaic*, vol. 3 (Leiden: Brill, 1962).

41. Zanchi, *In Hoseam* 1:3 (*Opera* 5:9): "Is sensit hanc fuisse meram allegoriam, ut nomine fornicariae simpliciter intelligatur Ecclesia Israel. Iubetur Propheta eam assumere, id est, ire ad hanc Ecclesiam tanquam ad suam uxorem sed fornicariam, et illi praedicare."

42. Especially crucial for both the *Targum Jonathan* and Zanchi is the view of Gomer as a literary personification of the elect among the Israelites (or in Zanchi's phrase, the Ecclesia Israelitica).

43. Zanchi, *In Hoseam* 1:3 (*Opera* 5:9).

44. Zanchi, *In Hoseam* 1:3 (*Opera* 5:9): "Altera tamen, quae dicit haec omnia fuisse in visione facta, magis amplector. . . ."

her the most shameful deed, so that I fathered children of harlotry. You
know, of course, that I did not actually do this, but this is how it
appeared to me in the vision. Through what happened to me in the
vision, the Lord wanted to show you, as if sketched on a tablet, the
public disgrace and spiritual fornication in which you and your parents
have been involved. . . .[45]

Having cast his lot with the school of interpretation outlined in
Targum Jonathan, Zanchi consistently interprets the Gomer affair in a
spiritual rather than a literal or historical way. In so doing, he is making
common cause not only with the rabbinic tradition but also with the views
of both Luther and Calvin. Like them, he rejects Jerome's literal/historical
interpretation out of concerns having to do with the dignity of the prophetic office. Zanchi safeguards God's prophet from scandal by insisting
that Hosea's obedience to the divine mandate was precisely as visionary
as the mandate itself: Hosea was joined to a harlot only in his own vision
(in visione tantum), not in actual fact *(reapse).*[46] The names of Diblaim
and Gomer, he insists, do not point to historical personalities but are
instead figures of speech that make a prophetic point, since in the Palestin-
ian context the Hebrew names "Diblaim" and "Gomer" suggest the corruption of rotten figs.[47] They are thus rhetorical artifacts, not the names

45. Zanchi, *In Hoseam* 1:3 (*Opera* 5:9): "Audite, Israel, quid iusserit Dominus me ad
vos referre. In visione apparuit mihi Dominus et iussit ut scortum mihi assumerem, cum illo
scortarer, et filios haberem ex scortatione natos, in hoc finem, ut Ego vobis essem ceu
speculum in quo contemplaremini publicam huius terrae turpitudinem et fornicationem. Et
ita mihi visus sum in ea visione accepisse insigne quoddam scortum nomine Gomer, filiam
Diblaiim . . . et turpissimam rem cum eo egisse et filios ex scortatione natos suscepisse. Vos
scitis hanc turpitudinem re ipsa me non comississe, sed ita visus sum in visione, quia Dominus
voluit per hanc visionem in mea persona, tanquam in depicta tabella, vobis indicare vestram
maiorumque vestrorum publicam turpitudinem et spiritualem fornicationem. . . ." Zanchi's
preference for this way of reading the text is grounded in the reasoning outlined in his
discussion of arguments for and against the first two opinions ("propter rationes superius
allatas").

46. Zanchi, *In Hoseam* 1:3 (*Opera* 5:9): "Hoseam in visione, etiam hoindicat, Hoseam
in visione tantum accessisse ad illud insigne scortum et in visione suscepisse ex ea filium.
Nam statim in eadem visione Dominus mandat ei quo nomine debeat appellare filium qui
in visione conceptus et natus esse videtur." On Et abiit Zanchi comments: "scilicet in visione,
hoc est, sibi visus est accepisse." "Et concepit illa Gomer imaginaria et peperit ei filium, id
est, visa est concepisse et peperisse ei Hoseae." A gloss on Gomer filiam Diblaiim reflects the
same angle of approach: "id est, mulierem et scortum insigne, cui videbatur esse nomen
Gomer, et videbatur esse filia parentis qui appellaretur Diblaiim."

47. Cf. Calvin on Hos. 1.3, lect. 2, CO 42:206.

of an actual man and his daughter.[48] What we are dealing with in Hosea 1–3, Zanchi claims, is not historical narrative but prophetic metaphor.[49]

III. From Egypt to Eternity: *Heilsgeschichte* with a Feminine Face

Zanchi's refusal to read Hosea 1–3 literally means that Gomer was not a "victim of violence," although it may still be argued that to some extent she was — both in Hosea's prophecy and in Zanchi's commentary — a "victim of metaphor." Zanchi insists that Gomer was not an actual historical figure physically threatened and abused by her husband in obedience to a divine mandate. The troubling language of Hosea 2, in which Gomer is threatened with physical violence and public sexual humiliation, becomes for Zanchi an allegorical expression of God's "severe mercy" toward the elect.[50] When Hosea threatens Gomer with a public stripping that will leave her genitals exposed to public view, Zanchi understands the theme of nakedness in terms of the spiritual condition that results when idolatry and superstition remove the garment of righteousness from the soul or from the public life of a community. He insists that "naked" (*nudam,* Hos. 2:3) must be understood spiritually (*quoad spiritum*). In its spiritual sense, the word describes not an abused woman but a disoriented community whose "mother" (that is, its spiritual and civil leadership)[51] has already left the people exposed and vulnerable through a policy of promoting idolatry.

48. Zanchi, *In Hoseam* 1:3 (*Opera* 5:9): "Haec duo nomina sunt fictitia, ut ante dixi. Significant ambo simul massam ficuum seu carycarum corruptam. Nam Gomer est corruptio, et Diblaiim carycae in unum corpus compressae. Usus vero est hac metaphora quia frequentes sunt carycae in illa regione Palestinae, ac si non corrumpantur suavissimae sunt, si corrumptantur pessimae."

49. Zanchi proceeds to treat the three children's names metaphorically; in contrast to Luther, he claims that the naming of the children, no less than the union of Hosea and Gomer, took place *in visione tantum.*

50. This is a theme that pervades Zanchi's discussion of Gomer. Commenting on Hosea 3:1, e.g., Zanchi speaks of "poenae cum clementia tamen coniunctae"; ". . . quoniam adultera et voluptuosa facta est, velit [Dominus] eam castigare; quoniam vero a se est amata, nolit eam perdere sed ita duriter, quia adulteram, eam tractare ut tamen clementer, quia dilecta, velit cum ea agere." Zanchi, *In Hoseam* 3:1 (*Opera* 5:59).

51. Zanchi, *In Hoseam* 2:3 (*Opera* 5:30): "In Scripturis enim illi qui alios, in religione praesertim, instutuunt patres et matres appellantur. . . ." "Hic revera inprimis perstringit utrumque magistratum, cum ait matrem esse scortum duplicis scortationis. Quarum una erat in religione, ipsa idolatria, altera in politia, confederatio cum idolatris, cum regibus Syriae. . . ."

Indeed, the threat of nakedness is part of what is implied in Yahweh's prediction that Gomer/Israel will be reduced to the conditions that marked the day of her nativity (Hos. 2:5: *Et ponam eam secundum diem nativitatis suae*); Zanchi finds here a reference to the birth not of a human female but of Israel herself.[52]

Once it is understood that Zanchi treats the text metaphorically, it becomes evident that he is not using the text — intentionally, at least — in support of misogyny. Zanchi's use of the metaphor provided by the Gomer materials may have the effect of reinforcing sexual stereotypes, but that is clearly not his intent. Indeed, the "woman" to whom these threats are addressed (Hos. 2:3, 6-7) is none other than the whole body of the elect.[53] Zanchi explains that the elect, not through malice but out of ignorance or immaturity or a certain prudence of the flesh, often fall back into spiritual fornication. These are the ones for whom God reserves the "severe mercy" to which Zanchi points in his comments on the thorns *(spinis)* and threats of confinement in Hos. 2:6. But to the reprobate, who embrace idolatry out of deliberate malice, God offers no obstacles: what is desperate about the condition of the reprobate is that God permits them to dash unimpeded toward damnation *(sinit illis liberas habenas)*. Only the elect receive the grace of thorns; only to the elect does God send the calamities and hindrances that the Spirit uses to lure them away from their own self-destructiveness.[54]

Zanchi incorporates the stern language of Hos. 2:3, 6, whose literal interpretation might seem to sanction spouse abuse, into what I have described elsewhere as "a theodicy for the Reformed diaspora."[55] He points to Saul's experience on the road to Damascus (Acts 9:1-19) as an example of God's use of adversity to bring the elect to salvation. This reference to

---

52. Zanchi, *In Hoseam* 2:3 (*Opera* 5:32): "Sensus est, 'Ne redigam eam in eas miserias extremas, in quibus erat cum nata est. Nam quis est dies nativitatis populi huius? Est dies seu tempus quo, ex Aegypto liberatus, natus est in novum populum, hoc est, in populum Dei sub lege."

53. Zanchi, *In Hoseam* 2:6 (*Opera* 5:34): ". . . notandum est hunc et reliquos qui sequuntur versus non posse intelligi nisi de electis."

54. Zanchi, *In Hoseam* 2:6 (*Opera* 5:34): "Quare? quia decrevit eos omnino salvare, ideo vias illis ad peccandum et ad idola colenda praecludit." The role of the Spirit is crucial. Zanchi insists that sufferings and hardships per se, apart from the influence of the Spirit, will never bring about real repentance. Zanchi, *In Hoseam* 2:9 (*Opera* 5:35): ". . . cum electi instrumento crucis ad veram resipiscentiam revocantur, hoc illis contingere ex singulari Spiritu sancti instinctu, non ex vi crucis."

55. John L. Farthing, "Christ and the Eschaton: The Reformed Eschatology of Jerome Zanchi," in W. Fred Graham (ed.), *Later Calvinism: An International Perspective* (Kirksville, Mo.: Sixteenth Century Journal Publishers, 1994), pp. 336-40.

the Damascus Road experience is fairly conventional. What is surprising — given Zanchi's commitment to a Reformed perspective and the thoroughness with which he criticizes Lutheran doctrine in other contexts[56] — is his use of Luther's conversion as an illustration of the way in which thorns are God's gift to the elect.[57] But it is entirely in keeping with his desire to cultivate piety in the hearts of his readers[58] that Zanchi then shifts toward examples closer to home:

> Or look at ourselves, for example. How many of us, pursuing our own self-interest, have decided to stay within the Papacy. And we said in our hearts, "I will go after my lovers" [Hos. 1:5]. . . . For it seemed to us that the way of superstition offered an abundance of wool and linen, bread and wine. But what did the Lord do? Because we had been chosen, and the Lord had decreed something different for us, God opposed us and closed off our paths. He aroused the persecution of the Roman pontiff against us; we were forced to abandon our "lovers."[59]

Far from constituting abuse that arouses terror, the cross of suffering is a sign of God's love that arouses in the elect a sense of assurance in times of tribulation: it is, in fact, "a special privilege that God extends to the elect"[60] as an instrument of their salvation.

Since Gomer signifies the elect of both the Old and New Covenants, Zanchi feels free to rewrite the history of salvation, from Egypt to the eschaton, in feminine terms:

> For the Israelite synagogue, like a little girl *(puella)*, was conceived in Israel, carried, as it were, in the womb in Egypt, born in the departure

---

56. See, e.g., the *locus tertius* attached to his commentary on Ephesians 5 (*Opera* 6:234-50). Cf. Farthing, "Zanchi on Ephesians 5," esp. pp. 627-34.

57. Zanchi, *In Hoseam* 2:6 (*Opera* 5:35). "Exemplum in Luthero. Initio postquam etiam cognovit Christum in Euangelio, tamen cogitabat redire ad Papatum et componere res suas. Quid Dominus? Diversis spinis et impedimentis interclusit viam eius, ne inveniret semitiam suam. . . ."

58. Cf. Farthing, "Zanchi on Ephesians 5," p. 650; "Christ and the Eschaton," pp. 346-50; and "*Foedus evangelicum:* Jerome Zanchi on the Covenant," *CTJ* 29 (1994): 160-61.

59. Zanchi, *In Hoseam* 2:5, 9 (*Opera* 5:35): "Exemplum in nobis. Quot nostrum sunt qui, rebus suis compositis, decreverint manere in Papatu? Et diximus in cordibus nostris, 'Ibo post amatores meos.' Quare amatores? Quia status ille superstitiosus videbatur nobis praebere copiose lanam, linum, vinum, panem. Quid Dominus? Quia electi eramus et aliud ipse decreverat de nobis, ideo se opposuit et spinis inclusit viam. Excitavit persecutionem Romani Pontificis contra nos, coacti fuimus deserere amatores nostros."

60. Zanchi, *In Hoseam* 2:6 (*Opera* 5:35).

from Egypt, reared in the wilderness, married on Mount Sinai when God entered into the covenant of law with her, brought as a wife into the house of her husband when she came into the land of Canaan, clothed and adorned, enriched when God expelled the heathen kings and gave her such kingdoms, power, riches, glory, and the priesthood. She committed adultery when she worshipped idols . . . ; the Lord divorced her, rejected her as his people, stripped her naked and reduced her to the condition of her earliest nativity when through the Assyrians he deprived her of her kingdom, power, glory, and liberty, and dispersed her among the Gentiles. But God took her again as his wife when many returned from Babylon with the Jews and when, after the coming of Christ, he received her into glory and restored the Kingdom and gives her eternal life and the other things that pertain to it.[61]

The story of Gomer offers Zanchi an opportunity to draw analogies between the history of God's people and the life cycle of a woman; he renders virtually the entire *Heilsgeschichte*, from Egypt to the eschaton, in feminine terms that embrace both the bad news of human faithlessness and the good news of God's saving purpose for the elect. In the infancy of Israel, God's people are described not simply as a child *(puer)* but as a girl *(puella)*. Hosea portrays Israel as a woman — faithless, indeed, but pursued and finally redeemed by the relentless love of Yahweh. Zanchi finds in this feminine imagery a clear depiction of spiritual Israel, the church of the elect.[62] Like Gomer, the elect find that not even their own faithlessness can finally frustrate God's sovereign will to redeem.[63]

It would be a vast overstatement to dismiss Zanchi's exposition of the Gomer story as an exercise in misogyny. In the rare instances in which he

---

61. Zanchi, *In Hoseam* 2:3 (*Opera* 5:32): "Nam Synagoga Israelitica tanquam puella, concepta in Israel, gestata tanquam in utero in Aegypto, nata in egressu ex Aegypto, educta in deserto, ducta in uxorem cum foedus legis cum illa iniit Deus in monte Sinai, introducta sponsa in domum sponsi cum introducta in terram Chanaan, vestita et ornata, ditata, cum expulsis regibus dedit ei tot regna, potentiam, divitias, gloriam, sacerdotium. Adulterata est cum adoravit idola, praesertim cum erexit duos vitulos, factum divortium cum eam, reiecit ne esset populus, spoilata nuda et ad conditionem primae nativitatis redacta, cum eam spoliavit per Assyrios regno, potentia, et gloria et libertate, atque inter gentes expulit, resumta in uxorem cum ex Babylone multi cum Iudaeis redierunt cumque post Christum eam recepit in gratiam, restituit regnum, cum dat vitam aeternam et alia quae ad aeternum vitam pertinent."

62. In contrast, Zanchi observes that *vir* in Hos. 2:12 denotes *idolum:* see *In Hoseam* 2:12 (*Opera* 5:38).

63. Zanchi, *In Hoseam* 3:1 (*Opera* 5:60): "Ait enim, Ama iuxta amorem Dei erga filios Israel, id est amore constanti, firmo, aeterno, qui neque peccatis impediri potest."

seems to speak of "girl" *(puella),* "woman" *(mulier),* or "wife" *(uxor)* disparagingly,[64] there is always strong textual evidence suggesting that something other than the feminine per se is the object of his criticism. It is not women as such but "unsophisticated and graceless women" who are portrayed in a negative light. "Wife" and "woman" are never used pejoratively in Zanchi's interpretation of Hosea 1–3. He employs feminine language, after all, to describe not the reprobate but the elect, who are pilgrims *(viatores)* on a journey toward eschatological perfection:

> When Hosea is commanded to love this woman, even though she is promiscuous, God indicates that he goes on loving this Israelite Church even though she is promiscuous. This certainly cannot be understood except as a reference to the Church of the elect. For it is these alone, whom he has loved from eternity, that he never ceases to pursue with his love.[65]

Zanchi makes it clear that the elect constitute the feminine party in the marriage with Christ *(nos filiae et sponsae Christi).*[66] Those who leave the spiritual fornication of Rome and return to Christ thereby fulfill the true role of his Bride.[67] Zanchi identifies the whole body of the pilgrim-elect as the Lord's "wife" *(uxorem).*[68] In all of Zanchi's comments on Gomer, there is not a single instance in which he brands all women as weak, evil, faithless, or fickle. Gomer, instead, represents the whole church of the elect,[69] inclu-

---

64. E.g., Zanchi, *In Hoseam* 2:3 (*Opera* 5:32): "Caeterum puella haec, ut solent fere rusticae et ingratae mulieres, ad gloriam et potentiam per maritum evecta, oblita qualis fuerit ab initio atque e quibus parentibus et in quantis sordibus nata, insolescere atque in tam magna fortuna superbire coepit, et contemto Dei mariti sui verbo, idola est prosecuta."

65. Zanchi, *In Hoseam* 3:1 (*Opera* 5:59-60): "Cum iubetur Hoseas amare hanc mulierem, etiamsi sit fornicaria, indicavit Deus quod hanc Ecclesiam Israeliticam, licet fornicaria sit, amare tamen pergat. Hoc certe non nisi de electorum Ecclesia intelligi potest. Hos enim solos, quos ab aeterno amavit, suo nunquam amore prosequi desinit." The threats of retaliation (Hos. 2:3, 6) are designed to bring the promiscuous wife to a soundness of mind in which the real source of her life and prosperity will be acknowledged with gratitude. "Not all, however, are recalled to a sound mind, but only the elect. Therefore she must be understood only in relation to the elect." ("Non revocati autem sunt omnes ad sanam mentem, sed tantum electi. Ergo de electis tantum intelligenda est.")

66. Zanchi, *In Hoseam* 2:7 (*Opera* 5:35): "Nam in baptismate fide fueramus desponsatae Christo." Note the combination here of a first person plural verb with a feminine plural attribute. Zanchi depicts the situation of the elect in feminine terms: cf. nn. 67 and 78 below.

67. Zanchi, *In Hoseam* 2:7 (*Opera* 5:35): "Facimus officium bonae uxoris."

68. Zanchi, *In Hoseam* 3:3 (*Opera* 5:63).

69. Cf. n. 53 above.

sive of both men and women, who, though faithless, are nonetheless pursued by a sovereign love that refuses to accept defeat.

IV. Exegesis and Polemics: *"Mater et Lena Nostra"*

The generous, nonpartisan tone of Zanchi's theological project is in considerable contrast to the polemical spirit of his age.[70] In his commentary on Hosea 1–3, Zanchi's ecumenical approach is apparent at several points. He goes out of his way, for instance, to show respect for opinions with which he disagrees.[71] He speaks of Luther in positive terms, and when he does reject Luther's position he scarcely calls attention to that fact.

In the Hosea commentary, however, his anti-Roman polemic is quite sharp, although he does acknowledge the genuine piety of some who are still within the Roman Church *(pii veri in Papatu)*.[72] For a critique of Tridentine Catholicism, the imagery of Hosea 1–3 offers a variety of rhetorical possibilities, which Zanchi is quick to exploit. For instance, when Hosea urges Gomer to put away "harlotry" from her face and "adultery" from between her breasts (Hos. 2:4), Zanchi hears a reference to the external adornment by which a prostitute shamelessly publicizes her professional interests and entices customers to join her immoral behavior. "That is what impudent idolaters do, such as are the Papists."[73] Zanchi can speak in this way because he sees a parallel between the attire and adornment by which a harlot advertises her services and the elaborate vestments and decorations featured in the liturgical pomp of "the Roman whore" *(meretrix Romana)*.[74] Thus the indictment of Gomer in Hos. 2.7 becomes a judgment against Rome's idolatrous devotion to the images or relics of saints (bowing before them with the head uncovered, lighting candles before them, kissing them,

---

70. Tylenda speaks of "Zanchi's ecumenical dream, his nonpartisan theology," his "spirit of peace and harmony," and "his hopes for a Catholic Evangelical Church"; see "Zanchi and Calvin," p. 122.

71. We have noted the caution with which Zanchi registers his dissent from Irenaeus and Augustine. Cf. *Opera* 5:30, where, noting an alternative to his interpretation of *mater* and *filii* in relation to Hos. 2:2, Zanchi shows his flexibility: "Si quis tamen volet nomine matris intelligi universam Ecclesiam simul, nomine vero filiorum singulos seorsum, non prohibeo."

72. Zanchi, *In Hoseam* 3, *argumentum* (*Opera* 5:60).

73. Zanchi, *In Hoseam* 2:2 (*Opera* 5:31).

74. Zanchi, *In Hoseam* 2:1 (*Opera* 5:39). The threats against Gomer Zanchi reads as a rejection of Catholicism's polluted worship ("hunc cultum meretricium").

etc.).[75] When Gomer declares that she will go after her "lovers" (Hos. 2:5), Zanchi comments, "that is, false gods" (although the only example he mentions is the cult of the Blessed Virgin).[76]

Zanchi's polemic against Catholicism reaches its most audacious level when, with considerable irony, he presses the sexual metaphor to the point of claiming that Rome has become not just a prostitute *(meretrix)* but a pimp *(lena)*. She is "our shameless mother and our pimp, the holy mother Church of Rome" *(nostra impudica mater et lena nostra, sancta mater Ecclesia Romana)*:[77]

> She it was who made us, the daughter and bride *(filiae et sponsae)* of Christ, commit fornication with idols. For in baptism we had been espoused *(desponsatae)* to Christ in faith. . . . But later, when we became adulterous, our shameless mother obtained for us many handsome youths so that we might take pleasure in committing fornication with them, so that along with her we might make our living in this shameful way. These handsome youths were idols beautifully adorned, lovely temples, various superstitions, and especially the idolatrous mass. . . . For what are these if not the lovely partners in fornication procured for us by our mother, the Roman Church?[78]

The "holy mother church" turns out to be a pimp who not only procures lovers for her children but also entices them with promises of rewards for their harlotry: forgiveness of sins, answers to prayers, health, and the like. Zanchi waxes ironic in his portrayal of a mother luring her daughters to take part in her own fornication:

> How does she do this? With promises of various benefits. For example: "If you will just worship that image or that idol in the mass, you will receive remission for all your sins. If you will visit seven churches or

75. Zanchi, *In Hoseam* 2:5 (*Opera* 5:33).
76. Zanchi, *In Hoseam* 2:5 (*Opera* 5:34): "Putant se amari superstitiosi a Diva Maria, si eam adorent et colant et eius imagines venerentur."
77. Zanchi, *In Hoseam* 2:5 (*Opera* 5:36).
78. Zanchi, *In Hoseam* 2:8 (*Opera* 5:35): "Illa enim erat et fuit autor ut cum idolis fornicaremur nos filiae et sponsae Christi. Nam in baptismate fide fueramus desponsatae Christo. Hic est primus maritus. Postea ubi facti fuimus adultiores, illa nostra mater impudica obtulit nobis multos formosos iuvenes, ut cum illis fornicando voluptatem inde caperemus, ut quaestum faceremus, tum illa tum nos, turpem. Hi formosi iuvenes fuerunt idola bene ornata, templa illa formosa, variae superstitiones atque inprimis idolum Missae, seu ipsa Missa tam bene ornata. Quid enim haec sunt nisi formosi fornicatores a lena matre nostra Romana Ecclesia nobis ad fornicandum oblati?"

altars during the times of indulgence, and bow before these idols and prostitute yourselves to them (like a prostitute to her customer), you will have infinite rewards, forgiveness of sins both for you and for your departed, and liberation from the pains of purgatory. What's more, if you will invoke St. Barbara, you will obtain healthy teeth; St. Lucia, healthy eyes," and countless other things of this sort.[79]

Enticed by these promises, we — Rome's daughters — followed our mother into harlotry.[80] So alluring, indeed, are the blandishments offered by our mother-prostitute-pimp that only God's severe mercy *(occlusit viam spinis)* could bring us to our senses.[81]

It is important to notice here that the tone of Zanchi's language, especially in his use of verbs and pronouns in the first person plural, is autobiographical, even confessional: we ourselves are the ones who have forsaken our true husband, but have been pursued by his love until we returned to him. Gomer and her daughters include not just "them" but "us." Zanchi sees himself in Gomer; her story illuminates the history of his own community. For Zanchi, therefore, making sense of Gomer's situation is an act of self-understanding. That is what makes his polemic, even at its most severe, something more than just a conventional anti-Roman diatribe.

V. Holy Harlotry and Reformed Exegesis

A careful reading of Zanchi's commentary on Hosea 1–3 prompts three main observations.

First of all, Zanchi brings to his exegetical work formidable linguistic and literary skills, a solid grasp of the Catholic tradition, and the fruits of his ongoing conversation with Protestant biblical interpreters, especially Calvin, Luther, and Musculus (all cited by name). His command of the

79. Zanchi, *In Hoseam* 2:8 (*Opera* 5:35): "Quomodo? Promissionibus variorum munusculorum. Verbi exemplum: Quod si adoremus illam imaginem vel illud idolum in Massa, remissionem habebis omnium poeccatorum. Si temporibus indulgentiarum visites 7 Ecclesias aut altaria, et ante idola illa procumbas et te illis prostituas, sicut meretrix suo amasio, habebis infinita munera, remissionem peccatorum pro te et pro mortuis tuis, item liberationem a poenis purgatorii. Item si invoces D. Barbaram, impetrabit tibi sanitatem dentium. Si B. Lucia, lumen et sanitatem oculorum, et infinita alia." In my judgment, "lover" is too intimate a translation for *amasio* in this context.

80. Zanchi, *In Hoseam* 2:8 (*Opera* 5:35): "Prostituimus et animas et corpora nostra idolis."

81. Zanchi, *In Hoseam* 2:8 (*Opera* 5:35): "Sed quid Dominus? Occlusit viam spinis, aperuit nobis oculos, agnovimus nos defecisse a vero marito, rediimus ad priorem maritum."

Hebrew is often evident. Not only does Zanchi read the Hebrew text but he also consults the rabbinic exegetical tradition (especially Ibn Ezra, David Kimhi, and *Targum Jonathan*). He cites not only the canonical Scriptures but also, occasionally, the Apocrypha. In deploying materials drawn from Jewish, Catholic, and Protestant sources, Zanchi exhibits a critical spirit that enables him to draw from the wide range of materials available to him without being overly dependent on any of them.

Clearly Zanchi is competent in literary as well as linguistic criticism; he is quick to exploit the figures of speech, such as synecdoche, that save exegesis from a wooden literalism. A sensitivity to multiple levels of linguistic meaning combines with a concern for moral exhortation and spiritual growth to dispose Zanchi toward a typological reading of the text. He believes that the literal-historical exegesis of the Gomer materials is not only embarrassing; it is also less fruitful for purposes of cultivating piety (or sharpening anti-Roman polemics). The entire story, in Zanchi's view, is a typological depiction of God's redemptive love for Israel.[82] At a deeper level, Zanchi's Christocentrism finds expression in his claim that Hosea, in his union with Gomer, is a type of Christ in his union with the elect.[83]

It is clear, secondly, that Zanchi finds in the feminine and sexual imagery of Hosea 1–3 abundant resources for his articulation of the Reformed agenda. Marital and sexual metaphors, which are crucial to his doctrines of church[84] and covenant,[85] mark the point at which Zanchi's theological imagination is most prolific. Zanchi sees that the metaphorical power of the Gomer narrative depends on a sense of the marital intimacy between Christ and the elect, to which idolatry — spiritual fornication — is the ultimate threat.[86] Here Zanchi's exegesis is at its best, whether in service to his polemic (defending Reformed believers against the entice-

---

82. Zanchi, *In Hoseam* 1:2 (*Opera* 5:6): ". . . quod iubetur facere Propheta typus est illius quod facit Dominus." Elsewhere I have noted the fruitfulness of Zanchi's typological exegesis. Cf. Farthing, "Zanchi on Ephesians 5," pp. 624-27.

83. Zanchi, *In Hoseam* 3:1 (*Opera* 5:60): "De cuius mariti amore loquebatur cum dixit, 'Ama mulierem a suo marito amatam'? De amore Dei in Christo. . . . Summa consilii Domini in hoc versu est ut Israel . . . certo tamen sciant se esse caros Deo et novo connubio tandem desponsatum iri Christo, cuius typus erat Hoseas." Zanchi sees the purpose of God's ordering Hosea to love a promiscuous woman in terms of a prophetic promise centered in Christ: "indicare voluit quod ipse Deus Israelitas electos, idololatras etiam effectos, velit constanter et perpetuo amore prosequi in Propheta ipso, id est, Christo."

84. Cf. Farthing, "Zanchi on Ephesians 5," esp. pp. 650-52.

85. Cf. Farthing, "Zanchi on the Covenant," esp. pp. 157-62.

86. Zanchi, *In Hoseam* 1:2 (*Opera* 5:6): ". . . et ratio huius metaphorae est quoniam sicut cum colimus verum Deum, vera pietate et cultu, cum Deo coniungimur, sicut sponso sponsa."

ments of Rome) or to his constructive spirituality (probing the union between Christ and the elect). Here one finds a warmth and vibrancy that belie the image of the Reformed Orthodox as tedious or pedantic or barren.

Finally, no discussion of Zanchi's interpretation of Hosea 1–3 can avoid confronting the morally troubling aspects of Gomer's story. We began by noting a variety of objections to Hosea's account of his union with Gomer. It is fitting, then, to conclude by asking how Zanchi's exegesis fares under feminist scrutiny.

Even from a perspective that takes into account the feminist critique, Zanchi's failings are almost entirely matters of omission; for example, he seems utterly insensitive to the oppressive potential of Hosea's metaphor (whereby the masculine is associated with God and the feminine with sin). But given the parameters of the hermeneutical situation in his own lifetime (*sola Scriptura*), that is not at all remarkable. Zanchi believes that the Bible is God's Word, that Hosea is God's prophet, and that it is safe to trust what we find written in Holy Scripture. As a man of the sixteenth century, Zanchi could hardly have engaged in a radical feminist criticism of Hosea's gender-stereotyped metaphor — a criticism that was not available in the West until quite recently.

What is truly noteworthy is that Zanchi does not turn the rhetoric of Hosea 1–3 into a pretext for woman-bashing. Since he is a citizen of the cultural world of sixteenth-century Europe, it is not surprising that he does (albeit rarely) speak of the relationships between men and women in terms of male initiative and female dependency, the husband's providing and the wife's receiving.[87] It would be remarkable to find a man of the sixteenth century who did not conceive of gender roles in that way. What is striking about Zanchi's exegesis, however, is the rarity with which he indulges in the arguably misogynistic rhetoric and stereotyping that are so pervasive in ancient, medieval, and early modern Christianity.

Far from objectifying or demonizing Gomer, Zanchi identifies with her: Gomer's story mirrors what has happened in Zanchi's own experience and in the history of the pilgrim church. In Gomer, Zanchi sees his own history. Hosea depicts Israel — faithless yet beloved, pursued, reconciled, redeemed — as a woman. Zanchi finds that image helpful in probing the dynamics of life in the church here and now, while at the same time intimating the assured outcome of her journey toward eschatological perfection. Accordingly, for Zanchi — perhaps even more than for Hosea — human history before God and with God is also in some sense the story of a feminine experience.

---

87. Zanchi pictures an aggrieved husband saying to his ungrateful wife (*In Hoseam* 2:3 [*Opera* 5:32]): ". . . faciam ut mimineris te non semper fuisse qualis iam es per me."

The Doctrine of Christ in
Nikolaus Selnecker's Interpretation
of Psalms 8, 22, and 110

ROBERT KOLB

MARTIN LUTHER IDENTIFIED Psalm 110 as "a prophecy of Christ, how he was to be an eternal king and priest, and in addition, true God, sitting at the right hand of God." He added, "there is nothing like it in all of Scripture."[1] Luther's christological or "prophetic-literal" hermeneutic for Old Testament interpretation is well known, as is his love for the Psalms.[2] Luther found in the Psalter a summary of the entire Bible, particularly because it "so clearly promised Christ's death and resurrection";[3] from its songs of prayer and praise he mined the riches of biblical teaching. It is thus no surprise that commenting and preaching upon the Psalms occupied many of his students and followers in the next generation.

Among them was Nikolaus Selnecker (1530-92), court preacher in Saxony and Braunschweig-Wolfenbüttel, professor in Leipzig and Jena, ecclesiastical superintendent in Leipzig and Hildesheim, and prolific author of both biblical commentaries and works of systematic and polemical theology. He represented electoral Saxony in the negotiations that led to the Formula

---

1. Luther, "Summarien über die Psalmen. . . , 1531-33," WA 38:54.29-32.

2. See, e.g., James S. Preus, *From Shadow to Promise: Old Testament Interpretation from Augustine to the Young Luther* (Cambridge: Harvard University Press, 1969); Heinrich Bornkamm, *Luther und das Alte Testament* (Tübingen: J. C. B. Mohr [Paul Siebeck], 1948), esp. pp. 86-102; and Marc Lienhard, *Martin Luthers christologisches Zeugnis, Entwicklung und Grundzüge seiner Christologie* (Göttingen: Vandenhoeck & Ruprecht, 1979).

3. Luther, "Preface to the Psalms," WADB 101:99.22-27.

of Concord in 1577, and he defended this document through his contribution to the *Apology of the Book of Concord*.[4] His loyalty to his "Preceptor" Philip Melanchthon and his association with the Preceptor's prize student, Martin Chemnitz, and the other formulators of Concord make him one of the most illuminating figures of the German Late Reformation. The significance of Selnecker's massive homiletical exposition of entire Psalter is indicated by the fact that it experienced at least six further editions in the subsequent three decades after its appearance in three volumes in 1563-64.[5] His interpretation of three "christological" psalms, 8, 22, and 110, provides a glimpse of how the second generation of the Reformation carried on Luther's and Melanchthon's exegetical tradition and how they used the biblical text to bring the comfort of the gospel to their people in a pastoral way and to address specific doctrinal problems besetting their church.

I. Selnecker's Developing Christology

Selnecker's homiletical-exegetical studies of the Psalms first appeared in the mid-1560s, at a time when many of Melanchthon's students, those later grouped in the "Philippist" camp, were edging toward public discussion of

---

4. Selnecker's contributions are analyzed in Jobst Ebel, "Die Herkunft des Konzepts der Konkordienformel. Die Funktionen der fünf Verfasser neben Andreae beim Zustandekommen der Formel," *Zeitschrift für Kirchengeschichte* 91 (1980): 237-282, and Irene Dingel, "Concordia und Kontroverse. Das Ringen um konfessionelle Pluralität und bekenntnismäßige Einheit im Spiegel der öffentlichen Diskussionen um Konkordienformel und Konkordienbuch" (Habilitationsschrift, Ruprecht-Karls University Heidelberg, 1993), pp. 557-638. This work will appear in print as *Concordia controversa. Die öffentlichen Diskussionen um das Konkordienwerk am Ende des 16. Jahrhunderts* (Gütersloh: Mohn, 1996).

5. Selnecker, *Das Erst Buch des Psalters Davidis/Nemlich/die ersten Fu[e]nffzig Psalmen/ordentlichen nach einander/dem gemeinen Mann/vnd Frommen/einfa[e]ltiger Christen zu gut/vnd in dieser elenden zeit zu Trost vnd Vnterricht/außgelegt vnd geprediget* (Nuremberg: Christoff Heußler, 1563); *Das Ander Buch des Psalter Davids/Von dem Ein vnd fu[e]nffzigsten biß auff den Hunderten Psalm . . . außgelegt* (Nuremberg: Christoff Heußler, 1564); and *Das Dritt Buch vnd letzte Theil des Psalter Davids/Außgelegt* (Nuremberg: Christoff Heußler, 1564) [the third volume is falsely dated 1566 by Guido Fuchs, *Psalmdeutung im Lied, Die Interpretation der "Feinde" bei Nikolaus Selnecker (1530-1592)* (Göttingen: Vandenhoeck & Ruprecht, 1993), p. 70]; for this and later editions, see *Verzeichnis der im deutschen Sprachbereich erschienenen Drucke des XVI. Jahrhunderts*, ed. Bayerische Staatsbibliothek in Munich and the Herzog August Bibliothek in Wolfenbüttel, vol. 19 (Stuttgart: Hiersemann, 1992), #5637-47. Fuchs reports another edition in 1589 as well. It appeared at least twice in the seventeenth century, in Leipzig, 1621, and also from the press of Justus Janson in Leipzig, 1623. Fuchs provides an overview of Selnecker's other work on the psalms, pp. 68-87.

the implications of the Preceptor's Christology for their own doctrines of the person of Christ. This discussion was provoked by controversies over the Lord's Supper but was not restricted to that arena. One of the first external provocations for the development of Philippist Christology, the Maulbronn Colloquium between the Lutherans of Württemberg and other South German principalities and the Calvinizing theologians of the Palatinate,[6] contributed to the alienation of the Philippists of Saxony from the Württemberg theologians who followed Johann Brenz's "ubiquitist" Christology. The Colloquy took place in April 1564, as Selnecker was composing his sermons on the Psalms; although it had little if any direct influence on them, its agenda did. For the issue of "ubiquity" commanded his attention as he commented, for example, on Psalm 110.[7] Already in 1561 Selnecker had expressed a Christology that reflected his antisacramentarian stance but also insisted, with Melanchthon, that an attribution of divine characteristics to an abstract human nature, considered apart from the hypostatic union, is untenable.[8] By 1570 he would encounter problems with stricter Lutherans such as Martin Chemnitz and Jakob Andreae because of his participation in an academic exercise at Wittenberg in 1570. Along with four other Wittenberg theologians, all of whom later rejected the Christology that Selnecker came to share with Chemnitz, he defended some 130 propositions on a variety of subjects. One thesis on the communication of attributes diverged from Chemnitz's and Andreae's position,[9] the position

---

6. Ernst Bizer, *Studien zur Geschichte des Abendmahlstreits im 16. Jahrhundert* (Gütersloh: Bertelsmann, 1940), pp. 335-62.

7. Selnecker, *Dritt Buch*, pp. cxli-b–cxlii-a.

8. Selnecker, *Libellvs brevis et vtilis de coena Domini editus* (Strassburg: Christian Mylius, 1561).

9. Thesis 30 of "Propositiones complectentes summam praecipvorvm capitvm doctrinae Christianae, sonantis, Dei beneficio, in Academia & Ecclesia VVitbergensi," in *De praecipvis horvm temporvm controversiis propositiones, orationes et qvaestiones . . .* (Wittenberg: Johannes Schwergel, 1570), sig. E3a-b, subtly but obviously rejected the Christology of Andreae that had been advanced in a formula for Lutheran concord presented at a conference at Zerbst in 1570; see Robert Kolb, *Andreae and the Formula of Concord* (Saint Louis: Concordia, 1977), pp. 43-48. On Selnecker's difficulties with Chemnitz and Andreae, with whom he was working at the time on the introduction of the Reformation in Braunschweig-Wolfenbüttel, see Ebel, "Herkunft," pp. 266-69. Ebel's judgment that Selnecker's *Paedagogia christiana* was "gut Philippistisch" on Christology must be acknowledged but with two observations: Selnecker's position was still developing at this time, and both the Philippists and their opponents among the Gnesio-Lutherans and Württembergers were just beginning to formulate the precise questions and lines of division that would make their positions specific. This is demonstrated by positions found in Selnecker's Psalms commentary, as discussed below. Cf. Franz Dibelius, "Selnecker, Nikolaus," *Realencyklopädie für protestantische Theologie und Kirche* 18:187.

Selnecker would affirm as he helped them compose Article VIII of the Formula of Concord.[10] To clarify his position, he issued a short German treatise on the subject in 1571.[11]

The critical issue centered around the *communicatio idiomatum* — the sharing of characteristics between Christ's divine and human natures within the unity of his person — and particularly what would later be called the *genus maiestaticum*. This *genus* made precise the definition of the communication of attributes that distinguished the stricter Lutherans not only from the Calvinists but also from many Philippists. According to the *genus maiestaticum*, within the hypostatic union of Christ's divine and human natures, the divine characteristics are fully shared with and conveyed to the human nature. All Evangelicals agreed that the characteristics of both natures were to be ascribed to the the entire person of Christ (this ascription was called the *genus idiomatum*) and that his redeeming work is to be ascribed to the one person of Christ acting in both his natures *(genus apotelesmaticum)*.[12] But many Philippists and the Calvinists rejected the "abstract" ascription of divine characteristics to the human nature of the person of Christ, insisting that this sharing of characteristics not be discussed apart from the "concrete" person of Jesus Christ, Son of God and Son of Man. In 1563/64 Selnecker obviously could not anticipate where the test points of the christological discussion would come in the next few years, but he represented a position that tried to remain faithful to Luther's Christology while holding fast to Melanchthon's resolve to avoid the "abstract" language of the sharing of divine characteristics with the humanity, rather than with the person, Jesus of Nazareth.[13]

Since Luther's confrontation with Zwingli in the mid-1520s, he and many of his followers had based their understanding of the communication of attributes, specifically of the divine attributes to the human nature, on

10. *Die Bekenntnisschriften der evangelisch-lutherischen Kirche,* 11th ed. (Göttingen: Vandenhoeck & Ruprecht, 1992), pp. 1017-49; *Biblischer Commentar über das Alte Testament,* pp. 591-610.

11. *Kurtze/Wahre vnd Einfeltige Bekantnus D. Nic. Selnecceri Von der Maiestet/Auffarth/Sitzen zur Rechten Gottes/vnd vom Abendmal vnsers HERRN Jhesu Christi . . .* (Heinrichstadt, 1571).

12. Dingel, "Concordia und Kontroverse," 601-21; Theodor Mahlmann, *Das neue Dogma der lutherischen Christologie* (Gütersloh: Mohn, 1969), pp. 62-92; Paul Tschackert, *Die Entstehung der lutherischen und der reformierten Kirchenlehre samt ihren innerprotestantischen Gegensätzen* (1910; Göttingen: Vandenhoeck & Ruprecht, 1979), pp. 553-57; Edmund Schlink, *Theologie der lutherischen Bekenntnisschriften,* 3d ed. (Munich: Kaiser, 1948), pp. 259-63.

13. On Melanchthon's treatment of the concept, see Mahlmann, *Neue Dogma,* pp. 65-69; on Selnecker's, pp. 239-43.

two points: (1) the union of the two natures in the hypostatic or personal union; and (2) the definition of the biblical term "right hand of God," which thus became one "test case" for this aspect of Lutheran Christology. Zwingli defined it as a place in heaven; for Luther and his followers, it was the almighty power of God. The ascension did not, therefore, fix the immobile human nature of Christ in heaven; instead, it returned the entire person of Christ — not only the divine nature but also the human nature — to the full exercise of his divine attributes, including omnipotence, omniscience, and omnipresence. The God-man in both natures could be present wherever he wanted, in whatever form he wanted, whenever he wanted.[14] Although in the quarter-century following Luther's death, Wittenberg Philippists objected to the attribution of this divine characteristic of "omnipresence" to humanity in the abstract, some of them could agree with those Lutherans who held that the God-man, the person Jesus Christ, by virtue of the hypostatic union, possessed this presence. This argument was particularly important in reference to the Lord's Supper. In the Formula of Concord, Chemnitz tried to come to accord with the Philippists through his formula, "multivolipresence," but he failed to win the more stalwart among them. Selnecker himself presented arguments similar to those advanced for a *genus maiestaticum* in the Psalms commentary, but relating the divine attributes always in concrete terms applied to the whole person of Christ rather than to the human nature.

Selnecker's own theological development moved him slowly away from many of his Philippist comrades,[15] in a direction that would enable him to work with and learn from Chemnitz, when the two joined Andreae in organizing the Reformation of Braunschweig-Wolfenbüttel at the end of the 1560s. Selnecker's comments on Psalms 8, 22, and 110 show that his Christology was in a certain "philippistic" stage in 1564, when he published the Psalms commentary, sharing the fundamental position from which some fellow-Philippists would develop a variety of formulations of the doctrine of Christ's person, thereby separating themselves from those of Luther's fol-

---

14. Bizer, *Studien,* pp. 352-62; Mahlmann, *Neue Dogma,* passim. Luther's critique of Zwingli's doctrine is presented in detail in "Vom Abendmahl Christi, Bekenntnis, 1528," in WA 26:317.6–349.34. Cf. *Handbuch der Dogmen- und Theologiegeschichte, 2. Band: Die Lehrentwicklung im Rahmen der Konfessionalität,* ed. Carl Andresen (Göttingen: Vandenhoeck & Ruprecht, 1980), pp. 56-60.

15. It is important to note that although the "Philippists" bore Melanchthon's name and did follow him more closely and completely than did their opposite numbers, the "Gnesio-Lutherans," the latter were also shaped by Melanchthon's instruction and method of theology.

lowers who united around the Formula of Concord thirteen years later.[16] Three years after the appearance of the Psalms commentary, Selnecker produced his detailed summary of Christian doctrine, following the outline of Luther's catechisms, his *Paedagogia christiana*. There he insisted with Melanchthon that a monophysite confusion of the two natures would destroy the human nature and therefore must be rejected. Moreover, he steadfastly maintained the Melanchthonian rejection of any abstract formulation of the *communicatio idiomatum*, which would attribute Christ's divine characteristics to his human nature instead of to the Son of Man within the hypostatic union. In 1567 he could simply state, "In the concrete we say of his person, God is this human creature, God suffered, was crucified, died. . . . God was born of the Virgin Mary."[17] He defined the right hand of God unequivocally "not as a physical place or some earthly place, but the majesty and omnipotence of God; . . . to sit at God's right hand is to rule with divine power and majesty which is the same as God's."[18] He posed the question whether Christ can be everywhere according to his physical body and concluded, "Christ is everywhere, according to the communication of attributes, which is real, not merely verbal. . . . Even if it cannot be said simply about the human nature in the abstract. . . , 'the body is everywhere,' nevertheless, in the concrete, or concerning Christ's person, it may be rightly said that Christ is everywhere, and everywhere where Christ is, there he is true God and a true human creature because it dare never be asserted or thought that Christ is where he is not both God and a human creature, without confusion of his natures and without a division of his person."[19] This Christology, which Selnecker would refine as he worked with Chemnitz, Andreae, and their colleagues on the Formula of Concord, is reflected in his Psalms commentary, and with a special kind of pastoral concern for the care of believers.

II. The Method of Selnecker's Commentary on the Psalms

The Psalms commentary, as formidable as it is, was put on paper in a fairly short time. Selnecker stated that it arose out of a sermon he had preached

16. Dingel, "Concordia und Kontroverse," chs. B5–7, and conclusion, pp. 601-21.

17. *Paedagogia Christiana continens capita et locos doctrinae Christianae, forma & serie catechetica uerè & perspicuè explicata . . .* (Frankfurt/Main, 1567), p. 544.

18. Selnecker, *Paedagogia Christiana*, pp. 595-96; on the *communicatio idiomatum* in general, see pp. 535-94. The preface indicates that this work was written in 1564.

19. Selnecker, *Paedagogia Christiana*, pp. 619-20.

on September 23, 1561, while court preacher in Dresden,[20] and he put the finishing touches on the last fifty psalms there on Trinity Sunday 1564.[21] Its pages reflect one — still philippistic — stage in the continuing development of his view of Christ's person and work.

Addressing such doctrinal issues within his commentary came naturally to Selnecker, as a Wittenberg student. His Psalms commentary was the second of his larger exegetical efforts.[22] In 1569 the mammoth Genesis commentary would follow, and his commentary on all the epistles of the New Testament would appear posthumously.[23] Particularly in the two latter, massive folio volumes Selnecker presented extensive instructions on how to teach or preach the text in the form of long *loci communes*. (For example, the locus on the person of Christ providing guidance on how to treat Gen. 49:10, "until Shiloh comes," runs some forty-nine folio pages.[24]) Selnecker's treatment of the Psalms followed a homiletical model closer to Luther's mode of narrative, discursive university lecture than the Melanchthonian model of tightly structured, analytical academic exegetical treatment that Selnecker would later adopt.[25] Nonetheless, the doctrinal organization of the ideas of the text into loci was a method waiting to burst from this narrative, homiletical style. He often indulged in the preacher's excursus, and thus his exposition of Psalms 8, 22, and 110 provided clues to his developing Christology with brief comments and with detailed development of his doctrine.

Selnecker's exegetical method reflects both his mentors' styles and principles of interpretation and at some points their very interpretations

---

20. Selnecker, *Erst Buch*, ♣iiij-a.

21. Selnecker, *Dritt Buch*, ☞iiij-b.

22. Earlier he had produced *Homiliae breves et vtiles in epistolas Ioannis apostoli* (Leipzig: Ernst Vögelin, 1561), and soon would follow *In Divi Petri apostoli epistolas, Carmen paraphrasticvm, et homiliae sev conciones* (Jena: Thomas Rebart, 1567).

23. *In omnes epistolas D. Pauli apostoli commentarius plenissimus* . . . (Leipzig: Johannes Apel, 1595).

24. *In Genesin, primvm librvm Moysi, Commentarius ita scriptvs, vt docentibvs et discentibvs coelestem doctrinam magno vsui esse possit* . . . (Leipzig: [Johannes Rhamba], 1569; 2d ed., 1578), pp. 818-66. Selnecker reproduced sixty-eight theses entitled "Quid sit communicatio idiomatum," in *In Genesin*, pp. 855-66, in his dogmatics textbook *Institutionis Christianae religionis, pars prima continens explicationem locorvm Theologicorum* . . . (Frankfurt/Main: [Martin Lechler], 1573), pp. 177-96.

25. The intention of such loci in the commentaries of Melanchthon and his students was to aid the reader/preacher in explicating the text for his people. Some of Philipp's students employed the one-sentence locus, a teaching tip; others, like Selnecker, followed a second Melanchthonian model and wrote extended doctrinal treatments of the points that the text should bring to mind; see Robert Kolb, "Teaching the Text, The Commonplace Method in Sixteenth Century Lutheran Biblical Commentary," *BHR* 49 (1987): 571-85.

of individual texts. In the preface of the first volume on the Psalms he identified himself as a "Lutheran" exegete. For him that meant, "I have not followed only my own interpretation or my own thoughts, nor have I sought something strange and inappropriate, but instead I have sought to preserve the correct understanding and the genuine, grammatical meaning. That is to say (the way the papists talk), I am properly Lutheran [*gut Lutherisch*]."[26] He openly acknowledged his debt to Luther, Johannes Bugenhagen,[27] Melanchthon's *Argumentum* or introductory overview of the Psalms, and the works of the Wittenberg Hebraist Georg Förster and his older contemporary, Hieronymus Weller, school superintendent in Freiberg in Saxony. His method intended to avoid not only reliance on his own thoughts alone but also on allegories and absurd interpretations; it remained with the simple words of the text and gathered comforting material from reading or listening to others.[28] Not only the incipient doctrinal loci scattered throughout his exposition but also his citation of the ancient fathers[29] and his construction of elaborate lists of points that would help unfold the text didactically and homiletically[30] reflect the milieu at Wittenberg in which he learned to interpret the biblical text.

Theologically, a point of orientation akin to Luther's theology of the cross guided Selnecker's interpretation again and again. Its cardinal point, that God reveals himself in what seems weakness and foolishness, particularly on the cross, helped Selnecker explain how the Word of God functions in the life of God's people. Examples abound in the three psalms under consideration here. He illumined Psalm 8:2 with allusions to the power of the weak Word of the Lord.[31] He specifically mentioned Paul's reference to God's hiding his wisdom in foolishness (1 Cor. 1:18–2:16) as he explored the meaning of the title of Psalm 22, "the Hind of the Dawn," in which "the Holy Spirit had hidden rich insights" into his revelation of God's person

---

26. Selnecker, *Erst Buch*, ♣iij-b.

27. Bugenhagen, *Psalter wol verteutscht auß der heyliger sprach. Verklerung des Psalters/fast klar vnd nutzlich* (1524; I have used: Basel: Adam Petri, 1526). In the passages discussed in this essay Bugenhagen's commentary did not, in fact, influence Selnecker.

28. Selnecker, *Erst Buch*, ♣iiij-b.

29. E.g., in Psalm 22, Selnecker, *Erst Buch*, pp. clxvi-b–cxlvii-a (Jerome), cl-b (Origen), clii-b (Hesychius), clx-b (Augustine). He also knew Jewish comment, perhaps through Nicholas of Lyra; see *Erst Buch*, cxlv-b.

30. Among countless examples, in Selnecker, *Erst Buch*, clviii-b–clix-a (six reasons why Christ had to suffer), clxv-b (five elements in Christ's cry from the cross to his Father), clxvii-b–clxvii-a (four foci of Christ's redemptive work, three reasons for it, and five impacts of it).

31. Selnecker, *Erst Buch*, pp. xxiiii-b–xxxc-a.

and work.[32] Paul's Corinthian *theologia crucis* was mentioned explicitly as Selnecker treated the suffering of Christ's kingdom in this world at Ps. 22:24.[33] God's kingdom is a kingdom of the cross, of suffering in this world, as Selnecker observed in comments on Ps. 110:2.[34] In addition, the cross of Christ emerges as a major theme in the commentary, as seen particularly in Psalm 22. On the basis of this *theologia crucis,* that God's power and wisdom reveal themselves in what is weak and foolish to the world, Selnecker set forth the doctrine of the revelation of God in the human creature, Jesus Christ, as he found prophecies of that revelation through the incarnation in the Psalms.

III. Selnecker's Christological Reflections in Psalms 8 and 22

Even though the christological interpretation of Psalm 8 had ancient roots[35] and Luther had treated it extensively as a prophecy of Christ, Selnecker made only a passing reference to the suffering of the Son of Man, Jesus Christ, in his brief exposition of verse 4, "What is man that thou art mindful of him, and the son of man that thou dost care for him?" There he described Christ's suffering in terms of Isaiah 53 and Ps. 22:6, and his exaltation in terms of Ps. 110:1 and Col. 2:15-20. Without treating the communication of attributes, Selnecker simply confessed that this Son of Man sits at God's right hand as a true human creature and is eternally almighty along with God his Father and the Holy Spirit.[36] It is possible that as Selnecker began his Psalms commentary in 1561, Christology was not yet a burning issue for him and his colleagues.

Certain christological excurses in Psalm 22 may reflect a growing interest in Christology — or the demands of the text, which Selnecker understood as a prophecy of the sufferings of the God-man, Jesus Christ.[37]

---

32. Selnecker, *Erst Buch,* pp. cxlv-b–cxlvi-a.

33. Selnecker, *Erst Buch,* p. clxxiiii-a.

34. Selnecker, *Dritt Buch,* pp. cxxv-b–cxxvi-a.

35. For the *Gloss* on Psalm 8, see *Biblia sacra cvm glossa ordinaria, Tomvs tertivs* (Antwerp: Joannes Mercerius, 1639), pp. 511-14.

36. Selnecker, *Erst Buch,* pp. xxxvii-b–xxxviii-a. See a more thorough development of this line of thinking in the context of the christological heresies of the early church at Ps. 72:1; Selnecker, *Ander Buch,* pp. cxlviii-b–cli-a.

37. When Selnecker wrote a special sermon on Psalm 22 for his Passion History twenty years later, all references to the hypostatic union were omitted; *Passio. Christliche/kurtze vnd tro[e]stliche Erklerung der Historien von dem Leiden vnd Sterben vnsers Herrn vnd Heylands Jesu Christi . . .* (Leipzig: [Zacharias Berwald], 1587, sig. Ee ij-a–Oo iij-a.

Although their treatments of this psalm diverged in detail, Selnecker followed the tradition that Luther put to use in interpreting the title of the Psalm, "the Hind of the Dawn," in his *Operationes in Psalmos* (1519), repeating his teacher's observation that the hind referred to Christ's human nature and the dawn to his divine nature.[38]

The psalm's first verse, "My God, my God, why have you forsaken me?" — with its expression of God's abandonment of the Son of God, who is God himself — demanded further explanation of the relationship of the divine and human natures. How could the one who is almighty God himself have suffered on the cross? In his exegesis of the verse Selnecker alluded three times to the relationship of the two natures. He placed in Christ's own mouth the confession that he was Son of God and image of the Father. He affirmed that the two natures are united in one person, like body and soul, and the divine nature shines through the human nature as a fire lights up a glowing piece of iron. In other words, the divine and human natures are related to each other in a manner similar to that of fire and iron: they retain their different characteristics and at the same time permeate each other, without giving up their own specific attributes. "As a true human creature, the Son of God hungered, thirsted, grew up, slept, cried, and carried on other activities, all without sin." Selnecker explained how it was possible for Christ to bear the sins of the world in his human nature only because he was God and almighty at the same time.[39] To make that clear, at verses 9 and 10 Selnecker treated the virgin birth, from which one person, Immanuel, God with us, true God and true human creature, was born.[40] His pastoral concern expressed itself in this effort to preserve the unity of the two natures in the person of Christ; whether consciously or not, he observed Melanchthon's general christological concern and avoided attributing divine characteristics abstractly to the human nature.

Throughout this exposition Selnecker's pastoral concern asserted itself; he was writing for preachers and wanted to aid them in applying the psalms to their people's lives. Thus, he wandered into a discussion of an assertion that he labeled "godless": Christ must not be God since God cannot die, and Christ did. In attempting to answer this syllogism, he employed an argument like that of the *genus apotelesmaticum,* arguing

38. Selnecker, *Erst Buch,* pp. cxlvii-b; cf. Luther's remarks at WA 5:598.32–600.6. Augustine had referred the hind to the human nature of Christ, as had Lyra; see *Biblia sacra* on Ps. 22:1 (3:592-94). Psalm 22 in its entirety had been treated as messianic throughout the history of Christian interpretation; *Biblia Sacra* 3:591-608.

39. Selnecker, *Erst Buch,* pp. cl-a, cliiii-b.

40. Selnecker, *Erst Buch,* pp. clix-a–clx-b.

exegetically on the basis of 1 Pet. 3:18 (in the words of his paraphrase), "Christ suffered for us in the flesh, and was put to death according to the flesh, that is, the human nature." "The divine nature did not suffer nor did it die." Selnecker cited Irenaeus, "Christ was crucified and died in such a manner that the divine nature or the Word in him held still and rested, so that the human nature in him could suffer and die," and appealed to Phil. 2:6-11 and Heb. 4:15b for support.[41] Selnecker elaborated with a reference to the two goats used as offerings to the Lord in Lev. 16:6-10; with an allegorical touch, he saw in them an explanation of how the two natures functioned in the atonement. One goat had been slaughtered as a sin offering while the other was presented live to the Lord.

> This figure is a reference to the two natures in the Lord Christ. His human nature suffers and dies; it pours out its blood as an offering for sin. It reconciles God the Lord with us poor sinners and wins for us free access to God's throne of grace. But his divinity remains as it has from eternity to eternity in eternal life, in eternal glory and omnipotence.

Nonetheless, Selnecker concluded, "The entire person of Christ bears our sins as true God and a true human creature, that they may never be reckoned to us again."[42] Selnecker was wrestling with the pastoral problem posed by the question, "How can God save in weakness?" His answer was forged on the basis of his *theologia crucis* with christological reflections. By the time he treated Psalm 110, some months later, polemical considerations joined the pastoral in shaping his exegesis.

IV. Selnecker's Christological Reflections on Psalm 110

The messianic interpretation of Psalm 110 had a long history before the Lutherans claimed it as a place to repeat their convictions concerning the hypostatic union and the relationship of the two natures.[43] Without extensive reference to the Real Presence in the Lord's Supper (the occasion for Luther's original development of this part of his Christology), Selnecker met "sacramentarian" and "schwärmerisch" interpretations of the personal union

41. Selnecker, *Erst Buch,* p. clii-a.
42. Selnecker, *Erst Buch,* p. clii-a.
43. See *Biblia sacra* on Ps. 110:1 (3:1293-1300). The *Glossa ordinaria* begins with a word from Cassiodorus, "Psalmus iste septimus de duabus naturis in Christo, plene & breviter de incarnatione, & omnipotenti divinitati Christi."

head-on; whether he had encountered them within the ranks of his own comrades is unclear. His opposition to them is not. The conversation between God the Father and the Messiah in Ps. 110:1 compels Christians "to give Christ the Lord his honor and speak of his person as of [one person], God and this human creature, inseparable." He sharply rejected "new, offensive, seductive thoughts and ways of speaking" that would "separate Christ as though he were true God and human creature at the same time in one certain place but in another [place] only God, thus making two persons, and separating and tearing the two natures apart from each other." This Selnecker regarded as a serious error and blasphemy.[44] He supported his conclusion by repudiating the sacramentarian position that interpreted God's right hand as a locality in heaven. The text itself demanded an interpretation of the concept of the right hand of God, and Selnecker obliged.

> God's right hand is not a particular place, where a person could be. It is instead the almighty power of God, which is unlimited, immeasurable, incomprehensible, outside everything and above everything that is or can be. He is in his essence everywhere, present everywhere, and he creates, effects, and preserves everything, . . . in every part and place of the creation.

Human reason cannot fathom this mystery, "but faith knows it and gives God honor" by trusting his word regarding the incarnation. The Father bestowed this power upon Christ, the Son of Man, "as a true human creature."[45]

Selnecker was not the first Lutheran to treat the mystery of the hypostatic union in Ps. 110:1. "For here is Christ the Lord addressed by God the Father as a true human creature." The Psalm states, "The LORD says to my lord"![46] In his "argumentum ac dispositio" on Psalm 110 Melanchthon had summarized the subject matter of the psalm as "the declaration of the promise of the coming Messiah," which the Psalmist developed in two points. The first was that the Messiah is one person, the eternal Son of God but David's descendant. The second point described Christ's work of suffering, assuming rule as victor, and gathering his church.[47] Although Melanch-

---

44. Selnecker, *Dritt Buch*, pp. cxxiii-a-b.

45. Selnecker, *Dritt Buch*, pp. cxxiii-b–cxxiiii-a. Cf. Luther's formulation, n. 14 above.

46. Selnecker, *Dritt Buch*, p. cxxiii-b.

47. Melanchthon, *Psalterivm Davidis integrvm, in qvo Psalmi octoginta tres illustrati sunt argumentis & enarratione . . .* (Wittenberg: Johannes Crato, 1561), pp. 244b-45b; edited in CR 13:1152-53.

thon avoided specific development of the doctrine of the two natures and the personal union here, his student Hieronymus Weller, whose work Selnecker consulted, did not: writing in 1558, he had observed, "This verse contains the clearest testimony that Christ is true God and a true human creature, and that the two natures, divine and human, are united in the person of Christ according to the hypostatic union, as the ancients said."[48] Weller did not originate the association himself. His and Selnecker's texts reflect Luther as well. In 1535 Luther had preached a series of sermons on Psalm 110 that were published in 1539. In treating verse 1 of the psalm, Luther had emphasized how difficult it is to believe that this human creature, Jesus Christ, is "at the same time true, eternal, almighty God."[49] Although Selnecker ignored much of Luther's treatment of this text and wandered far from his mentor's exegesis as he developed his own, on this point the similarity is striking.

It was from Luther, too, that Selnecker probably paraphrased a citation from Bernard of Clairvaux, which brought the consolatory aspect of the doctrine of the personal union into focus. "It is for us a great comfort that we know, as Bernard said before his end, that our flesh and blood sits at God's right hand, with equal power and might. Who could be afraid if he believes that? Away with our unbelief and doubt."[50] Christology is ever a matter of *Seelsorge*.

In a lengthy christological excursus Selnecker answered two questions raised by verse 1. "Why did David not call the Lord Christ Jehovah?" "Why did he call Christ his Lord when Christ was in fact his son?" The first question treated the doctrine of the Trinity. Selnecker was not engaged in dispute over the Trinity, and he answered the question in less than half a folio page: the persons of Father and Son must be kept distinct.[51] But the questions that had led to the Maulbronn Colloquy were also demanding the refinement of Wittenberg Christology. The answer to the christological question required detailed treatment.

David recognized that the Messiah was to come from his own loins. Nonetheless, he recognized him as his Lord. With a series of seven assertions

---

48. Weller, *Brevis enarratio aliqvot Psalmorvm. Libellvs de modo concionandi, pro studiosis Theologiae* (Wittenberg: Johannes Crato, 1558), p. 597.

49. Luther, "Predigten des Jahres 1535," WA 41:89-93, esp. 89.3-28. Selnecker could have had the 1539 printing at hand; he also had these sermons in the Wittenberg (3 [1550], II, 207a-52b) or Jena (7, 297a-349a [1558]) editions of Luther's German works.

50. Selnecker, *Dritt Buch*, p. cxxiiii-b; cf. Luther, "Predigten des Jahrs 1535," WA 41:101.6-12.

51. Selnecker, *Dritt Buch*, p. cxxxiii-a-b.

Selnecker explained why. Christ is, first of all, the eternal image of the divine essence and the eternal reflection of his glory. The nature of God dwells in him essentially and perfectly (Col. 1:19), and therefore he must be true God. Third, the entire Scripture testifies to the difference between the eternally begotten Son of God and other children of God. Creation is the work of God alone, but it is ascribed to the Son of God (John 1:3). Everything that the Father does "ad extra" (outside the relationships of the persons of the Trinity), the Son does with the same power and omnipotence: he makes alive and awakens the dead; he is the resurrection and the life (John 11:25). All Scripture testifies that we are to call upon the Messiah, worship him, and trust in him alone. Finally, the witness of the Holy Spirit in our hearts confirms that the Messiah is true God.[52] In this manner Selnecker was able to aid his readers as they prepared to preach and teach the text to their people, even if he did not plumb the depths of the christological issues.

The christological implications of verse 1 of this psalm had to be developed further. Selnecker proceeded to Ps. 110:3b, "Your children will be born to you as the dew from the dawn."[53] Citing Epiphanius,[54] he proposed that this word speaks first of the

> eternal birth of Christ, that he is eternal, true God, through whom the world was made, Hebrews 1[:2], the first born of all creation, through whom all things were made in heaven and on earth . . . Colossians 1[:15-16]. For just as dew does not come from the earth but falls from above, so Christ's birth comes from heaven, for, as John the Baptist said, he comes from above (John 3:31), and as John the evangelist wrote, the Word was in the beginning; he was with God and he was God himself (John 1:1).[55]

Selnecker did not mention to the "common man and pious, simple Christians" for whom he wrote what Weller told "the students of theology"

---

52. Selnecker, *Dritt Buch*, pp. cxxxiii-b–cxxxv-b.

53. In interpreting v. 3 Selnecker also displayed the synergistic position of the Philippists, which he would later reject, but which got him into trouble with the Gnesio-Lutheran opponents of this position and contributed to his dismissal from the University of Jena in 1567; see Dibelius, "Selnecker," p. 186.

54. He mentioned that Epiphanius had offered six different explanations of the verse. Epiphanius had concluded that the verse was written "ut ex eo sermone cognoscas Deum Verbum hypostasi propria praeditum a Patre esse genitum, nullo neque initio, neque tempore, priusquam aliquid aliud exsisteret. . . ," in *Haereses* 2.II, "Contra Paulum Samosatenum," PG 42:18.

55. Selnecker, *Dritt Buch*, pp. cxxviii-b–cxxix-a.

who were the intended audience of his little volume, namely, that Luther and Melanchthon presented different interpretations of this passage.[56] Luther applied this "new birth from the dew" only to the new creation of Christians from above, through baptismal water and Word.[57] Philip had understood this new birth as the Messiah's birth from the virgin's womb. He spoke of the descent of "God's Son, who is the coeternal image of the Father, to us who are in utter misery," but he avoided any deeper exploration of the personal union and the two natures of Christ.[58] Selnecker did not mention his Preceptor's exegesis in his lengthy explication of this passage. He found that Luther's interpretation provided the fundamental understanding of the verse. Nonetheless, he could not pass up another opportunity to comment on the mystery of the incarnation and the two natures.

In a later summary of the first part of the psalm, Selnecker offered a more complete analysis of the doctrine of Christ's session at the Father's right hand. This analysis indicates that Selnecker had not been drawn into the polarization that had become evident at Maulbronn between the Württemberg "ubiquitist" Christology and that of their calvinizing opponents in the Palatinate. Like the Württembergers, Selnecker rejected a "circumscribed" definition of the term "right hand" as a coarse anthropomorphism without embracing their specific understanding of the *genus maiestaticum* that the human nature of Christ was everywhere *(ubique)* present. Instead, "sitting means carrying out a certain office, ruling, exercising lordship, administering justice and righteousness," as Paul explained in Eph. 4:10 and Phil. 2:9-11.

Why did the Father say to the Son, "Sit at my right hand"? Selnecker asked. Not to bestow upon this human creature (at this point for the first time) divinity and omnipotence, for these he had had from eternity. Rather, the Father here makes clear that "this true human Creature, Christ, David's and Mary's son, sits at God's right hand with the same omnipotence and majesty as God himself, and is also true God, Lord of all creatures, worshipped and praised by all angels." Selnecker supported his conclusions with more biblical evidence: Christ, Mary's son, could claim that all power in heaven and on earth had been given to him (Matt. 28:18) and could pray to the Father, "glorify me in your presence with the glory that I had in your presence before the world existed" (John 17:5).[59] Nonetheless, Selnecker

---

56. Weller, *Brevis enarratio,* p. 612.
57. Luther, "Predigten des Jahrs 1535," WA 41:158.20–167.20.
58. Melanchthon, *Psalterium Davidis,* fol. 247^r; CR 13:1154-55.
59. Selnecker, *Dritt Buch,* pp. cxxxviii-a–cxxxix-b.

did not interpret such statements as a basis for a doctrine of the abstract communication of divine attributes *to the human nature as such*. He consistently emphasized that the entire person of Christ, within the hypostatic union, exercises the divine characteristics of omnipotence, omnipresence, and so on. Even though Eph. 4:10 states that the ascended Christ fills all things, this does not mean for Selnecker an omnipresence of the human nature itself, but an omnipresence of the entire person of Christ, true God and true human creature. Wherever Christ is as true God, he is there as human creature also, *"vbique retenta proprietate vtriusque naturae"* — retaining everywhere the characteristic of both natures. The characteristics of each nature remain inalterably.

In Selnecker's argumentation the hypostatic union retains priority. He repeated, "Christ is true God and true human creature, inseparable in one person, and where he is present as true God and true human creature, he is there without confusion of the natures, and without a division of his person, and this person retains everywhere the characteristic of both natures."[60] Selnecker did not deduce the *genus maiestaticum* from Christ's ascension but used it instead to support the *genus idiomatum*.

From this Selnecker did deduce that sacramentarian argumentation regarding the Lord's Supper based upon what is possible according to the rules of Aristotelian physics is false. He emphatically rejected the proposition that the human nature of Christ must be bound to a specific place, according to such rules. Without initiating an explicit discussion of the doctrine of the Lord's Supper, he argued that there could be no question that Christ's humanity is present in the Lord's Supper. But the basis for this argument lay not in the communication of divine attributes to the human nature, as the Württembergers had argued in connection with the exaltation of the human nature to God's right hand. In Selnecker's understanding Christ's body is present because God is present in the Lord's Supper — and "here there can be no disputing regarding the human body [the human nature] in the abstract, but we speak of the entire person [of the God-man]."[61] Selnecker met the reproach of Calvin's adherents against the ubiquity of the human nature of Christ with his own concept of the ubiquity of the God-man as the redeemer.[62]

---

60. Selnecker, *Dritt Buch,* pp. cxxxix-b–cxl-a.

61. Selnecker, *Dritt Buch,* pp. cxxxix-b–cxl-a, with details of the argument against the "sacramentarians" and Anabaptists continuing to p. clxiii-a.

62. Selnecker, *Dritt Buch,* p. cxli-b. Cf. pp. cxliii-a and cxl-a, as well as Selnecker's similar criticism of sacramentarians on Psalm 89, *Ander Buch,* p. cclxvii-a-b.

Selnecker found this unity of the two natures a source of pastoral comfort. For it assures believers that their own human brother, Jesus Christ, is their only true mediator, who, according to the words of institution, is present for them also in the Lord's Supper and prays for them as the *God*-man.[63] Polemical as much of his argument was, it always aimed at the comfort and consolation of believers.

Psalm 110:1 gave commentators the opportunity to treat Christ as Messiah; verse 4 gave them occasion to treat his office as priest: "You are a priest forever after the order of Melchizedek." In explaining this verse, Selnecker used what would be called the *genus apotelesmaticum* to help his readers understand that this person is "an eternal priest, in one person the true, eternal God and a true human creature, and he fulfills his priestly office through both natures, divine and human. For the work of redemption is not ascribed to one nature only in the Lord Christ but to his entire person."[64] Neither Luther nor Melanchthon had felt compelled to treat the hypostatic union in their exposition of Ps. 110:4.[65] What challenge provoked Selnecker to introduce the subject here remains unclear. His exposition of Psalm 110 formed a basis for the further development of the doctrine of the person of Christ and the communication of attributes that he would later represent in the drafting of the Formula of Concord and its defense.[66] Woven within Selnecker's attempt to mine the riches of the text for the use of his readers' hearers is his pastoral concern to build faith and console consciences.

V. The Work of Christ

For Selnecker, as for all Christian theologians since Paul, to speak of Christ's person is to speak of his work as well. His Psalms commentary reflects his Lutheran rootage as he used Psalms texts to illumine God's act of salvation in the God-man Jesus Christ. In contrast to most of his contemporaries among Luther's heirs, Selnecker explicitly employed Luther's language of

---

63. Selnecker, *Dritt Buch*, p. cxli-a.

64. Selnecker, *Dritt Buch*, p. clvi-b, a thoroughly noncontroversial use of the *genus apotelesmaticum*.

65. Selnecker's exegesis of the verse does show similarities with the interpretations of the priesthood of Melchizedek as a type of Christ's priesthood that his mentors presented at other points; see Luther, "Predigten des Jahrs 1535," WA 41:167-214, and Melanchthon, *Psalterium Davidis*, pp. 248a-56b; CR 13:1155-65.

66. Dingel, "Concordia und Kontroverse," pp. 599-636.

the "joyous exchange" of human sinfulness for Christ's righteousness in describing what Christ had wrought through the suffering and death prophetically described in Psalm 22.

> As the Son of God suffered for our sins, which he took upon himself, so we rejoice and comfort ourselves with his righteousness, with which we are dressed and clothed. This very comforting exchange with the Son of God trades death for life, wrath for grace, sin for righteousness, damnation for salvation, sickness for health, restlessness for peace, sadness for joy.[67]

At verse 22, Selnecker confessed,

> We are free from the devil, innocent of our sins, free from eternal death, because Christ, our brother, is flesh and bone of our flesh and bone. Everything which belongs to him is ours, so that nothing shall harm us anymore: neither sin, nor death, nor devil, nor hell, nor the world, since Christ, our brother, has conquered all our enemies, and we conquer continually these same enemies throughout our whole life in him and through him.[68]

Psalm 22 permitted Selnecker to deal in detail with the sufferings of Christ, and he coordinated its descriptions with those of Isaiah 53, without, however, indulging in Anselmian satisfaction speculation.[69] He focused strongly on the victory of Christ:

> Christ overcame and cast down the devil and destroyed his work. He eradicated all our sins. He broke the power of death, and he brings and bestows upon us life, 2 Timothy 1. He demolished the power of the tyrants who opposed his Word and his people. . . . He thwarts the sectarian spirits and establishes his reign by laying all his enemies under his feet.[70]

---

67. Selnecker, *Erst Buch*, p. cliii-b.
68. Selnecker, *Erst Buch*, p. clxxi-a.
69. E.g., Selnecker, *Erst Buch*, pp. clvii-a–clvii-b. This is even the case when Selnecker treats the high priest Christ as an offering himself, *Dritt Buch*, pp. clix-a-b. He comes closer to an Anselmian doctrine at Ps. 72:1; *Ander Buch*, pp. cxlviii-a–cxlix-a. On the use of the "vicarious satisfaction" theories in the Late Reformation, see Robert Kolb, " 'Not Without the Satisfaction of God's Righteousness,' The Atonement and the Generation Gap between Luther and His Students," *ARG Sonderband: Die Reformation in Deutschland und Europa, Interpretation und Debatten,* ed. Hans R. Guggisberg and Gottfried G. Krodel (Gütersloh: Gütersloher Verlagshaus, 1993), pp. 136-56. Selnecker stands in this regard somewhat apart from many contemporaries and thus closer to Luther.
70. Selnecker, *Dritt Buch*, p. cxiiii-a-b.

Verse 18, "they divide my garments among them, and for my raiment they cast lots," concludes Psalm 22's description of suffering. Selnecker used it as the occasion for a summary of Christ's redeeming activity, for he applied the psalm as a direct foretelling of Christ's passion. He emphasized Christ's obedience to his Father through which he fulfilled prophecies such as that of the psalm. Christ acted in behalf of "the poor human race, which he redeemed with his sacrifice," and he acted against "the devil and his tyranny, which he destroyed and conquered." The redeeming activity of Christ was part of a three-part plan of God, which explains why God sent his Son into the world. The plan is rooted in eternity, in God's inalterable righteousness and his fatherly, indescribable mercy. It was executed in bringing sinful creatures out of their sin to faith in the Son of God and thus to righteousness and salvation. It concludes with the destruction of the devil's rule, power, and rage.[71]

Although Lutheran dogmatics did not formally develop "orders of salvation," Selnecker also fit Christ's redeeming activity into something like an *ordo salutis* as he treated Psalm 110. He developed it from Rom. 8:29-30 as part of his explanation of how the atonement brings the chosen of God together. God first foresaw those whom he wanted to accept into grace for the sake of his Son, Christ Jesus. Selnecker here emphasized that God wants all to be saved without attempting to address the tension between the universal promise and God's election. Second, God ordained those to eternal life whom he had foreseen (and thus designated) as recipients of his grace. Third, God revealed his foreseeing and predestining through the call to repentance and the Gospel. Fourth, God justified those whom he called, forgave their sins, and clothed them in the righteousness of his Son, bestowing upon them the Holy Spirit and eternal life. Fifth, he granted them eternal glory.[72]

For this purpose Christ had come. All christological teaching had as its goal for Selnecker the proclamation of this gospel. Discussions of Christ's person had to lead to a proclamation of his work.

VI. Conclusion

Nikolaus Selnecker claimed to be a "Lutheran" interpreter of Scripture, and that he was. In his treatment of three selected psalms, he proved that in

---

71. Selnecker, *Erst Buch*, p. clxvii-b.
72. Selnecker, *Dritt Buch*, pp. cxxix-a–cxxx-a.

several ways. That he did not always replicate Luther's interpretation of specific passages says nothing about his being a "Lutheran exegete." In his commentaries on Genesis and Galatians his exegesis demonstrated even less of Luther's direct influence upon his understanding of specific passages than is the case in these psalms. That was the case for all other interpreters of these two books among Selnecker's generation of the heirs of Luther and Melanchthon.[73] It was also the case in Selnecker's treatment of Psalm 101.[74] Exegetes interpret the biblical text within their own historical contexts. Selnecker had to address the concerns of his own age, not of Luther's generation.

Selnecker demonstrated that he was a Lutheran exegete rather in his pursuit of what he thought of as the simple grammatical sense of the text, which he understood to mean that a text points to the coming Messiah, Jesus of Nazareth, whenever possible. Luther's *theologia crucis* provided orientation for his interpretation, and he found Luther's concept of the "joyous exchange" a helpful framework for commenting on the work of Christ. Furthermore, in these three psalms Selnecker proved himself a Lutheran exegete by engaging the question of the relationship between Christ's human nature and his divine nature in a manner that reflected not only his own Philippist orientation but also much of the broad consensus of Lutheran theology on the eve of open conflict over the christological legacy of Luther and Melanchthon. In 1564 he was on the way to a specific confessional position; at this point, his replication of Luther's understanding of the importance of the hypostatic union and of the "right hand of God" places him firmly within the Lutheran tradition, albeit with a clearly recognizable Philippist shading. In more ways than one, Selnecker proved himself "gut Lutherisch" as he provided an accent in the doctrine of Christ that could serve as an integrating force in the discussion to come.

---

73. See Robert Kolb, "Sixteenth-Century Lutheran Commentary on Genesis and the Genesis Commentary of Martin Luther," in *Théorie et pratique de l'exégèse,* ed. Irena Backus and Francis Higman (Geneva: Droz, 1990), pp. 243-58; and "The Influence of Luther's Galatians Commentary of 1535 on Later Sixteenth-Century Lutheran Commentaries on Galatians," *ARG* 84 (1993): 156-84.

74. As Wolfgang Sommer has observed, correctly noting that Selnecker regarded Luther's interpretation of Psalm 101 as so masterful and continuingly relevant that its insights did not need to be repeated, and, perhaps more importantly, that the times had changed in regard to the relationship of prince and preacher in Lutheran Germany (the subject of both the commentaries on Psalm 101); *Gottesfurcht und Fürstenherrschaft* (Göttingen: Vanden-hoeck & Ruprecht, 1988), pp. 90-93, 103-4.

PART IV

CONCLUSION

· 16 ·

The Significance of Precritical Exegesis:
Retrospect and Prospect

RICHARD A. MULLER
JOHN L. THOMPSON

ALTHOUGH SCHOLARS MAY be found who insist that objectivity is neither possible nor desirable for understanding the past, most historians find it exceedingly desirable, if never fully possible, to attempt to control — or at least to ascertain — their methodological biases and the predilections to which their culture, time, and circumstances dispose them. "Precritical exegesis," however, like such descriptors as "gothic" and "Dark Ages," never served anyone as a self-referential term; it was neither coined nor embraced by those supposed to have practiced it. Instead, it was spawned by an era and a method that held these earlier practitioners in some contempt; as such, the term represents a profound (and, one may add, uncontrolled) bias in the historical literature. For although the biblical exegesis with which this volume has been concerned does indeed stand prior to historical-critical exegesis, it is by no means therefore also uncritical, and to equate "precritical" with "uncritical" in this context is simply to commit an anachronism.

"Precritical" exegetes, in other words, were not bereft of method merely because they followed a different method. Nor should they be deemed insufficiently critical because their standards do not always reflect our own, as if they had no standards for self-evaluation — indeed, as if peer review and the harsh judgments of the marketplace were inoperative prior to the Enlightenment! No. They saw the text in a different light, and employed their own criteria in examination of the text. Sometimes their concerns mirror our own; sometimes they are said to "anticipate" critical exegesis, which often is itself an uncritical comment. But despite some parallels to the criteria used by the modern exegete, precritical exegetes also exhibit substantial differences over against the methods of modern "higher criticism."

The time has come, therefore, to move beyond the "chronological snobbery" so often displayed by modern exegesis toward its own forebears. Indeed, many of the modern histories of precritical exegesis have themselves spent far more time vilifying these earlier interpreters than understanding them. Would it not be more fruitful, and fairer, and certainly less facile, to reread this story here as not the triumph of truth over error but instead as a confrontation between divergent methods and their divergent results? The essays in the present volume have attempted to demonstrate, in various ways, that the allegedly "precritical" exegesis of the Reformation era is of more than antiquarian interest, yet to do so without simply strip-mining it to unearth elements deemed valuable sheerly because they remind us of modern "critical" history and exegesis. By way of conclusion, then, we wish to offer some reflections on the significance of precritical exegesis both in light of the limitations of historical-critical exegesis and in its own right.

*   *   *

The career of historical-critical exegesis in the twentieth century is fraught with irony. Historical-critical exegesis has been lionized as the key to unlocking the past, even as it has been vilified as the source of a reductionism that effectively dismisses the past by dissolving it into its various cultural, economic, social, and psychological components. Protests against such reductionism have been regularly voiced; those of Martin Kähler and Karl Barth are two of the best known, but lists both longer and more up-to-date could easily be compiled. Significantly, however, support for such a protest has more recently begun to develop out of an increasing disillusionment with historical criticism not on the part of outsiders but among those who have been most dedicated to its practice.

Moreover, the cracks that have appeared in the edifice of historical criticism reveal not only that modern exegesis is often overburdened but also that not all modern exegetes willingly dismiss their forebears. Signs of second thoughts have begun to appear, and several of the post–historical-critical hermeneutical and methodological stances of the late twentieth century have either overtly recognized the insights of older exegesis or have generated ways of understanding the text that stand in continuity more with the precritical than with the so-called "critical" approach. For example, approaches such as "canonical" and "rhetorical" criticism have led to a new and deliberate appreciation of precritical understandings of the scope and unity of the biblical text and of the necessity of understanding the meaning of a particular passage not only in terms of its immediate context but also in light of its inclusion in the canon of Scripture.[1] On the other hand, recent hermeneutical theorists as diverse as E. D. Hirsch, Hans-Georg Gadamer, and Anthony Thiselton have recognized that the interpretive task — and, therefore, the meaning and significance of the text itself — derives not only from the text in its original *Sitz im Leben* but also from the reader of the text and the tradition in which he or she stands. Consequently, much contemporary interpretation has come to admit that it can no longer discount the older tradition as an aid to the interpretation to the understanding of the text.[2] As Karlfried Froehlich has elsewhere summarized the issue, "In order to understand a text, its posthistory is as important as its prehistory and *Sitz im Leben*."[3]

Here is where the contrast between the "critical" and "precritical" approaches could scarcely be greater. The critical approach looks to the most primitive meaning of the text, often disparaging the work of Scripture's alleged redactors as "unenlightening," in order to locate meaning in a precanonical and therefore also prescriptural (if not preliterary) reconstruction of the text. The larger context of the canon is lost, and the final,

---

1. See Gerald T. Sheppard, "Between Reformation and Modern Commentary: The Perception of the Scope of Biblical Books," in William Perkins, *A Commentary on Galatians with Introductory Essays*, ed. Gerald T. Sheppard (New York: Pilgrim Press, 1989), pp. xlviii-lxxvii; Henning Graf Reventlow, *The Authority of the Bible and the Rise of the Modern World* (London: SCM Press, 1984), pp. 91-184; Brevard S. Childs, *Biblical Theology in Crisis* (Philadelphia: Westminster, 1970); idem, *The New Testament as Canon: An Introduction* (Philadelphia: Fortress, 1985); and Gene M. Tucker, David L. Petersen, and Robert R. Wilson (eds.), *Canon, Theology, and Old Testament Interpretation: Essays in Honor of Brevard S. Childs* (Philadelphia: Fortress, 1988). Also note the discussion of patterns of patristic exegesis in David Dockery, *Biblical Interpretation Then and Now: Contemporary Hermeneutics in the Light of the Early Church* (Grand Rapids: Baker, 1992).

2. E. D. Hirsch, *Validity in Interpretation* (New Haven: Yale University Press, 1967); idem, *The Aims of Interpretation* (Chicago: University of Chicago Press, 1976); Hans-Georg Gadamer, *Truth and Method* (London: Sheed and Ward, 1976); Anthony C. Thiselton, *The Two Horizons: New Testament Hermeneutics and Philosophical Description* (Grand Rapids: Eerdmans, 1980); idem, *New Horizons in Hermeneutics: The Theory and Practice of Transforming Biblical Reading* (Grand Rapids: Zondervan, 1992).

3. Karlfried Froehlich, "Biblical Hermeneutics on the Move," in *A Guide to Contemporary Hermeneutics: Major Trends in Biblical Interpretation*, ed. Donald K. McKim (Grand Rapids: Eerdmans, 1986), pp. 188-89.

canonical form of a biblical book drops out of the interpretive picture —
as does the community that received and then treasured these writings as
Scripture. Of course, whether or not this precanonical reconstruction is
historically correct (itself a highly questionable conclusion!), the text that
it finally posits as a historical source is no longer the church's book. Indeed,
it is scarcely a book that belongs to anyone, not even to the academy, for
it is "known" only to those critics who prize one particular reconstruction
or hypothesis over others, and as such it may well be "owned" by no one
at all. Whereas the critical approach often undermines the canon of Scripture and the role of the canon in biblical interpretation, the latter respects
it and takes it with utmost seriousness. Indeed, the precritical approach
assumes not only the relevance of the whole book to the interpretation
of a part, but also the relevance of the whole book to a community of
readers that the book itself maintains in a measure of continuity over
time.

Although, as noted, there have been many challenges to the hegemony
and reductionism of modern critical exegesis, for many recent historians
and exegetes David Steinmetz's essay "The Superiority of Pre-Critical Exegesis" served as a catalyst in recognizing the values of the older forms of
exegetical investigation. As Steinmetz observed, much contemporary exegesis assumes that "the most primitive meaning of the text is its only valid
meaning, and the historical-critical method is the only key that can unlock
it." By contrast, "medieval theologians defended the proposition, so alien
to modern biblical studies, that the meaning of Scripture in the mind of
the prophet who first uttered it is only one of its possible meanings and
may not, in certain circumstances, even be its primary or most important
meaning."[4] Finally, Steinmetz also pointed out, over against the modern
misconception of medieval exegetes as practitioners of unrestrained allegorical fantasy, that once the framework for understanding a text was
acknowledged, medieval exegetes were just as restrained in their approach
to the text as "any comparable group of modern scholars."[5]

An example of such critical restraint may be derived from the seemingly perennial controversy over how to translate Isa. 7:14. Modern critical
exegetes have often assumed that the text must be translated as "a young
woman shall conceive and bear a son." Accordingly, the traditional rendering of 'almah as "virgin" is deemed erroneous, and Isaiah's words therefore

---

4. David C. Steinmetz, "The Superiority of Pre-Critical Exegesis," *Theology Today*
(April 1980), p. 28.

5. Steinmetz, "Superiority of Pre-Critical Exegesis," p. 33.

cannot be taken in their original context as a prophecy of Christ. Yet this controversy is by no means unknown to the older exegetical tradition. To the contrary: these exegetes were well aware that "a young woman shall conceive" was textually possible, but such a reading did not in itself rule out a christological understanding of the text.[6] They thus accepted as a matter of principle what historical-critical exegetes often dismiss as a matter of principle, namely, that the text could have more than one level of meaning. In the case at hand, the prophet, as the human author of the text, may himself have been unaware of his words' prophetic significance; or, alternatively, he may have intentionally proffered a contemporary image as a figure of Christ's advent.[7] Modern exegesis adds few if any new ingredients to the treatment of this text, for the medieval and Reformation commentators are just as keen to consider the enduring problems of philology and context. Where the two groups part company is not over critical method but over critical presuppositions, indeed, over the matter of who constitutes the community of interpretation and what comprises its ethos. For the "precritical" exegetes, a truly critical understanding must include a scrutiny of the text in the light of the broader scope of Isaiah's prophecy and of the relationship of the Old Testament to the New.

In fact, among the many differences between the fundamental assumptions governing precritical versus historical-critical exegesis, four stand forth as crucial to understanding the precritical address to the text of Scripture and the relative unity or community of exegesis in the history of the church prior to the eighteenth century. First, unlike the historical-critical exegesis of the eighteenth, nineteenth, and twentieth centuries, the older exegesis (whether of the patristic, medieval, or Reformation eras) understood the *historia* — that is, the story that the text is properly understood to recount — to be resident in the text and not under or behind it. In other words, the "story" is identified with the literal or grammatical sense. This point is made in first phrase of the old couplet about the fourfold

---

6. Calvin, e.g., knew of the reading offered by some of his predecessors in the Christian exegetical tradition that Isaiah referred to a child born under ordinary circumstances at the time of his prophecy, "by whom, as by an obscure picture, Christ was foreshadowed"; see his *Comm. Isaiah* 7:14 (CO 36:155; CTS 1:245).

7. This view was rejected by Calvin in favor of identifying the text as a direct prophecy of Christ. Calvin believed that the imposing character of the revelatory event in the text of the prophecy itself ruled out identifying its object as a contemporary child. Thus Calvin rejected a reading of the text related to Lyra's double-literal sense in favor of a reading akin to Lefèvre's spiritual-literal understanding of the Old Testament, but on the basis of a series of textual considerations.

sense of scripture: "The letter teaches what happened."[8] And however strongly one might wish to pose the opposition between Reformation-era exegetes and their medieval predecessors concerning the three spiritual senses — allegorical, moral or tropological, and anagogical — virtually no difference can be discerned in their understanding of the literal sense.[9]

Second, quite in contrast to modern historical-critical exegesis, the older exegesis assumed that the meaning of a particular text is governed not by a hypothetically isolable unit of text having a *Sitz im Leben* distinguishable from surrounding texts or from the biblical book in which it is lodged. Instead, the meaning of a text is governed by the scope and goal of the biblical book in the context of the scope and goal of the canonical revelation of God. In other words, Christian exegetes traditionally have assumed that a divine purpose and divine authorship unite the text of the entire canon. To be sure, Reformation-era exegetes were well aware of differences in style and in content between the various biblical books. Yet they still assumed that the exegete needed to come to terms with the historical and theological unity of the whole of Scripture as an integral part of the attempt to understand a particular book or passage. The point is perhaps best illustrated by the constant use of Scripture to explain Scripture — an interpretive technique that well supported the *sola Scriptura* of the Reformation but one that was also characteristic of patristic and medieval exegesis. Thus (for example) the text of the Old Testament is illuminated by its fulfillment in the New Testament; the Psalter is illuminated by the use of the Psalter in the Gospels, the Acts, and the Epistles; the story of creation in Genesis 1 is illuminated by the first chapter of the Gospel of John; and so on.

Third, the older exegetes understood the primary reference of the literal or grammatical sense of the text not as the historical community that gave rise to the text, but as the believing community that once received

---

8. This oft-quoted verse reads in full: *Littera gesta docet, / quid credas allegoria, / moralis quid agas, / quo tendas anagogia.* See pp. 9 and 42, above. The same point is also made in the more precise definition of the literal meaning offered by Alexander of Hales: "Intelligitur in prima facie litterae, hoc est *per significationem verbi*, et sic est litteralis sive historicus; historia enim est rerum gestarum narratio quae in prima facie litterae continentur"; see Alexander of Hales, *Summa Theologica*, I, q. 1, cap. iv, a. 4, 4 vols. (Quaracchi: Collegium S. Bonaventurae, 1924-48), as cited in Ceslaus Spicq, *Esquisse d'une histoire de l'exégèse latine au moyen âge* (Paris: J. Vrin, 1944), pp. 268-69.

9. See Brevard S. Childs, "The Sensus Literalis of Scripture: An Ancient and Modern Problem," in *Beiträge zur alttestamentlichen Theologie*, ed. Herbert Donner, Robert Hanhart, and Rudolf Smend (Fs. Walther Zimmerli; Göttingen: Vandenhoeck & Ruprecht, 1977), pp. 80-93.

and continues to receive the text. The text is of interest above all because it bears a divinely inspired message to an ongoing community of faith and not because it happens also to be a repository of the religious relics of a past age. And yet this crucial preference in no way conflicts with the concomitant interest among precritical exegetes in the immediate and concrete historical context out of which a prophet or an apostle spoke. Aquinas, for example, offers as much detail concerning the historical context of Romans as most Reformation interpreters of the text; Alcuin of York ponders in detail the situation that produced the Pastoral Epistles; virtually all precritical exegetes recognized what has come to be called the "synoptic problem";[10] and many of the older exegetes recognized the redacted character of the Pentateuch and of the historical books from Joshua through 2 Kings. The precritical exegete, however, did not understand these historical or contextual issues as providing the final point of reference for the significance of the text. Or, to make the point in a somewhat different way, the precritical exegete understood the text, by its very nature as sacred text, as pointing beyond its original context into the life of the church. "Literal," therefore, had a rather different (and fuller) connotation for the older exegetical tradition than it does for many today.

A fourth point amplifies the third. The Reformation-era exegete, like his medieval and patristic forebears, never conceived of his task as the work of an isolated scholar on the shoulders of whose opinion the entire exegetical result could be established and carried. Instead, the exegete of the Reformation era — indeed, even the Protestant exegete of the later sixteenth-century, who held as a matter of doctrine that Scripture was ultimately self-authenticating as the highest norm of theology — understood the interpretive task as an interpretive conversation in the context of the historical community of belief. Modern Protestant understandings of *sola Scriptura* have often obscured and caricatured this characteristic of older exegesis by individualizing exegesis in the name of freedom of conscience. Admittedly, the Reformers considered the biblical text to be clear and authoritative in itself, capable of

---

10. Thus Calvin, in his *Commentary on a Harmony of the Evangelists* (CO 45:3-4; CTS 1:xxxviii-xxxix), weighs in against the reliance of Mark on Matthew. Matthew Poole (*A Commentary on the Holy Bible* [1683-85; repr. 3 vols., London: Banner of Truth, 1962], 3:147), however, indicates in the "argument" to his commentary on Mark that the Evangelist "seemeth much to have compared notes with Matthew, and hath a few things which Matthew hath not," even as he puzzles with no result over the possible sources of Luke (*ibid.*, p. 185). The same concern is voiced by Hugo Grotius's *Annotationes in Novum Testamentum* (Leipzig, 1755), pp. 11, 13, 591, 593, 674-75 (Matthew, cap. 1, praef.; Mark 1:1, in loc.; Luke 1:1, in loc.); there, Matthean priority is argued, with Mark and Luke both relying in part on Matthew.

being interpreted both grammatically and canonically by the comparison of difficult passages with clearer passages. But interpretation, for them, was not a conversation between a lonely exegete and a hermetically sealed text! The preceding essays have amply documented many of the resources used in the sixteenth century, from medieval works such as the *Glossa ordinaria*, to Nicholas of Lyra's *Postilla*, as well as to individual commentaries by exegetes as diverse as Bonaventure, Aquinas, and Denis the Carthusian. The Reformation of the church implied neither a refusal to examine such works nor a consistently negative response to them; indeed, the Reformers shared with earlier eras a vision of interpretation that was communal in nature, insofar as it drew on the "cloud of witnesses" comprised of the church and its exegetes throughout the ages. In other words, the older exegesis assumed that the exegete lived and functioned not as part of an academic guild but as a "doctor" or teacher of the church in a long line of churchly teachers. As in the case of the older dogmatic theology — whether of the patristic, medieval, or Reformation era — the notion of new, original, or individualistic interpretation was both foreign and alarming to precritical exegesis. Reformation exegetes were also quite capable of discovering their predecessors' errors and of offering corrections based on more careful philology, or on more accurate geography, or on more accurate knowledge of cultural backgrounds — all as part of their commitment to an ongoing exegetical conversation. By the same token, modern exegesis has become a far lonelier task than it ever was for these older exegetes.

Other contrasts between precritical and modern exegesis could be isolated, but the lesson to be drawn here is, once again, simply that precritical exegesis is not necessarily uncritical in its methods or values. While it is often appropriate to recognize that traditionary readings of the text are erroneous on the grounds offered by the historical-critical method, we ought also to recognize that the conclusions offered by historical-critical exegesis may themselves be quite erroneous on the grounds provided by the exegesis of the patristic, medieval, and Reformation periods. We further ought to acknowledge that the higher-critical result may not be capable of speaking to the living community of belief, whereas the precritical result addresses the living community of belief directly. That historical-critical exegetes dismiss many traditional questions out of hand may well say more about their own context and constituency than about the questions themselves. And that such questions have lately begun to arise anew even within the guild of historical-critical exegetes surely indicates that the valuation of the text as Scripture that is expressed by the older exegesis has never been fully extinguished.

By all accounts, the sixteenth century marked an epoch in the history of exegesis, for the combined force of the philological and textual interests of Renaissance humanism and the theologically critical, scriptural demands of the Reformation led to a flowering of editions, translations, and interpretations of the biblical text. The essays assembled here, however, have also contributed to the conclusion that many of the generalizations found in much of the older scholarship concerning this epochal event have misunderstood its nature and character. In particular, the "standard" English-language studies — ranging from Farrar's well-known *History of Interpretation*[11] to the *Cambridge History of the Bible* — have typically claimed a dramatic disjuncture between medieval and Reformation patterns of interpretation, and a similar contrast between the exegetical work of the Reformation and that of the post-Reformation era. Indeed, it was Farrar's judgment that the medieval church was so clogged with absurd allegories as to offer Reformation exegetes little useful precedent, and the Protestant orthodox were so similarly preoccupied with dogmatic system as to have virtually no relation to the biblical interpretation of the Reformation era. In Farrar's view, shared in large part by the third volume of the *Cambridge History*,[12] the Reformation appears as a rather isolated outpost of literal, grammatical exegesis on the difficult (but now vindicated) path toward the historical-critical method.[13]

But when the history of exegesis is examined with the sort of care and detail that this volume has sought to exemplify, these long-standing caricatures lose their punch. Medieval exegesis cannot, in fact, be reduced to allegorism. Moreover, the assumptions underlying the fourfold pattern of exegesis did not simply disappear, whether in the later Middle Ages with

11. Frederic W. Farrar, *History of Interpretation* (New York: Dutton, 1886; repr. Grand Rapids: Baker Book House, 1961).

12. But note the excellent essays by Raphael J. Loewe, "The Medieval History of the Latin Vulgate" (*CHB* 2:102-54), and Beryl Smalley, "The Bible in the Medieval Schools" (*CHB* 2:197-220).

13. Such an approach to the history of exegesis is suspiciously similar to the timeworn caricature of the Reformation as a sudden rupture with medieval superstition — and akin to the frequent claim that later Protestantism "forgot" the insights of the Reformers and reverted to a scholastic dogmatism, just in time to be chastened by the protests of the Pietists. But when placed into a larger historiographical context, the approaches of Farrar and the *Cambridge History* to Reformation-era exegesis are easily seen to be defective, if only because their understandings of precritical exegesis were tailored entirely to the standards of modern historical-critical method. See Steinmetz, "Superiority of Pre-Critical Exegesis," pp. 27-38; and idem, "John Calvin on Isaiah 6: A Problem in the History of Exegesis," *Interpretation* 36 (1982): 156-70.

the rise of various alternative patterns of interpretation or with the humanists' and the Reformers' emphasis on the literal meaning of the text in the sixteenth century. On the one hand, not only does medieval exegesis manifest a considerable variety of interpretive patterns, but it also displays what can only be called an increasing interest in both the text and its literal sense and thereby situates itself along a trajectory pointing toward the Reformation rather than away from it.[14] On the other hand, when the medieval fourfold method is understood less under the general rubric of allegory (which is, of course, a misunderstanding of the method) and more as an attempt to express that — beyond the basic literal and grammatical reading of the text — Scripture also speaks to the teaching, to the morality, and to the expectation of the believing community, then the continuity of intention between the various medieval approaches and the methods of the Reformers also becomes far more obvious.[15] Naturally, this is not to imply that one cannot also distinguish between patristic and medieval exegesis, between medieval and Renaissance exegesis, between Renaissance and Reformation exegesis, or between Reformation and post-Reformation Protestant exegesis. As demonstrated by several of the essays in this volume, there are such differences, and they can be substantial. Nonetheless, as also demonstrated, often by these very same essays, there remain continuities of assumption about the sacred text, its scope, and its import that unite the exegetes of these several eras despite the variety of their methods and results.

*   *   *

What is the value or significance of precritical exegesis for today? For those who stand within the Christian tradition, "precritical" exegesis is at once strange and yet strangely familiar. This is as it should be. To trade the

14. This assertion is amply corroborated by the best studies in the history of exegesis, including Henri De Lubac, *Exégèse mediaevale: les quatre sens de l'Ecriture*, 4 vols. (Paris: Aubier, 1959-64); Spicq, *Esquisse d'une histoire de l'exégèse latine au moyen âge*; James S. Preus, *From Shadow to Promise: Old Testament Interpretation from Augustine to the Young Luther* (Cambridge, Mass.: Harvard University Press, 1969); Beryl Smalley, *The Study of the Bible in the Middle Ages* (Notre Dame: University of Notre Dame Press, 1964); and Gillian Evans, *The Language and Logic of the Bible*, 2 vols. (Cambridge: Cambridge University Press, 1984-85).

15. A similar parallel could be traced between the formats employed by medieval and Reformation interpreters. Accordingly, the medieval fondness for a running gloss accompanied by more detailed scholia or postils not only carried over into the practices of the young Luther but also found echoes in the tendency of Reformers such as Bullinger and Musculus to offer both a running commentary on the text and a series of specific (if excursive) doctrinal *loci* developed from the text.

344

traditionary exegesis for a mess of historical-critical pottage would assuredly leave one hungry in the long run, for the "meaning" of Scripture per se is not the goal of historical criticism. And yet to refuse to learn from historical-criticism would distance one from the tradition and from traditional and precritical exegetes still more, for they, too, are concerned about matters of historical context, intention, and philology. If the several authors contributing to this volume are correct in the view that the older exegesis has been misunderstood and misinterpreted, and if, moreover, they are correct in their assumption that exegesis is a churchly exercise that must take place in a such a way that particular texts are understood nonreductionistically — that is to say, understood in their immediate context and in their canonical relationships, indeed, understood in terms both of their original grammatical meaning and of their historical reception in the ongoing community of belief — then "precritical" exegesis may well offer some invaluable guidance for how historical-critical exegesis may be employed alongside and in the service of a more holistic and ecclesial approach to the text of Scripture. To appreciate the significance and value of precritical exegesis does not require a naive faith in the infallibility of its findings, much less a Luddite or antiquarian mentality. For it is far less the specific findings or positions of precritical exegesis that should command attention than its commitment to an exegesis at once careful (one could easily say "critical") and yet also contemporary. Precritical exegesis was not always correct in its assertions, nor certainly univocal in its views; but it was always concerned to locate biblical exegesis within the community of those who valued the text as more than a curiosity, indeed, as inspired Scripture. For moderns and postmoderns alike, then, the traditionary path of "precritical" exegesis may well be the only track that joins the present-day interpreter to the sacred text and that brings the sacred text forward again to us as having significance, not only for the dead but also for the living.

A Chronological Bibliography
of the Writings of David C. Steinmetz

compiled by
MICKEY L. MATTOX

Books

Misericordia Dei: The Theology of Johannes von Staupitz in Its Late Medieval Setting. Studies in Medieval and Reformation Thought, IV. Leiden: E. J. Brill, 1968.

Reformers in the Wings. Philadelphia: Fortress, 1971.

Luther and Staupitz: An Essay in the Intellectual Origins of the Protestant Reformation. Durham, N.C.: Duke University Press, 1980.

Luther in Context. Bloomington: Indiana University Press, 1986.

Memory and Mission: Theological Reflections on the Christian Past. Nashville: Abingdon Press, 1988.

Editor. *The Interpretation of the Bible in the Sixteenth Century.* Durham, N.C.: Duke University Press, 1990.

Calvin in Context. New York: Oxford University Press, 1995.

Editor. *Die Patristik in der Bibelexegese des 16. Jahrhunderts.* Wolfenbüttler Abhandlungen zur Renaissanceforschung. Wiesbaden: Otto Harrassowitz, 1996.

Divided by a Common Past: An Intellectual History of the Reformation. New York and Oxford: Oxford University Press. Forthcoming.

The Intellectual History of the Reformation: A Reader. New York and Oxford: Oxford University Press. Forthcoming.

Articles

"The Nature of Ordination in the Light of Tradition." *Lancaster Theological Seminary Bulletin* 3 (1969): 8-19.

"The Making of a Theologian." *Lancaster Theological Seminary Bulletin* 4 (1969): 11-20.

"Scholasticism and Radical Reform: Nominalist Motifs in the Theology of Balthasar Hubmaier." *The Mennonite Quarterly Review* 45 (1971): 123-44.

"*Libertas Christiana:* Studies in the Theology of John Pupper of Goch (d. 1475)." *The Harvard Theological Review* 65 (1972): 191-230.

"Luther and the Late Medieval Augustinians: Another Look." *Concordia Theological Monthly* 44 (1973): 245-60.

"Woe to me if I do not preach the Gospel!" *The Duke Divinity School Review* 39 (1974): 1-9.

"Mary Reconsidered." *Christianity Today* 20 (1975): 240-43.

Entries in *The New International Dictionary of the Christian Church,* ed. J. D. Douglas. Exeter: Paternoster Press and Grand Rapids: Zondervan Press, 1975. [Catherine of Genoa; Durandus of St. Pourçain; Evangelical and Reformed Church; Evangelical Church (Albright Brethren); Emanuel Vogel Gerhart; Gerhoh of Reichersberg; Johann Karl Ludwig Geiseler; Karl Joseph Hefele; Holy Office; Cornelius Otto Jansen; Jansenism; John of Wesel; John the Constant; Martin Kaehler; Johann Peter Lange; Merit; Julius Müller; Nicholas of Myra; Karl Immanuel Nitzsch; Protestantism; Purgatory; Articles of Schwabach; Servites; Sulpicians; August Friederich Christian Vilmar; Vincent of Lerins; Walter of St. Victor; Johann Hinrich Wichern; Francesco Zabarella]

"Asbury's Doctrine of the Ministry." *The Duke Divinity School Review* 40 (1975): 10-17.

"Ordination and the Theology of the Cross." *The Duke Divinity School Review* 41 (1976): 36-40.

"The Necessity of the Past." *Theology Today* 33 (July 1976): 168-76.

"Theological Reflections on the Reformation and the Status of Women." *The Duke Divinity School Review* 41 (1976): 197-207.

"Luther ausserhalb des Luthertums: Reformierte Sicht." *Concilium* 12 (October 1976): 505-8. Also in French, Dutch, Italian, Spanish, and Portuguese editions.

"Late Medieval Nominalism and the *Clerk's Tale*." *The Chaucer Review* 12 (1977): 38-54.

"Theology and Exegesis: Ten Theses" and "Discussion Agenda for the Session on Theology and Exegesis." In *Histoire de l'exégèse au XVIe siècle. Etudes de philologie et d'histoire*, 34. Geneva: Librairie Droz, 1978. Pp. 383-84. Reprinted in *A Guide to Contemporary Hermeneutics: Major Trends in Biblical Interpretation*. Ed. Donald K. McKim. Grand Rapids: Wm. B. Eerdmans, 1986. Pp. 27.

"Reformation and Conversion." *Theology Today* 35 (April 1978): 25-32.

"The Baptism of John and the Baptism of Jesus in Huldrych Zwingli, Balthasar Hubmaier and Late Medieval Theology." In *Continuity and Discontinuity in Church History*, ed. by F. Church and T. George. Studies in the History of Christian Thought 19. Leiden: E. J. Brill, 1979. Pp. 169-81.

"Hermeneutic and Old Testament Interpretation in Staupitz and the Young Martin Luther." *Archiv für Reformationsgeschichte* 70 (1979): 24-58.

"The Nature of Luther's Reform." *Duke Divinity School Review* 44 (1979): 3-13.

"The Exposition of Matthew 25:14-30." *Interpretation* 34 (1980): 172-76.

"The Superiority of Pre-Critical Exegesis." *Theology Today* 27 (1980): 27-38.

"Religious Ecstasy in Staupitz and the Young Luther." *The Sixteenth Century Journal* 11 (1980): 23-37.

"John Calvin on Isaiah 6: A Problem in the History of Exegesis." *Interpretation* 36 (1982): 156-70.

"The Theology of Calvin and Calvinism." *Reformation Europe: A Guide to Research*. Ed. Steven E. Ozment. St. Louis: Center for Reformation Research, 1982. Pp. 211-32.

"The Protestant Minister and the Teaching Office of the Church." *Theological Education* (Spring 1983): 45-59.

"Jean Gerson" and "Devotio Moderna." *Dictionary of Christian Spirituality*. Ed. Gordon S. Wakefield. London: SCM Press and Philadelphia: Westminster Press, 1983.

"Scripture and the Lord's Supper in Luther's Theology." *Interpretation* 37 (1983): 253-65.

"Luther und Hubmaier im Streit um die Freiheit des menschlichen Willens." *Evangelische Theologie* 43 (November/December 1983): 512-26.

"Abraham and the Reformation: The Controversy over Pauline Interpretation in the Early Sixteenth Century." *Medieval and Renaissance Studies* 10. Ed. G. M. Masters. Chapel Hill: University of North Carolina Press, 1984. Pp. 94-114.

"Luther and Calvin on Church and Tradition." *Michigan Germanic Studies* 10 (Spring/Fall 1984): 98-111.

"The Superiority of Pre-Critical Exegesis." *Theology Today* 37 (1980-81): 27-38; reprinted in *Ex Auditu* 1 (1985): 74-82 and in *A Guide to Contemporary Hermeneutics: Major Trends in Biblical Interpretation*. Ed. Donald K. McKim. Grand Rapids: Eerdmans, 1986. Pp. 65-87.

"Luther and the Ascent of Jacob's Ladder." *Church History* 55 (1986): 179-92.

"Calvin and Melanchthon on Romans 13:1-7." *Ex Auditu* 2 (1986): 74-81.

"Calvin and the Absolute Power of God." *The Journal of Medieval and Renaissance Studies* 18 (1988): 65-79.

"Calvin and Abraham: The Interpretation of Romans 4 in the Sixteenth Century." *Church History* 57 (1988): 443-55.

"The Reformation and the Ten Commandments." *Interpretation* 43 (1989): 256-66.

"Calvin and the Patristic Exegesis of Paul." In *The Bible in the Sixteenth Century*. Duke Monographs in Medieval and Renaissance Studies 11. Ed. David C. Steinmetz. Durham and London: Duke University Press, 1990. Pp. 100-118.

"Calvin and His Lutheran Critics." *The Lutheran Quarterly* 4.2 (Summer 1990): 179-94.

"Calvin and the Divided Self of Romans 7." In *Augustine, the Harvest, and Theology (1300-1650): Essays Dedicated to Heiko Augustinus Oberman in Honor of His Sixtieth Birthday*. Ed. Kenneth Hagen. Leiden: E. J. Brill, 1990. Pp. 300-313.

"Calvin and the Natural Knowledge of God." In *Via Augustini: Augustine in the Later Middle Ages, Renaissance and Reformation. Essays in Honor of Damasus Trapp, OSA*. Ed. Heiko A. Oberman and Frank A. James III. Leiden: E. J. Brill, 1991. Pp. 142-56.

"Calvin among the Thomists." In *Biblical Hermeneutics in Historical Perspective*. Ed. M. S. Burrows and P. Rorem. Grand Rapids: Wm. B. Eerdmans, 1991. Pp. 198-214.

"Calvin and the Monastic Ideal." In *Anticlericalism in Late Medieval and Early Modern Europe*. Ed. Peter A. Dykema and Heiko A. Oberman. Leiden: E. J. Brill, 1992. Pp. 605-16.

"Luther and Loyola." In *Ignacio de Loyola y su Tiempo*. Bilbao: Universidad de Deusto, 1992. Pp. 791-800. Also in *Interpretation* 47 (1993): 5-13.

"Luther and Tamar." *Lutheran Theological Seminary Bulletin* 73 (1993): 3-15.

"Martin Luther." In the Abingdon *Dictionary of Biblical Interpretation*. Ed. John H. Hayes. Nashville: Abingdon Press, 1994.

"Teológia és Egzegésis, Tíz Tézis" and "A Prekritikai Írásmagyar zat Elsödlegessé." In *Paradigmaváltások a Biblia Értelmezésében*. Ed. Tibor Fabiny. Budapest, 1994. Pp. 5-20.

"Luther és Támár." *Protestáns Szemle* 56 (Budapest, 1994): 81-89.

"Der Intellektuelle Reiz der Reformation." In *Rechtfertigung und Erfahrung*. Ed. Ernstpeter Maurer, Hans Ulrich, Michael Beintker, and Hinrich Stoevesandt. Munich: Christian Kaiser Verlag, 1995.

"Johannes von Staupitz," s.v. in *Oxford Encyclopedia of the Reformation*. New York and Oxford: Oxford University Press, 1995.

Book Reviews

Review of *Readings in Christian Thought*, by Hugh T. Kerr. *Theology and Life* 9 (1966): 277-78.

Review of *Later Medieval France: The Polity*, by Peter Shervey Lewis. *Church History* 38 (1969): 264-65.

Review of *Gottschalk Hollen, O.E.S.A.: Leben, Werke und Sakramentenlehre*, by Willigis Eckermann. *Zeitschrift für Kirchengeschichte* 80 (1969): 411-15.

Review of *The School of Peter Abelard: The Influence of Abelard's Thought in the Early Scholastic Period*, by David E. Luscombe. *Church History* 39 (1970): 109-10.

Review of *Wort und Stunde*, Vol. 3, *Beiträge zum Verständnis Luthers*, by Hermann Dörries. *Church History* 39 (1970): 548-49.

Review of *A Theology of Testament in the Young Luther: The Lectures on Hebrews*, by Kenneth Hagen. *Church History* 44 (1975): 406.

Review of *Ökumenische Kirchengeschichte*, ed. R. Kottje and B. Moeller. *Journal of Ecclesiastical History* 26 (1975): 327-28.

Review of *Ecclesia in Via: Ecclesiological Developments in Medieval Psalms Exegesis and the* Dictata Super Psalterium *(1513-1515) of Martin Luther*, by Scott H. Hendrix. *Renaissance Quarterly* 29 (1976): 399-401.

Review of *Luther's Theology of the Cross*, by Walter von Loewenich. *Interpretation* 31 (1977): 305-7.

Review of *Luther and the False Brethren*, by Mark U. Edwards. *Journal of Religion* (1977): 99-101.

Review of *Luther and the Mystics*, by Bengt R. Hoffman. *Interpretation* 31 (1977): 305-7.

Review of *Calvinism and Scholasticism in Vermigli's Doctrine of Man and Grace*, by J. P. Donnelly. *Renaissance Quarterly* 30 (1977): 377-79.

Review of *Wrestling with Luther: Introduction to the Study of His Thought,* by J. R. Loeschen. *Interpretation* 31 (1977): 305-7.

Review of *Documenta anabaptistica neerlandica,* Vol. 1, *Friesland en Groningen (1530-1550),* ed. A. F. Mellink. *Church History* 47 (1978): 223-24.

Review of *Sin and Confession on the Eve of the Reformation,* by Thomas N. Tentler. *Church History* 47 (1978): 448.

Review of *The Concept of Grace in the Radical Reformation,* by A. J. Beachy. *Renaissance Quarterly* 31 (1978): 379-82.

Review of *Stadt und Kirche im spätmittelalterlichen Würzburg,* by Karl Trüdinger. *Catholic Historical Review* 67 (1981): 90-91.

Review of *Calvin wider die Neugierde: Ein Beitrag zum Vergleich zwischen reformatorischen und patristischen Denken,* by E. P. Meijering. *Renaissance Quarterly* 35 (1982): 622-23.

Review of *The Christian Tradition: A History of the Development of Doctrine,* Vol. 4, *Reformation of Church and Dogma (1300-1700),* by Jaroslav Pelikan. *American Historical Review* 91 (1986): 97-98.

Review of *The Theology of Huldrych Zwingli,* by W. P. Stephens. *Theology Today* 44 (1987): 396-97.

Review of *Théorie et pratique de l'exégèse: Actes du 3e colloque international sur l'exégèse biblique au 16e siècle 1988,* ed. Irena Backus and Francis Higman. *Sixteenth Century Journal* 23 (1992): 862-63.

Translations

Gerhard Ebeling, "The Hermeneutical Locus of the Doctrine of God in Peter Lombard and Thomas Aquinas." In Ernst Käsemann et al. *Distinctive Protestant and Catholic Themes Reconsidered.* New York: Harper and Row, 1967.

Walter Bauer, "The Confrontation between Orthodoxy and Heresy: General Characteristics and Operating Procedures." In *Orthodoxy and Heresy in Earliest Christianity.* Philadelphia: Fortress, 1971.

Other Contributions

Senior Editor. *The Oxford Encyclopedia of the Reformation.* New York and Oxford: Oxford University Press, 1995.